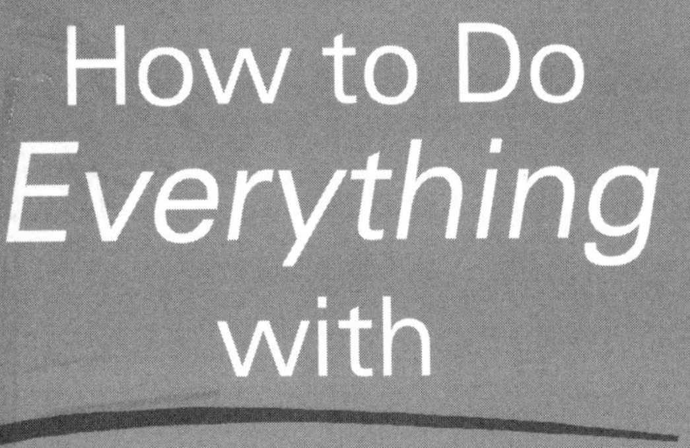

MP3 and
Digi

C

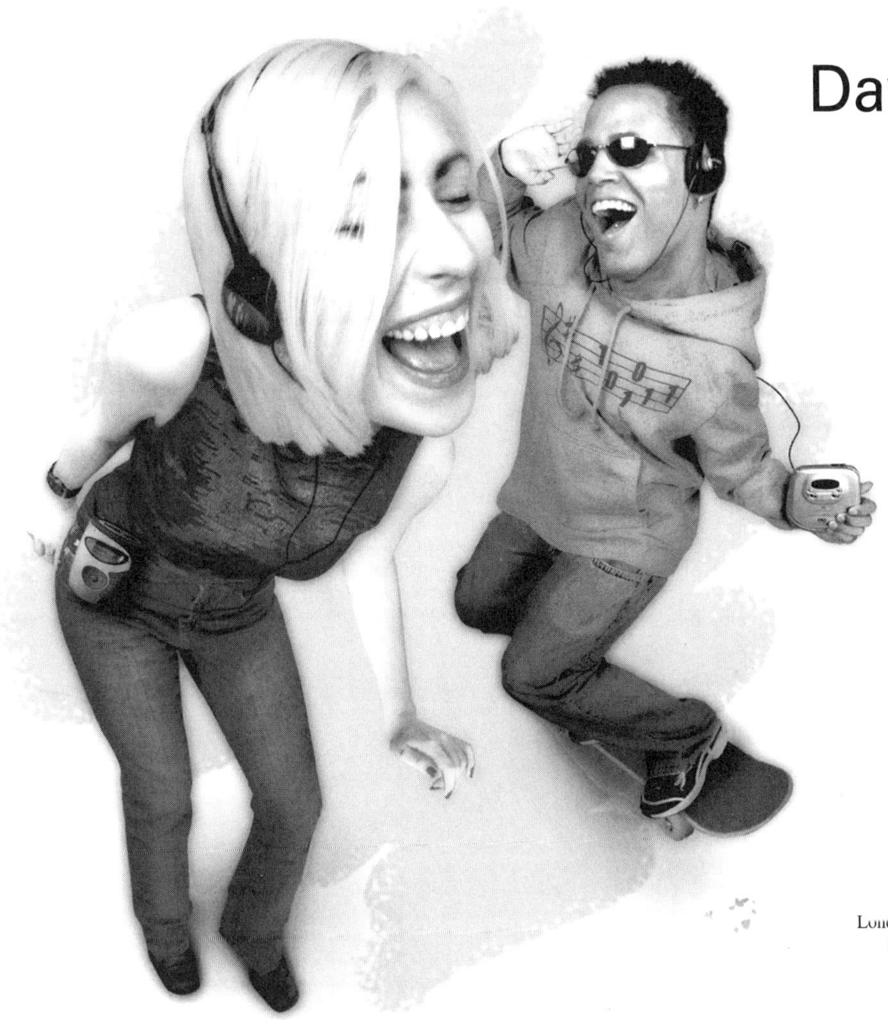

Dave Johnson
Rick Broida

McGraw-Hill/Osborne

New York Chicago San Francisco Lisbon
London Madrid Mexico City Milan New Delhi
San Juan Seoul Singapore Sydney Toronto

McGraw-Hill/Osborne
2600 Tenth Street
Berkeley, California 94710
U.S.A.

To arrange bulk purchase discounts for sales promotions, premiums, or fund-raisers, please contact **McGraw-Hill**/Osborne at the above address. For information on translations or book distributors outside the U.S.A., please see the International Contact Information page immediately following the index of this book.

How to Do Everything with MP3 and Digital Music

1234567890 FGR FGR 01987654321

ISBN 0-07-219413-8

Publisher: Brandon A. Nordin
Associate Publisher & Editor-in-Chief: Scott Rogers
Acquisitions Editor: Marjorie S. McAneny
Project Editor: Elizabeth Seymour
Acquisitions Coordinator: Tana Diminyatz
Technical Editor: Brian Nadel
Copy Editor: Chrisa Hotchkiss
Proofreader: Paul Tyler
Indexer: James Minkin
Production and Editorial: Apollo Publishing Services
Series Design: Mickey Galicia
Cover Series Design: Dodie Shoemaker
Cover Illustration: Tom Willis and Joseph Humphrey

This book was composed with Corel VENTURA™ Publisher.

Dedication

We humbly dedicate this work to the thousands of innocent victims who lost their lives in the heinous terrorist act of September 11, 2001—an event that put the closing weeks of this book into perspective for us. We embrace music as a source of solace during this time of terrible grief, and invite all mourners to do the same.

About the Authors

Dave Johnson writes about technology from his home in the Rocky Mountains. As a newsletter editor he covers digital photography for PC World and mobile computing for IT World. He's also an award-winning wildlife photographer and the author of 18 books, including *The Wild Cookie*, an interactive kids' story on CD-ROM.

Dave is a dedicated but entirely talentless guitarist, though he tries to make up for that deficiency by dressing like Pink Floyd's Roger Waters.

Before Dave started writing, his somewhat unfocused career included flying satellites, driving an ice cream truck, photographing a rock band, stocking shelves at Quick Check, teaching rocket science, and writing about intergalactic space penguins. Today, he relaxes by photographing wolves; he's also a scuba Divemaster and Assistant Instructor.

Rick Broida has written about computers and technology for over ten years. A regular contributor to *Computer Shopper* and *ZDNet*, he specializes in mobile technology. In 1997, recognizing the Palm PDA's unparalleled popularity and the need for a printed resource covering the platform, Rick founded *Tap Magazine*. It later became *Handheld Computing*, and it remains North America's only magazine devoted to Palm OS products.

While dabbling in flute and saxophone during his formative years, Rick developed a love for classical music and jazz. To help preserve the integrity of both genres, he gave up the instruments after college. Today, Rick's preferred musical hobby is making fun of Dave's musical tastes.

Rick lives in Michigan, where he works as a writer and handheld-computing consultant and instructor.

Contents at a Glance

PART I **The ABCs of MP3**

1 Welcome to MP3 and Digital Audio 3
2 Getting Your Computer Ready 15
3 MP3 and the Law 31

PART II **Playing Digital Music**

4 Finding Digital Music Online 45
5 Listening on the PC 69
6 Dialing into Internet Radio 95
7 Taking It on the Road 113
8 MP3 Around the House 139
9 Getting the Best Sound 153

PART III **Creating Your Own Music Files**

10 Ripping Music from a CD 169
11 Transferring Analog Sources to MP3 193
12 Editing, Correcting, and Tweaking Your Audio 221
13 Organizing Your Music Files 239

PART IV **Sharing Your Digital Music**

14 Converting Music to CD and Streaming Audio 261
15 Sharing Your Music Online 285
16 Promoting Your Sound 295

A Internet Radio Stations 317
B Top Web Sites for MP3 Dowloads 343
C In Search of Storage Space 353
D Portable Player Memory Cards 359

Index 363

Contents

Acknowledgments xvii
Introduction xix

PART I The ABCs of MP3

CHAPTER 1 **Welcome to MP3 and Digital Audio** **3**
A Brief History of Recorded Time 4
What Is MP3? 5
What's the Big Deal about Compression? 6
Where Do MP3 Files Come From? 7
What Can You Do with MP3? 8
What about All the Legal Stuff? 8
How to Listen to MP3 Files 9
Your Computer 9
Portable Players 9
A Car Player 11
A Home Stereo 12
Our Favorite TV Show Theme Songs 13
The Difference Between MP3 and Digital Audio 14

CHAPTER 2 **Getting Your Computer Ready** **15**
Must-Have Hardware 16
Processor and RAM 17
Notes for Macintosh Users 17
The Hard Drive 18
The Sound Card 19
Speakers 20
Universal Serial Bus Ports 20
The CD-RW Drive 22
Operating System Issues 26
Our Five Favorite Funky Songs 27
MP3 in Windows 95 28

MP3 in Windows 3.1 28
MP3 in Macintoshes 28
Your Internet Connection 29

CHAPTER 3 **MP3 and the Law 31**
A Brief History of MP3 Controversy 32
Blame It on Rio 33
The Rise and Fall (and Rise) of MP3.com 34
The Napster Effect 35
How to Not Break the Law 37
Rick vs. Dave: MP3 Ethics 37
Definitely Legal Activities 38
Illegal Activities 38
"Legal" Alternatives to Napster 39
The Dawning Age of Copy Protection 39
Our Favorite Songs from the '80s 40

PART II **Playing Digital Music**

CHAPTER 4 **Finding Digital Music Online 45**
Music Sites 47
Amazon.com 47
What Is Liquid Audio? 48
MP3.com 50
Our Favorite Portable MP3 Players 54
The Best $13.98 You Can Spend on Your Kids 55
File-Sharing Services 58
File-Sharing Fundamentals 59
How to Use LimeWire 60
If I Share My MP3 Files, Can Someone Hack into All My Files? 60

CHAPTER 5 **Listening on the PC 69**
How to... 70
Choosing an MP3 Player 70
Finding an MP3 Player 71
Music Players for Windows 72
Get Hip to the Lingo, Digi-Cat 73
Winamp 75
Windows Media Player 76
RealJukebox Plus 80
MusicMatch Jukebox 6 82
Music Players for the Mac 85
iTunes 85

MPLAY 87
MusicMatch Jukebox 88
Setting Your Volume 90
Changing Skins 90
See Your Music 92

CHAPTER 6 **Dialing into Internet Radio 95**
Understanding Internet Radio 96
Where Internet Radio Comes From 97
How You Listen to Internet Radio 97
The Importance of High-Speed Internet Access 99
Internet-Radio Sound Quality 99
Why a Slow Connection Equals Dead Air 99
How to Find Internet Radio Stations 100
Tune In with Windows Media Player 103
Creating Your Own Preset Lists 103
Searching for Stations 104
Build Custom Radio Shows with RadioMOI.com 105
Tune In with RealJukebox 108
Should You Pay for MusicMatch Radio MX? 109
Sharing with SHOUTcast 110
Other Software and Sites 111

CHAPTER 7 **Taking It on the Road 113**
Choosing a Portable Music Player 114
How Much Memory Does the MP3 Player Have? 115
How Does the MP3 Player Connect to the PC? 116
What about the Batteries? 117
What Other Goodies Does the MP3 Player Have? 118
The MP3 Tree 119
The Right MP3 Player for You 120
MP3s on a Budget 120
If You Need a Voice Recorder 121
Longer Playing Time 122
Listening in Your Car 122
If You're a CD Fanatic 123
Getting Massive Amounts of Music 124
MP3 for Your Car 124
In-Dash Receivers with MP3 125
Hard Disk MP3 Players 126
Cassette Adapters 127
Go Wireless 129
Understanding Memory Card Formats 130

CompactFlash 130
SmartMedia 131
Secure Digital and MultiMediaCard 131
Memory Stick 132
Dave's MP3 Auto Experience 132
What Do Memory Cards Cost? 133
Playing MP3s on a Personal Digital Assistant 133
MP3s on a Pocket PC 134
Pocket PC Choices 135
MP3s on a Palm OS Device 136

CHAPTER 8 **MP3 Around the House 139**
From PC to Stereo (Same Room) 140
From PC to Stereo (Different Rooms) 142
Kinda Like Mr. Microphone—for MP3 143
X10 Marks the Spot 145
Make Your Stereo Part of Your Computer Network 145
Internet Radio to Go 147
From PC to Any Other Room 148
From MP3 Player to Stereo 149
Other Cool MP3 Options for the Home 150
Where to Find It 151

CHAPTER 9 **Getting the Best Sound 153**
Converting Your Audio Files 154
Normalizing Your Audio Files 156
All about Equalizers 158
Using Winamp's Equalizer 159
Using the Windows Media Player Equalizer 161
Choose a Killer Set of Speakers 162
Choose a Killer Set of Headphones 165
Headphones That Roam Free 165

PART III **Creating Your Own Music Files**

CHAPTER 10 **Ripping Music from a CD 169**
Inside Digital Audio 170
Sound Waves 101 171
The Age-Old Debate: Digital or Analog? 173
Digital File Formats 177
WAV vs. MP3 179
When to Use WAV and MP3 179
Choosing a CD Ripper 180
Ripping Music 181

- Using a Jukebox 182
- Dealing with Glitches 188

CHAPTER 11 **Transferring Analog Sources to MP3 . . . . . 193**
- Making the Connection 194
  - Sound Card Inputs 196
  - Analog Source Outputs 198
  - Cabling It All Together 200
- Audio Recording Software 204
- Making the Recording 208
  - Setting the Recording Device 208
  - Setting Sound Levels 210
  - Recording Audio 212
  - Recording Strategies 214
  - Do It All with Easy CD Creator 216

CHAPTER 12 **Editing, Correcting, and Tweaking Your Audio 221**
- Starting Clean 222
- Touring an Audio Editor 223
- Cutting Up Your Music 224
  - Deleting Silent Leader 225
  - Inserting Silent Leader 226
  - Splitting a File into Tracks 228
  - Gluing Tracks Together 230
  - Fading Your Songs 231
  - Taking Jazz Head On 232
- Cleaning Up Noisy Audio 233
- Optimizing the Dynamic Range 237

CHAPTER 13 **Organizing Your Music Files 239**
- Planning for MP3 Storage 241
- Organizing Your Songs 242
  - Controlling Playback with Filenames 243
  - Selecting a Folder Strategy 243
  - Selecting Filenames 246
- Editing Music File ID Tags 249
  - Changing Several Tracks at Once 252
- Fixing the File Type Association 254
  - The Desert Island Test 257

PART IV **Sharing Your Digital Music**

CHAPTER 14 **Converting Music to CD and Streaming Audio 261**
- Getting Started with CD Recording 262

- Prepping Your Computer . . . 263
- Choosing Your Discs . . . 265
- CD-R Speed . . . 266
- Choosing a Data Format . . . 267
- Recording with Easy CD Creator . . . 269
  - Choosing Recording Options . . . 269
  - Burning a CD . . . 272
  - Making an MP3 CD . . . 276
  - The Monkees Weren't so Bad . . . 277
- Streaming Your Music from the Web . . . 278
  - Stream Without Extra Software . . . 278
  - Using Streaming Production Software . . . 281

CHAPTER 15 **Sharing Your Music Online . . . 285**

- What MP3.com Can Do for You . . . 286
  - The Premium Artist Service . . . 287
  - Payback for Playback . . . 287
  - The Copyright Wizard . . . 287
  - The Music Licensing Program . . . 287
  - The CD Program . . . 288
  - Promo Auctions . . . 288
- Promoting Your Music on Ampcast.com . . . 288
  - Royalties . . . 289
  - The CD Program . . . 289
  - Five Best Band Names We Just Made Up . . . 289
  - Ad-Free Pages . . . 290
  - Ratings and Sales Data . . . 290
  - Fast Song Approval . . . 290
  - Concert and Event Calendars . . . 290
- Getting Your Songs on Internet Radio . . . 291
  - Create Your Own Internet Radio Station on SHOUTcast . 291

CHAPTER 16 **Promoting Your Sound . . . 295**

- Selling Your CD . . . 296
  - Online Stores That'll Sell Your CD . . . 296
  - Accepting Payment . . . 298
  - Essential Resources for Musicians . . . 298
  - Finishing Touches for Your CD . . . 300
- Promoting Yourself . . . 302
  - Write a Press Release . . . 302
  - Cool Things to Do with Your Site . . . 303
  - Write to Your Fans . . . 304
- From the Experts . . . 305

Music That Burns Your Fingers 305
Kristin Hersh 306
Peter Himmelman 308
Diana Darby 310
Cherish Alexander, The Painkillers 312
Dana Mase 314

APPENDIX A **Internet Radio Stations** **317**
General/Networks 318
News/Sports/Talk 319
Classical 324
Country 326
Hip-Hop/Electronic/Dance 327
JAZZ 332
R&B/Soul 334
Rock/Pop 335

APPENDIX B **Top Web Sites for MP3 Dowloads** **343**
Napster 345
Morpheus 346
Aimster 347
iMesh 348
KaZaA 349
Audiogalaxy 350
BearShare 351
WinMX 352

APPENDIX C **In Search of Storage Space** **353**
Optical Storage 354
External Hard Disks 355
Online Storage 356
Storage Schemes at a Glance **357**

APPENDIX D **Portable Player Memory Cards** **359**
Memory Cards 101 360
CompactFlash 360
SmartMedia 361
Memory Stick 361
Secure Digital/MultiMediaCards 361
Security and Memory Cards 362
Memory Cards at a Glance 362

Index **363**

Acknowledgments

This book was a painless writing experience largely because of the great team at Osborne. Our heartfelt thanks go out to Margie McAneny, Tana Diminyatz, Jane Brownlow, Elizabeth Seymour and Emma Acker. Finally, we're indebted to the ever-insightful Brian Nadel, who spotted numerous areas in need of fleshing out and added some excellent copy to the book.

Dave adds:

I had originally intended to dedicate this book to a few of the people that, though they have no idea of their impact, have had a most profound effect on my life. I'm referring to Ray Page, my high school teacher who opened my eyes to a world of culture I might otherwise never have experienced. I'm referring to John Lennon and Paul McCartney—enough said. And to contemporary geniuses Kristin Hersh and Peter Himmelman, whose art resonates in my heart each and every day. Circumstances led us to steer the dedication in a different direction, but I'd be remiss if I didn't acknowledge you here. Thanks to everyone who forms part of the daily soundtrack to my life and who provided such valuable insight for the book: Kristin, Peter, Diana, Cherish, and Dana. Also, thanks, Rick—as always, you're a true friend.

Rick adds:

Endless thanks to my wife, Shawna, whose unyielding support reminds me why I married her, and to my daughter, Sarah, whose infectious laughter makes all the hard work worthwhile. Thanks, too, to my family—Mom, Dad, Caroline, Bill, Baxter, and Davis—who made the move worthwhile and who fill my heart with happiness. Finally, I offer my appreciation to Mike Valeski and Craig Zurcher, who, by throwing each other's tape collection down the hall, taught me a valuable lesson about music.

Introduction

Digital music is more than just downloading songs from Web sites and playing tunes on your portable MP3 player. It is the beginning of a new era in art, entertainment, and technology. When a music fan first uploaded a song to the Internet and shared it with the world, he had absolutely no idea how profound and far-reaching the effect would actually be.

We're not exaggerating. Consider this: In the past, people tended to think of a music purchase as buying a thing—an LP, a cassette, or a CD. You owned a thing, and had to carry the thing with you to listen to music when you were away from home. Sure, you could make a copy (and the copyright law afforded you that opportunity) but few people copied music very often. It just wasn't a common practice.

Flash forward and you'll find that digital audio is making people reconsider what it means to buy music. It's becoming less of a thing and more of a license to listen. Take MP3.com's Instant Listening program, for instance. If you can prove that you own a CD, MP3.com lets you listen to it via your PC from anywhere you can establish an Internet connection.

That's just the start. File formats like MP3 and WMA have made music files so small that you can carry the equivalent of 500 CDs in your pocket. Having access to thousands of songs wherever you go sounds like science fiction, but it's a reality—and it, too, changes everything. Don't forget about the artists. If you create music, digital audio affords you some unique opportunities—and some challenges.

We wrote *How to Do Everything with MP3 and Digital Music* to help put all this in perspective. The book covers the essentials of ripping music from CDs and LPs, cleaning up that music, and playing it on a PC and on the road. It also shows you how to get the most out of this technology revolution if you're a musician.

Part One is where to turn for an introduction to the basics of digital music. Here you'll find out how to get your computer ready for MP3 and learn about digital music and the law.

In Part Two, we dive into the essentials of playing music. We'll teach you how to wring free and commercial music from the Internet, as well as how to choose and use music players for both the PC and the Mac. Digital music extends far beyond the desktop, so we also look at portable players and pumping digital music to home stereos.

If you want to rip songs from CDs and analog sources like LPs and cassettes, make sure you read Part Three. You'll even find advice on cleaning up noisy music and restoring the sound of your needle-worn, 30-year-old Santana album.

The book concludes with Part Four, which we wrote expressly for anyone who wants to learn to share. We talk about pressing your own CDs, making the modern equivalent of mix tapes on CD, and uploading and streaming your audio on the Internet. And we've got something you won't find anywhere else—after conducting exclusive interviews with five of the most exciting independent musicians on the national stage, we included tips and advice from artists like Kristin Hersh, Peter Himmelman, The Painkillers, Diana Darby, and Dana Mase on how you can succeed as a musician today.

Every Chapter Has a Head to Head

Dave: Rick and I rarely see eye to eye. He has the musical taste of a 14-year-old girl, and his idea of high literature is reading *Entertainment Weekly*. So we face off 16 times in this book. Within these H2H sidebars, nothing is sacred, but hopefully you'll find them amusing.

Rick: I don't know what "high literature" is, but at least *Entertainment Weekly*'s writers can construct a grammatically correct sentence. Dave, I should warn readers now, doesn't like jazz, so you have to take everything he says with a grain of salt. And, for the record, I have the musical taste of a *15*-year-old girl, thank you very much.

We wrote this book so you could sit down and read it through like a novel. But if you're looking for specific information, we made it easy to find. Plus, you can find special elements to help you get the most out of the book:

- **How To...** These special boxes explain, in a nutshell, how to accomplish key tasks. Read them to discover important points covered in each chapter.
- **Did You Know?** These special boxes provide information on fascinating but probably potentially useless trivia.
- **Notes** These provide extra information that is vital to gain understanding of a particular topic.
- **Tips** These tell you how to do something smarter or faster.
- **Sidebars** Here we address related—and, sometimes, unrelated—topics. Sidebars can be pretty interesting, if only to see us bicker like an old married couple.

Can't get enough of Dave and Rick and their wacky arguments? See the back page of *Handheld Computing Magazine*, where we continue our lively Head2Head column (though it's typically not about music). You can also send questions and comments to us at *dave@bydavejohnson.com* and *rick@broida.com*. Thanks, and enjoy the book!

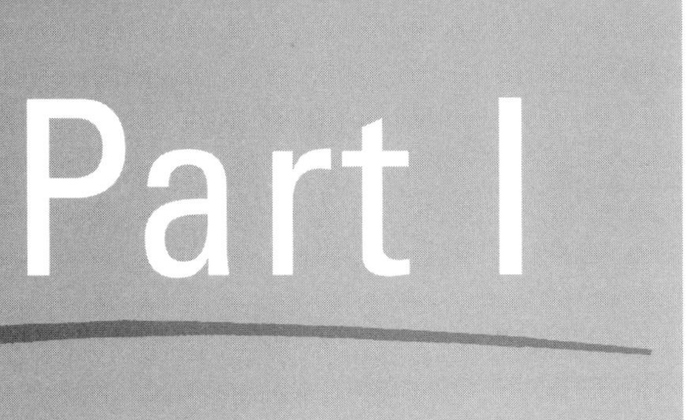

The ABCs of MP3

Chapter 1

Welcome to MP3 and Digital Audio

How to...

- Define MP3
- Understand the importance of compression
- Find MP3 files
- Decide between MP3 and other standards
- Listen to MP3 files on your PC
- Listen to MP3 files on a portable player
- Listen to MP3 files on your home stereo
- Listen to MP3 files in your car
- Avoid legal complications

"Without music to decorate it, time is just a bunch of boring production deadlines or dates by which bills must be paid." —Frank Zappa, *musician*

"Music and wine are one." —Ralph Waldo Emerson, *essayist*

"This one goes to eleven." —Spinal Tap

With so many great words already written on the subject of music, we don't feel compelled to reinvent the wheel. We like music. You like music. That's why we're all here (in this book, not on this planet—that's a totally different discussion). Call it art, call it entertainment, call it business—music is magic.

So is the technology that enables us to record, play, and share music. In the late twentieth century, the world of music changed forever with the advent of MP3 technology, and that evolution is still underway. Just what is this MP3 thing, where did it come from, and how can you leverage it to improve your music life?

A Brief History of Recorded Time

The evolution of recorded music goes something like this: In 1877, at his Menlo Park laboratory, Thomas Edison invented the phonograph. Then, for a long while, nothing happened. At least, nothing new.

For nearly a century, the phonograph remained the preferred means of recording and listening to music. But in the last three decades of the twentieth century, the music industry experienced a technological revolution that produced the 8-track tape, the audiocassette, the compact disc, and, finally, digital audio.

By 1997, Edison's invention had come full circle, when a man named Tomislav Uzelac unveiled *Amp*—a computer program designed to play MP3 files. No media was required—at least not in the traditional sense. No wax record, no thin spool of magnetic tape, no shiny silver disc. Music had become digital, electronic, computerized. Liberated.

Today, the MP3 file is the de facto standard for sharing music, and it's rapidly gaining ground on the CD player as the preferred means for listening to music. In fact, the next car, home stereo, or portable music player you buy is likely to support MP3 technology in one way or another. The age of digital music has arrived.

What Is MP3?

First things first: The *M* in MP3 doesn't stand for music. The *P* doesn't stand for power, platinum, or anything cool like that. And the *3* has nothing to do with triangles or Three Dog Night. *MP3* is a simple, albeit catchy, abbreviation for a kind of compression technology, one that has become universally popular for sharing, downloading, and transporting songs. (Think of someone zapping a 45-rpm record and turning it into zeroes and ones.)

If you're really interested in the technical description, MP3 stands for *MPEG Audio Layer-3.* What the heck is MPEG? It stands for *Moving Picture Experts Group,* a consortium of companies and organizations that develops compression, decompression, and processing standards for audio and video. So, all spelled out, those innocuous three characters become *Moving Picture Experts Group Audio Layer-3.*

Whew—glad that's out of the way. That's just about the most complicated aspect of MP3, and it's not even important that you remember it. Here's a more real-world explanation: an MP3 file is a song, usually taken from a CD, that's converted into an electronic format and compressed to become very small. It can then be played on a PC, a portable Walkman-like player, or any number of other devices.

By "electronic," we generally mean in a digital format, without the involvement of any kind of media (record, 8-track tape, CD, etc.). This should not be confused with "electronic music," the kind that Dave likes to jam to on his Casio keyboard.

What's the Big Deal about Compression?

Remember trash compactors? They were popular in homes built in the '70s. Basically, you'd toss your garbage into a drawer, and the compactor would smash it all down into a little cube. Efficient, practical, and kinda cool. (The fact that they aren't still in use today is a source of disappointment to environment-conscious Rick.)

When you copy a song from a CD to your computer using a traditional file format like WAV, the resulting file is usually upwards of 40–50MB in size. Figure ten songs to an album, and now you're talking about nearly 500MB of hard drive space for *Abbey Road* alone. That's twice the space needed by the entire Microsoft Office XP suite! Even if you have a 20GB hard drive, it doesn't take a math genius to see how impractical it is to store music electronically.

In case you're unfamiliar with it, WAV is the longtime standard for audio files in Windows. It's also the format used when you turn MP3 files into audio CDs, which we discuss in greater detail in Chapter 14.

By *compressing* (the digital equivalent of trash compacting) a "raw" song file into an MP3 file, it becomes roughly 12 times smaller, with little or no discernible loss in sound quality. Now the B-52s' "Love Shack" is 4.9MB instead of 59MB. Suddenly, you can store a *lot* more music on your computer. And you can carry songs in a portable MP3 player. This, friends, is the big deal about compression.

An MP3 file can actually be as much as 96 times smaller than the original file, depending on compression rate. We explore this subject in detail in Chapter 10.

Windows Media Audio: The MP3 Alternative

MP3 is not the first compression standard for music files, nor will it be the last. It is, however, the most popular, despite competition from a Microsoft-backed alternative: *Windows Media Audio* (WMA). This technology is similar to MP3, but with a couple of notable advantages. First, according to Microsoft, WMA delivers CD-quality sound at a much lower bit rate than MP3 (64 Kbps vs. 128 Kbps). Theoretically, that means a portable player could store twice as much music in the same space (assuming it supported the WMA format). What's more, WMA includes a digital rights management system, which can help deter piracy. We talk more about WMA in later chapters.

Where Do MP3 Files Come From?

Where do these supercompressed, bookworthy music files come from? Obviously, you can download them from the Internet, but where did they come from before that? Most commonly, MP3 files originate on ordinary audio CDs. Dave, for instance, recently completed the awesome task of converting his 400-plus CDs into MP3 files, meaning he now has some 5,000 songs littering up his hard drive. Why did he do this? To make his music collection highly portable.

Rick hasn't invested quite as much time in turning his CDs into an MP3 library, but instead has collected music from outside sources—namely, the Internet. Thanks to file-sharing services like Napster and Audiogalaxy Satellite (discussed in Chapter 4), Rick has traded songs with music lovers from all across the globe.

Yes, there are indeed some legal—and ethical—issues involved with this kind of music sharing. But it is possible to trade MP3 files without breaking the law—or being a bad person. Read all about it in Chapter 3.

To answer the big question then, MP3 files can come from your own music collection or from online sources. They can also be created from the recordings you made with your band (if you have a band)—a topic we discuss at length in Part IV.

What Can You Do with MP3?

Sure, MP3 is a neat technology, but how is it going to improve your life? You'll find out in the chapters to come. In the meantime, here's an overview of some of the benefits:

- **Discover new music** Traditionally, most people encounter new music on the radio. With MP3, you can download songs from unknown bands and artists based on the categories of music you like.
- **Create music compilations** If you've ever spent an hour or two making a tape of your favorite songs from CDs or record albums, you'll appreciate how quick and easy it is to create a compilation of MP3 tunes.
- **Find rare songs and bootleg recordings** It beats rifling through the bins at used record stores—but there are definite legal issues to consider, which we discuss in Chapter 3.
- **Take your entire music collection anywhere** Imagine all 200 of your CDs stored in a player no larger than a deck of cards. It's possible.
- **Get discovered** So you've laid down some tracks and think you're ready for the radio. Internet MP3 services let you share your sound with not just the local listening area, but the entire world.
- **Listen to the world** With a fast Internet connection, you can tune into Web radio stations from around the world. Find out more in Chapter 6.

What about All the Legal Stuff?

Unless you're a basement-dwelling hermit like Dave, chances are good you've heard of Napster and the eruption of controversy it sparked. It's an extremely complicated issue, one the courts are still wrangling with. We talk more about it in Chapter 3, but in the meantime, here's what you need to know to keep your conscience clear:

- If you own a CD, you have the right to make a tape of it, extract the songs as MP3 files, or use it as a Christmas tree ornament. Basically, anything that qualifies as "personal use" is A-OK. What you can't do is sell the MP3 files or make them publicly available. As for trading them with friends (and strangers), well, that's where things get sticky. See Chapter 3.

- If you download an MP3 file from the Internet, it's perfectly OK as long as the song was authorized for distribution by the artist. If it wasn't, you've violated copyright laws. There's probably no need to hire a lawyer, but there are ethical consequences to consider. See Chapter 3.

How to Listen to MP3 Files

Because MP3 files are electronic, and because MP3 is a widely accepted standard, you can listen to them in any number of places using a myriad of devices. All modern desktop and notebook computers, for instance, include software for playing MP3 files. Many handheld PCs (like Compaq's iPAQ Pocket PC) can play them as well, and dozens of portable MP3 players are designed expressly with music playback in mind. Let's take a look at the hardware that makes MP3 listening possible.

Your Computer

Given that your computer is the place where you download MP3 files from the Internet and "rip" them from your CDs (that is, convert them to digital format), it should come as no surprise that it can also play the files (see Figure 1-1). On Windows systems, you can use the built-in Windows Media Player or any number of third-party "jukebox" programs. The newest Macintosh systems come preloaded with Apple's iTunes player, and there are numerous third-party players available as well. Find out more about turning your PC into a full-blown stereo system in Chapter 5.

Portable Players

We're particularly keen on portable players, which have numerous advantages over their Walkman-style forebears. For starters, they tend to be very compact—some make a deck of cards look big (see Figure 1-2). Better still, they have no moving parts, meaning they won't skip under any circumstances and last a lot longer on a pair of batteries. We're both runners (actually, Rick runs, Dave just stumbles and complains rapidly), and we've both found portable MP3 players to be ideal accessories. They're small and light enough to slip into a pocket (or clip to a waistband) without bouncing around too much, and they never skip!

FIGURE 1-1 With a pair of speakers and the right software, any PC can play MP3 music as though it were a stereo.

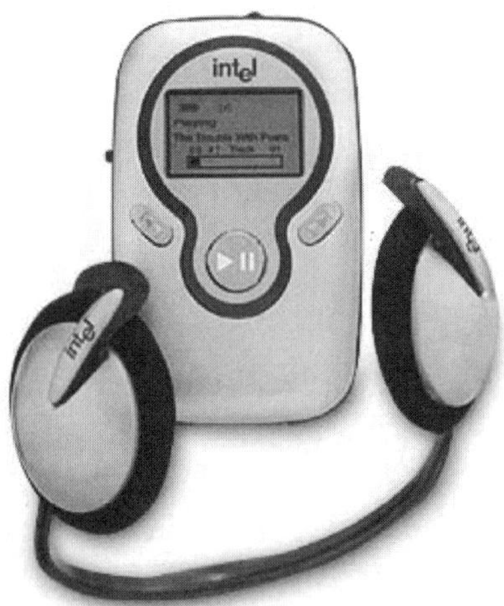

FIGURE 1-2 Portable MP3 players like this one recall the venerable Sony Walkman, but they're much smaller and have better battery life. Plus, the music never skips.

We give you the skinny on portable players in Chapter 7.

A Car Player

Who's up for a little math? An ordinary CD can hold roughly 74 minutes' worth of music—upwards of 20 average-length songs. An ordinary CD can also hold about 650MB of computer data. Now, using the math we learned earlier in this chapter, let's compute: 650MB is enough space for 130 MP3 songs at 5MB each. That's about 10 hours of music squeezed on a single CD. Sound good?

NOTE *Newer CDs can hold 80 minutes of music or 700MB of data.*

Of course it does, especially if you're in the car and don't want to deal with swapping CDs every hour or so. The wrinkle is that most car CD players and changers can't recognize CD-R or CD-RW media—the kind used to hold MP3 files. Fortunately, you have options, in the form of new players that *will* play MP3-packed discs (see Figure 1-3).

FIGURE 1-3 The Kenwood Z919 is a *CD-MP3 receiver* for your car: it can play ordinary audio CDs and MP3-packed CDs.

Of course, your computer's hard disk can store way more than 130 songs. Wouldn't it be great if you could put your PC in your car? You can, in a way, thanks to car-based MP3 systems like the PhatNoise (see Figure 1-4). It stores music on a cartridge-like hard disk and works with existing car-stereo head units. Find out more about car players like these in Chapter 7.

A Home Stereo

So you already own this monster stereo system. You're not going to be happy sitting at your PC while you listen to your MP3 collection. Wouldn't it be great if you could pipe music from your computer to your stereo? You can, thanks to an inventive array of products discussed in Chapter 8. Even if you don't have an earthshaking stereo, you can enjoy MP3 audio in nearly any room in your house. That capability comes courtesy of products like the Rio Receiver (see Figure 1-5), which streams music from your PC to a special receiver via—believe it or not—your home phone lines. See Chapter 8 for more information.

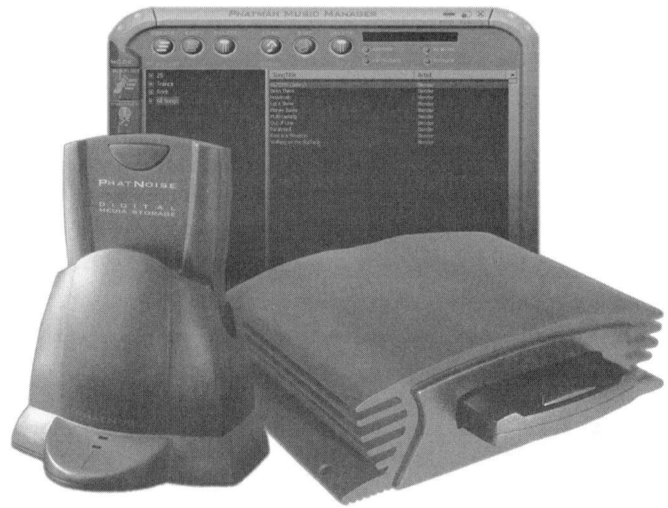

FIGURE 1-4 The PhatNoise Car Audio System puts gigabytes of MP3 storage in your trunk.

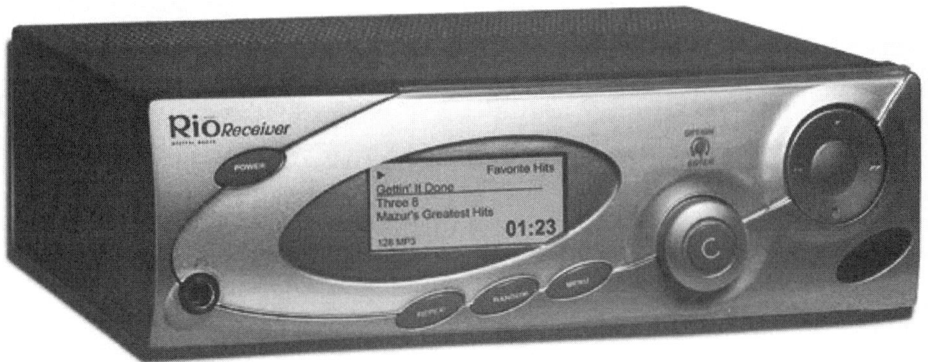

FIGURE 1-5 The Rio Receiver lets you listen to your MP3 collection in any room that has a phone jack.

Our Favorite TV Show Theme Songs

Music ain't just The Beatles and Velvet Underground (though try telling Dave that). It comes in all shapes and sizes—like, say, the catchy little themes from TV shows. Which ones do we like best? Aw, it's kind of you to ask. In fact, we're so flattered, we're going to share a whole bunch of our "favorites" throughout the book, just so you get a better idea what makes us tick. It's pretty scary.

Rick: Personally, I can't help humming the theme from *Get Smart* whenever I walk through a pair of sliding doors at the mall. In terms of sheer musical quality, one must admire the strains that accompany *I Love Lucy* and *thirtysomething*. And, finally, in the interest of revealing my true geek self, I really like the opening theme from *Star Trek: The Next Generation* (though it is not, repeat, *not* my preferred Trek show).

Dave: The last time I agreed with Rick I was heavily medicated, though I have to admit that *Get Smart* had one of the coolest themes ever. But he fails to mention *The Greatest American Hero.* I never get tired of that song. With the exception of the theme from *Friends,* which is now so uncool you can get rocks thrown at you for suggesting it's actually a pretty good song, TV shows have largely lost the ability to make infectiously good theme music.

Believe it or not, I'm walking on air...

The Difference Between MP3 and Digital Audio

While this book places a heavy emphasis on creating, listening to, and sharing MP3 files, it also looks at the larger digital-audio picture. We talk about Microsoft's WMA format. We show you how to turn a batch of MP3 files into a standard audio CD that you can play in any CD player. We look at Internet radio, which turns MP3 files into streaming audio delivered via modem. And we show aspiring musicians how to promote their sound—everything from mass-producing audio CDs to drawing attention to an MP3 demo tape.

In other words, MP3 is just one cog—a large one, admittedly—in the digital audio machine. Or, more accurately, one bit in the digital audio stream.

Chapter 2

Getting Your Computer Ready

How to...

- Identify necessary hardware
- Upgrade your computer (if necessary)
- Add a second hard drive
- Choose a CD-RW drive
- Install a CD-RW drive
- Make sure your sound card is sufficient
- Choose a set of speakers
- Work with older operating systems
- Optimize your Internet connection
- Find broadband service in your area

Before we dive into all the fun stuff—portable MP3 players, CD burning, and so on—you need to make sure your computer is sufficiently equipped for the tasks at hand. For instance, do you have enough hard drive space for a library of MP3 files? Sure, they're reasonably small, but if you wind up with several hundred of them (a fairly common scenario), you may find your system cramped for storage. Then there's the CD-RW drive, a mandatory peripheral for anyone planning to create custom CDs. Does your system already have one? If not, how do you choose and install one?

Let's take a closer look at the hardware and software that play key roles in the world of digital music.

Must-Have Hardware

Here's the good news: if you purchased a PC within the last two or three years (say, 1999 or later), it's probably ready to rock and roll (both figuratively and

Notes for Macintosh Users

Because roughly 90 percent of computers worldwide employ one of the many iterations of the Windows operating system, the information in this book is tailored accordingly. However, we've neither forgotten nor neglected the Macintosh platform. Where necessary we pop in to spotlight relevant Mac information. In the meantime, you can find loads of great material at MP3 for the Mac (www.mp3-mac.com), a site devoted to Mac-specific MP3 news, software, and hardware.

literally). The simple task of playing an MP3 file requires little raw computing power, so even older systems should have no trouble. In fact, the operating system installed on your PC probably plays a larger role than the speed of the processor or the amount of RAM you have. (We talk more about operating system requirements in "Operating System Issues" later in the chapter.) That said, you should give your system a once-over to check for potentially vital features like universal serial bus (USB) ports and a capable sound card.

Processor and RAM

You don't need a state-of-the-art system to play, rip, or even record MP3 files. Take Windows Media Player 7.1, the latest version of the popular player that's bundled with the Windows operating system. (See Chapter 6 for more information.) It requires only a 166 MHz processor and 32MB of RAM (though a 266 MHz processor and 64MB of RAM are recommended). Roxio's Easy CD Creator 5 Platinum, the immensely popular CD/MP3 recording package (see Chapters 11 and 12), has similar minimum and recommended system requirements.

TIP

How can you tell how much RAM is installed in your PC? In Windows, right-click the My Computer icon, and then choose Properties. The resulting window shows the amount of memory the machine has. It also shows the type of processor (Pentium III, Athlon, or something similar), but unfortunately, not the speed. On a Mac, click the Apple icon in the upper-left corner of the desktop, and then choose Apple System Profiler (or About This Mac if you use OS X).

If your machine has only 32MB of memory (or, horrors, less), you may find an upgrade very worthwhile. Moving to 64MB or even 128MB of RAM will improve system performance, at the same time gaining you compatibility with a wider range of software. At press time, you could buy a 128MB memory module for as little as $25—a shocking price for those of us who remember paying $40 for a 4MB module.

If you think a RAM upgrade is in order, consult your system manufacturer to find out which type of memory modules you should buy (dozens of different varieties are out there) and how much memory your computer's motherboard can handle.

If your motherboard has no room for additional memory modules, you might want to try a SIMM doubler, *which turns one memory socket into two. They're inexpensive and easy to install.*

The Hard Drive

As the old saying goes, you can never be too rich or too thin—or have too much hard drive space. Consider Dave, who recently turned a collection of about 400 CDs into roughly 20GB worth of MP3 files. Fortunately, while financial security and a trim waistline are often lifelong endeavors, extra hard drive space can be had in about 30 minutes.

Most desktop PCs have room inside for two hard drives. If your machine has only a few gigabytes of storage available, you may want to consider adding a second drive. It's a fairly painless operation, even if you've never been "under the hood" of your machine before.

NOTE

A gigabyte is 1024 megabytes (MB) of storage space. If the average MP3 file is 4MB, you can store about 256 songs—or roughly 20 CDs—in a gigabyte of space. If you have a 10GB hard drive and it's 80-percent full, you still have lots of room—but don't be surprised if you run out soon.

As with RAM, hard drive prices have dropped dramatically in recent years. For about $170, you can buy a speedy 60GB drive, and a mere $99 buys you a 20GB drive. (Both prices came from a quick check on www.insight.com.) Holy mackerel —does anyone else remember paying $300 for a 250*MB* drive?!

TIP *If you'd rather not monkey around with installing a new hard drive, consider an external solution like the Iomega Peerless drive. It uses 10GB and 20GB removable cartridges (for virtually limitless storage), and it connects to your PC via a USB or FireWire port. The drive is expensive, though, and the cartridges cost a small fortune (about $200 for 20GB).*

The Sound Card

Virtually every computer built within the last decade has a *sound card,* which is all you need to listen to MP3 files on your system. (OK, you need speakers, too.) For most users, the sound card is a nonissue—but for some users, it's a pivotal component. Music production, for instance, demands features like digital-to-analog and analog-to-digital converters, built-in audio effects, MIDI in/out ports, and more.

The more likely scenario is deciding to turn your PC into a surrogate stereo and upgrading your speaker system in the process. If you buy a fancy surround-sound package with four or more speakers, you need a sound card with dual output jacks (see Figure 2-1).

Many PCs that have *integrated* (that is, built-in) sound circuitry lack dual jacks, and not every sound card has them either. Fortunately, it's pretty easy to pop out the old card (or disable the integrated hardware) and pop in a replacement. We recommend the $99 Sound Blaster Audigy MP3+ (www.soundblaster.com), a

FIGURE 2-1 A sound card with dual output jacks enables you to connect a four- or five-piece speaker system.

robust card that supports a wide variety of speaker hookups. It also comes with a wealth of music-oriented software.

Speakers

It goes without saying (we hope) that you need at least one pair of speakers to enjoy MP3 audio on your PC (or any other kind of audio, for that matter). We'd bet that 99 percent of you already have speakers connected to your PC, so there's not much more to say on the subject. However, many computer makers bundle—how shall we say—cheap, low-quality speakers with their systems. If you're ready to rattle the floorboards and annoy the neighbors, it's time to invest in a better set. We recommend the following:

Price Range	Speakers	Manufacturer	URL	Notes
Under $100	AVS500	Altec Lansing	www.alteclansing.com	This is a surprisingly good five-piece system for just $60.
$100-199	ProMedia 2.1	Klipsch	www.klipsch.com	Dave calls this "the best three-piece speaker system ever made."
Over $200	ProMedia 2.5	Klipsch	www.klipsch.com	Dave calls this "the best five-piece speaker system ever made."

For information on choosing speakers (see Figure 2-2) and getting the best sound from your PC, see Chapter 10.

Universal Serial Bus Ports

Most computers built within the last several years have at least one USB port, if not two or four. What does an expansion port (see Figure 2-3) have to do with MP3 files? Plenty, actually, if you're planning to work with portable players and other external devices.

FIGURE 2-2 A speaker system like the Altec Lansing AVS500 lets you enjoy surround-sound audio for a modest price.

Most MP3 players and devices employ USB connectors, although a few older and oddball products snag your computer's parallel port (the same one used by your printer, which is why we'd almost never recommend any such products). Whether you're using an Intel Pocket Concert or a Compaq iPaq Pocket PC, you need a USB port to make the connection to your PC. It's through that connection that MP3 files are transferred from PC to player.

TIP *If you don't have room to connect an MP3 player, meaning your PC's USB ports are already occupied by other devices, consider adding a four-port USB hub. These little boxes effectively turn one USB port into four. We recommend something like the Belkin 4-Port USB Hub (www.belkin.com), which sells for under $40 and is compatible with Windows and Macintosh systems.*

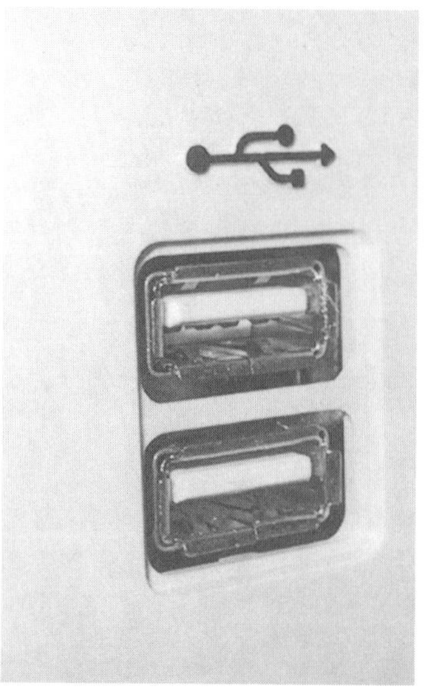

FIGURE 2-3 Ideally, your PC should have at least one USB port, because most portable players require one.

It's worth noting that if your PC has USB ports but is running Windows 95, you should strongly consider upgrading to Windows 98—or at least Windows 95 OSR2. The first version of Windows 95 has very limited support for USB hardware and may pose problems with your MP3 device.

The CD-RW Drive

Finally, we come to the CD-RW drive—also known as the *CD burner*—a cornerstone piece of equipment in the MP3 universe. You're probably already familiar with the *CD* part—the compact disc has been home to software and music for well over a decade. The *RW* part stands for *rewritable,* which means you can record information (be it data or music) to a CD more than once.

In Chapter 14, we tell you everything you need to know about using CD-RW drives to create your own music compilations, the differences between CD-R and CD-RW media, and much more. But right now, we're going to help you choose and install a CD-RW drive (assuming you don't already own one).

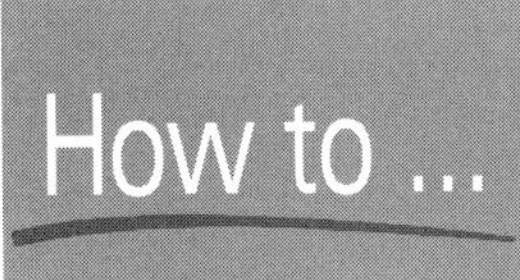

Turn Your PDA into an MP3 Player

In Chapter 7, we tell you all about portable MP3 devices, including a few you might not expect: Palm and Pocket PC handhelds. Yes, your favorite PDA can double as an MP3 player. Pocket PCs like the Compaq iPAQ and Hewlett-Packard Jornada, for instance, come with a streamlined version of Windows Media Player, which lets you play MP3 files through the built-in speaker or plug-in headphones. If you own a Palm m100 or m105, you can outfit it with the Shinei Porteson (www.porteson.com), a clip-on MP3 player. For the Palm V series, there's the PyroPro 256 (www.pocketpyro.com), which has a whopping 256MB of storage space. Handspring Visor owners, meanwhile, should check out the MiniJam (www.innogear.com) and SoundsGood (www.palmgear.com) Springboard modules.

NOTE *How can you tell if the CD-ROM drive in your computer is actually a CD-RW drive? Look at the label on the front of the slide-out tray. It should read something like "compact disc recordable rewritable." If it's blank or reads "DVD-ROM," it's not a CD-RW drive.*

Choosing a CD-RW Drive

During the last few years, CD-RW drives have grown immensely popular, and their prices have plummeted accordingly. As recently as 1999, you could expect to pay upwards of $400 for a state-of-the-art drive—which, ironically, was quite a bit slower than the drive you can buy today for $99.

At press time, prices for internal CD-RW drives ranged from as low as $60 to around $250. Why the discrepancy? As with most computer hardware, speed is usually the key factor. The fastest, newest drives fetch a premium price, while last year's models often wind up as clearance or close-out bargains.

Let's take a look at the key considerations in choosing a CD-RW drive:

- **Internal or external** There are advantages and disadvantages to both. Internal drives tend to cost less and offer faster performance, but they require more time and effort to install in your PC. External drives, on the other hand, are easy to install and can be used on more than one PC. Opt for one with a FireWire interface, assuming your computer has the ports to match.
- **Speed** CD-RW drives have three rated speeds, usually expressed like this: 8x/4x/24x. The first number is the speed for writing to a CD. The second is for rewriting to a CD. The third is for reading from a CD. (This number is akin to typical CD-ROM drive speed ratings.) The higher the first two numbers, the faster the drive will burn CDs. At press time, the fastest drives available offered 24x/10x/40x speeds and sold for upwards of $250. Can you get by with an 8x/4x/32x drive that's only $70? Absolutely, but see the next item.

- **Built-in buffer** As you'll learn in Chapter 14, a *buffer underrun* can ruin a CD burn, leaving you with a disc that's good for coaster duty and little more. Although this problem plagued many early CD-RW drives, the latest models include a built-in buffer (also known as a *cache*) that virtually eliminates it. Trust us when we say it's worth spending extra on a drive that has one.
- **Bundled software** Most drives come with at least some sort of CD-creation software suite, but the age and comprehensiveness of it can vary. A common inclusion is Adaptec Easy CD Creator 4, which is a capable program but rather out-of-date. We prefer something like Roxio (formerly Adaptec) Easy CD Creator 5, a much more current and versatile package (see Chapter 14). At the very least, you want software that enables you to use your drive to copy CDs, create music CDs, and back up data.

If you're looking for a bargain on a CD-RW drive and don't know where to shop, start with PriceGrabber (www.pricegrabber.com). It helps steer you to the best Web deals on drives and other computer equipment.

Installing a CD-RW Drive

Assuming you decided on an internal drive, you now face the somewhat daunting task of installing it in your PC. That means prying open the case, fiddling with wires, and risking the collapse of modern civilization. Okay, we exaggerated a bit on that last part, but for anyone who's never been inside a computer before, it can seem that scary.

The drive you bought came with installation instructions, which we won't attempt to rehash here. (With so many different computer systems and configurations in the world, it's virtually impossible to cover every scenario.) However, we will offer some key advice:

- **You need an open drive bay** The new drive needs a home inside your PC—specifically, a 5.25-inch drive bay. Many computers have at least one such bay available, in which case you can install the CD-RW drive alongside your existing CD-ROM or DVD-ROM drive. If there's no bay available, you have two choices: return the CD-RW and opt for an external model, or install it in place of the existing drive.

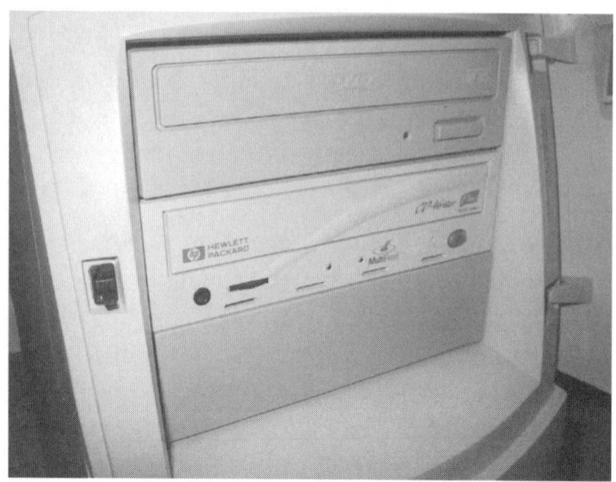

- **Pay attention to the audio cable** Inside your PC, there's a small cable that runs from your CD or DVD-ROM drive to your sound card (or to the motherboard, depending on whether your sound card is integrated). This cable allows standard audio CDs to be played through your computer's speakers. If you replace your existing drive with the CD-RW, be sure to reattach this cable. If the CD-RW is a secondary drive, you may want to relocate the audio cable to it. Whichever drive has it connected is the one that will be able to play music CDs. (Discs filled with MP3 files can be played in any drive because software—not hardware—handles the playback chores.)

Operating System Issues

Earlier in this chapter, we told you that you don't need a state-of-the-art computer to work with MP3 files. Nor do you need a state-of-the-art operating system on that computer—but it helps. The most recent versions of Windows (namely, Windows XP) and the Mac OS (namely, OS X) were designed to reflect the growing popularity of digital music, and as such, include some robust software for MP3 playback and recording.

Windows XP, for instance, comes with Windows Media Player 8, while OS X includes iTunes (both detailed in Chapter 5). These players let you listen to your MP3 files, tune into Internet radio, burn your own CDs, and more. In short, they're worth having.

We're not saying you should spend money on a newer OS just to net some MP3 utilities. Quite the contrary—there's plenty of great MP3 software available for earlier versions of Windows and Mac operating systems. However, depending

Our Five Favorite Funky Songs

You know the kind we mean—the songs that make you want to put the top down and crank the volume. The songs with riffs that get under your skin. The songs that make you beat the steering wheel like a bongo drum.

Rick: I'm not sure "funky" is in Dave's musical lexicon (apparently, he thinks Bon Jovi fits the definition), but I'm a sucker for a driving beat or jazzy brass riff (both in the same song, ideally). My picks:

- "Woke Up This Morning" (Theme from *The Sopranos*) — Alabama 3
- "Start the Commotion" — Wiseguys
- "Ray of Light" — Madonna
- "Bang the Drum All Day" — Todd Rundgren
- "Dorothy the Dinosaur" — The Wiggles (just one of this great kids' group's infectious tunes)

Dave: Oh my God; I've never heard of even a single song in Rick's list. Look—I'm a normal guy. I'm in my 30s, occasionally listen to the radio, grew up in New Jersey, and have a sizable collection of audio CDs. In fact, music is one of my life's overarching obsessions. Music for me isn't just a tune playing in the background; it's a defining art form that shapes my life. Which leads to the inevitable conclusion—Rick's musical taste closely parallels that of 14-year-old girls, the only demographic with which I'm entirely unfamiliar. That said, I'm not sure if these songs meet Rick's definition of "funky," but they definitely have a good beat and are great songs for blasting from my convertible on a sunny day:

- "Let the Day Begin" — The Call
- "Bang a Gong" — T. Rex
- "Big City" — The Pretty Things
- "After Midnight" ('90s version) — Eric Clapton
- "Bad Medicine" — Bon Jovi

on just how early a version you have, there may be some more compelling reasons to upgrade. For instance, you want an operating system that's compatible with not only the latest MP3 software, but the latest portable MP3 players as well. Read on.

MP3 in Windows 95

Yes, yes, we know—Windows 98 offered no major improvements over Windows 95, so you never got around to upgrading. Well, guess what—it's time to upgrade. For starters, you may encounter some MP3 software that requires Windows 98 or later. Microsoft's latest versions of Windows Media Player, for instance, don't run under Windows 95. What's more, many MP3 devices—particularly those with USB interfaces—require Windows 98 or later, because Windows 95 has somewhat flaky USB support.

If you do decide to upgrade, pay close attention to the system requirements of the new OS. Windows XP, for instance, recommends a 300 MHz processor and at least 128MB of RAM—more than many Windows 95 systems have. For the price of upgrading your hardware and buying the new OS, you might be better off just buying a whole new system (one with Windows XP already loaded).

MP3 in Windows 3.1

Just because you're still using Windows 3.1 doesn't mean you're a raving lunatic—but it's time for a new computer already! Although it may be possible to find MP3 software that supports your aging OS, none of the latest and greatest players (Winamp, Windows Media Player, MusicMatch Jukebox, and so on) do. We scoured the Internet high and low just for you and came up empty-handed. Plus, you can forget about working with portable MP3 players and other MP3 hardware. Virtually none of it supports Windows 3.1. Honestly, if you're serious about MP3, you're going to need a newer version of Windows—and probably a new PC.

MP3 in Macintoshes

Your Macintosh came preloaded with a media player called QuickTime. If it's version 4.0 or later, it can play MP3 files. If it's not, you can download the latest version free from Apple (www.apple.com).

As you'll learn in Chapter 5, Apple's newer iTunes is the preferred application for MP3 listening and recording on a Macintosh. However, the free software requires OS 9.0.4 or later, which leaves out a large segment of Mac owners. Naturally, you can upgrade to a newer version of the operating system (OS X is pretty cool, we must admit), or you can look for MP3 players that support your version. Panic's Audion (www.panic.com), for instance, works with OS 8.5, as does Winamp for Mac (www.winamp.com).

Your Internet Connection

Your computer is half the MP3 battle—your Internet connection is the other half. Much of what we discuss in this book involves uploading and downloading files and listening to Internet radio. There's no way to sugarcoat this, so we're just going to come right out and say it: If you have a *broadband* Internet connection (cable, Digital Subscriber Line (DSL), a T1 line, or something similar), you're sitting pretty. If you're using a dial-up modem, well, you may want to sit down.

NOTE

A dial-up modem *is one that connects to an ordinary phone line and achieves a maximum connection speed of 56 Kbps. (In terms of real-world performance, it's usually more like 40–45 Kbps.) Cable, DSL, and other broadband technologies start at around 384 Kbps and often run as fast as 1,500 Kbps (or 1.5 Mbps).*

Because Internet radio involves "streaming" a lot of data to your computer, a dial-up connection generally isn't fast enough for an uninterrupted listening experience. What's more, the best audio quality you can expect is something on par with listening to AM radio through a long metal pipe. A broadband connection, meanwhile, usually delivers hiccup-free music with at least the quality of FM radio.

As for downloading MP3 files, a dial-up modem makes it a frustratingly slow process. It might take, say, 10 minutes to download a single song, versus a minute or less with a broadband connection. This is not to say that relying on dial-up

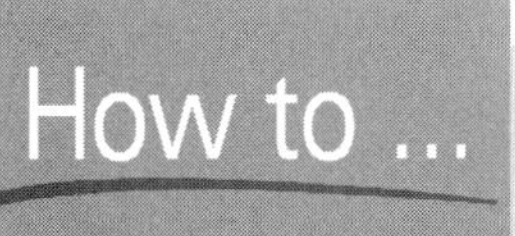

Find Broadband Service in Your Area

Ready for a broadband connection but not sure if service is available in your area? Two Web sites can help you uncover your options: DSLreports (www.dslreports.com) and LowerMyBills.com (www.lowermybills.com).

service will thwart your MP3 aspirations—just that you may find your patience stretched thin.

Fortunately, you can employ a few tricks to make the most of your modem connection:

- **Tweak the settings** Software utilities like BlazeNET, Modem Booster, and TweakDUN promise to configure your modem and dial-up settings to maximize connection speeds. Many of these programs are free or reasonably inexpensive, and those that cost money let you try before you buy. Find them all at Download.com (www.download.com).
- **Toss your Winmodem** Check with your PC manufacturer to see if your machine has a Winmodem installed. These inexpensive modems rely on your computer's processor for much of their operation, and therefore can reduce overall system performance. Replace yours with a conventional modem.
- **Use a download manager** A download manager can not only speed up file transfers, but resume interrupted downloads as well (great for anyone plagued by Call Waiting disconnects and other download downfalls). Keep in mind that download managers won't necessarily accelerate MP3 file sharing in programs like Aimster and Morpheus, which use their own file-transfer schemes, but they will speed up your downloads of the programs themselves. We recommend the freeware gem Download Accelerator Plus (www.mijenix.com), but you should also check out GoZilla and GetRight (both available from Download.com).

Chapter 3

MP3 and the Law

How to...

- Understand the basics of copyrights
- Interpret the Audio Home Recording Act
- Make sense of the Napster controversy
- Download music without breaking the law
- Share music without breaking the law
- Differentiate between legal and illegal MP3 files
- Make a moral decision about MP3 files
- Find information on current MP3 laws and litigation

When you buy a car, the last thing you want to do is read through the endless fine print on the lease agreement—you just want to get in the car and go. Same thing here: You probably want to jump right in and start ripping, playing, burning, and sharing MP3s. You have our permission to do exactly that—but we strongly recommend reading this chapter first. Buying a car is black and white: you pay your money, you get your car. But the world of digital music couldn't be grayer—it's rife with legal and even ethical issues.

For instance, you've no doubt heard of Napster and the controversy it created in the music biz. Maybe you even recall the legal proceedings that tried to stop Diamond Multimedia from making portable MP3 players. In this chapter, we tell you everything you need to know about the legalities of digital music and discuss the ethical concerns that go with them.

A Brief History of MP3 Controversy

Just what makes MP3 technology so controversial, anyway? After all, WAV files, which employ a similar audio-recording technology, existed for years before MP3 hit the scene, so why all the fuss? The answers can be found in three pivotal lawsuits, an act of Congress, and perhaps the Betamax VCR.

NOTE *We'd like to tell you that neither Dave nor Rick are lawyers. We're not married to lawyers. Our pets aren't lawyers. We have never even played lawyers on television, although Dave has played a secret agent named Dank Showcase on the radio. The bottom line: We've written this chapter to spell out some of the legal and political issues surrounding the MP3 debate, but nothing we say constitutes actual legal advice.*

Blame It on Rio

In 1998, Diamond Multimedia Systems introduced the Rio PMP300, a pager-sized descendant of the Sony Walkman that could play MP3 files downloaded from the Internet or "ripped" (that is, copied) from audio CDs. Ironically, before the device ever reached store shelves, the Recording Industry Association of America (RIAA) filed an injunction to prevent its release. The claim? That the Rio promoted the illegal distribution of copyrighted music.

The RIAA was aware that people were downloading copyrighted songs from the Internet and felt that the Rio player would encourage that behavior. Fortunately, the courts were smarter and allowed Diamond to ship the Rio. It became such a smash hit that Diamond eventually spun off a separate division devoted to the Rio line. (That division was later acquired by SonicBlue.)

In the interim, the courts ruled that portable MP3 players did not fall within the "digital recording device" definition used in the Audio Home Recording Act of 1992. (See the box "Congress Gets into the Act.") Thus, other companies were free to make their own MP3 players, and make them they did. At press time, we counted several dozen different models—and those were just the Rio clones. (The market now includes CD/MP3 players, in-dash car players, home-stereo players, MP3-playing cell phones, and more.)

Having failed to stop the hardware (which, to our thinking, has nothing to do with copyright issues), the RIAA then set its sights on the Internet services that were making an MP3 splash. The first target: MP3.com.

Did you know?

Congress Gets into the Act

The Audio Home Recording Act of 1992 was enacted long before MP3 hit the scene, but its doctrines are being examined for current legal actions. According to the AHRA, individuals cannot be prosecuted for making copies of copyrighted digital material, as long as they do so only for personal use. That clause enabled Diamond Multimedia to sell the Rio portable MP3 player—but it wasn't enough to keep Napster operating following the RIAA's lawsuit. Interestingly, analog devices such as cassette decks and Minidisc players are covered in the AHRA, but multipurpose devices (like computers and CD-RW drives) are not. That's one reason the waters are still so murky. You can find the full text of the AHRA at www.virtualrecordings.com/ahra.htm.

The Rise and Fall (and Rise) of MP3.com

MP3.com began life as a service that let unknown bands and artists promote themselves. Users could download free songs from these musicians and then buy their CDs if they liked what they heard. Great concept, and it worked: the service thrived, and Dave discovered several bands he likes.

NOTE *Despite its name, MP3.com had nothing to do with the creation of the MP3 format, nor is it ground zero for all things MP3. It just happens to have a name that reflects what it is. Not quite onomatopoeia, but close.*

Over the years, MP3.com evolved to offer a much broader range of music-related services—and turned into a lawsuit magnet in the process. In early 2000, the RIAA sued to put a stop to MP3.com's Instant Listening Service and Beam-it service, citing the creation of an unauthorized digital music catalog. (Instant Listening Service made it possible for users to listen immediately to CDs purchased from MP3.com's partner e-tailers, while Beam-it enabled users to listen to their existing CD collection on any Internet-connected computer.)

In a nutshell, MP3.com was storing a library of copyrighted material on its own servers and potentially making money from it (though both services were free upon their launch). MP3.com lost the lawsuit and had to pay roughly $160 million to various record companies, but was able to reinstate Beam-it and Instant Listening Service.

At press time, MP3.com had just been acquired by Vivendi Universal, which plans to use the service as a backbone for Pressplay, a music-subscription venture with Sony Music Entertainment. Yes, things continue to evolve rapidly in the ol' music biz. (See Chapter 4 for more information about MP3.com's excellent content and services.)

The Napster Effect

History will record Napster as the service that really put MP3 technology on the map—and as the catalyst of a litigation firestorm. The service debuted in 1999, the brainchild of college student Shawn Fanning, and quickly became popular on college campuses, where students used it to share—and augment—their MP3 collections. About a year later, a media frenzy erupted seemingly overnight, followed closely by high-profile legal action.

Unlike MP3.com, which ostensibly dealt with authorized songs, Napster enabled music lovers worldwide to exchange copyrighted songs in the form of MP3 files. The software was free, the service was free, the songs were free. This polarized the music industry like nothing before (not even Michael Jackson). Many artists—heavy-metal band Metallica the most notorious—denounced Napster as enabling theft of their work (the phrase "copyright infringement on a massive scale" was used regularly). Other artists came out in support of Napster, citing the possibilities of a wider audience for their music. The RIAA, unsurprisingly, went ballistic—and went to court.

See, the record companies don't make any money when you download songs from Napster (or a service like it). Even worse, the artists don't make anything either. Put simply, you're getting for free what you normally would have to buy, and that raises no end of legal and moral questions.

On the other hand—and this is where things get murky—the Audio Home Recording Act of 1992 gives consumers the right to make copies of commercial media, as long as it's for noncommercial use. (This is the very act that helped Diamond Multimedia win permission to make MP3 players.) Because Napster members weren't making money from the exchange of their MP3 files (even though they contained copyrighted material), one could argue that the law wasn't being broken. Hmmm.

While the record companies ply the courts with legal arguments, the rest of us must grapple with knotty ethical issues like these:

- **The One Song Argument** If you like a particular song but would never consider buying the entire album it's on, what's the harm in downloading it? The artist wasn't going to get your money anyway.
- **The Lost Song Argument** Suppose there's a song—or even an entire album—that you'd gladly buy, but you can't because it's out of print. If you can find it online as an MP3 file, why shouldn't you be able to download it? The artist wouldn't be getting any money anyway because the material is out of print.
- **The Greater Exposure Argument** In the old days, we were exposed to new music via the radio (or MTV, depending on what qualifies as "old days" for you). By being able to download a wide variety of music, you gain greater exposure to artists you might not have discovered otherwise—and you may wind up buying an album as a result.
- **The Bootleg Argument** Trading bootleg concert recordings is older than the Grateful Dead, so there's no harm in doing it electronically, right?
- **The VCR Argument** When you record a TV show or movie on your VCR, you're effectively copying copyrighted material. But a famous Supreme Court case held that movie studios could not outlaw a technology (in this case, the Betamax VCR) just because it was capable of copyright infringement. Most people, they ruled, would use it for noninfringing purposes. So, you can record whatever you want, and keep it for your personal use or share it with friends (or even strangers)—just as long as no money is changing hands. The same rules should apply to MP3 recording and sharing, right?
- **The Mix Tape Argument** People have compiled their favorite songs and "burned" them onto cassette tape for friends for as long as the cassette deck has existed—how is sharing songs on Napster fundamentally different? A computer is just an updated cassette recorder—albeit one that can make perfect copies.

At press time, Napster had been shut down for months after losing its court case, but was on the verge of relaunching as a fee-based membership service under the new ownership of BMG Entertainment, a major record label (talk about turning lemons into lemonade). Visit the site (www.napster.com) to find out the exact nature of the new service.

How to Not Break the Law

As we write, the courts are still wrangling over MP3-related copyright issues. In August 2001, MP3.com was facing yet another major copyright-infringement lawsuit, again over its Beam-it service. However, we know of no case in which an individual has been prosecuted for using a service like MP3.com or even Napster. And while we never say never, we think it's pretty unlikely that the FBI is going to bust down your door for downloading Britney Spears' latest radio hit (so you're safe, Dave).

That said, we've compiled lists of legal and illegal activities, so you know exactly what you're dealing with.

Rick vs. Dave: MP3 Ethics

Rick: You and I have had more than a few debates on this subject. My feeling is that if I own or have ever owned an album, a 45 record, an 8-track tape, or whatever, then I've already paid my money to the artist, and am therefore entitled to download those songs in MP3 format—regardless of where they come from. Anything else I download is piracy, plain and simple.

Dave: That makes perfect sense to me, and if I can change the subject a moment, that's what infuriated me about the way MP3.com's Instant Listening Service was litigated to death. If I already own a song, I should have the right to listen to it anywhere, anytime I like—and MP3.com simply made that possible. Grrr. Anyway, I'm perhaps a bit more liberal than you in this regard. I've used Napster to download songs I don't own. In the process, I've discovered new bands (like the Painkillers, featured in Chapter 16) and bought music I would never have otherwise been exposed to.

Definitely Legal Activities

Here's a list of stuff we know for sure is legal. This week.

- **Internet radio** The stuff that streams in off the Web (see Chapter 6) may be coming from some teenager who just knocked off a Musicland store, but you can't be held liable for listening to it. Seriously, most Internet radio stations are absolutely legal.
- **MP3 players** As the courts ruled in the landmark Diamond Multimedia case, there's nothing wrong with carrying music in a portable player. (Hadn't the RIAA ever heard of the Sony Walkman?)
- **CD-RW drives** The drives that enable you to burn and copy CDs are legal; otherwise, you wouldn't have been able to buy one at Wal-Mart. However, if you stand outside Wal-Mart selling copies of The Nightfly that you burned yourself, don't be surprised if you wind up serving 5–10. Remember, anything that qualifies as *personal use* is okay. You can copy your own CDs to play in your car and make music compilations for friends—you just can't make money from it.
- **Downloading authorized songs** "Legitimate" MP3 sites like MP3.com have extensive libraries of songs you can download legally, because the artists who created them gave their permission. See Chapter 4 for a list of "legal" download sites.

Illegal Activities

Here's a list of stuff we know is illegal:

- **Posting unauthorized songs online** If you run a Web site and make any unauthorized song available for others to download, you're breaking the law.
- **Selling MP3s** Hopefully this goes without saying, but if you try to sell MP3 copies of your CDs, songs, albums, and the like, you're breaking the law.

The truly gray area is swapping MP3 songs using file-sharing services like Napster and MusicCity Morpheus. On the one hand, you're getting copyrighted music for free. On the other, no money changed hands, so you didn't violate the letter of the law. Yes, this issue keeps us up nights. It's a toughie. Our advice: let your conscience be your guide. Artists deserve to be paid for their work.

"Legal" Alternatives to Napster

Napster isn't the only game in town. You can still download just about any song you want using a service like Audiogalaxy Satellite, BearShare, KaZaa Media Desktop, LimeWire, or MusicCity Morpheus. How is it that these services can deliver Napster-like functionality without incurring the wrath of the RIAA and others?

The answer lies in a technology that could almost be described as devious. You see, Napster operated around a central server, meaning it facilitated the exchange of copyrighted material. That's why it could be held liable for copyright infringement. The competing services rely on what's called *peer-to-peer* file sharing, meaning there's no central server in between your computer and everyone else's.

Here's another way to look at it. When you mail a letter, it goes through the post office before reaching its destination. Now, imagine taking the post office out of the equation: when you mail a letter, an unmarked truck picks it up and drives it to the recipient. That's peer-to-peer file sharing: no central office involved, just a direct exchange of data.

"Semantics!" cries the artist, who's still potentially losing money on record sales. "Same theft, different method." And she has a point.

Read more about these services in Chapter 4.

The Dawning Age of Copy Protection

In the not-too-distant future, the freedom we enjoy to rip songs from CDs, listen to them on any MP3 device, and share them with friends may vanish. The recording industry is hoping to stop copyright infringement by finding a foolproof method of copy protection. Perhaps you've heard of Macrovision, the copy-protection technology that prevents consumers from making copies of rented movies?

A similar technology (also from Macrovision) is being tested by record labels—it inserts audible clicks and pops into music files copied from CDs.

Meanwhile, in 2000, Sony tried pushing a proprietary music format—ATRAC3—as an alternative to MP3. It works only in Sony MP3 players and includes a robust (and decidedly user-unfriendly) copy-protection scheme—two reasons it flopped bigtime. Good riddance.

While it remains to be seen what will happen with all this, expect some radical changes in the future. It's in the record companies' best interests to stem the tide of CD and song copying, and copy protection is the only real solution. It may happen that Microsoft's WMA format takes over (see Chapter 1), as it offers smaller file sizes than MP3 and offers built-in copy protection.

Our Favorite Songs from the '80s

It actually came as a surprise to Dave that any songs were written in the '80s, as his music library doesn't extend past December 1979. On the other hand, Rick was an MTV-watching, pop-loving geek during most of that decade (and a good part of the next one), so who's he to talk? Here's a list of our faves from the days of Huey Lewis and Oingo Boingo.

Rick: Yeah, I took a lot of abuse from my college buddies for my bubble-gum taste in music. But at least I can say I evolved. I destroyed my Cyndi Lauper albums and now recognize the true gems of the '80s.

- "Don't You Forget About Me" — Simple Minds
- "Bang the Drum All Day" — Todd Rundgren
- "What I Like About You" — Romantics
- "Rebel Yell" — Billy Idol
- "Melt With You" — Modern English

Dave: Well, it was nice working with you, Rick, but there's absolutely no way I will ever speak to you again now that you've admitted a fondness for one of the ten most despicable songs ever written, Rundgren's "Bang the Drum All Day." Heck, I don't even know how we're going to finish the book at this point, but I'll let my lawyers worry about that. To clear the stench made by that horrible song, I offer these five songs:

- Something by Supertramp, maybe. Let's say "Breakfast in America."
- "Moving in Stereo" — The Cars
- Man, this is soooo hard. There was no good music in the '80s. "Rock of Ages," by Def Leppard, maybe?
- "Sunday Bloody Sunday" — U2. Whew, a classic from the '80s. A miracle.
- "Orange Crush" — REM. Might be a '90s song, though. This is so hard…

Playing Digital Music

Chapter 4

Finding Digital Music Online

How to...

- Download free music from Amazon.com
- Differentiate between various music file formats
- Find sites for downloading MP3 files
- Choose a file-sharing service
- Share only the files you want to share
- Understand the Gnutella Network
- Download MP3 files from MP3.com
- Find great kids' music online
- Share files with LimeWire

Now that your computer is ready and you've read about the legalities of MP3, it's time to start looking for the actual music files. As you learned in Chapter 1, there are two main sources for digital music: your personal collection and the Internet. In this chapter, we steer you to sites that offer legitimate (that is, authorized and legal) song files to download, as well as services that enable file sharing. This includes the notorious Napster, the service that started the ball rolling. (You should know right now that Napster as we once knew it no longer exists. At press time, it was being revamped and relaunched as a pay service. But plenty of file-sharing services have arisen to take its place, and some of them seem pretty lawsuit-proof.)

NOTE *This chapter focuses primarily on downloading and sharing MP3 and other song files. Chapter 5 tells you how to find and play music using various MP3 player applications, and Chapter 6 introduces you to Internet radio.*

Music Sites

There's no such thing as a free lunch, but the Internet is home to a seemingly endless supply of free music. For instance, you can connect to one of hundreds of Internet radio stations for free tunes around the clock (see Chapter 6). Or, if you're looking for actual music files you can play anytime or take anywhere, you'll find no shortage of offerings there, either. Just surf to one or more of the great music sites that inhabit the Web.

There are myriad advantages to obtaining music this way (as opposed to using one of the file-sharing services we profile in "File-Sharing Services" later in this chapter). First, you can be secure in the knowledge that the files you're downloading are legal, because they've been authorized for distribution by the artists and/or record label. Second, you can often find "special" tracks from your favorite artists that haven't been released elsewhere. And, finally, music sites open the door to discovery, allowing you to check out new and unknown bands and artists.

In the pages to come, we tell you about two of our favorite online destinations—Amazon.com and MP3.com. After that, we steer you to nearly a dozen other worthwhile sites (see Table 4-1). Get your modem connected and your hard drive spinning—let the download-fest begin!

Wait, wait, hold the download-fest for a second. There's one other piece of business to discuss. Although many of the files you find at these sites will be in the MP3 format, some will be Windows Media Audio (WMA) or Liquid Audio files. You can refresh your memory about WMA in Chapter 1. As for Liquid Audio, see the following sidebar, "What Is Liquid Audio?"

Amazon.com

You may be surprised to learn that Amazon.com—the famous seller of books, CDs, and other merchandise—is a source for thousands of authorized songs that are free for the download. And because of the site's prominence, it can offer tracks from artists ranging from Bob Dylan to U2, with plenty of renowned blues, country, folk, and new age performers in between.

What Is Liquid Audio?

While MP3 is the reigning standard for digital music, competing standards do exist. We've already talked briefly about WMA, the Microsoft-backed format that offers better compression and digital security. Another competitor is Liquid Audio (www.liquidaudio.com), which is actually older than MP3 and is supported by thousands of record labels and artists. As you surf the Web in search of music to download, chances are you'll encounter a lot of songs in the Liquid Audio format.

Although Liquid Audio bills itself as a "format-neutral distribution company" rather than as a simple audio-compression technology like MP3, the fact is that Liquid Audio tracks (files that have an "LQT" extension) are proprietary and incompatible with other formats. Therefore, if you plan to download Liquid tracks from, say, Amazon.com, you'll need either Liquid's own player software (a free version is available for download from the Liquid Audio Web site) or one of the Real players. As you'll learn in Chapter 5, we're partial to the RealJukebox audio player, which has the added benefit of supporting Liquid Audio files (though you must first download a plug-in that enables this functionality). RealJukebox supports virtually every other digital music format as well.

It's important to note that while you can listen to Liquid songs on your PC, you can't convert the files to MP3 or WAV format. That means you can't burn the songs onto a CD or copy them to most portable players. (A couple of Sony's players do support the Liquid format.) The upshot here is that although Liquid Audio is the one MP3 alternative with extensive music-industry support, it's nowhere near as flexible as MP3. That said, you can find hundreds of great songs to download at Web destinations like Amazon.com and CDNow (www.cdnow.com).

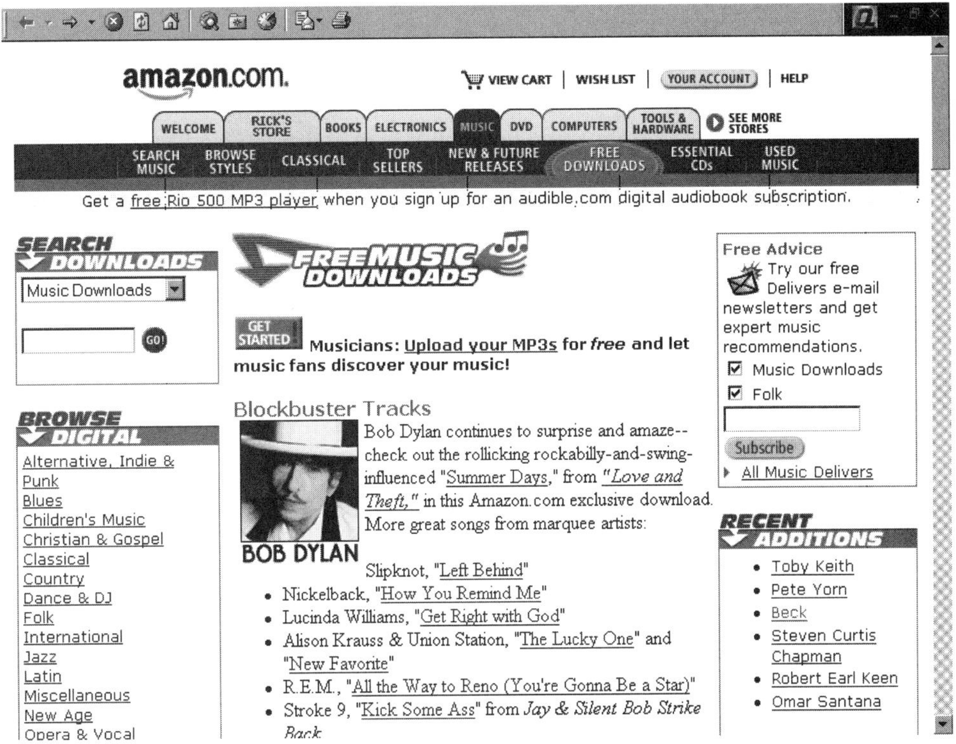

Make no mistake—we're not talking about the 30-second snippets you listen to when you're shopping for audio CDs (see "Did You Know?" at the end of this chapter). These are complete tracks for you to download and listen to on your PC, portable player, or wherever. The artists and their record companies offer these tracks as a promotional effort, the idea being that you'll like what you hear and decide to buy the CD.

Amazon.com's songs are available in one of two formats: Liquid Audio and MP3. It's easy enough to work with the latter—just download the files and play them on your computer or portable player (see Chapters 5 and 7, respectively). Liquid Audio is a different matter, however, one that merits a separate discussion (see "What Is Liquid Audio?").

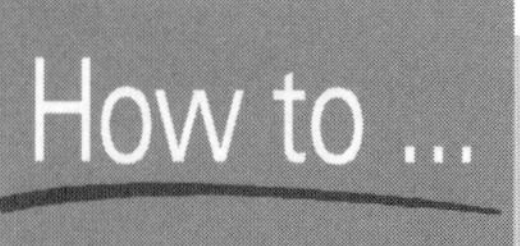

Play a Song You've Downloaded

Nothing too tricky here. We recommend that you download all your song files into the same folder on your hard drive, be it "My Music" or another easily identifiable location. Then you can simply navigate to the folder and double-click the icon for the song. If it's an MP3 file, it will automatically launch the default MP3 player on your computer (most often that's Windows Media Player). If it's a Liquid file, it will launch whichever appropriate software is installed: Liquid Player or RealJukebox. See Chapter 5 for more information on listening to music on your PC.

MP3.com

If you visit just one site after reading this chapter, make sure it's MP3.com (see Figure 4-1). A pioneer of the digital music industry and one of our favorite destinations, MP3.com offers a huge variety of freely downloadable MP3 files, to say nothing of streaming audio, MP3 software, hardware reviews, and unique services like Beam-it and Instant Listening. The site's catalog includes hundreds of high-profile bands and musicians (including David Bowie, Tina Turner, and Big Bad Voodoo Daddy, to name just a few), as well as a mammoth archive of independent artists. Thus, it's the place to go not only for music you know, but also for music you don't know.

NOTE *Music from the better-known commercial artists is likely to be available as streaming audio rather than a download. Thus, if you want to hear, say, Madonna's latest, you'll hear it played in real time as it streams to your computer—but you won't end up with a file you can keep and replay.*

Because MP3.com is ostensibly the single best source for authorized songs to download—songs you can listen to on your PC, transfer to a portable player, or do with as you please—we're going to walk you through the steps of finding and obtaining an MP3 file. Along the way, we'll highlight some of MP3.com's interesting options and capabilities.

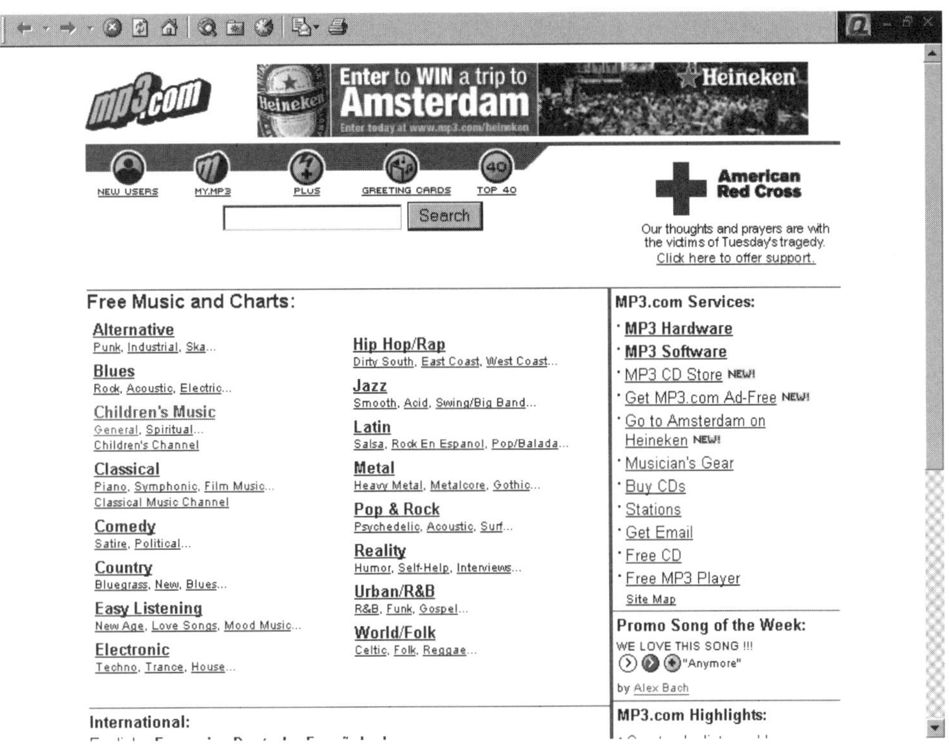

FIGURE 4-1 The MP3.com home page makes it easy to navigate to specific music genres.

NOTE *In late August 2001, as we were writing this book, MP3.com was acquired by Vivendi Universal, with the intent of using the service to power Pressplay, its online music-subscription joint venture with Sony. It's possible that the look and feel of MP3.com will change somewhat as a result, but we think the core content and capabilities will remain the same.*

Two Ways to Find Songs

When you first visit MP3.com, you can look for songs in two main ways. You can use the search engine, or simply browse the site by clicking here and there. Let's take a closer look at both strategies:

- **Search** On most MP3.com pages, there's a Search box where you can type the name of a song or artist.

- **Browse** If you've ever used Yahoo to "drill down" through links to find what you're looking for on the Web, you'll appreciate MP3.com's similar setup. The main page lists several dozen music genres and subgenres, making it quite easy to head in a desired direction. When you click a link, you're presented with lists of songs that fall into that category.

We should mention at this point that MP3.com continues to add new features all the time, and that we could probably devote an entire chapter to using the service—if not an entire book. Some experimentation may be required—not just because there's so much to wade through, but because the service can be confusing in some areas.

MP3.com can be befuddling at times. For instance, if you decide to add a CD to your online shopping cart and then choose to keep browsing, you later discover there's no easy way to get back to your cart to complete the purchase. The solution is to click the Buy button on some other CD. It won't get added to your cart right away, but you will finally see the View Cart option—where you can then finish buying the stuff you do want.

Locating and Downloading a Song

As just one of many possible scenarios, let's say you're looking for some dance music to play during your kickboxing workouts. Here's how to find great stuff on MP3.com.

If you download a lot of songs (or other files, for that matter), it's a good idea to use a download manager. This software can speed up your downloads and even resume them if there's an interruption. We highly recommend Download Accelerator Plus, a free program you can obtain from SpeedBit (www.speedbit.com).

What Is My.MP3?

To really get the most from MP3.com, you should sign up for the free My.MP3 service. It allows you to add, store, access, manage, and listen to your personal music collection, regardless of where you are (any Internet-connected computer will do). While you're browsing the site, for instance, you can click any free song to have it instantly added to your My.MP3 collection. Songs and albums you buy wind up there as well, as do tracks added using Beam-it (see the next section). You can build custom playlists of these songs, transfer them to a portable MP3 device, get recommendations of other music you might like, and download songs to your computer.

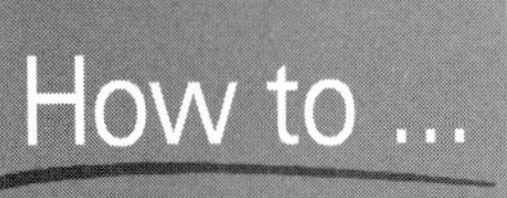

Find Music on MP3.com

1. Start on the MP3.com home page by clicking the Electronic link.
2. On the subsequent page, under the Electronic Charts heading, click the Dance link. You'll then see a page containing dozens of songs, and links to additional pages in the Dance group.
3. For any given song, you have several options. You can click Lo Fi Play to hear the song played immediately (it's routed through your MP3 player software as streaming audio), click Add To My.MP3 to have the song added to your personal library (more on My.MP3 in the next section), or click the name of the artist. For purposes of our example, pick an artist and click the link.

Our Favorite Portable MP3 Players

Rick: Dave, you probably think I'm going to champion a cheapy MP3 player that has only 32MB or 64MB of RAM, because most people can live with one or two hours of music. But this time I'm on your side, as I know which player is your favorite: the Archos Jukebox Recorder. This amazing little puppy stores 6GB of MP3 files (but, alas, not WMA files), and it's priced at just $349. That's only $50 more than the Intel Pocket Concert, which has only 128MB of storage capacity.

The only people who shouldn't buy the Archos are runners and other athletes, who should choose a model that's not hard-drive based (most MP3 players aren't, which makes them impervious to shock and, therefore, skipping).

Dave: You think you know me… But as usual, you're so far off base that you're actually playing hockey (that's a little sports metaphor for you). Honestly, the Archos Jukebox Recorder is a nifty little gadget and I love the fact that it lets you make MP3 recordings thanks to a line-in jack. But my personal portable MP3 player is, in fact, the Neo Jukebox from I/O Magic. Why? Even though it costs about the same as the Archos player, the Neo Jukebox is a 20GB player, meaning I can store my entire music collection; with the Archos, I still have to compromise and only carry part of my collection.

What if I'm in Toledo and desperately need to hear Neil Young's "Get Gone?" Or I find myself in Boston and have an insatiable desire to listen to "Crosstown Traffic" by Hendrix? What then? With the Neo, I know I can hear anything, anytime. Archos has a 20GB version of their MP3 player as well, but I don't recommend it as highly as the Neo because the batteries are a lot harder to change, making it a pain to swap power sources in the middle of a long plane flight.

What Is Beam-it?

So you have a massive collection of CDs at home. Wouldn't it be nice to listen to your music at the office, at a friend's house, or in a hotel while on a business trip?

The Best $13.98 You Can Spend on Your Kids

While working on this book, Rick discovered the Children's Music section at MP3.com. He downloaded a variety of songs for his 20-month-old daughter, Sarah, and burned them onto a CD for listening in the car. One of the artists he discovered was Graham Clarke, who sings some of the catchiest, funniest kids' tunes Rick has ever heard. Do yourself a favor and download "Old MacDonald Goes Crazy"—and then do what Rick did: buy Clarke's two "sampler" CDs (each containing about six songs) for $6.99 each. Your kids will love them, and Rick thinks you will, too.

With Beam-it, you can spin your CDs—virtually speaking—from anywhere there's Web access. At home, you simply slide a CD into your CD-ROM drive. Beam-it recognizes it and adds the tracks to your My.MP3 account. Repeat the process with every CD you own (yes, it could take a while). Now you can listen to your personal music collection—streamed to whatever computer you're using—from just about anywhere. (The usual caveats about connection speed still apply—a slow one will mean lower-quality playback and possible interruptions.)

NOTE *Owing to licensing restrictions, not all of your tracks or CDs may be accessible through Beam-it. Those that aren't will have a little padlock next to them in the My Music page.*

What Is Instant Listening?

When you order a CD from, say, Amazon.com, you have to wait a week or so for it to arrive in the mail. When you buy a CD from MP3.com, you can take advantage of Instant Listening to hear your new music immediately. The tracks are made available in your My.MP3 library for real-time play. Look for the little Instant Listening Enabled logo to see if a CD you're buying supports the Instant Listening option.

Deciphering MP3.com's Song Options

When you look at the listing for any given song, you're likely to see as many as eight different options—some of which might not make immediate sense. Let's define each one in turn.

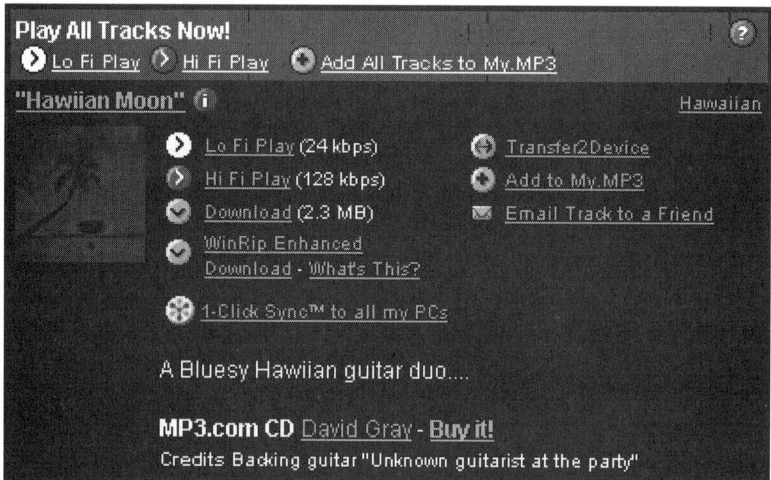

- **Lo Fi Play (24 Kbps)** This option will stream the song to your computer so you can listen to it in real time. The sound quality is roughly on par with AM radio—but if you have a dial-up Internet connection, this is the option you're stuck with.

- **Hi Fi Play (128 Kbps)** This option doesn't appear with all songs, but when it does, the streaming audio that comes to your computer will sound like it came from a CD. You need a broadband connection to make it happen, though.
- **Download** Just like it sounds, this option (not always available) downloads the MP3 file to your PC.
- **WinRip Enhanced Download** Imagine an MP3 file that included song lyrics, artist bios, touring information, concert photos, Web links, and more. That's the basic definition of a WinRip-Enhanced MP3 file. To play these fabulous files (which, understandably, are larger and thus take longer to download), you first need to download and install InterVideo's WinRip player (www.intervideo.com).
- **1-Click Sync to all my PCs** Powered by a third-party Web service called FusionOne (www.fusionone.com), this option downloads any given song to all your PCs, not just the one you're at. Thus, if you're at the office and want a song on your home system, this can save you from having to find and download it again.
- **Transfer2Device** If you have a portable MP3 player (see Chapter 7), clicking this option enables you to transfer songs directly to it. However, only about a dozen players are supported, so this option is of limited value.
- **Add to My.MP3** This option instantly adds the song to your My.MP3 library.
- **Email Track to a Friend** You found this song on MP3.com that you're absolutely wild about, and you want to share it with some friends. Rather than e-mailing the MP3 file itself (which, at 3MB on average, is a pretty sizable attachment), just click the "Email Track to a Friend" link next to the song title. That will send the appropriate Web address to your friends, allowing them to download or play the song at their leisure.

Table 4-1 lists other digital music sites you might like to explore.

Site	URL	What You'll Find There
ArtistDirect.com	www.artistdirect.com	Dozens of modern songs in Liquid, MP3, and WMA formats, plus music news, videos, shopping, and message boards
Liquid.com	www.liquid.com	The Liquid Audio player, plus a handful of songs to download
Listen.com	www.listen.com	Links to hundreds of free and pay tracks in Liquid, MP3, and WMA formats, plus music videos and Internet radio
MTV	www.mtv.com	Dozens of WMA songs from popular rock, rap, and indie artists
Real.com	www.real.com	In the Guide section, a handful of Liquid Audio downloads, plus links to dozens of sites where you can download Liquid and MP3 files
Rioport.com	www.rioport.com	Hundreds of promotional downloads in MP3 and WMA formats
Rolling Stone	www.rollingstone.com	Thousands of MP3 songs for streaming and downloading
Windows Media	www.windowsmedia.com	Music videos and downloads, the latter in WMA format
VH1	www.vh1.com	A few free tracks and many more pay tracks

TABLE 4-1 Digital Music Sites

File-Sharing Services

The fastest and easiest way to obtain MP3 files is by using a file-sharing service. You've probably heard of Napster, the notorious service that created a media frenzy and raised the ire of record companies. If you haven't already, please go back and read Chapter 3, which gives you some of the history of Napster and exposes the legal and ethical implications of trading MP3 files online.

We're not going to rehash that here. Instead, we're going to introduce you to some of the better file-sharing tools and services, and remind you that artists deserve to be paid for their work. Let your conscience be your guide.

File-Sharing Fundamentals

At press time, we counted nearly 100 programs expressly designed with MP3-swapping in mind. There may be 100 more by the time you read this. These programs employ a slightly different technology than Napster (again, see Chapter 3), but their core functionality is the same—they allow you to download MP3 files from other users. You type in the name of an artist or song you're looking for, the software finds the file, and you download it.

CAUTION *Virus alert! It's entirely possible to contract a virus from a file you download. Although we don't know of any that are specific to MP3 files, there's no reason a virus couldn't masquerade as an MP3. Play it safe—install a virus checker such as Norton AntiVirus, and be sure toupdate the virus definitions regularly. (Usually it's an automated process.)*

At the same time, your MP3 files are fair game for others to upload. At least, that's the idea. Because these programs allow you to specify the folder that contains the files you want to share, you have the option of keeping your collection totally private. In Web parlance, this makes you a "leech"—someone who takes files without giving any in return. If you're going to download, the least you can do is make your collection available to others.

In the following sections, we give you the lowdown on the most popular file-sharing programs, with detailed how-to information on one of our favorites: LimeWire. Many of these programs go beyond mere MP3 sharing, allowing you to swap photos, videos clips, text documents—you name it.

CAUTION *Parents, take note: People use file-sharing programs to share not only MP3 files, but pornographic material as well. Unmonitored kids may unwittingly—or wittingly—download inappropriate stuff. Even if you have software that's designed to prevent access to inappropriate Web sites, it probably won't filter the file-sharing programs. We don't presume to advise you on how to handle this situation—we just want you to know it's shockingly easy to access pornography using these programs.*

If I Share My MP3 Files, Can Someone Hack into *All* My Files?

In these days of Internet paranoia, that's a perfectly fair question. It seems logical to assume that if someone can tap into the folder that contains your MP3 files, he or she could gain access to your entire hard drive—with potentially devastating results. The good news is, it's virtually impossible for this to happen. File-sharing software not only limits access to a specific folder or set of folders, but also makes your computer invisible to all others. In other words, someone who's downloading an MP3 file from you doesn't know where it's coming from.

While a clever hacker may be able to bully his way into your machine, it's not likely that file-sharing software is going to facilitate the process. In any case, we recommend using a firewall utility like ZoneAlarm (www.zonealarm.com) for general protection, so you'll have absolutely nothing to worry about.

How to Use LimeWire

With its friendly interface and myriad features, LimeWire (see Figure 4-2) ranks as one of our favorite file-sharing programs. With it, you can swap audio, video, image, and document files, and even programs. What's more, because it was written in the Java language, it's compatible with virtually every platform: Windows, Macintosh (including OS X), Linux, and even Solaris.

You can download the appropriate version of LimeWire from the company's Web site (www.limewire.com). Like most file-sharing programs, this one is a freebie—as is the Gnutella Network it employs.

What Is the Gnutella Network?

Sounds like something out of *Star Trek* ("Captain, we can't take the ship into the Gnutella Network! The radiation would destroy the replicators!"), but it's actually a "peer-to-peer" network with no central computer or company coordinating file sharing.

Many of today's most popular file-sharing programs are essentially Gnutella *front ends,* meaning they provide an interface for accessing the network. LimeWire and Gnutella are just two of the file-sharing programs that link you to Gnutella.

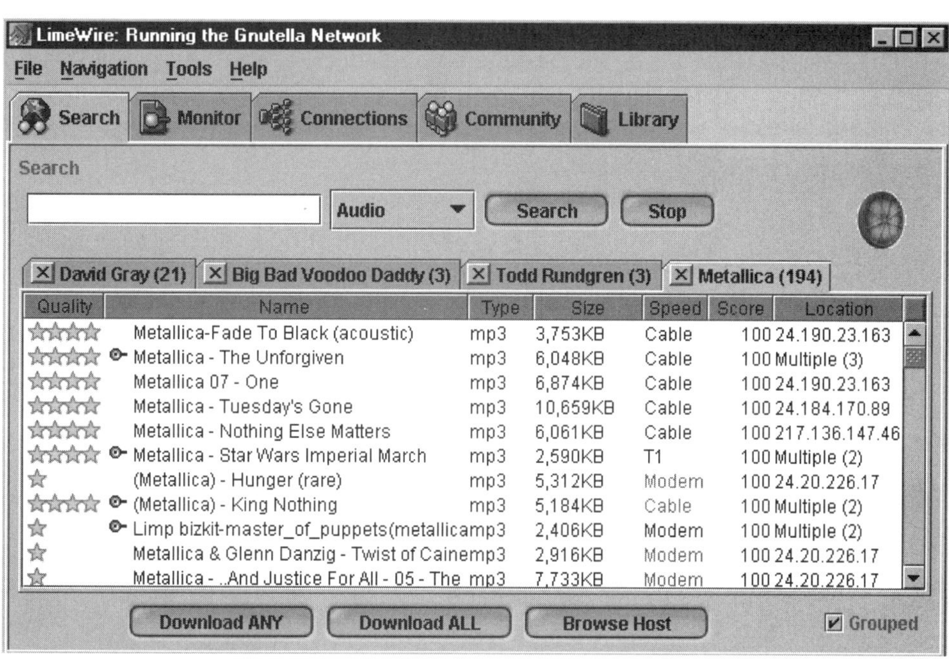

FIGURE 4-2 LimeWire is a great program for sharing files, as it's easy to use and compatible with multiple platforms.

LimeWire Installation

After you download the LimeWire program (making sure to remember where on your hard drive you saved the file), double-click it. During the installation process, you may be informed that your system needs the Java2 Runtime Environment—a separate piece of software that enables the use of Java programs like this one. Just follow the instructions to download and install Java2. It's all fairly automated, but if you have a slow Internet connection, it could take a while to download the 5MB file.

NOTE *We looked at LimeWire 1.6d. A newer version is likely to be available by the time you read this, but most of the basic operations should be the same.*

Getting Started with LimeWire

After installation is complete, you should have a LimeWire icon on your desktop. Double-click it to launch the program. You'll then see something that looks a lot like Figure 4-2. Notice the five tabs across the top of the screen:

- **Search** This is where you search for songs, artists, or whatever else you might be seeking. Notice the box labeled "Any Type" next to the Search field. Click it to pull down a menu that lets you narrow your search to documents, programs, audio, video, or images.
- **Monitor** You can use this tab to see which files are currently being uploaded from your computer by others.
- **Connections** For only the most advanced users, this tab reveals the servers to which you're connected and lets you add specific servers manually.
- **Community** Want to chat with other LimeWire users? That's the idea behind this tab. Unfortunately, at press time, we couldn't get it working.
- **Library** This tab provides quick access to your collection of existing and downloaded files, based on the folders you specify in the Options screen (discussed in the next paragraph).

Before you do anything else, you should tell the program which folders on your hard drive to use for downloading and sharing. Select Tools | Options, and then click the Sharing tab. In the field labeled Save Directory, enter the name of the folder where downloaded files should be stored (or click the Browse button to navigate to the folder).

In the field labeled File Sharing, click the Add Directory button, and then navigate to the folder that houses your MP3 files. You can add multiple directories to this list if you wish. When you're done, click OK.

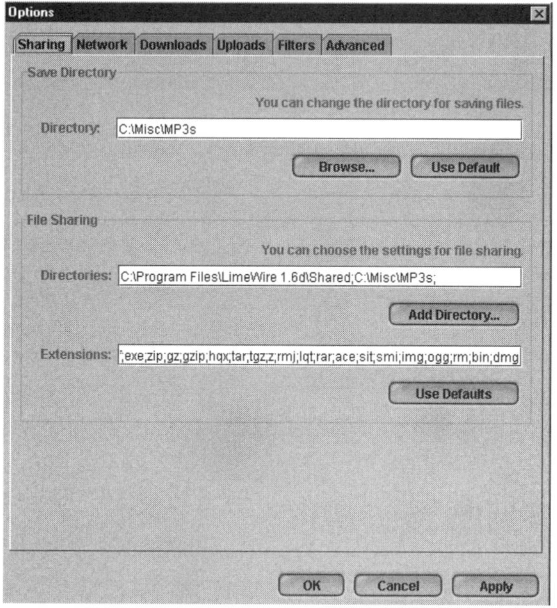

LimeWire's one significant shortcoming is that it doesn't tell you the bit rate of the file you're downloading (see Chapter 5 for more information on bit rates). Thus, you may wind up with a file that was ripped at 64 Kbps, which won't sound nearly as good as the original CD recording. Other services, like MusicCity Morpheus, do provide bit rate information, so you can download more selectively.

When you first start LimeWire, wait a minute or so before starting a search. It takes a while for the software to connect to all the servers out there, and the longer you wait, the more likely you are to find what you're looking for.

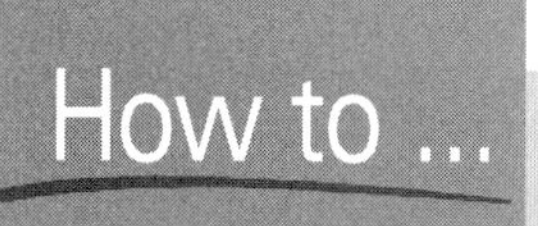

Download an MP3 File

Now let's try finding and downloading an MP3 file. For this example, we're going to use the George Michael song, "Too Funky." This is freely available from Amazon.com, so it's a song that's legal for distribution. Here's the step-by-step process:

1. Make sure the Search tab is active, and then type **Too Funky** into the Search field. Click the pull-down box next to it and select Audio from the list.

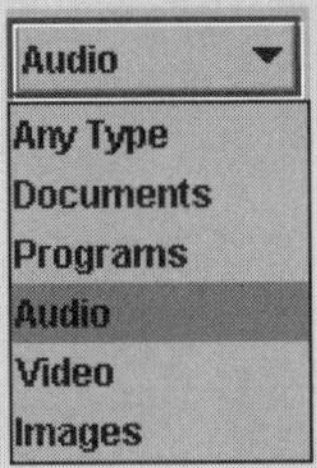

2. Click the Search button to start the process. In a few moments, you should see the song appear in the main search window. If it doesn't, try again by searching for George Michael.

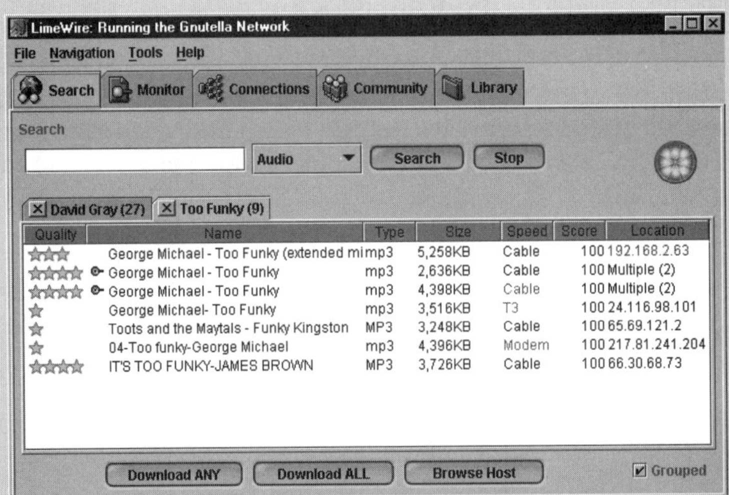

3. Once you find the song, simply double-click it to begin the download. It will then appear in the Downloads window at the bottom of the screen, along with the size of the file, its download status, and the transfer speed.

How Do I Know Which Version to Download? When you searched for the song "Too Funky," LimeWire probably found at least two or three instances of it—meaning at least two or three people were making the song available for sharing. Which one should you download? Start by looking at the Quality rating (see Figure 4-3), which is expressed as 1 to 4 stars. In this case, "quality" refers not to the song itself, but to the speed of the connection to the other computer. Thus, when choosing which version of the song to download, look for a three- or four-star connection. But don't be concerned if it you're limited to a one- or two-star download—it'll just take a little longer.

Why Are There Different File Sizes for the Same Song? It's common to see several different file sizes for the same song. When we searched for "Too Funky," for instance, we got one that was 2636KB, one that was 4398KB, and a third at 3516KB (see Figure 4-3). Why the discrepancies, and how do you know which one to choose? As you'll learn in Chapter 10, when people rip songs from their CDs, they do so at different bit rates. These rates affect not only sound quality, but also file size. If you have a fast connection and want the best sound quality, always download the largest version of any given song.

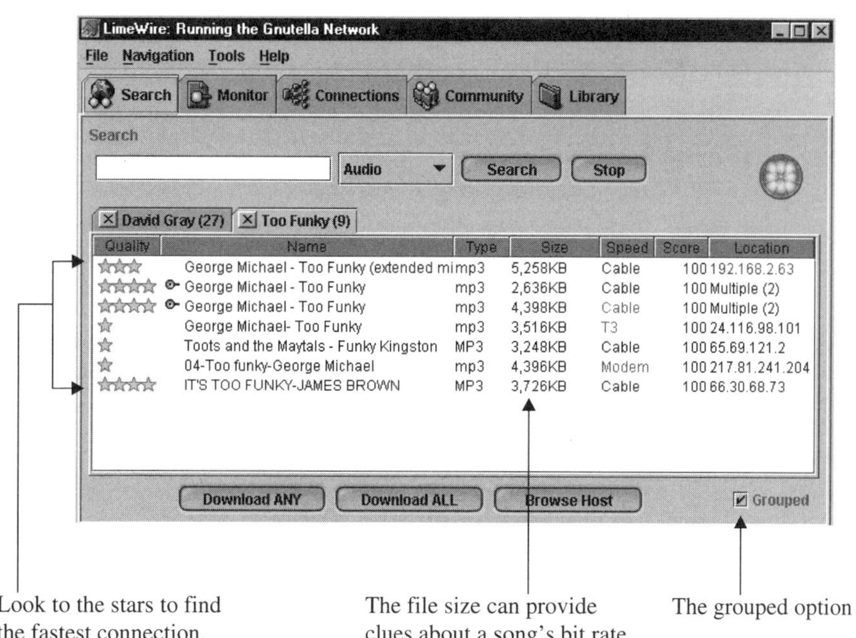

FIGURE 4-3 LimeWire uses star ratings to help you identify the fastest connections for your downloads.

What Does the Grouped Option Do? In Figure 4-3, notice the check box labeled Grouped. When checked (which it is by default), LimeWire will group together all versions of a song that have the exact same file size, rather than listing them individually (the idea being to keep the song list shorter and more manageable). You can click the little magnifying glass next to a song name to see the items in the group, or simply clear the Grouped box to remove groups altogether. Experiment to see which method you like best.

How should you choose a file-sharing service? Simple—try several of them. They're all free, and most are pretty easy to use (Aimster and Audiogalaxy Satellite being two exceptions). We think most users will be happy with LimeWire or MusicCity Morpheus, but we also encourage you to experiment with others to find your personal preference. You have nothing to lose!

Table 4-2, on the following page, gives you an overview of file-sharing services.

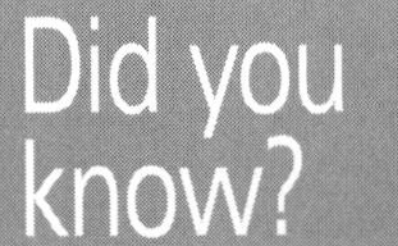

You Can Listen Before You Leap

When you shop online for audio CDs, you can usually listen to snippets of several tracks before making your purchases. This is thanks to *streaming audio,* which downloads a portion of a song—usually about 30 seconds—for you to hear in real time. Most of these snippets are delivered in the Real audio format—another reason we're partial to using RealJukebox as our music player (see Chapter 5). If you don't have a Real player installed on your system, you may not be able to listen to some of these samples.

Service	URL	Backbone	Sharing Capabilities	Can Resume Interrupted Downloads	Platforms Supported	Our Take
Aimster	www.aimster.com	Central server	All media files	No	Win/Mac	Confusing software; lawsuits pending
Audiogalaxy Satellite	www.audiogalaxy.com	Central server	Music files	Yes	Win/Linux	Works well, but the Web-based interface can be confusing
Gnotella	www.gnutella.com	Gnutella Network	All media files	Yes	Win	Definitely not the most user-friendly program, but very versatile
KaZaa Media Desktop	www.kazaa.com	Distributed peer-to-peer network	All media files	Yes	Win	Virtually identical to Morpheus, but we like the latter better
LimeWire	www.limewire.com	Gnutella Network	All media files	Yes	Win/Mac/Linux	Probably the most novice-friendly file sharing software
Morpheus	www.musiccity.com	Distributed peer-to-peer network	All media files	Yes	Win	Very fast and reasonably user-friendly
SwapNut	www.swapnut.com	Distributed peer-to-peer network	All media files	Yes	Win	A good choice for dial-up modem users
WinMX	www.winmx.com	Distributed peer-to-peer network and central servers	All media files	Yes	Win	Not one of our favorites. The interface is cluttered and confusing

TABLE 4-2 File-Sharing Services

Chapter 5 Listening on the PC

How to...

- Choose an MP3 player for your PC or Mac
- Decide on music player features
- Decode the lingo
- Play music with Winamp
- Use music players in Windows
- Use music players on the Mac
- Optimize your volume
- Create custom playlists of music
- Change the look of your player with skins
- See your music with visualizations

So you've got a collection of MP3 songs and you're hankering for a way to play them. Actually, only Rick would download songs before he thought about getting a program capable of playing them. Back in college, Rick didn't have the money to get a CD player, but he bought a somewhat sizable CD collection nonetheless. It was sad to visit his dorm room and see him tinkering with the "CD player" he had made from a cardboard box and shoestrings from an old pair of sneakers. He kept insisting it would work soon; he just needed to draw some more transistors inside the box.

Seriously, we know you've already got at least one MP3 player on your computer. If you have a Windows Millennium Edition (Me) or Windows XP system, for instance, it probably came with Microsoft's Windows Media Player, which isn't half-bad. In this chapter, though, we'll talk about your other music player options and the basics of using them.

Choosing an MP3 Player

MP3 players, for the most part, all do the same thing—they play music. But that's like saying that all cars get you to Dairy Queen or all TVs show repeats of *The Simpsons*. You should find the player that suits your personality and needs.

At the same time, remember that lots of people have several MP3 players and use different ones at different times or for different reasons. Take Dave, for instance: he primarily uses RealJukebox, but he switches to MusicMatch Jukebox when copying CDs to the PC. Why? He prefers the MusicMatch interface for changing batches of song titles at once (a lot more about that in Chapter 11). So you needn't stick with just one, especially if they're inexpensive or free.

Thankfully, most music players are classified as *shareware,* which means you can download and try them out before deciding to buy. Many shareware programs—like RealJukebox and MusicMatch Jukebox—let you use the most basic version of the player for free, forever. If you want more features, you'll have to pay a few dollars to get the enhanced version of the program. Other music players, like the popular Winamp, are completely free; this is known as *freeware.*

In addition, many new PCs come with MP3 players preinstalled on the hard disk. Hewlett-Packard, for instance, ships many of their PCs with the basic version of the MusicMatch player preinstalled. Even the newest version of Netscape Navigator, a Web browser, comes with MP3 software now (a version of Winamp).

Finding an MP3 Player

What if your computer doesn't have an MP3 player and you're not sure where to begin looking? In the next section, we'll highlight some of the most popular MP3 players for the PC and Macintosh. You can also find MP3 players at a number of Web sites. Visit MP3.com, for instance. This site has a respectable list of MP3 player software—complete with product reviews—right from a link on the home page. Or you can visit download.com. This comprehensive Web site lists thousands of programs that you can download. The MP3 & Audio section is home to many music players and other software. Another site, tucows.com, has a comprehensive collection of MP3 software as well.

Of course, all music players are not created equal. Some play just one or two music file formats, while others can play almost any file format that has yet been invented. Likewise, some music players do one thing and one thing only: play MP3s. More elaborate programs are known as *jukeboxes,* and these programs can typically do a bunch of different things, like play audio CDs, play streaming audio from the Internet, rip music from music CDs, and rip record tracks to blank, recordable CDs. Obviously, if you plan to make your own CDs with a CD-RW drive or if you have CDs that you want to transfer to your hard disk, you want to focus your attention on the more elaborate jukebox programs.

Which features should your music player actually have? Here's a short checklist of the most common features of desktop MP3 players today. You can use this list as a yardstick when choosing the MP3 player that you plan to use on your own computer:

- **Cost** Because many MP3 players are free, be careful about spending money on a commercial product. Make sure you try it out first. Personally, we are extremely leery of boxed music players in computer and office supply stores. If you ask us, many of them are very shoddy products that are trying to capitalize on the popularity of digital music. The Internet is the best place to find music players because you can download and try them out first, *before* you spend money.
- **Web savvy** The best music players have Web features built in. Our favorite features are the ability to look up information about the song that's currently playing, and the ability to check for program updates automatically.
- **Behavior** Music players are notoriously rude—you might want to try out any program you plan to buy to check its manners. How can music programs be rude? For starters, many are system resource hogs, slowing your system down and making it harder to multitask the longer the program runs. We've used music players that essentially bring the computer to its knees after four or five hours of playing music. Also, some music players are almost Zen-like in their obsession with playing all of the music file formats on your computer. You might have another program that you prefer to use, but you can't because this program keeps stealing the file associations. We'll show you how to fix that problem in "Fixing the File Type Association" in Chapter 13, by the way.
- **Appearance** Let's face it: we're all shallow people (well, at least Rick is), and appearances matter. Even if you like all the features in a particular music player, you may not like the way it looks. This problem has largely disappeared, though, thanks to a feature called *skins,* which let you dramatically change the appearance of your music player.

Music Players for Windows

Sometimes, it seems like just about anyone who knows how to program has created a music player for Windows. There are many to choose from, and many are free or quite inexpensive. A few years ago, perhaps it might have made sense to try many different players to find the one that fit you best. These days, we recommend taking one of the four or five most popular ones and getting on with your life. We highly recommend any one of the following programs.

Get Hip to the Lingo, Digi-Cat

Getting into digital music means learning a whole new vocabulary. Here are some common terms and features you'll find in most music players:

- **Skins** *Skins* are alternate interfaces for your music player. Although the program and its features remain unchanged, you can apply new, custom-designed skins to the program to radically change its appearance. You can use a skin to make the program take up less space on the desktop, to highlight the features you use most often, or just to make it look prettier.

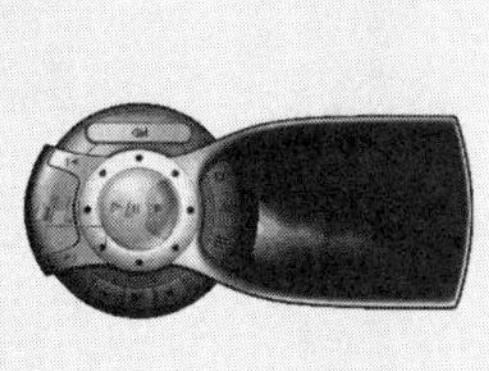

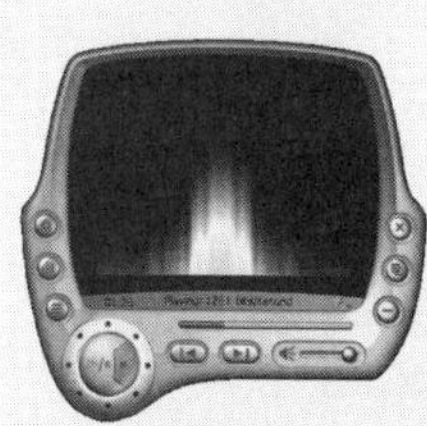

- **Playlists** *Playlists* are collections of songs that you plan to listen to. You can create custom playlists and load them quickly, giving you access to certain styles of music, your favorite tunes, songs by a certain artist, or any other personal preference. Playlists are the digital equivalent of mix tapes and come in handy for parties as well as personal listening.

- **Visualizations** Pure eye candy, *visualizations* are graphics that move, pulsate, or animate in response to the beat of the music. Most music players let you choose from a large number of visualization themes, and you can change them at will. You can make the visualization window small or as large as the monitor itself; it's up to you to customize the experience.

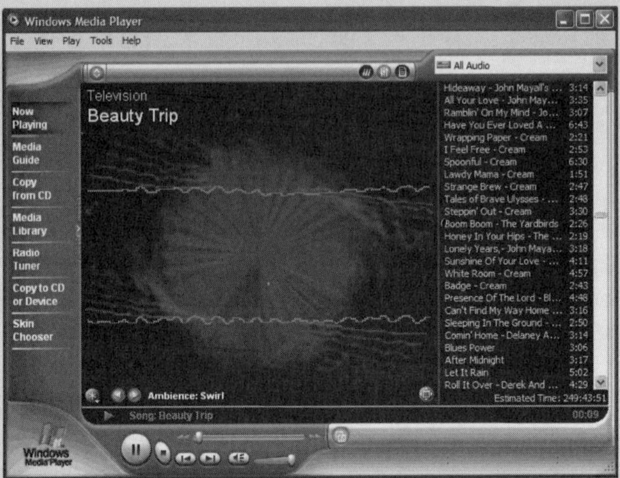

- **Equalizers** Graphic *equalizers* are a part of a stereo system or, in this case, MP3 player that divides the total dynamic range of music into a number of frequency bands—as few as three (highs, mids, and lows) or as many as a dozen. You can adjust equalizers to emphasize the bass, add presence to the high end, or cover up a muddy midrange. Read more about them in Chapter 9.

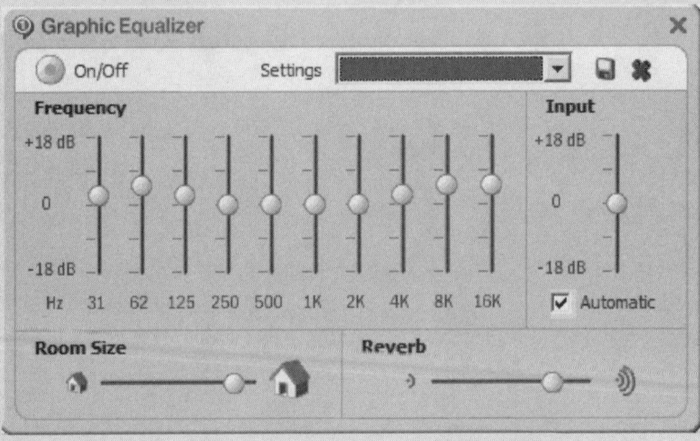

Winamp

Winamp could possibly be the most popular music player for the PC ever. Surprisingly, the program is still completely free, and it appears that it'll stay that way for quite some time to come. You can download your own copy from www.winamp.com. The program has four main components:

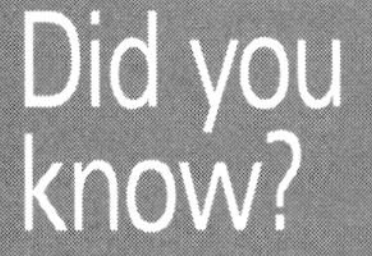

Buttons Explained

Winamp has a lot of controls, but no traditional Windows-style menus. Context-sensitive menus are available by right-clicking on the program screens, though. The following is a breakdown of the main controls in all four of the program's windows:

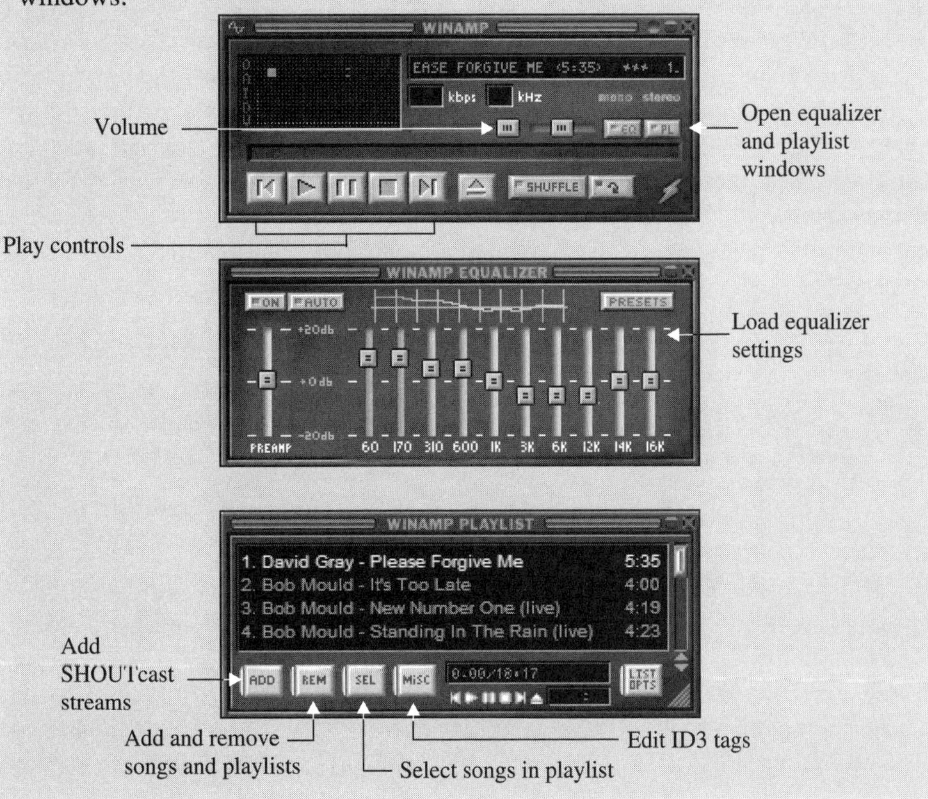

- **Player** This is the core of the program, and it lets you manage the playback of your music.
- **Playlist** This is your queue of songs waiting to play.
- **Equalizer** The program lets you adjust the sonic qualities of the music with a graphic equalizer. We talk about how to use equalizers in Chapter 9.
- **Minibrowser** This small TV-screen-shaped browser window lets you get information about music via the Internet.

Each of these four components appears as a separate window on your desktop. You can turn each of them on or off separately, allowing you to customize the display to your liking. You can also activate what Winamp calls the *window shade mode,* which rolls a window up into its title bar.

Playing Music with Winamp

There are two ways to start playing music with Winamp. On the Player screen, you can click the Eject button to display the Open Files dialog box. From here, just select one or more files to play and click OK. The music starts automatically.

If you have a lot of music, though, a better way to start it is via the Playlist window. Click the Add button to add to the playlist an entire folder of music on your hard disk—you can add your entire My Music folder, for instance, or just a folder of music within it. Once you have some files in the playlist, you can rearrange the play order by dragging files around with the mouse. Or, if you prefer, you can set the player to shuffle play, which randomizes the order.

TIP *You can bookmark your favorite songs and, like a bookmarked page in a book, access them quickly without thumbing through dozens or hundreds of entries. To bookmark a song, select it in the playlist and press* ALT-I *on the keyboard, or right-click and choose Bookmark Item(s) from the menu. Later, listen to the song by choosing Bookmarks from the menu.*

Windows Media Player

Once a poor substitute for a "real" music player, the latest version of the Windows Media Player could easily serve as your one-and-only. (Version 7 of Windows Media Player ships with Windows Me, and version 8 comes with Windows XP.) If you're using anything other than Windows Media Player 8, you should upgrade right away: it's a full-featured, jukebox-style player that performs essentially all the functions

Did you know?

Inside Playlists

Playlists are great. You can create an unlimited number of song lists that suit your various moods or that you tailor for special events like parties. You may not realize that playlists are typically not unique to a single program; if you create a playlist in Winamp, for instance, you can load it into Windows Media Player or RealJukebox and use it there. Therefore, you can use the same playlist in different music players and even on different PCs, provided your playlist points to valid music files on the new computer. You can carry music files on an external, USB-connected hard disk, for instance, to bring your music and playlists with you.

A playlist is a simple text file with the complete filename and path of each song in the list, which might look something like this:

```
C:\My Albums\Throwing Muses\In a Doghouse\Rabbits Dying.mp3

C:\My Albums\The Velvet Underground\Disc 2\All Tomorrow's Parties.mp3

C:\My Albums\Throwing Muses\House Tornado\Marriage Tree.mp3

C:\My Documents\My Music\Kristin Hersh\The Key.mp3
```

You can make your own playlist—or edit an existing one—in any word processor or text editor. Just remember to save the playlist as a plain text file.

as the other programs we talk about in this chapter, as well as video and animation. You can download it for free from Microsoft's Web site.

Not only does the Windows Media Player catalog and play MP3, but it also plays Windows Media Audio (WMA) files, audio CDs, and streaming audio from the Web.

NOTE *For more information on the WMA format, see Chapter 1.*

Playing Music

To begin playing music with the Windows Media Player, you should tell the program where to find your music collection. Select Tools | Search For Media Files, and either search your entire hard disk (which might take a while) or specify a folder in which to look for your collection.

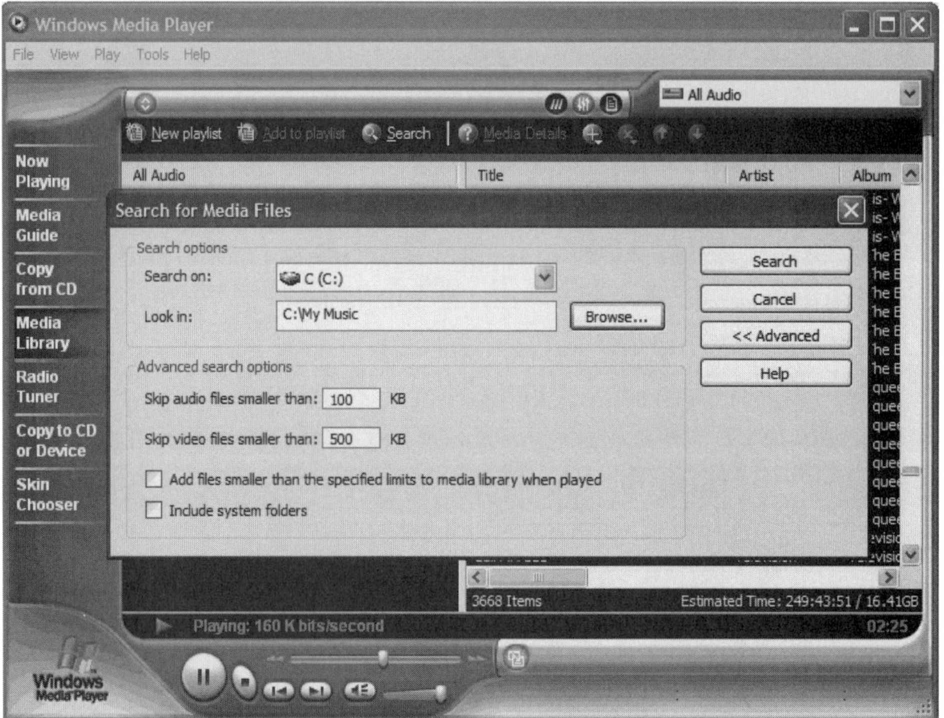

TIP *Unlike most programs, Windows Media Player version 8 can be set to ignore very small music files. These files, probably aborted fragments of songs that didn't completely download from the Internet, are best left out of your library. To control this option, click the Advanced button in the Search For Media Files dialog box.*

After your music collection has been cataloged by the program, click the Media Library button on the left side of the window. You should see a complete list of all the music on your hard disk. Double-click a song to play.

Windows Media Player lets you create custom song lists by dragging songs in the Media Library to a playlist file. Here's what you need to do:

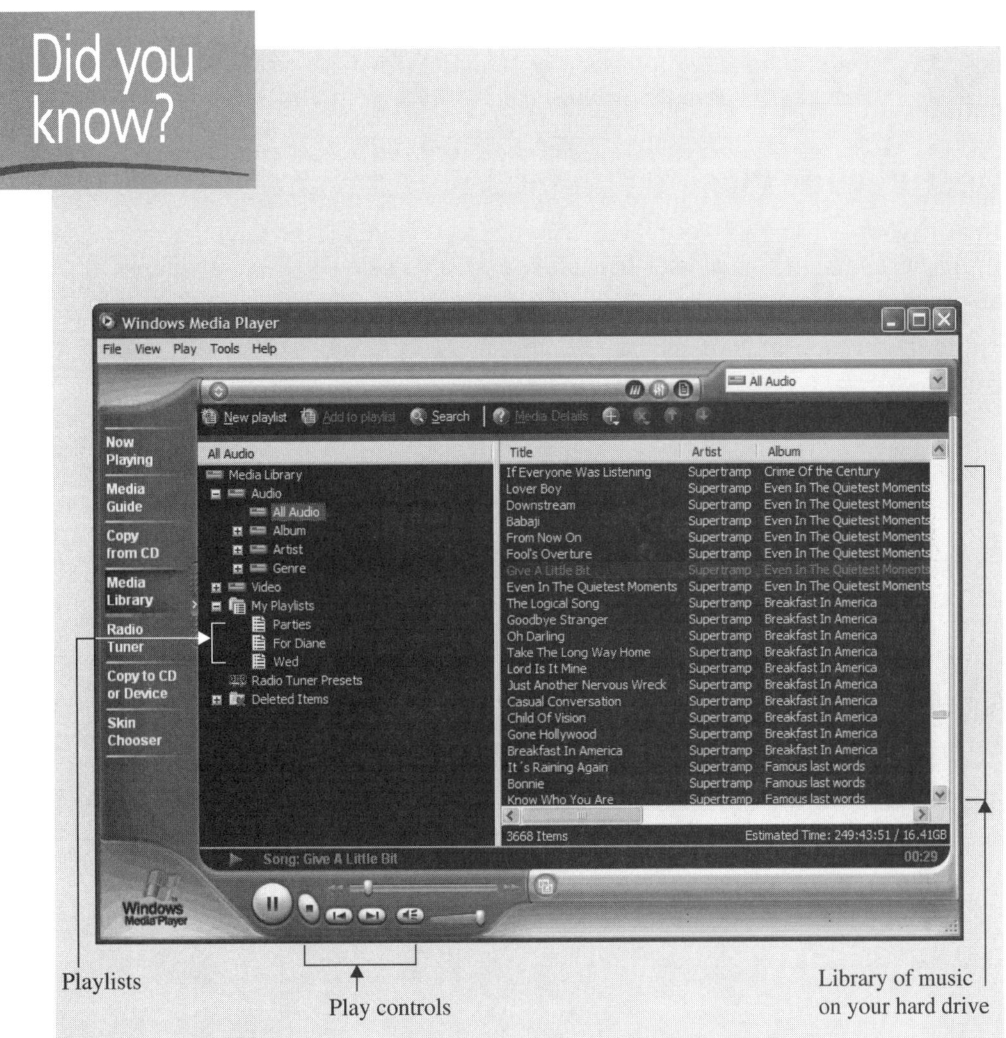

1. Click the New Playlist button on the toolbar.
2. Name the playlist and click OK.
3. Click All Audio in the Music Folder list so you can see all your music.
4. Select songs and drag them, one at a time or in groups, to the playlist you created in the folder list.

To play that playlist, just click on it and click the Play button.

You can't rearrange songs in the Media Library, but you can drag songs around in playlists to customize the play order.

RealJukebox Plus

RealJukebox is Dave's favorite music player, a program that he might describe as a "magical combination of user-friendliness, smart music playback features, and an excellent music track display." He also describes the Hot Roast Beef and

Did you know?

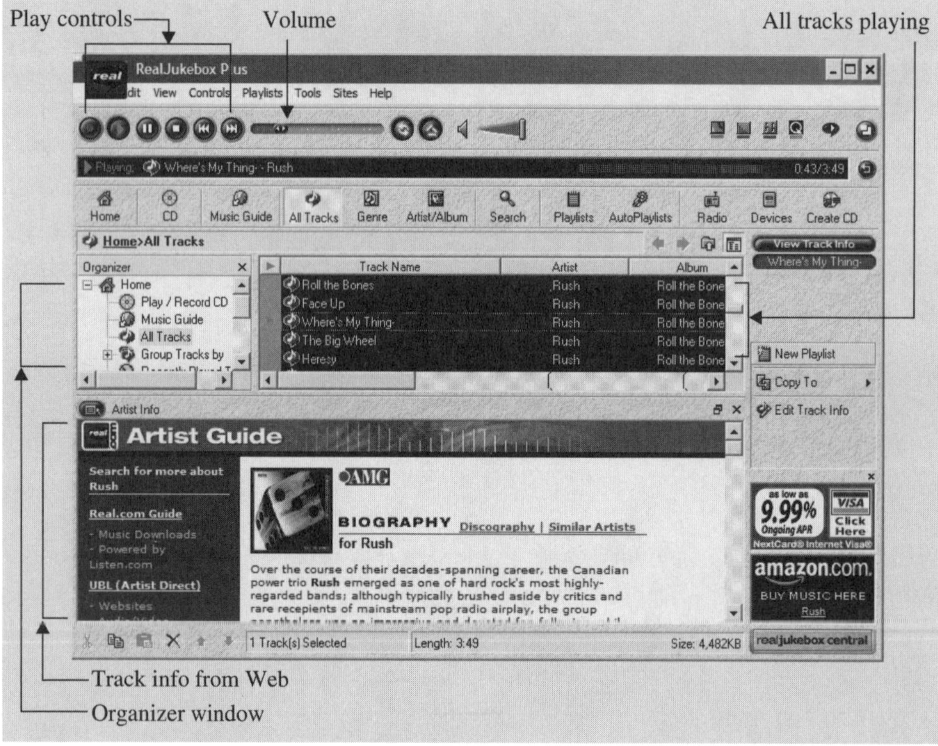

Play controls
Volume
All tracks playing
Track info from Web
Organizer window

Cheese sandwich from Blimpie's in exactly the same way, though, so we're not sure if you should put a lot of stock in that.

RealJukebox is a commercial product (costing about $30), but you can use the basic version for free. It never expires, although you will occasionally be bugged about upgrading. You can download it from www.real.com.

The program's interface is somewhat similar to Windows Media Player; in addition to music playback controls, there's a file and folder list called the Organizer as well as the track list in the middle of the window.

Although RealJukebox is just one big window (unlike Winamp, for instance, which is a modular concoction of several independent windows), you can turn various panes on and off to fully customize its appearance. With everything turned on, RealJukebox looks like this:

Clicking the small close box buttons, though, can eliminate the Special Offers, Visualization, Track Info, and Organizer. At its most minimal, the program looks like this:

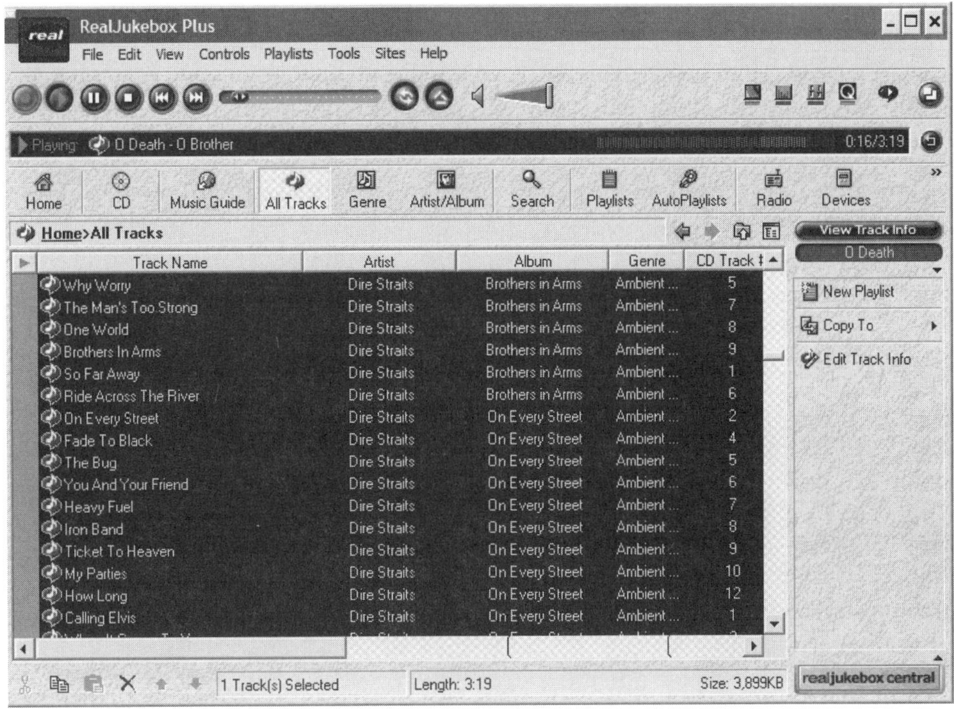

Playing Music

RealJukebox can keep a catalog of all the music on your hard disk. To store those file locations, select Tools | Configuration Wizard and let the program search your hard disk. RealJukebox makes it particularly easy to listen to your music—just choose All Tracks from the Organizer or toolbar and click the Play button. You can further fine-tune your musical choices by using the Organizer to sort songs by artist, genre, album, or other criteria.

RealJukebox is one of our favorite programs because we can select All Tracks, Shuffle Play (in the program's menu), and click the Play button, putting our entire music collection on random play faster than you can read this sentence.

In addition to playing tracks directly from your library of tunes, you can create two kinds of playlists:

- **Playlists** RealJukebox includes ordinary playlists, which you can build in a wizard-like fashion by clicking the New Playlist button on the right side of the window. Give the list a name and make an empty playlist (which you can fill by dragging songs into the playlist file in the Organizer), or let the program automatically grab tracks in the current view.
- **AutoPlaylists** RealJukebox can automatically select songs for this kind of playlist based on your genre and artists preferences. Just click New AutoPlaylist and follow the instructions in the wizard.

Use the Remix Now button to refresh your AutoPlaylist with new songs. It'll use your existing preferences regarding song length, artists, and genre, but give you new music that matches your criteria.

MusicMatch Jukebox 6

MusicMatch Jukebox is another incredibly popular music player for the PC. It resembles both Windows Media Player and RealJukebox in that it has the ability to play a variety of music formats as well as copy from audio CDs and create custom CDs. The interface is modular and can take up very little space on the desktop or expand to consume almost the entire screen. The interface is kind of cool, actually—

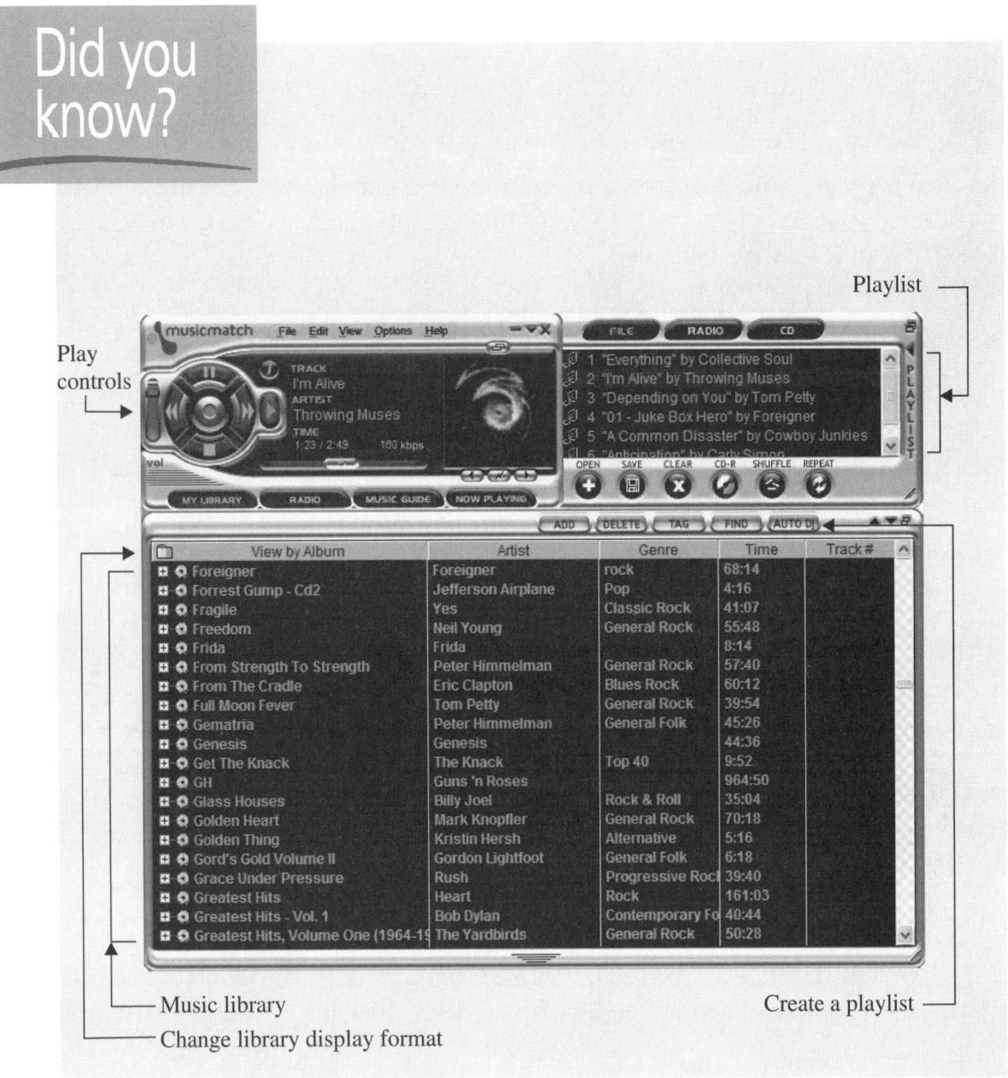

you can "detach" windows from MusicMatch and drag them around the desktop, or dock them so MusicMatch behaves like a single application.

MusicMatch is a commercial product; the complete MusicMatch Jukebox program costs about $20. It's available from www.musicmatch.com. You can use the basic version of MusicMatch Jukebox for free, though, and although the program will occasionally ask you to upgrade, it never stops working.

Playing Music

Getting started with MusicMatch Jukebox is a matter of telling the program where you keep your song files. Select File | Add New Track(s) To Music Library and specify a particular folder, or let the program search your entire hard disk.

When it's complete, you can drag songs from the My Library view to the Playlist view. Click play to hear your songs.

Unfortunately, getting MusicMatch to really sing for you is a bit more complex than in other programs, and that's why both Dave and Rick rate this program near the bottom of the most popular music players. Here's the problem:

- By default, MusicMatch displays your music by artist, which means you have to drill down to a level to see actual song titles—and you can't see all your music at once in this view.
- You can't tell MusicMatch to just start playing songs from your library—you must create a playlist first.

The first problem is easily fixed. Click the folder icon in the My Library view, and you'll see a menu that lists a number of different views. To see all of your songs in a single, complete list, choose All Tracks. Now that you can actually see your music, try listening to it. As we already mentioned, you must first create a playlist: MusicMatch can't play stuff directly out of the library. You can create a playlist in two ways: manually and automatically (similar to RealJukebox's Playlist and AutoPlaylist).

- **Manually** Drag songs from the My Library window to the Playlist window. Once there, you can drag the songs around with the mouse to put them in the order you like, or just set the player to Shuffle.
- **Automatically** This is a far easier solution than manually creating a playlist if you have hundreds or thousands of songs in your collection and you just want to get down to the business of listening to music. Click the Auto DJ button and follow the steps to create a playlist: Specify how many hours of music the program should generate; choose specific albums, artists, genres, and so on, or just click Select All; click the Get Tracks button. You'll see a dialog box that tells you how much music you've got. Click OK and start your tunes.

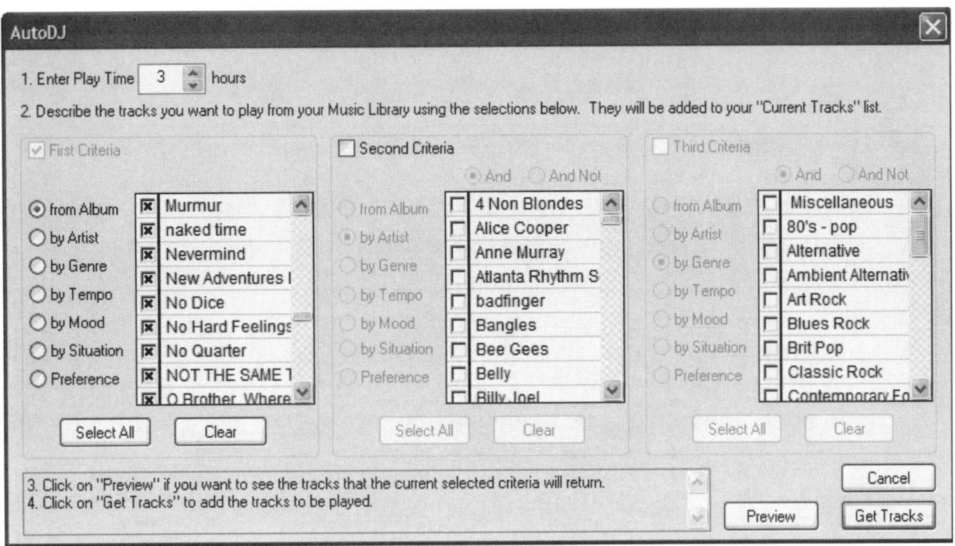

TIP *Once you create a playlist using either method, you can click the Save button to store it for another time. To open a playlist, click the Open button and click Playlists in the Open Music dialog box.*

Music Players for the Mac

Although it's not quite a desert out there, fewer really good music players are available for the Mac than for the PC. That's OK; you need only one or two good players to listen to your music. But watch out—you need to pay attention to whether particular players are designed for OS X or OS 8 and 9.

iTunes

It's not the most elaborate, but one of our favorite music players is iTunes, available for free from Apple's own Web site. The program packs into a single screen the ability to listen to MP3s and streaming audio from the Internet. The following illustration shows the two panes you work with in the iTunes window, the source pane and the song list:

Playing Music

To build your music library, select File | Add To Library. After iTunes searches your hard disk for songs, you'll see them appear in the main display. iTunes supports playlists as well. Click the Create A Playlist button and then drag songs to the playlist file in the source pane.

One of iTunes' best features is its great search and browse capability. If you're looking for a specific song, there are two ways to find it:

- **Search** Start typing a song title, artist, CD, or genre into the Search box. iTunes narrows down the search in real time, filtering the display to show you only the potential matches.
- **Browse** Click the Browse button and the display changes to three panes: as you click an artist in the first pane, all of the appropriate CDs appear in the next. Finally, click a CD to see all of the songs listed in the final pane.

MPLAY

You can listen to MP3s using QuickTime, but why would you? The QuickTime interface is poorly designed for music playback, with no playlists or music library capability. That's why deepNiner released MPLAY, an add-on to QuickTime that capitalizes on its music-playing abilities and adds party-savvy playlist features. The end result is a flawed but intriguing player that has a place on your hard disk for those occasions when you need its features.

Playing Music

MPLAY's biggest limitation is the lack of any music library capability. That means the playlist is king in MPLAY. Indeed, the program is designed to make you a DJ at a party, so you'll want to create some playlists for this program. Drag-and-drop songs into MPLAY and choose File | Save Playlist to retain your song list.

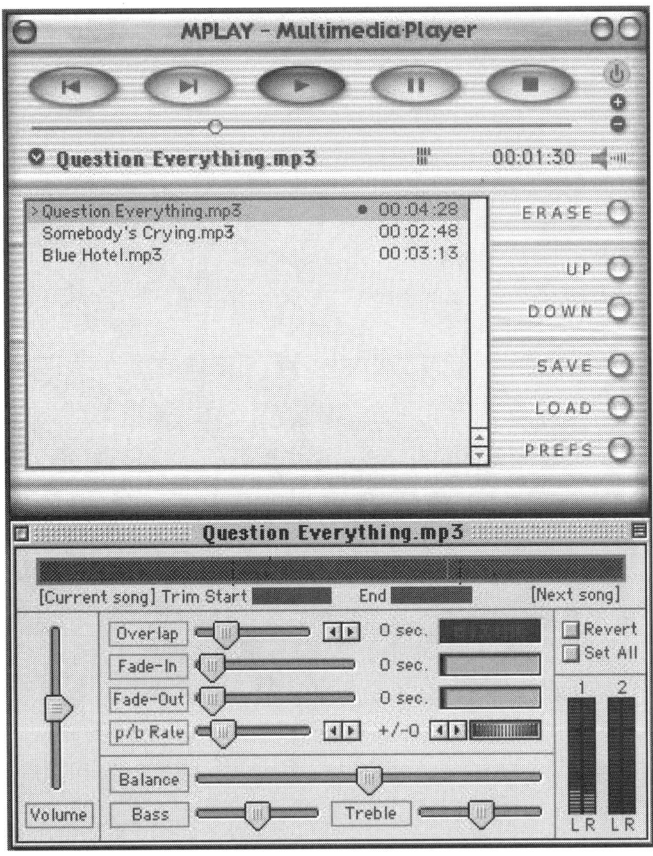

Once you have a playlist complete, though, MPLAY comes alive with a window called Track Mixer. This clever utility lets you control fading and overlap between songs like a professional DJ. It's fun to play with and handy for parties. You can even trim the silent parts out of the beginning of songs and change the playback rate of music—from painfully slow to beyond-Chipmunks fast.

MusicMatch Jukebox

A popular music player on the PC, MusicMatch Jukebox is also available for the Mac. The modular interface can be folded up to show just the player window or expanded to include other screens, like the music library and the current playlist.

It's a commercial product; the complete MusicMatch Jukebox program costs about $20. It's available from www.musicmatch.com. You can use the basic version of MusicMatch Jukebox for free, though, and although the program will occasionally ask you to upgrade, it never stops working. You can see the program's default interface in the following illustration:

Shirts or Skins

Dave: What's up with skins, anyway? Programmers are squandering the most clever and innovative idea in the history of personal computing. For centuries, people had to accept whatever horrible interface designs programmers gave them. Skins change all that—without changing the underlying "engine" that makes the software work, people can now slap on entirely new interfaces, customizing them like a Lego set! But what are people doing with skins? Making their music players look like butterflies or killer robots, and making the interface 100 times worse in the process. Half of the skins out there have buttons so small or illogically placed that I can't use them. What a shame.

Rick: It's understandable that someone of Dave's advanced age would be so grumpy. True, many skins are god-awful, but some of them are really cool and artistic. And there's something for every taste, from cars to Star Trek to Britney Spears. I find it interesting to see the wide variety of designs people create. Honestly, what other aspect of your life can you customize so easily? If I want my music player to have a Powerpuff Girls theme, well, then, my music player is going to have a Powerpuff Girls theme!

Dave: At least it'll match the rest of your office.

Playing Music

Getting started with MusicMatch Jukebox is a matter of telling the program where you keep your song files. Select File | Add Tracks and specify a particular folder, or let the program search your entire hard disk. When it's complete, you can drag songs from the My Library window to the Playlist window. Click Play to hear your songs.

One aspect of MusicMatch that we don't care for is the fact that you can't directly play tracks in your music library. Instead, you must create a playlist using one of two methods: either manually or automatically.

- **Manually** With this method, you drag songs from the My Library window to the Playlist window. Once there, you can drag the songs around with the mouse to put them in the order you like or just set the player to Shuffle.
- **Automatically** This is a far easier solution if you have hundreds or thousands of songs in your collection and you just want to get down to the business of listening to music. Click the Auto DJ button and follow the steps to create a playlist: Specify how many hours of music the

program should generate; choose specific albums, artists, genres, and so on, or just click Select All; click the Get Tracks button. You'll see a dialog box that tells you how much music you've got. Click OK and start your tunes.

Once you create a playlist using either method, you can click the Save button to store it for another time. To open a playlist, click the Open button and click Playlists in the Open Music dialog box.

Setting Your Volume

There are typically three places to set the volume when you're working with music players: the player's volume control, the Windows volume control for Wave files (this refers to any sound generated by the PC), and the control on the speakers themselves.

Try to set these three different levels to achieve two effects:

- The overall volume of your PC shouldn't fluctuate much no matter which kind of audio you're listening to, including MP3 files and CDs.
- Any potential distortion is minimized or eliminated.

To meet these standards, start by making sure the speaker volume is reasonably low; otherwise, you can easily overdrive hardware and get distortion. The speakers should never be set all the way to the max. A better position is between 25 percent and 50 percent. Next, set the volume in your music player to approximately 50 percent. That way, you can use the music player to fine-tune volume daily. Finally, open the Windows Control Panel's sound volume dialog box (that's the icon called Sound and Audio Devices in the Control Panel). Set the Wave level near 100 percent, but switch to an audio CD and make sure there isn't a huge difference in volume between the two. When everything's in balance, use the music player for moderate changes in volume.

Changing Skins

One of the most exciting developments in software design today is the concept of skins. While originally applied only to music players, skins stand a good chance of revolutionizing every aspect of personal computing. Imagine, for instance, the ability to radically modify the interface of your favorite word processor, Personal Digital Assistant (PDA), and desktop operating system just by clicking a button. You can make your software work the way you want it to work instead of the way the programmer envisioned it. And if you like, you can slip a different skin onto your program every day, or switch back to the original just as easily.

Anyway, that's the idea. Skins are the outer layer of music players—the arrangement of buttons and menus, for instance, as well as the program's physical layout and graphic design. Changing skins is as much about the look and feel of the program as it is about the operation of the controls. Figure 5-1 shows an assortment of skins for RealJukebox. Every major music player is compatible with alternate skins, which you can download from the Web or even design yourself.

FIGURE 5-1 Transform your music player by using downloadable skins—or create your own by using the guidelines available on the music player's Web site.

Each program that supports skins has a mechanism for installing new skins, and they're always free. You can download new skins in a matter of minutes and switch among your library of skins at will.

See Your Music

Visualizations have no real function except that they're fun to look at. You can keep them small, like a tiny TV, while you work at your PC, or blast them the size of your entire monitor for parties, when the music takes center stage.

In most music software, you can not only download and install additional visualizations, but you can also tweak the way they perform. The following illustration shows the Visualization dialog boxes from MusicMatch Jukebox and RealJukebox. They illustrate the ways you can edit the visualization's performance. They have little effect on the music, but visualizations are fun to mess around with.

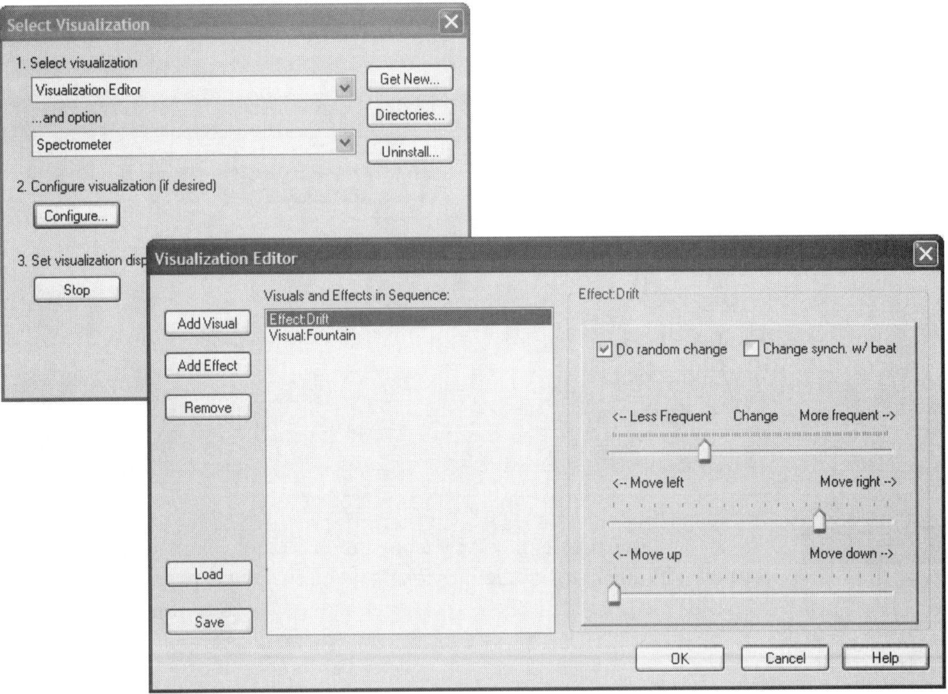

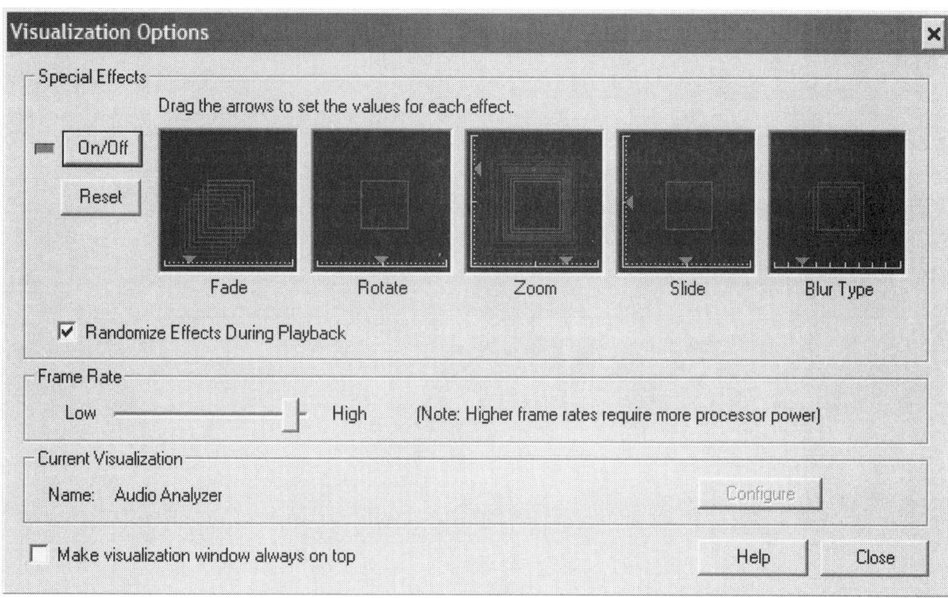

TIP *If you have an older PC and you notice that the music skips, breaks up, beeps, pops, or has any other sort of audio glitch, try closing the Visualization window. That will often solve the problem—slow processors are overtaxed trying to play music and display fancy graphics at the same time.*

Chapter 6

Dialing into Internet Radio

How to...

- Define streaming audio
- Find Internet radio stations
- Use Windows Media Player to listen to Internet radio
- Build a custom radio station with RadioMOI.com
- Listen to thousands of stations using RealJukebox
- Listen to high-quality, ad-free music with MusicMatch Radio MX
- Build your own radio station and broadcast it on the Web

One of the Internet's most magical capabilities—and, we think, best-kept secrets—is streaming audio. Imagine listening to a beloved radio station from your old hometown, tuning into London's BBC for the latest European news, or enjoying around-the-clock sports coverage on the ESPN Radio Network. Just as the Internet gives you access to information from around the world, so does it open the door to a global network of radio stations.

In this chapter, we tell you how to get started with Internet radio: what you need, what you can find, and where you can find it. When you're done, your PC may never be silent again.

Understanding Internet Radio

The core concept behind Internet radio is not much different from that of ordinary radio. Traditionally, a station broadcasts a signal that travels through the airwaves on a particular frequency, and you tune into that frequency with a device (a radio) that converts the signal into sound. With Internet radio, the signal travels through the Internet in the form of small digital *packets*—instead of through the air—and you use your PC and special software to tune into desired stations. This process is referred to as *streaming audio.*

Listening to streaming audio is not the same as downloading an MP3 file and listening to it on your PC or a portable device. Rather, you're listening to the audio *as* it's being received, not after. Unlike a file download, streaming audio doesn't permanently store anything on your hard drive. Think of streaming audio as radio that's delivered electronically or as MP3 music that you listen to in realtime, and you should have a clear mental picture.

So, if streaming audio isn't the same as MP3 files, what is it (and what is it doing in this book)? Put simply, streaming audio is just another form of digital audio, one with a different delivery method. And because Internet radio is just so impossibly cool, we'd be doing you a major disservice by not covering it in these pages.

Where Internet Radio Comes From

Internet radio comes from two main sources:

- **Actual radio stations** An increasing number of traditional radio stations have taken to *simultaneous online broadcasting,* meaning that the same signal that's pushed into the airwaves is also available on the Internet. That means if you're out of range of a favorite station or just want to listen to what's going on halfway across the country (or the world), you can easily tune in.
- **Internet-only stations** Thousands of radio stations exist *solely online,* meaning that they were created expressly for Internet listening. Some of these stations are, like their traditional radio counterparts, supported by advertising, while others are produced by everyday users just like you. (We tell you how to create your own station later in this chapter.)

You may be surprised to learn that both kinds of stations, tallied together, number in the thousands. That's great, because it means you can probably find any kind of radio show you want (music, talk, sports, and so on) at any time of the day or night. The only potential downside is sifting through so many stations to find what you're looking for. In the pages to come, we show you the most effective ways to tune in.

How You Listen to Internet Radio

Just as listening to broadcast radio requires, well, a radio, listening to Internet radio requires a computer. More than that, it requires an Internet connection (the faster the better) and special software. Chances are good you've already got the latter, especially if you've already read Chapter 5—most popular MP3 player software (such as RealJukebox and Windows Media Player) includes Internet radio capabilities.

NOTE *When you first tune into an Internet station, it may be in the middle of a song or show. It's no different from flipping the dial on a regular radio. However, some stations "feed" shows to you from the beginning, most likely to placate the advertisers who helped pay for what you're hearing.*

It's important to note that some Internet radio stations rely on specific kinds of streaming audio, and may therefore require you to download a specific player or

Just Happy to Be Listening?

Dave: For me, this is one of those nonnegotiable aspects of listening to music: it has to sound good or it's just not worth listening to at all. That's why I don't "get" music stations on the AM band. Sure, AM is fine for talk radio, but the fidelity is so low it's actually painful to listen to music. Streaming audio is no different. If you're listening to Net music that's limping in at 28.8 Kbps, the sound is simply pathetic. The music is compressed so aggressively there's essentially nothing left but a nasty whooshing effect, a trebly whine, and a few skittish frequencies from the midrange. On top of that, it's sure to stutter worse than Rick on his first date. How can you enjoy such a depressing caricature of the original tune? Here's my advice: if you don't have a broadband Internet connection, don't bother with streaming audio at all. Likewise, if you find a Net radio station that doesn't broadcast a high bit rate, move on. Why listen to the digital equivalent of AM?

Rick: Dave is what we in the music biz like to refer to as a fidelity snob. He considers it an insult to his ears if low-fidelity audio passes through them. As for me, I would never say "don't bother with streaming audio" just because you don't have broadband. By all means, give it a try! Sure, it may sound like AM radio, but you still get to listen to stations from around the world for free. Of course, speaking as someone who just recently made the move to broadband, I can affirm that the difference is like night and day. But don't be discouraged if you can't afford it or it's not available in your area. There's no shame in AM radio. Dave doesn't even like blueberries, so what does he know?

plug-in (a bit of software that adds capabilities to an existing program) before you can listen. Many stations, for instance, employ the RealMusic format, meaning that you must have a RealAudio player (such as RealJukebox) installed on your PC before the music will play.

The Importance of High-Speed Internet Access

As you learned in Chapter 4, broadband (that is, cable, DSL, and satellite) Internet service is the key to MP3 happiness. This is particularly true where Internet radio is concerned, as it usually means the difference between frustration and fun. While dial-up modem users can certainly tune into Web stations, they're likely to experience mediocre sound quality and frequent interruptions.

Internet-Radio Sound Quality

In Chapter 5, we told you about MP3 *bit rates* and how they impact sound quality. The higher the rate, the better the sound. Internet radio is somewhat similar: if you have a fast connection, you can tune into stations that broadcast at a higher bit rate. If you're like Dave, you may find anything lower than a 96-Kbps audio stream unacceptable. Rick, who's just grateful to have all this great music at his fingertips for free, is happy to "tough it out" at 56 Kbps or even 28 Kbps.

Why a Slow Connection Equals Dead Air

Arguably more important than sound quality is the stability of your connection. Even at a low bit rate, streaming audio sends a lot of data to your PC. If you have broadband Internet access, you should enjoy virtually flawless playback 99 percent of the time. But if you have a dial-up modem, you are quite likely to experience interruptions—sometimes momentary, sometimes lengthy, always irksome. What's happening is that the audio stream isn't arriving at your PC fast enough to allow continuous playback.

Fortunately, you have nothing to lose by experimenting. Some stations may deliver more reliable playback than others, and you may encounter fewer interruptions if you're online when Internet traffic is lower—like during weekdays. However, the fact remains that to make the most of what Internet radio has to offer, you need a broadband connection. Consider this the perfect excuse to take the plunge on cable or DSL service.

Rick Makes an Internet Radio Discovery

Before he met Dave, Rick never knew there were people who didn't like jazz. He still can't believe it. Anyway, while working on this chapter, he discovered the dulcet voice of Lavay Smith, a modern-day swing-music singer who evokes comparison to Billie Holiday, Ella Fitzgerald, and other jazz greats. Rick first encountered her while listening to a swing station on CyberRadio2000.com—and immediately fell in love. An accompanying link enabled him to order one of her CDs. Even better, a quick visit to her Web site revealed that she was performing near his hometown just three weeks hence. (He ordered tickets online on the spot.) This, friends, is why we love the Internet.

How to Find Internet Radio Stations

One of the best ways to get started with Internet radio is with the MP3 player software you already have. Windows Media Player, for instance, has a Radio Tuner feature that lets you search for—and play, of course—stations based on format, genre, band, and various other criteria. RealJukebox goes a step further by letting you narrow your search to specific cities, states, and/or countries—helpful if you're trying to find a station in, say, your hometown or Paraguay.

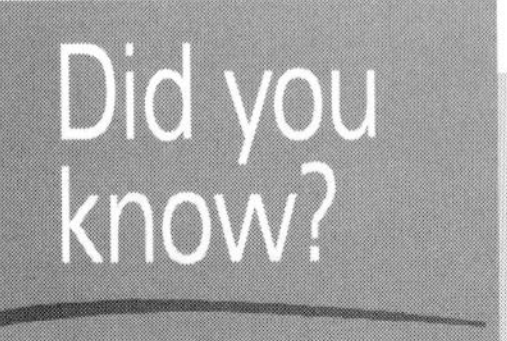

Internet Radio to Go

If you're thinking about how great it would be if you could listen to streaming audio in your car, get ready for XM Radio (www.xmradio.com). This new satellite-based service promises to beam 100 digital radio channels to your car stereo (it has to be an XM model, of course), including jazz, country, classical, news, kids, comedy, and more. Better yet, because the channels come from a satellite rather than an antenna, they're available nationwide—no matter where you drive. If the service takes off, watch for XM Radio receivers for your home as well.

One of the key benefits of using programs like these is that you don't have to worry about file formats or plug-ins. All the stations listed in RealJukebox, for instance, provide streaming audio in the RealMusic format, and because you obviously already have the compatible player installed on your computer, you're all set to listen.

You can also go directly to Web sites that host Internet radio services, like Bonzaroo.com (www.bonzaroo.com) and Sonicnet.com (www.sonicnet.com). These sites often make it easier to find the kind of stations you're looking for, although you may not find quite as many stations in each genre. What's more, when you try to play a station, you may discover that you first need to download some software—which can be annoying and even a little confusing. Novice users might do better to use one of the aforementioned MP3 players.

In the pages to come, we show you how to use various Internet radio sites, services, and software programs.

FIGURE 6-1 Click the Radio Tuner button in Windows Media Player to enter the wonderful world of Internet radio.

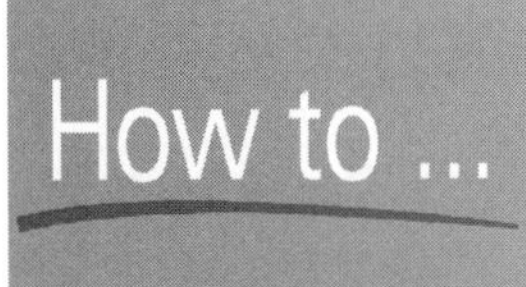

Listen to Radio with WMP

1. Click the Start button, then find and click the Windows Media Player icon. (If you use a dial-up modem rather than an always-on cable or DSL modem, now would be the right time to connect to your ISP.)
2. By default, WMP first opens the Now Playing screen. Click the Radio Tuner button (see Figure 6-1).
3. You now see the screen divided into two panes: Presets and Station Finder. Double-click the NPR National Public Radio listing under Presets. This action has two effects: it launches the NPR Web site in a separate window (you can close it or view it, your choice), and it begins streaming content from NPR. It could take upwards of a minute or more

before you actually hear any audio—be patient. Even with a broadband connection, it takes time to link to a radio server.

That's all there is to it. To change to another station, simply double-click it. You can use the Station Finder pane to locate stations based on format, band (AM, FM, or Internet only), language, location, and more (just click the pull-down menu labeled Format to see a list of your sorting options, and then select the one you want). Sorting by format then enables you to choose from over two dozen different station groupings, from adult contemporary to world music. Within each format, you'll find anywhere from a handful to several dozen stations.

Tune In with Windows Media Player

With the introduction of Windows Media Player 7.0 (WMP), which came bundled with the Windows Me operating system but is available as a free download (www.windowsmedia.com), Microsoft added a Radio Tuner option (see Figure 6-1) that makes it easy to access a wide variety of Internet stations. Let's take a look at this feature of WMP, which many of you probably already have installed on your computers.

For purposes of this tutorial, we'll focus on WMP 7.0. Windows XP comes with version 8.0, but its radio features are generally similar.

Creating Your Own Preset Lists

WMP 7.0 allows you to create customized lists of favorite stations (culled from its own extensive listings). It refers to these lists as *Presets,* probably in deference to the lingo used by stereos and car radios. As you noticed when you first clicked Radio Tuner, WMP includes a Featured list that contains ten general-interest Presets. When you click the Featured pull-down menu in the Presets pane, you'll find that there's already a My Presets item, which you can use to quickly build a list of favorite stations. Alternately, you can click the Edit button to create your own Preset category (such as "classic rock" or "swing music").

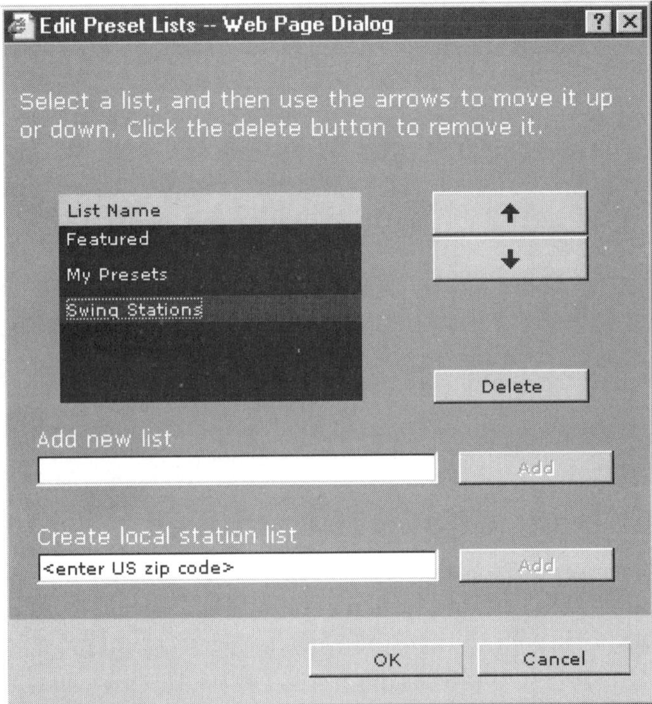

It's a simple matter to add or remove stations from any given Preset list. To add one, click the desired station name as it appears in the Station Finder list (the right-hand pane), and then click the left-arrows button. You'll see the station name appear immediately in your list. To remove it (or any other station), just reverse the process: click the name of the station in the Preset list, and then click the right-arrows button. (It doesn't matter what's listed in the right-hand pane.)

Searching for Stations

Want to find those stations that play, say, Madonna? Big Bad Voodoo Daddy? Rockabilly music? Click the Search button near the upper-right corner of the Radio Tuner window. You can narrow your search by selecting from a variety of options, and then typing in a keyword to specify what you're seeking. A list of relevant stations appears in the Station Finder pane.

Music for Jazz Lovers

Blue Note Records is a household name among jazz lovers, having produced much of the 20th century's greatest jazz music. Blue Note Radio (www.bluenote.com) is the label's "in-house" Internet station—it delivers tunes from Blue Note's stable of bands and artists. The music plays in a special Web browser window, so there's no special software required. Better still, if you hear something you really like, it's a simple matter to click the Get CD option. You're instantly taken to a Web storefront where you can place an order.

Build Custom Radio Shows with RadioMOI.com

Ever since he crossed over into the wonderful world of broadband, Dave has been a big fan of RadioMOI.com—a free service that not only delivers a wide selection of Internet radio stations, but also lets you create entire libraries of songs for a totally customized listening experience. It's a great solution if you've ever wanted to fill a jukebox with only the tunes you like.

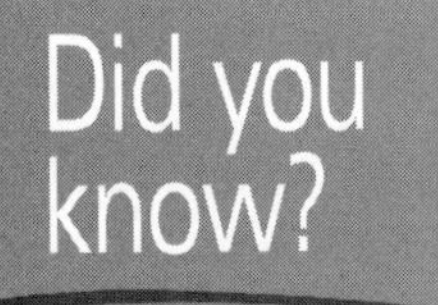

Internet Radio Around the House

If you find yourself becoming a major fan of Internet radio, you may be interested in devices that let you listen to it away from your PC. The Rio Receiver, for instance, links to your computer (and its Internet connection) via the phone lines in your home, thereby allowing you to tune into Internet radio from just about any room. The Acer iRhythm, meanwhile, wirelessly broadcasts the tunes from your PC to your home stereo for a world-class listening experience. Find out more about this kind of hardware in Chapter 8.

Just be prepared for one of the most awkward and confusing Web experiences of your life. RadioMOI.com offers almost zero help or how-to information, and its interface was undoubtedly constructed by whichever class of monkey is the dumbest. That's pretty sad for a site that has only a handful of options. Still, you may decide it's worth slogging through the soup to get to the meaty bits, so here's a quick RadioMOI.com primer.

- **Time Machine** RadioMOI.com's only uncomplicated feature, Time Machine lets you pick one of a couple dozen stations, then specify a range of years you want to hear. Thus, you could listen to jazz from 1943–1945, punk rock from 1980–1985, or whatever permutation you desire.

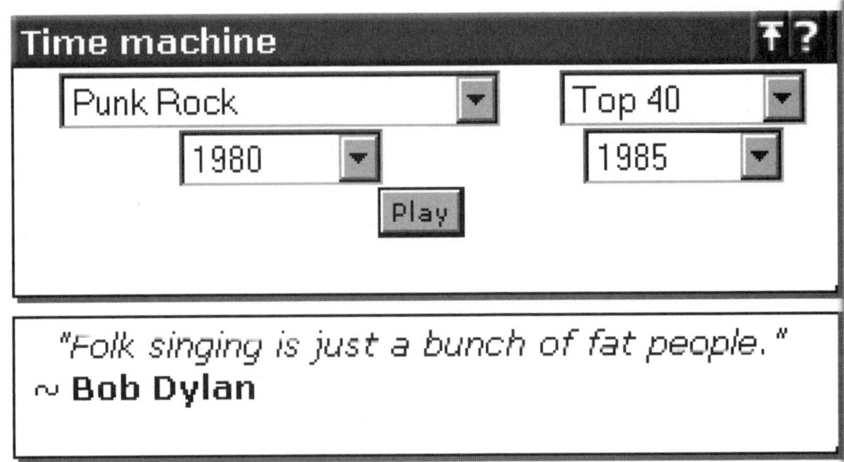

- **My Shows** This feature is the core of the service, where you create shows filled with whatever mix of music you want. First, you click the MyRadioMOI button, then the My Shows link. After you provide a name for your new show and click Add Show, click the Edit button. The next step is the really confusing part: to add songs to your show, you must search for them by using some or all of the criteria in the Search Only For Tracks I Can Add To My Shows area. You can't just browse RadioMOI.com's song library, picking and choosing titles as you go. Plan on experimenting with the search feature to determine how best to locate the songs—or types of songs—you want for your shows.

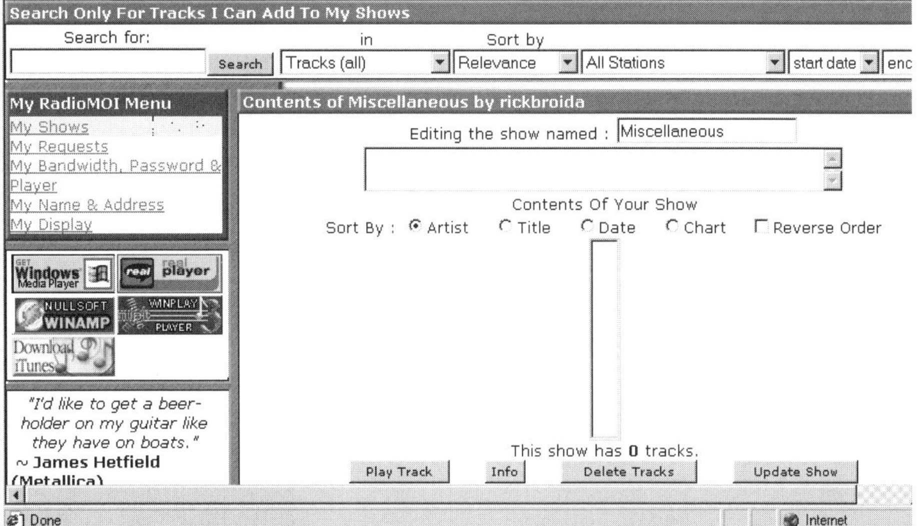

- **My Requests** As you browse the RadioMOI.com site, perusing channels, songs, and artists, you'll notice a little heart button next to most listings. When you click it, the channel, song, or artist gets added to your My Requests list. This pool of tracks has a higher chance of being heard when you listen to specific channels—including randomly generated shows like Time Machine and Category Shows. To us, this is kind of kooky—like calling a radio station to request a song, and then listening all day on the chance that they'll play it.

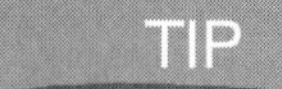

When you're looking at a lengthy list of songs you may want to add, you can select multiple songs at once by holding down the CTRL *key on your keyboard while clicking song titles. Or, you can select the entire list—click the first song, scroll down to the bottom, hold down the* CTRL *and* SHIFT *keys, and then click the last song. If you did it right, every song in the list will be highlighted.*

It's worth noting that any show you create with RadioMOI.com can be shared, meaning other users of the service can listen to it. To share one of your shows, click the little gray button with the four arrows.

It's also worth noting that RadioMOI.com seems to have some internal problems. For starters, although we changed our preferences to reflect 56-Kbps stereo sound rather than the default 16 Kbps, music continued to stream in at the lower bandwidth (and sounded decidedly mediocre). When we attempted to e-mail the company for tech support, our missive was bounced back as "undeliverable." User beware: RadioMOI.com is an annoying, poorly supported service that may send you scurrying back to the security of your Walkman.

At press time, we were unable to get RadioMOI.com to work with Windows XP.

Tune In with RealJukebox

As you learned in Chapter 5, RealJukebox is our favorite MP3 player software, and it's no slouch when it comes to Internet radio. It's exceptionally easy to use, too—just click the Radio button, then choose one of the Featured stations or use the Find A Station tool. The latter is kind of neat: you choose a genre, language, city, state, country, and/or keyword, and the search engine produces a list of matches. Thus, you could look up stations that broadcast, say, baseball games in Spanish or college music from East Lansing, Michigan. (Go Spartans!)

One nice touch is the option of adding any station(s) to your list of favorites (accessible by clicking the My Favorites tab). Just click the little blue "plus" sign. You can also visit the Web site (if there is one) for a station by clicking the little blue Web site icon.

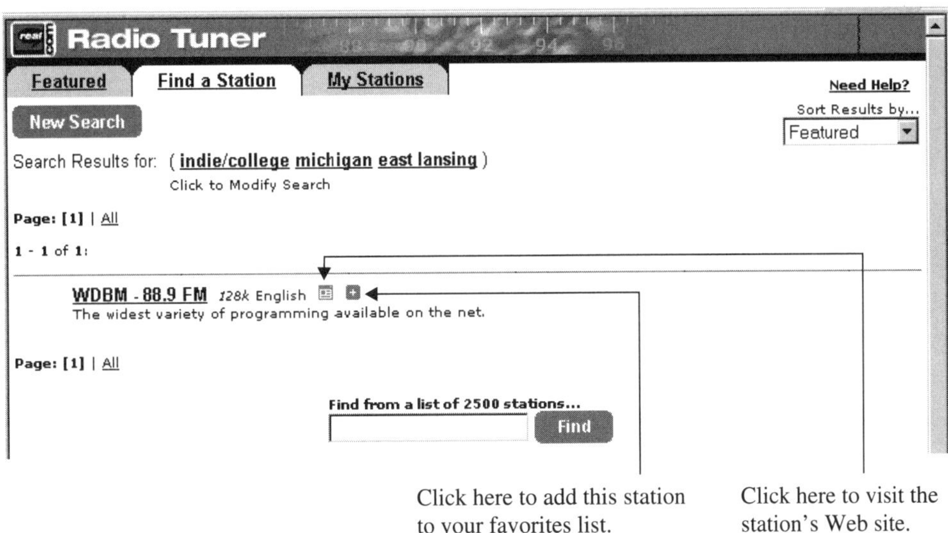

Click here to add this station to your favorites list.

Click here to visit the station's Web site.

Should You Pay for MusicMatch Radio MX?

While most Internet radio stations are free, MusicMatch Radio MX charges a small fee. MusicMatch Jukebox, as you may recall from Chapter 5, is a capable (but often confusing) MP3 player that has Internet radio features already built in. So why pay extra for Radio MX? Good question. Here's what you get for $4.95 per month, $12.95 per quarter, or $39.95 per year:

- **ArtistMatch** You can build stations with up to 25 of your favorite artists.
- **Era stations** You can listen to music from any time period (excluding eras when music wasn't recorded, like, you know, the Renaissance).
- **CD-quality sound** By default, MusicMatch Jukebox broadcasts Internet radio at a relatively low bandwidth. With Radio MX, you can listen at a CD-quality 128 Kbps (assuming you have a fast enough Internet connection to support it).
- **Ad-free listening** You will suffer no more of those annoying ads every five songs or so.

Is all this worth paying for? At the very least, you should sign up for the 14-day free trial. (Just remember to cancel your membership at the end of it so you don't automatically get billed.) Although other Internet radio services offer some of Radio MX's features, none mix them together under one roof. The interface remains a pain in the neck, but the benefits can be worth the discomfort.

Sharing with SHOUTcast

Remember Winamp, the megapopular MP3 player we discussed in Chapter 5? Turns out it's not just for listening to MP3 files. Nullsoft, the company behind Winamp, created a "distributed streaming audio system" called SHOUTcast—a radio system by users, for users.

When you visit SHOUTcast.com (www.shoutcast.com), you can immediately tune into stations created by other users. (The service recommends that you use Winamp, but the music will play using the default MP3 player on your machine.) The stations are divided into dozens of different genres, and you can search for specific artists or station titles. You can also sort stations by bit rate, so you don't wind up tuning into those that require a faster connection than your modem can handle.

The service also invites you to become a broadcaster, sharing your own station with the world. This so-called *Webcasting* can be a little complicated, but you can find documentation (and the necessary software) at the SHOUTcast Web site. Be sure to check out Chapter 15 as well, where we help you get started with the SHOUTcast software.

Other Software and Sites

The Internet is home to a seemingly endless supply of radio software and sites. If we haven't yet addressed a topic of interest, or you just want to explore further without wandering aimlessly on the Web, check out our handy chart.

If you want…	Use…
An easy introduction to Internet radio	Listen.com
National Public Radio	Windows Media Player
Custom-built radio shows	RadioMOI.com
Era-specific music	MusicMatch Radio MX, RadioMOI.com
Club music	Hotclubmix.com
Big band/swing	Bigbandmix.com
Classical music	Bestclassicalmix.com
A little of everything	Bonzaroo.com, Cablemusic.com, CyberRadio2000.com, Sonicnet.com
Stations created by other users	SHOUTcast.com
To broadcast your own music over the Web	SHOUTcast.com
Sports	ESPNradio.com

Chapter 7

Taking It on the Road

How to...

- Choose a portable MP3 player
- Transfer songs from the PC to your music player
- Play music in your car
- Understand memory card formats
- Play MP3s on your Pocket PC
- Listen to music on a Sony Clie or Handspring Visor

Although we spend a lot of time talking about MP3 and digital music playback on a desktop (or notebook) computer, don't lose sight of the fact that MP3 is a *portable* music file. With songs weighing in at about 3–5MB each, you can carry around a few hours' worth in your pocket with little trouble. Consequently, the portable MP3 market is hot right now, with a dozen popular players from which to choose.

Some of us—well, Dave, specifically—dream of a world in which all music exists in digital form. You can carry your entire music collection with you all the time and listen to anything you own, whether you're at home on the couch, driving in your car, or walking around town. If you live on the bleeding edge, it's already possible to do just that, as you will see in this chapter.

Even if you don't eat, breathe, and sweat music, there's plenty in this chapter for you. We'll talk about various ways of taking music on the road and tell you what you need to know to make the experience as enjoyable as possible.

Choosing a Portable Music Player

Only a few years ago, the Rio was pretty much the only portable MP3 player on the market. These days, a single trip to an electronics store is probably enough to convince you that this is no longer the case: portable MP3 players are popular. Very popular.

You can divide the market into four kinds of players:

- **Ultraportable players** These are small MP3 players with a very limited amount of memory, usually integrated into the device. The advantage is that they're inexpensive, but you can't swap memory cards to listen to different music. A good example of an ultraportable is the Sony VAIO

Music Clip MC-P10, about the size of a highlighting marker. It holds 64MB and sells for under $200.

NOTE *An increasingly common player style features an MP3 player integrated into a set of headphones. The Evolution NeckPhone, for instance, has a 64MB MP3 player and FM radio in an over-the-neck headphone design.*

- **Standard players** This kind of MP3 player is what most people end up buying. Because the memory card is removable, you can carry different music collections and swap out music to suit your mood. These players might also include additional features, like an integrated radio tuner. Intel's Pocket Concert player holds 128MB of memory and has an integrated FM radio. It sells for about $200.
- **CD players** A few portable CD players play MP3s as well. These are bulky compared to the standard players, but they give you a lot more flexibility—you can play audio CDs, and you can also store hundreds of MP3 songs on CD and have hours of music available at your fingertips. Without a doubt, the most common example of a CD/MP3 player is the Rio Volt. It sells for about $200.
- **High-capacity players** When it comes to sheer running time, the top of the food chain is dominated by a crop of MP3 players that use small, portable hard disks to store dozens or even hundreds of hours of music. These devices typically start with 6GB hard disks and can range up to 20GB or more. Take the Neo Jukebox, for instance, which has a 20GB hard disk and sells for about $350.

Which criteria should you use to choose an MP3 player? The following sections provide a rundown on the important elements we think you should consider.

How Much Memory Does the MP3 Player Have?

How much music you can fit on a player is absolutely the most important aspect to think about. Consider this: MP3 music is typically encoded at 128 Kbps, which lets you store, on average, about an hour of music in 64MB of storage space.

TIP *Here's a good rule of thumb: you can store about a minute per megabyte in 128 Kbps MP3 format.*

How much music do you want to carry with you? There's no right answer to this: it's a matter of personal taste. Rick, for instance, is reasonably happy with an hour of music, whereas Dave wants to have several hours available all the time.

Some MP3 players come exclusively with internal, nonremovable memory. Some players have a memory slot so you can add more storage space. And yet others have no internal memory at all; whatever you put in the memory slot is what you have to work with. One thing's for sure: we recommend avoiding inexpensive ultraportables that give you a fixed 32MB or 64MB. It's like buying a cassette player that has a single cassette tape permanently installed, and the only way to listen to different music is to bring it home and use your stereo to record new songs onto it. Instead, we suggest that you make sure you can add memory via an expansion slot.

A related question is, which kind of removable memory does the player use? There's CompactFlash, SmartMedia, Secure Digital/Multimedia Card (SD/MMC), and Memory Stick. You may care, especially if you already have memory cards for another portable device, like a digital camera. Of course, you should also factor in the cost of memory. You may want to carry a gigabyte of memory, but it may not suit your budget. Memory cards aren't cheap, but they're dropping in price very quickly. See "Understanding Memory Card Formats" later in this chapter for more details on memory cards and their prices.

How Does the MP3 Player Connect to the PC?

These days, most MP3 players use industry-standard universal serial bus (USB) cables to transfer music from the desktop. A few serial cable-based players are still out there, though, and they aren't compatible with Macintoshes. While we're on the subject, check out the player's system requirements carefully because not all players work with Macs or older PCs.

In addition, you may have upgraded to the new Windows XP operating system, and occasionally, we've seen some multimedia products that don't work right on XP. If the box doesn't specify—and you're not sure if it'll work on XP—visit the company's Web site or call them up. It's easier to find out ahead of time than to try to return the product afterwards.

We're also sticklers for the way you actually transfer songs to the player. Many players use removable memory cards, and if you have a memory card reader like the one in Figure 7-1, you can put the card in the reader and drag-and-drop files onto the card as if it were a floppy disk or external hard disk. That's the easiest way.

There are other options as well. Many players are compatible with jukebox programs like RealJukebox. With the player attached to your PC, you can drag-

FIGURE 7-1 Memory card readers let you drag-and-drop songs from the PC directly to your memory card—a method we recommend.

and-drop songs from the music library to the player, and they'll be copied automatically for you.

Of course, most players come with their own music transfer software, but these programs can be complicated and intrusive. We use them as a last resort, if none of the other solutions work.

What about the Batteries?

Players come in all shapes and sizes and use batteries of every imaginable configuration. We've seen players with AAA, AA, and Lithium Ion batteries, for instance. Rechargeables are generally best, but even if your player uses AA batteries, you can substitute a pair of AA-style Ni-MH rechargeable batteries (see Figure 7-2). It'll save you money over the long haul.

TIP *You can buy Ni-MH rechargeable batteries from almost any computer or electronics store. An excellent source is igo.com, which seems to offer just about every kind of battery in the known galaxy.*

FIGURE 7-2 Batteries come in all shapes and sizes, but if your player uses standard AA-sized batteries, they're easier to charge or replace than unusually shaped proprietary batteries.

If your player comes with a single rechargeable battery, you might want to buy a spare from the company that sells the player. Many rechargeable batteries aren't standardized, so you might not be able to find a compatible battery unless you get it from the same folks who sold you the player. Dave carries a spare, fully charged Lithium Ion rechargeable battery when he travels with his MP3 player, which gives him about six hours of music for those really long plane rides.

What Other Goodies Does the MP3 Player Have?

If recorded music isn't good enough for you, some MP3 players come with built-in AM/FM tuners. If you've ever had a Walkman, you know the drill—you can switch from MP3 to radio broadcasts at the flip of a button.

Some portable MP3 players also have line-in or microphone inputs for making your own MP3 recordings. This feature is handy if you want to convert your LP collection to MP3, for instance, but your home stereo and desktop computer are too far apart to do it the ordinary way. If there's a microphone, you can even use the player as a digital voice recorder.

A line-out jack is handy as well, because it allows you to plug your MP3 player into your stereo or, if you're really lucky, your car stereo. In general, it's not a good idea to connect your MP3 player to another stereo using the headphone jack. The headphone level is much higher than a line-out level, and you could damage the hardware you're jacking it into.

If you plan to exercise with an MP3 player, look for one that has a lock switch. Otherwise, the controls may get bumped as you work out, and the player will start skipping tracks, pausing, or changing volume from routine jostling.

The MP3 Tree

As you can see, MP3s come in a wide variety of shapes, sizes, and capabilities. Just about the only thing you can count on them having in common is a bundled

Going on a Trip

Heading out of town? Take your MP3 player. Here's a checklist of what you should do to get your music ready for a plane ride or a few days out of town:

- Change or charge your batteries so your player can run for a few hours without interruption.
- Pack a spare set of batteries and a charger if you're using rechargeable batteries.
- Bring an AC adapter for your MP3 player so you don't have to rely on batteries when you're in the hotel room.
- Copy fresh music to your memory card. If you have more than one memory card, you can create several playlists.
- Don't forget the headphones. Rick did once, and he had to buy a new pair at the airport before boarding the plane.
- If you travel with a traditional laptop, you can put your music on there as well. Bring a connection cable so you can move music from the laptop to the MP3 player as needed.

set of headphones. Where do you start? If you're shopping online, you can find excellent information on current models at these Web sites:

- www.mp3.com
- www.cnet.com
- www.dealtime.com

We've highlighted several MP3 players and categorized them according to the different kinds of users who might like them.

The Right MP3 Player for You

Which features are most important to you? We've created this little chart that you can use to figure out which kind of MP3 player you should be looking for based on your lifestyle. If you travel a lot, for instance, an ultrasmall player probably won't satisfy you; it can't hold enough music.

Use	Batteries	Memory	Size
Exercise	Alkaline are OK because you're not going very far.	Internal memory is adequate because you'll use the player for short bursts of time.	Ultracompact designs are best because you'll want to clip it to your clothing or stick it in a pocket.
Around town	Use long-life rechargeables if you listen to music for hours at a time.	Internal memory will suffice.	A small player is less obtrusive.
Out-of-town trips	Long-life rechargeables are the only reasonable option.	Hard disk or removable memory cards give you longer play time.	Larger sizes are OK because they're part of your luggage.
On-the-go recording	Long-life rechargeables can keep you from running out of juice in the middle of a recording.	A hard disk is needed to make long recordings.	You probably don't have any choice but to use a big player/recorder.

MP3s on a Budget

Rio is the original name in MP3 players. When Diamond Multimedia first introduced the Rio back in 1998, virtually no one else was making portable music players capable of accessing MP3 audio. Today, the original Rio design lives on in the form of the Rio One, a small player with 32MB of built-in memory and the option of upgrading to as much as 160MB via SmartMedia cards. It gives you only about a half-hour of music right out of the box, but priced at under $100, it's a good deal for starting out in digital music.

If You Need a Voice Recorder

The Rio 800 comes in three flavors: with 64MB, 128MB, or 384MB of internal memory. There's no expansion card, but snap-on memory backpacks let you add additional memory if you want to. The backpacks also include rechargeable batteries for longer play time.

This MP3 player's coolest feature, though, is a built-in microphone, which turns this player into a digital voice recorder. If you want to listen to music and take voice notes, the Rio 800 does both.

Longer Playing Time

If you like the idea of carrying a small, portable MP3 player, but you want more listening time than you can get from a simple 32MB unit, you have a lot of options. One of our favorites is the RCA Lyra RD2211. This MP3 player has no built-in memory, but it uses the CompactFlash memory format so you can, for instance, carry several 128MB memory cards and get hours and hours of playback. It also features several Digital Signal Processing (DSP) modes for fine-tuning your music.

Listening in Your Car

Few car stereos have input jacks for listening to external music players through the car's speakers. So if you want an MP3 player that works for both general-purpose listening and one you can use in your car, there's the Digisette Duo-64 (www.digisette.com). This gadget works best if you have a cassette player in your car; the player is shaped like a traditional audiocassette, and you simply insert it into the deck to hear MP3s through the car stereo.

NOTE *Rick is partial to this player because it's supported by Audible.com, and therefore allows him to listen to both music and audiobooks in his car.*

If You're a CD Fanatic

A few portable MP3 players are starting to appear in the form of CD players. The Rio Volt, for instance, is a compact CD player barely larger than the CD itself. The Volt can play audio CDs as well as MP3s that are stored on CD-R and CD-RW discs. Whereas a regular audio CD holds about a dozen songs, a CD-R loaded with MP3s can hold hundreds of songs. To take advantage of one of these players, you'll need a computer with a CD-RW drive so you can make your own MP3 discs. Check out Chapter 14 for details on creating CDs from MP3.

Getting Massive Amounts of Music

Dave can't be troubled by MP3 players that store just an hour or two of music; he uses I/O Magic's Neo Jukebox. This player, about the size of two decks of cards placed side by side, is an MP3 player with a 20GB hard disk and a rechargeable Lithium Ion battery.

The Neo Jukebox attaches to the PC via a USB cable and acts like a standard external hard disk. That means you can use the Jukebox to store not just MP3s, but other kinds of files as well. During playback, the MP3 player ignores anything that's not a true digital music file.

If you like the idea of a hard disk–powered MP3 player but don't need a full 20GB of capacity, you might want to try the Archos Jukebox instead. This player is similar to the I/O Magic player, but it has 6GB of storage.

MP3 for Your Car

Right now, MP3 playback in automobiles is still in its infancy. If you want to play MP3s in your car, you have perhaps a half-dozen options at best, and they're largely first-generation as well, which means you may have to make some compromises or pay more than your neighbor would consider rational for the privilege. That said, Dave installed an MP3 player in his car several months ago, and he is thrilled. (See "Dave's MP3 Auto Experience" later in this chapter.) Here's a rundown of the options available to you right now.

In-Dash Receivers with MP3

Several companies make in-dash receivers with AM/FM radio and single-disc in-dash CD players that read MP3 tracks (see Figure 7-3). Here's what we're talking about: most CD players understand music that's written only in traditional audio CD format, but some new players can read CD-R and CD-RW discs that have been loaded with MP3s. The difference in capacity is startling. Whereas a regular audio CD holds perhaps a dozen songs, or 70 minutes of music, a CD-R packed with MP3s can hold hundreds of songs or a dozen hours of music. A single CD-R can hold all of the Beatles' dozen studio albums, for instance.

To take advantage of one of these gadgets, you'll need a computer with a CD-RW drive so you can make your own MP3 discs. To find out how to create MP3 CDs for these kinds of players, check out Chapter 14.

The following table describes the most popular models currently available:

Model	Price	MP3 Playback	Reads ID3 Tags	Front Audio Input
Aiwa CDC-MP32	$349	CD-R and CD-RW	No	No
Clarion DXZ815MP	$399	CD-R and CD-RW	No	No
Jensen MP3510	$299	CD-R and CD-RW	No	Yes
JVC KD-SH99	$399	CD-R and CD-RW	Yes	Yes
Kenwood eXcelon Z828	$700	CD-R and CD-RW	Yes	No
Panasonic CQ-DP171U	$279	CD-R and CD-RW	No	No
Rockford Fosgate RFX9000	$450	CD-R and CD-RW	No	No
Sony CDX-MP450X	$330	CD-R	No	No

What's the front audio input for? Glad you asked! If your stereo has an audio input, you can plug your portable MP3 player into the stereo and listen to music that way as well. Unfortunately, very few in-dash players have audio inputs.

ID3 is a component of the MP3 file that stores information about the song. Stuff like artists, album name, genre, lyrics, album art, and a number of other items can be stored here. Stereos that recognize ID3 tags can show information like artists, album, and song name on the display.

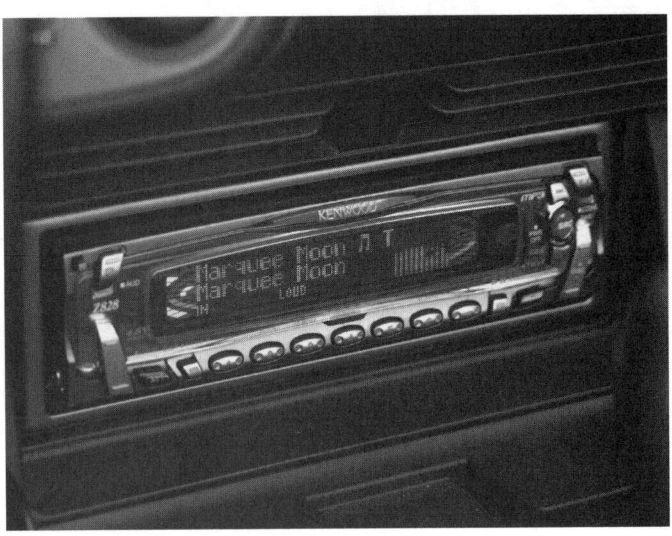

FIGURE 7-3 In-dash MP3 players like this Kenwood read MP3 tracks off of CD-R discs and can play for hours without swapping discs.

Hard Disk MP3 Players

Although this could potentially be a huge market, right now, only a few products are around that add a massive hard disk full o' MP3s to your car.

Perhaps the most ambitious one is called the Rio Car (www.riohome.com); it's a removable in-dash unit that offers a truly massive amount of storage space for all of your digital music. Unlike in-dash CD units, the Rio Car is just a hard disk, so it puts all of your music at your fingertips in a truly dynamic way. There's no disc swapping to listen to your music. To install music, you remove the Rio Car (it's designed to slip out of the car easily) and connect it via USB, serial, or Ethernet to your PC. When you're done transferring your music, slip it back into the car and go.

Although the Rio Car fits in a single standard *DIN slot* (the slot that car stereo units slip into), the fact that it doesn't include an AM/FM tuner may give you pause. You'll need to leave your original car stereo in the vehicle and add this as a second head unit, or learn to live without radio. (An FM tuner upgrade is promised for Rio Car units, but it's not available as of this writing.) On top of that, the Rio Car is a little expensive. The 10GB version costs about $1000, and bigger units take off into the stratosphere—you'll pay about $1800 for the 60GB version. We're as MP3-greedy as the next music fanatic, but at those prices, we'll wait a while.

Flying with an MP3 Player

As security concerns have a greater impact on air travel, you should plan ahead to make sure that your MP3 player doesn't cause a problem on the plane.

If you carry your MP3 player onto the plane, it might be checked by hand to make sure it really is what it seems. Most often, that means a security professional will ask you to demonstrate that it works. This means you should have the headphones easily accessible and fresh batteries installed. If you can't prove that it plays music, you may be delayed or forced to leave the player behind.

In addition, remember that you won't be allowed to use the player for the first few minutes and last few minutes of the flight.

Another alternative is the PhatNoise Car Audio System (www.phatnoise.com). PhatNoise has the advantage of working with—instead of replacing—your existing car stereo. It requires some trunk space, however. The PhatBox is a large hard disk that sits in the back of the car and connects to your stereo head unit. Your stereo gets disc and song names from the PhatBox and displays them on the stereo display.

PhatNoise comes in several versions ranging from 5GB to 30GB, and it's priced much more reasonably: around $600.

NOTE *If you've heard of the empeg-car and wondered why we didn't write about it, we actually did. Thanks to Sonic Blue, maker of Rio music players, empeg-car has become Rio Car.*

Cassette Adapters

Remember the early days of CD players? Companies sold cassette-shaped adapters that you put into the cassette deck of your car, and the audio from your portable CD player would then play through your car's speakers. That old idea hasn't gone away; it has simply been reborn in the age of MP3s.

The Duo-64 from Digisette (www.digisette.com), for instance, is a clever MP3 player shaped like a traditional audiocassette. You can listen to music using it as a stand-alone MP3 player, or insert it into a cassette deck and play your music that way. The Duo-64 uses removable SD/MMC memory cards. It's a great interim solution for listening to MP3s in the car if you're not planning to upgrade your car stereo soon.

Naked Before the Song

Dave: At the risk of sounding a bit pretentious, I think there are two broad categories of music. As in any artistic medium, there's both decoration and serious art. If you're looking for a painting, you can go to a country fair and find a lot of decorations. Go to the MOMA, and you're more likely to encounter serious art.

What's the difference? Decorative songs have a good beat, are fun to listen to, or—as Rick might say—sound "funky." In the hands of a serious musician, however, you find yourself standing naked before the song, utterly exposed and completely vulnerable to its truths. A decoration is pretty and may keep your attention for a few minutes, but ultimately, it's a formula that's about nothing at all; or, at best, it's about the performer who wrote it.

Art is not about the artist, but about the listener. It asks and answers profound questions, sometimes without even involving a vocalist. It's great because art transcends formula. It doesn't grow tired with repeated listening the way mere decoration does because it's more than a beat, a rhythm, and a melody. It's about you. It's about life. It's about that inner strength or weakness that we all bury deep within ourselves. A great song speaks, and we are compelled to listen.

That said, there's absolutely nothing wrong with decorative songs. They're usually just not for me.

Let's cast our votes for the songs that are most meaningful to each of us personally. You can list anything here, but after my lengthy preamble, I humbly suggest that "Your Auntie Grizelda," by The Monkees, probably doesn't belong on this list.

- "Fall Down," from *Hunkpapa* — The Throwing Muses
- "The Gunner's Dream," from *The Final Cut* — Pink Floyd
- "Pale Blue Eyes," from *Loaded* — The Velvet Underground
- "Within You Without You," from *Sgt. Pepper's Lonely Hearts Club Band* — The Beatles
- "Measure," from *From Strength to Strength* — Peter Himmelman

Rick: There are very few things before which I will stand naked, and songs are not among them. Dave, as you may have guessed, is just plain kooky—but

I respect that music has a different meaning for him than it does for me. When I hear a particularly lively version of Benny Goodman's "Sing, Sing, Sing," it lifts my spirits and gets my toes a-tappin'. It's also a thrill when I hear Courtney Love belt out "Violet," or when I'm singin' along with David Gray in the car. In short, I'm not looking for deep or hidden meanings in the lyrics, nor am I interested in prodding the heart hanging from the songwriter's sleeve. I just want to jam, or sing, or get swept away by a great melody. End of story.

Songs that have personal meaning, huh? Apparently "Your Auntie Grizelda" is too trivial for Mr. Art-Deco Music Man, so I'll try to look a little deeper.

- "Come Rain or Come Shine" — Ray Charles
- "At Last" — Etta James
- "I Melt with You" — Modern English
- "Cat's in the Cradle" — Harry Chapin
- "Wild Child" — The Untouchables

Dave: For what it's worth, Rick's house is filled with pictures of dogs playing poker.

You can buy those old cassette adapters that were popular with portable CD players and plug them into your MP3 player's headphone jack. They're available for around $20 from your neighborhood department store.

Go Wireless

Last, but not least, we've run across an intriguing new product from Kima Wireless (www.akoo.com) that deserves some attention, even though it wasn't quite ready to ship when we wrote this chapter. Called Link-It, it's a wireless transmitter for your MP3 player that broadcasts your music over the FM band, enabling you to receive your music on your car stereo (or any other stereo, for that matter).

If Link-It works as advertised, it'll be a great way to turn your portable MP3 player into a personal radio station that you can tune into any time you're traveling. The downside, of course, is that you have no control over the playlist once you leave the house.

Understanding Memory Card Formats

No matter which kind of portable music player you choose, you will no doubt have to deal with the concept of memory cards. There's a handful of competing memory formats around today, and they're all largely incompatible. If you buy an MP3 player that uses CompactFlash memory, for instance, you can't simply insert a SmartMedia or Memory Stick instead. Check out Figure 7-4 to see all of the most popular memory card formats side by side.

CompactFlash

CompactFlash cards, sometimes referred to as CF cards, are just about the oldest memory cards currently in use in MP3 players. They ship in a wide variety of densities, from an almost unusably tiny 8MB all the way up to about 512MB. Although small, they're rigid enough to resist most kinds of casual damage. These cards are manufactured by several companies, including Viking, Kingston, SanDisk, and Lexar.

FIGURE 7-4 You can easily see the size of each memory card in relation to a floppy disk and paper clip.

If you like the idea of massive storage, you should consider a special kind of CompactFlash card made by IBM and Iomega. Called the Microdrive, it's a true hard disk in a CompactFlash casing. The Microdrive comes in a variety of capacities, including 340MB, 500MB, and 1GB—and 2GB may follow soon. Before buying a Microdrive, check with the MP3 player manufacturer to see if it's compatible. Microdrives require more power than ordinary CF cards, and that means they don't work in all devices.

SmartMedia

SmartMedia—originally known by the somewhat cumbersome name of Solid State Floppy Disk Card (SSFDC)—is the thinnest of all memory formats, measuring a mere .75 mm thick. SmartMedia has been around as long as CompactFlash and has long been its biggest competitor. Because it's so thin, SmartMedia has no on-board intelligence; it relies on the parent device (such as your MP3 player) to provide control. While it's more streamlined, the SmartMedia's nonintegrated design poses a potential problem. Some older gadgets may not be able to accept larger-density SmartMedia cards as they're introduced because the device wasn't programmed to understand those higher-capacity SmartMedia cards. A number of companies sell SmartMedia cards, including Kingston, SanDisk, Lexar, and Iomega.

Secure Digital and MultiMediaCard

Secure Digital (SD) and MultiMediaCard (MMC) are the newest challengers to the CompactFlash and SmartMedia dynasty. These cards offer digital devices high memory capacities in a footprint only slightly thicker than SmartMedia and no bigger than a thumbnail. They're so small, in fact, that we constantly worry about losing them.

Because both SD cards and MMC cards share the same overall dimensions (although SD cards are slightly thicker than MMC cards), most devices are designed to accommodate both formats interchangeably. The principal difference is data encryption: SD cards allow vendors to deliver copyrighted data to the end user while ensuring that it can't be illegally copied.

SD/MMC cards are becoming popular because of their tiny size, and we wouldn't be surprised to see most new MP3 players making use of SD/MMC memory next year. The format's only major downside is the limited memory capacity: because it's so new, it's currently available in formats up to only 64MB. Higher capacities should emerge next year.

Dave's MP3 Auto Experience

Although my car had a 6-disc changer in the trunk, I simply wasn't happy. The problem? I really disliked removing CDs from my Sony CD jukebox in the home stereo. CDs have a tendency to get lost that way, and Lenny Kravitz's *Mama Said* would never be in the CD player when I needed it. So, overcome with a yearning to have my entire 350-CD music collection in my car at all times, I shopped for and installed an MP3 player in my car.

Unfortunately, I was limited by the car's design. I have a Honda S2000, a small two-seat roadster that isn't designed for lots of audio upgrades. While I was intrigued by the potential of the Rio Car, which would have put my entire music collection on a big hard disk, I didn't have $1000.

Instead, I determined I needed to get an in-dash CD player that would also play MP3 tracks from CD-R discs. I settled on the Kenwood eXcelon. It's compatible with a CD changer, but it will recognize MP3s only from the disc in the dash. So I opted not to spend the extra money on the trunk-mounted changer.

In the final analysis, I love my MP3-enabled car. I've burned my music collection onto CD and can listen to every Beatles album, for instance, in sequence from a single disc, and then change discs and hear all of the Rolling Stones. The changer displays the album title and track name, so I can see exactly what I'm listening to. The only downside? It takes a few seconds to change tracks as the ID3 tag data is read off the disc, and there's a pause between tracks, even when they were originally intended to flow together. I've got a dozen CDs arranged over my head on the sun visor and another dozen or so CDs in a box in the glove compartment. Between them, they add up to almost every song I own. And that's pretty cool.

Memory Stick

If you ask us, Sony has a history of introducing proprietary or semiproprietary technologies that fail because they aren't dramatically better than the competition —just different. There was Betamax in the VCR wars, Minidisk in the home stereo format battles, Digital8 versus DV among camcorders, and now the Memory Stick.

The Memory Stick concept is a clever one: it's a small memory card that's ubiquitous across Sony's entire product line. Take a picture with a Sony digital camera, for instance, and you can insert it into a Sony laptop, Clie handheld, digital picture frame, or desktop Memory Stick Reader. The stick itself is a thin blue card, about the same width as and only slightly longer than an SD/MMC card. (Most people liken it to a stick of chewing gum.)

Although Memory Stick products are still rare—at least compared to other memory formats—there are, indeed, MP3 players on the market that use Memory Sticks. Memory Sticks are now available in a 128MB density, and Sony is planning to roll out two new kinds of Memory Sticks: Magic Gate Memory Sticks, which encrypt copyrighted data (much like the SD card), and Memory Stick peripherals, which are more than just flash memory and extend the functionality of connected devices.

What Do Memory Cards Cost?

Here's a comparison of memory card prices as of September 2001. If you're considering a portable MP3 player, you might want to factor in the cost of adding memory cards before you make your final decision.

Memory	CompactFlash	SmartMedia	SD/MMC	Memory Stick
32MB	$38	$30	$55	$42
64MB	$60	$55	$99	$75
128MB	$99	$110	$230	$140
256MB	$300	N/A	N/A	N/A

Playing MP3s on a Personal Digital Assistant

Portable MP3 players look cool, but you may not need one. If you've got a handheld PC of some sort, you may already have everything you need to listen to music on the go. Electronic organizers and portable PCs like the Palm, Handspring Visor, and Pocket PC are all increasingly emphasizing multimedia prowess.

Today's portable PCs fall broadly into two main classes: Pocket PC devices based on the Microsoft Pocket PC operating system, and Palm OS devices based on the operating system from Palm, Inc. Microsoft designed the Pocket PC OS to accommodate multimedia right from the outset—so your Compaq iPAQ or HP Jornada is designed to play digital music and even play video files from the moment you take it out of the box. Palm, on the other hand, has traditionally designed its operating system to be much simpler, and allowed its hardware partners to add their own multimedia capabilities.

There are compromises associated with listening to music on a PDA like the Pocket PC or Handspring Visor. First and foremost, it's designed to be a computer, not a musical jukebox, so the controls are not optimized for music. You may also find that the battery life is limited and it may not have as much memory for storing music as you'd like.

Most important, your Personal Digital Assistant (PDA) is a significant investment. You probably won't want to go jogging with a $500 Pocket PC in your hand or take it to the beach to hear some tunes while lying in the sand. Even if you occasionally use your PDA for music playback, you may end up getting a portable music player anyway for some of those reasons.

MP3s on a Pocket PC

Like we already mentioned, Pocket PC devices like the ones in Figure 7-5 are designed to play digital music. Indeed, they all come with a "pocket" version of Microsoft's Windows Media Player. To play music on your Pocket PC device, you simply need to copy songs onto the device when it's in the ActiveSync cradle. Because only a few songs will quickly exhaust the small amount of memory in your Pocket PC, you'll almost certainly want to install a CompactFlash memory card and add your music to the card instead of main memory.

TIP

If you're copying songs to a memory card, a quirk in the Pocket PC operating system requires that you copy the music to the card's My Documents folder. If you drag the songs to a different folder, your Pocket PC won't be able to find and play the files.

Pocket PC handhelds are really handy; you can use one not only for all of your daily organizer and mobile computing tasks, but you can use it as an MP3 player as well. We've found one very serious limitation with the Pocket PC, though: because of the way MP3 files are stored on the handheld, it can take hours to copy a few songs to the device via the ActiveSync cradle. That snag makes it highly inconvenient to just throw a few songs on the device before you head out at lunchtime.

FIGURE 7-5 The HP Jornada and Compaq iPAQ both play MP3s right out of the box.

Pocket PC Choices

At the moment, only a small selection of Pocket PC devices are available. They all play MP3s via the Windows Media Player. Here's a chart that summarizes your options:

Model	Company	Memory	Color	Internal Memory
Cassiopeia E-125	Casio	CompactFlash	Yes	32MB
Genio e570	Toshiba	CompactFlash and SD	Yes	64MB
iPAQ H3100	Compaq	CompactFlash or PC Card	No	16MB
iPAQ H3600	Compaq	CompactFlash or PC Card	Yes	32MB
Jornada 525	HP	CompactFlash	Yes	16MB
Jornada 545	HP	CompactFlash	Yes	32MB

MP3s on a Palm OS Device

It's too bad that Palm doesn't have a catchy name like Pocket PC, because the only way we can talk about "all of the Palm gadgets, not just the ones made by Palm," is to say the equally long mouthful, "Palm OS devices." In the old days, of course, these gadgets were called PalmPilots, and many folks still call them that. But to be technically accurate (and that's something we've had to do ever since Rick made that drunken wager on the radio, offering a million bucks to anyone who could spot an error in one of our books), we'll call them Palms.

Right now, there are two ways to get multimedia capabilities on a Palm device. You can buy a Sony Clie N760C or choose a Handspring Visor. First, let's take a quick look at the Clie.

The Sony Clie is a Palm OS device that has Sony's magic multimedia touch. It uses Sony's unique Memory Stick expansion card format for additional memory, and one of the models includes built-in MP3 software and a headphone jack for private listening. When we wrote this chapter, three Clie models were available:

Model	MP3 Capability	Screen
PEG-N760C	This is the guy with the built-in MP3 player—but we're sure you'll see this feature in a lot of future models as well.	High-resolution color display
PEG-N610C	No.	High-resolution color display
PEG-S320	No.	Standard-resolution monochrome display

The Visor doesn't have MP3 capability built in, but that's OK; you can add it. The Visor's expansion capability—called a Springboard slot—is where you insert all sorts of gadgets that change the way your Visor works. In a sense, it's like building a PDA out of Legos with just the features you personally need. Springboard modules are available that turn the Visor into a cell phone, Global Positioning System (GPS) receiver, barcode scanner, digital camera, and more.

Thanks to a pair of MP3 player modules, the InnoGear MiniJam (see the illustration) and the SoundsGood audio player, you can also turn your Visor into an MP3 player. They both slip into the Springboard slot and can play music even when you're using the Visor for some other application. Here's how they differ:

Features	MiniJam	SoundsGood
Price	$199	$149
Memory	Two independent SD/MMC card slots for virtually unlimited storage	64MB of permanent internal storage (about an hour of audio)
Size	Slightly thicker than Visor	Mounts flush with top and back of Visor

We have to admit that given a choice, we prefer the MiniJam. Its pair of SD/MMC cards gives the module the ability to play hours and hours of music. The SoundsGood module runs out of steam after a single hour, and you can't swap memory cards to hear something different—you have to take it home and HotSync to get new music. Yuck.

NOTE *If you're a fan of audiobooks, check out the Audible Advisor. It's a Visor module that enables you to listen to audio content downloaded from Audible.com. This isn't technically MP3 technology, but it's close.*

Chapter 8

MP3 Around the House

How to…

- Listen to MP3 music in any room
- Listen to MP3 music on your home stereo
- Listen to MP3 music on an FM radio
- Listen to MP3 music while moving around the house
- Plug your portable MP3 player into a stereo or boombox
- Buy a DVD player that doubles as an MP3 player

Let's review. In Chapter 5, you learned how to turn your PC into a jukebox for playing MP3 tunes. In Chapter 6, you added Internet radio to the mix. In Chapter 7, you learned how to make MP3 files mobile, to give them a life outside your PC. Here in Chapter 8, it's time to focus on the home front. When you're done, you'll be able to listen to your MP3 collection at your bedside, on your home stereo, or in virtually any room in the house.

From PC to Stereo (Same Room)

If you're like Dave, your home stereo has speakers the size of telephone booths. If you're like Rick, your home stereo fits on a bookshelf. Either way, chances are good your stereo sounds a lot better than your PC (unless you've upgraded to some serious speakers, as discussed in Chapter 9). Wouldn't it be great, then, to pipe MP3 music from your computer to your stereo?

You can do just that, thanks to a small metal box called Stereo-link (see Figure 8-1). This device, which is compatible with both Windows and Macintosh systems, establishes a physical connection between computer and stereo—meaning, of course, that they must be in the same room. The package includes roughly 18 feet of cable, so consider the location of your equipment before purchasing this rather pricey accessory ($159).

The Stereo-link relies on a USB connection (see Figure 8-2), so your computer must be new enough to have USB ports. The key benefit behind this technology is that your digital audio stays digital until it reaches the stereo, ostensibly resulting in better sound quality than if it were routed through a sound card first. Thus, even if you have a high-end speaker system for your PC, the discriminating ear may prefer the combination of Stereo-link and a home stereo.

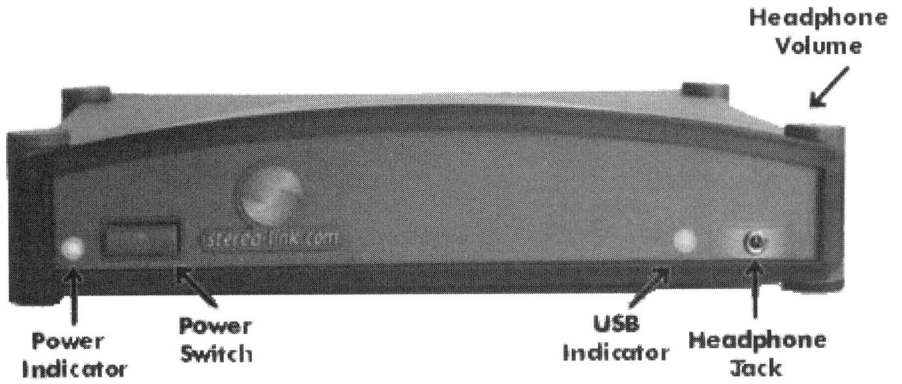

FIGURE 8-1 The Stereo-link bridges the gap between your computer and your stereo—provided they're in the same room.

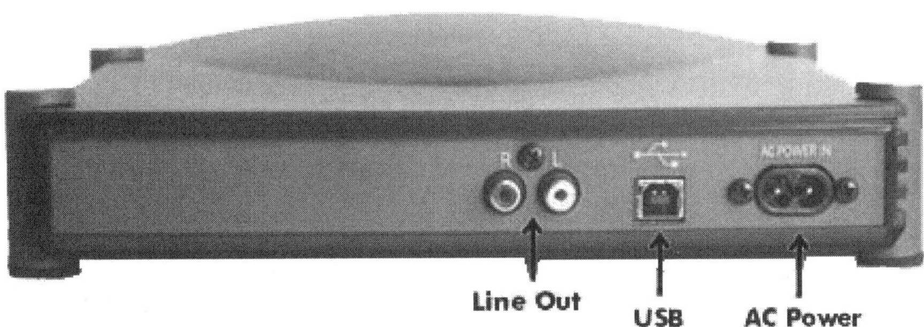

FIGURE 8-2 To use Stereo-link, your computer must have at least one available USB port and an up-to-date operating system.

Can't I Just Run an Audio Cable from My PC to My Stereo?

Sure you can—in fact, it may be worth a try. A few PC sound cards have RCA-out jacks (instead of the more traditional 1/8-inch phono jacks), meaning that you could just buy a long RCA cable and run it from your sound card to your stereo's AUX or line-in jacks. You can also buy a phono-to-RCA cable if your sound card has only phono (also known as "stereo") jacks, although finding an acceptable length could be difficult. Check your local Radio Shack for options. The more important issue is sound quality: a number of factors (including signal degradation, computer noise, and so on) may diminish it. Even so, you may want to try this direct approach. The $10 or so you spend on a cable is a lot less than the $160 you'll spend on Stereo-link.

The Stereo-link plugs into your stereo via RCA line-in jacks (CD, AUX, tape, VCR—they're all fair game). All modern receivers—and most higher-end bookshelf and boombox stereos—have them, so compatibility shouldn't be an issue unless you have really old or cheapo equipment.

The Stereo-link will feed any computer-generated audio to your stereo, so it's useful not just for MP3 files, but also for Internet radio and even games. It also supports audio CDs played in your CD-ROM drive, provided the latter supports *digital audio extraction*. Check with the drive's manufacturer to determine if it does.

We tried Stereo-link and liked it. But it's an expensive solution, which is why you may prefer something like the Akoo Kima KS-110 (see the next section). It not only costs less, but it also lets you link to stereos that are in other rooms of the house.

From PC to Stereo (Different Rooms)

Not everyone has their stereo in the same room with their PC. Rick, for instance, works from a basement office, but his stereo is located one floor up in the family room. Is he prohibited from enjoying his MP3 collection and Internet radio on his lovely new stereo? Heavens, no. Thanks to a variety of wireless products, he can listen to PC audio just about anywhere in the house.

Dave would like to state for the record that he thinks wireless systems are god-awful, while Rick thinks they're good enough for all but discriminating audiophiles.

Kinda Like Mr. Microphone—for MP3

Remember those wacky Mr. Microphone commercials from decades ago? "Hey, good lookin', we'll be back to pick you up later!" Yes, we mourn the '70s, too. This novelty product enabled you to broadcast your voice over the radio by transmitting at a specific frequency. Akoo's Kima KS-110 Wireless Audio System works on the same principle, effectively turning any FM radio in your house into a receiver for music "broadcast" from your PC.

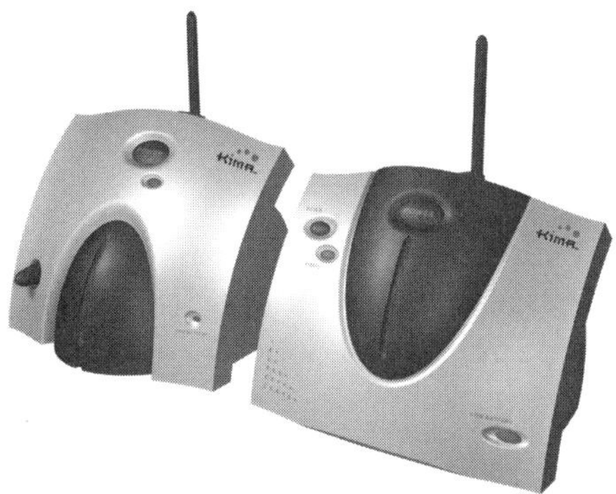

The package consists of an attractive, futuristic-looking transmitter and a nearly identical receiver. The former connects to your PC's sound card (and cleverly includes a passthrough connector so you can continue to use your speakers), while the latter sits near your radio or receiver. What's particularly neat is that the Kima receiver can plug into one of your stereo receiver's input jacks (such as AUX), or it can simply use a wireless radio connection. In that case, all you do is tune your radio or receiver to a specific frequency. Presto—an easy, effective, wireless link between your PC and your stereo.

The Kima broadcasts on a 900 MHz frequency. What happens if you have other 900 MHz devices in your home, such as a cordless telephone? The Kima has four channel options, so if there's interference, you can simply switch to another channel. What's more, the base unit and receiver can operate off AC power (adapters are included) or four AAA batteries—the latter a plus if you like to keep wire clutter to a minimum.

In our tests, the Kima worked extremely well. We like the fact that the receiver can sit up to 10 feet away from your radio or stereo. We also like the price, a reasonable $99.95.

Music Today Just Plain Stinks!

Dave: Ah, I see from the heading that I'm supposed to be a crotchety old man and dismiss as garbage the music that the kids of today listen to. Well, that shouldn't be hard, because honestly, music today has no soul, no spirit, no integrity. Hits are pumped out of the corporate machine by cynical boy bands like 'N Sync and the Backstreet Boys and by teenage girls like Christina whatever-her-name-is. Those kids don't care about the music they make; heck, they can't even play musical instruments. They sing songs other people write for them and learn dance steps mapped out by their choreographer.

Real music—music with heart and substance—survives, but only in tiny pockets of the music world, far away from teen demographics. But for every Kristin Hersh or Bob Mould in the world, there's a dozen Barenaked Ladies and Big Bad Voodoo Daddies, cashing in on a popular musical trend just to make a quick buck. But I know you, Rick. You're going to say that music doesn't need a sense of integrity or a glimmer of originality. It just needs a good beat and to follow the same darned three-chord formula used by every other popular performer this year.

Rick: Whew—it must be tough work being that cranky. I don't even know where to start, but I will agree with your sole valid point: today's money-grubbing corporate band production is obnoxious. That said, one could argue that your basic 'N Sync is not much different from the Beach Boys 35 years ago—it's just this generation's form of pop music. As for instruments, the Monkees didn't play any, and I happen to know you like the Monkees (against all reasoning). As for integrity and originality, I don't discriminate: if there's a song I like, I'm not going to stop liking it just because of its origins. And I laugh at the coffeehouse beatnik snobbery that decries three-chord songs, which says that for music to be good, it must be complex. Please.

TIP

When we first set up the Kima, the audio level on the base unit wouldn't go high enough, even though we cranked the volume dial to maximum. Then we opened Windows' volume control panel (double-click the Speaker icon in your System Tray) and raised the Wave/DirectSound slider. That did the trick.

X10 Marks the Spot

If you're into home automation, you probably recognize the name X10. The company makes a wide variety of nifty products, from wireless surveillance cameras to automated lighting systems.

The X10 MP3 Anywhere 2000 is similar to the aforementioned Akoo Kima, but it costs $20 less. The kit also includes a universal remote that can control up to eight devices, as well as an MP3 software interface for your computer called BOOM2. This combination gives you remote control over MP3 playback, including skipping tracks and pausing songs. What's more, the MP3 Anywhere 2000 operates on a 2.4 GHz frequency, so it's less likely to experience signal interference.

On the downside, X10 products have a tendency to be user-unfriendly, so novices may want to steer clear.

Make Your Stereo Part of Your Computer Network

Your library of MP3 files is stored on your PC. Products like the Kima and X10 MP3 Anywhere 2000 simply beam the music from your PC to your stereo, without giving you much control over the library. AudioTron, on the other hand, is like an extension of your PC that connects to your stereo. With it, you can select songs by name, play songs in a specific order or randomly, and control every other aspect of playback. (A remote is included as part of the package.)

The AudioTron is not a wireless product. Rather, it links to your PC by way of Ethernet or Home Phoneline Networking Alliance (HPNA) networking—and this is a potential limitation. Your stereo must be in relatively close proximity to an Ethernet jack or a phone jack. (We'd say no further than 10 feet, unless you're OK with wires running all over your floors.) Most homes aren't wired for Ethernet, so you'll probably need to go the phone-jack route.

See, it's possible to create a computer network in your home using ordinary phone lines. This technology was developed by the HPNA, and the AudioTron sort of pretends to be a computer on the network. Put simply, it talks to your PC—the one with all the MP3 files stored on it—via the phone line. The good news is, it doesn't interrupt the line while it's active. You can still make and receive phone calls. The bad news is, you have to buy an HPNA card for your machine (but you can buy them for as little as $30), and you have to deal with some of the potential hassles that go with setting up a network.

Cool as the AudioTron is for the audiophile who wants total control over his or her MP3 collection, we're not sure we'd spend $300 on it. Sure, it saves you from having to run to your PC every time you want to pause the music or change Internet radio stations, but for $300, we're willing to run a little.

Internet Radio to Go

If you were tantalized by the Internet radio offerings presented in Chapter 6, you may be wondering how you can enjoy the global network around the house. Although the Akoo Kima and X10 MP3 Anywhere 2000 can pipe Internet radio to your stereo, neither is expressly designed with that in mind. Enter iRhythm, which could best be described as a portable Internet radio appliance.

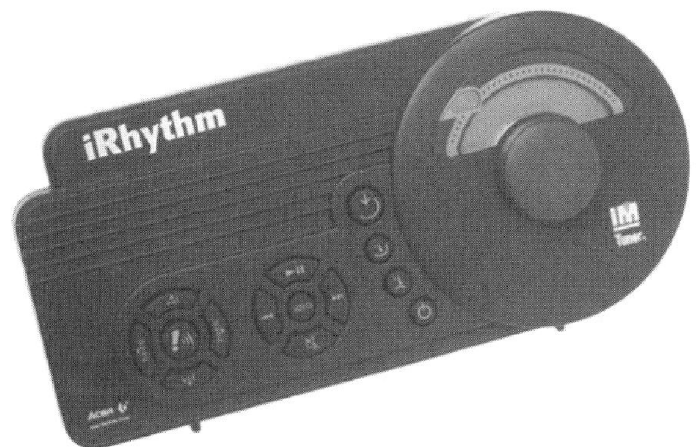

Before we tell you anything more, we should mention that the iRhythm is currently in a state of flux. It used to be sold by Acer's NeWeb division, but that's gone. It's now supported by iM Networks, where it's officially known as the iRhythm Remote and sold exclusively through Amazon.com. Sad to say, it could be discontinued by the time you read this, which is a shame because it's a neat product.

The package consists of a 900 MHz transmitter, two receivers, and a remote. The transmitter plugs into one of your PC's USB ports and your sound card's line-out jack. The main receiver plugs into your stereo's AUX input jacks. (The secondary receiver is a pager-like device that lets you plug in an ordinary pair of headphones for listening while moving around the house. Very slick.) The remote "tunes in" Internet radio stations from the 25 preselected categories (including rock, country, news, and the like).

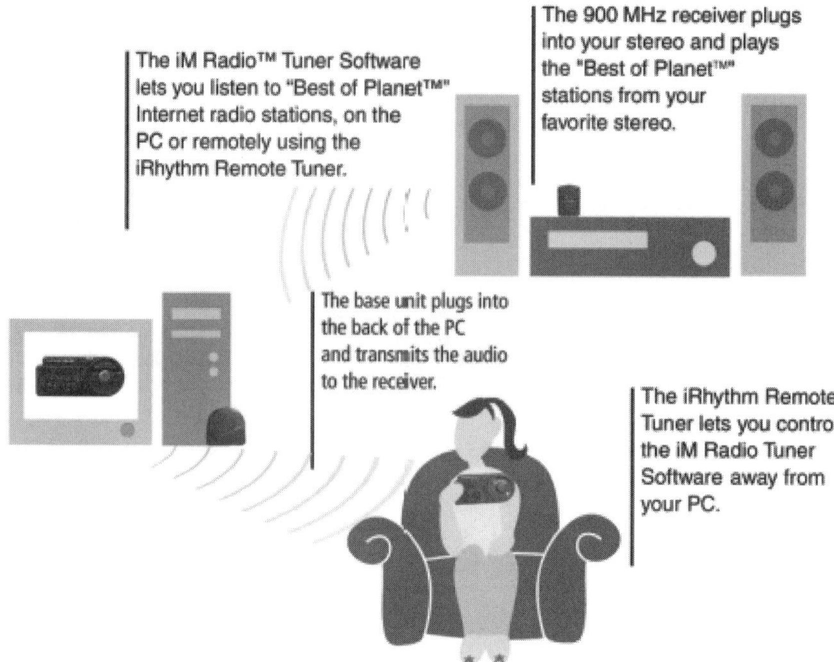

The iRhythm will work with a 56 Kbps dial-up connection, but it works a whole lot better with broadband. The remote is duplicated by Windows software that you can download and try even without buying the package—something we recommend to see how you like the iM Networks "experience." For the record, we thought it was pretty cool.

From PC to Any Other Room

Not everyone has a fancy-schmancy stereo system. And certainly few of us have one in every room. Suppose, for instance, that you want to listen to MP3 tunes in your bedroom or basement, where there's neither a PC nor a stereo. That's where the Rio Receiver comes in (see Figure 8-3).

This device is very similar to the AudioTron (see "Make Your Stereo Part of Your Computer Network" earlier in this chapter), in that it links to your PC via an Ethernet or HPNA connection. But there are two key differences: the Rio Receiver

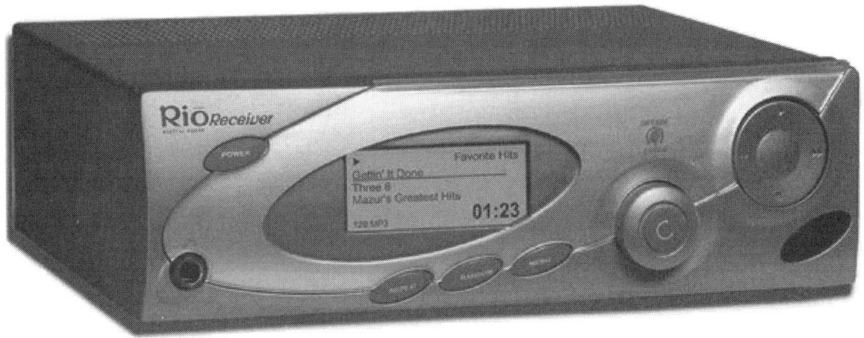

FIGURE 8-3 The Rio Receiver integrates with your stereo or stand-alone speakers and provides detailed information about the songs it plays.

comes with an HPNA card, and it supports the use of powered stand-alone speakers. The latter means that you can use it in just about any room of the house, without needing a full-blown stereo system.

Unfortunately, the Rio Receiver costs the same as the AudioTron ($300) and comes with the same potential setup hassles. Nevertheless, it's a pretty decent product, and it's an intriguing option for those who want MP3 in a room without a stereo. (But we still think most users would be better off with something like the $100 Akoo Kima.)

From MP3 Player to Stereo

Psst! We're going to let you in on a little secret. You know that pager-sized MP3 player you bought? You can plug it right into your home stereo for a little MP3 music on the fly. The headphone jack on all portable MP3 (and CD/MP3) players is the same 1/8-inch phono jack that's been around for years, so it's simple to run a cable from that jack to your stereo's AUX connectors.

The cable in question can be found at Radio Shack—it's called the 6' Specialty Y-Adapter, catalog #42-2483. As of press time, it was selling for $7.99.

TIP *There's no reason not to leave the cable plugged into the back of your stereo, even when your MP3 player is elsewhere. When you do want to connect the player, just fish out the cable and plug it in.*

Other Cool MP3 Options for the Home

In case you haven't already purchased a DVD player for your home entertainment system, make sure you get one that supports MP3. That way, you can spin CDs burned with MP3 files. It's like getting two players for the price of one.

Take, for instance, the Panasonic DVDRV31K (see Figure 8-4). It plays not only DVD movies, but also CD-R and CD-RW media. At press time, it was

DVDs Support CDs

Portable DVD players have grown increasingly popular in recent months. What you probably didn't know is that many of them support CDs burned with MP3 audio files. Thus, you're getting not only a portable movie studio, but a portable jukebox as well. Neat!

FIGURE 8-4 DVD players like this one make great additions to your home entertainment system because they can play MP3-packed CDs.

commonly available for under $200—no more expensive than DVD players that don't support MP3.

Where to Find It

Web Site	Address	What's There
Stereo-link	www.stereo-link.com	Stereo-link
Akoo	www.akoo.com	Kima KS-110
X10	www.x10.com	MP3 Anywhere 2000
AudioTron	www.audiotron.net	AudioTron
iM Networks	www.imnetworks.com	iRhythm
RioHome	www.riohome.com	Rio Receiver
Radio Shack	www.radioshack.com	6' Specialty Y-Adapter cable
Panasonic	www.panasonic.com	Panasonic DVDRV31K DVD/MP3 player

Getting the Best Sound

How to...

- Normalize the volume levels of your MP3 files
- Convert WMA files to MP3 and vice versa
- Use graphic equalizers
- Find sound-enhancing plug-ins for Winamp
- Choose the best bit rates
- Choose a set of speakers
- Choose a pair of headphones

Wow, look at you! Downloading MP3 files from the Internet, listening to them on your PC, copying them to your portable player—you're becoming quite the expert. But lest you feel like tossing this book out the window with a snide "Bah! I don't need you guys anymore," pay attention—we're not done yet. For instance, you don't know how to convert MP3 files to the Windows Media Audio (WMA) format, do you? Huh, smarty-pants? And what about speakers? You think you can just walk into a store and buy the speakers in the prettiest box? Ha! Close that window, pardner, and read on.

In this chapter, we help you get the best sound from your music files by normalizing their volume and trimming extra silence from the beginning and end. We also introduce you to the equalizers in Winamp and Windows Media Player, as well as Winamp's music-enhancing plug-ins. Plus, we delve into file conversion, bit rates, and speaker selection—all in this one tidy chapter.

Converting Your Audio Files

Here's a common scenario: You've got a mammoth collection of MP3 files, but your portable MP3 player has just 64MB of memory—enough for about an hour's worth of songs. Fortunately, the player also supports WMA files, which take up about half the space of MP3 files. If you could convert your music to WMA format, you could fit twice as many songs on your player!

A similar scenario: You've downloaded some songs in the WMA format, but your portable player doesn't support it. You need to convert the songs to MP3 format so you can listen to them on the go.

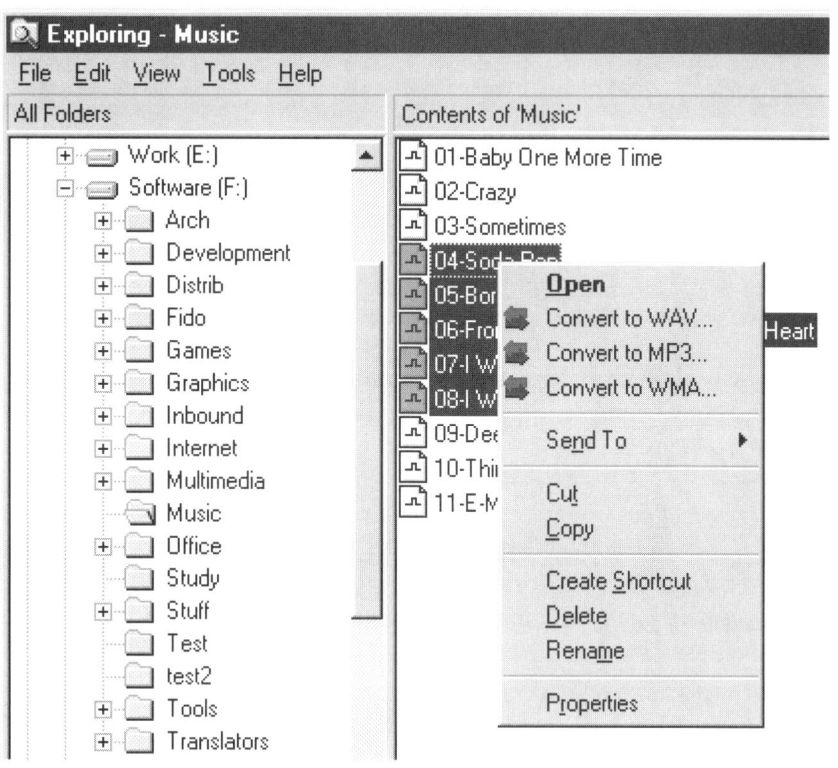

FIGURE 9-1 One-Click Audio Converter works its magic with MP3, WAV, and WMA files.

There are plenty of other situations in which you might want to convert songs among the MP3, WMA, and WAV formats (the last is the one used when burning songs onto audio CDs, as described in Chapter 14). Fortunately, there's a terrific Windows software utility that makes conversion as easy as a few mouse clicks. It's called One-Click Audio Converter (see Figure 9-1), and it's available from Streamware Development (www.streamware-dev.com).

The software integrates with Windows Explorer, meaning that it has no stand-alone interface like most programs. Rather, you right-click a music file, then select the desired conversion option from the pop-up menu that appears (see Figure 9-1). From there, a small option window appears, in which you can make changes to the sound quality of the file that's about to be created. (Most users will probably want to stick with the default settings.)

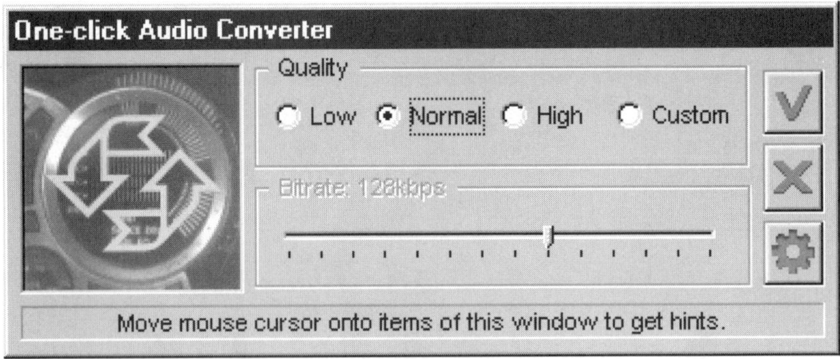

One-Click Audio Converter costs $21 to register, but you can use the demo version for 40 conversions before it expires. That's a good way to get your feet wet with the program and make sure it meets your needs.

You needn't convert your files one at a time—One-Click Audio Converter supports batch conversions. Thus, you can select multiple song files, then right-click to access the conversion menu. Any changes you make to the options will be applied to all the selected songs.

Macintosh users should check out SoundApp (www.download.com), an MP3 player that also performs file conversions. It's freeware!

Normalizing Your Audio Files

When you rip songs from your own CDs, the resulting MP3 files are likely to be at the same volume level. Most ripping software includes the capability to *normalize* the volume of songs as it rips them, so the levels remain equal (see Chapters 10 and 12). But what about songs you download from the Internet? You may discover that the volume level varies significantly between songs (which can lead to the annoying need to fumble with the volume control). Fortunately, there's a solution: you can use software to normalize the audio levels of your song files, ostensibly making them all equal.

Technically speaking, normalizing an audio file increases the volume of that file as far as possible without distorting the sound.

If you're a Winamp user and you listen to music mostly on your PC, download a plug-in called RockSteady. It's a simple volume equalizer that monitors and

After a Long, Hard Day...

You know the kind we mean—everything goes wrong, your blood pressure is through the roof, you think your head is about to explode. We have two suggestions for coping with such days: kickboxing, and unwinding with our favorite "decompression" music.

Rick: I can remember specific moments when I was so aggravated I wanted to go postal. Fortunately, music was my solace. Here are the tunes I turn to when I hit the boiling point:

- "Ode to My Family" — The Cranberries
- "Please Forgive Me" — David Gray
- "Adagio for Strings" — Samuel Barber
- "Violet" — Hole

Dave: I wonder what it takes to make Doctor Mellow (you know him as Rick) go postal. This much I know—regardless of what's on his list, a few minutes with *Soul Train* is enough to make him right as rain. And while I know what Rick is going for here, I have to admit that any of my music has a therapeutic effect on me—I don't have to mellow out to a sappy ballad to feel better. Nonetheless, in the spirit of Rick's topic, here are a few of my decompression tunes:

- "The Mummer's Dance" — Loreena McKennit
- "Maybe I'm Amazed" — Paul McCartney
- "December" — Collective Soul
- "Mission of My Soul" — Peter Himmelman
- "Day after Day" — Badfinger

adjusts playback so that all songs sound roughly the same. It's available in the software section of MP3.com (www.mp3.com). If you want even more control over Winamp's volume controls, download the AudioStocker plug-in (surf.to/mp3stock). It allows you to adjust the range of amplification for soft songs, the frequency balance equalization, and the compression (which determines whether you get

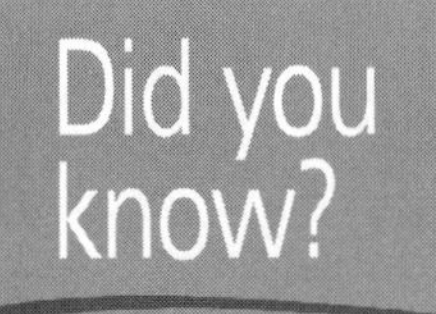

A Few Words about Bit Rates

We've discussed bit rates in several chapters already, and you'll learn more about them in Chapter 10. But because this topic is so important, it bears repeating in any chapter devoted to sound quality. Put simply, the higher the bit rate of any digital music file—MP3, WMA, or whatever—the better it will sound. If you're downloading or creating MP3 files expressly for listening on your PC, always opt for a 128 Kbps bit rate—or, better still, 160 Kbps. On the other hand, if you have a portable player with a fixed amount of memory, it's not unthinkable (unless you're Dave) to work with 96 Kbps files.

sound faithful to the original recording or something that's "very loud and massive," like FM radio).

NOTE *These plug-ins don't modify the MP3 files themselves—only their volume when played on your computer. Thus, don't expect normalized volume when you transport them to your MP3 player.*

Plug-ins like these can put a greater strain on your computer's processor. If you have a slow machine (something built in the mid-to-late '90s), you may find that using the plug-ins creates an unacceptable performance hit.

See Chapter 12 for information on normalizing audio levels when burning songs to a CD.

All about Equalizers

As you know from reading Chapter 5, RealJukebox is our favorite MP3 player. One feature it lacks, however, is a *graphic equalizer*—a kind of fine-tuning system for the various frequencies of audio playback (think bass and treble controls on steroids). That's something you can find in two other popular players: Winamp and Windows Media Player. Let's take a quick look at how they work.

NOTE *Actually, the registered version of RealJukebox does have an equalizer, but the otherwise versatile freeware version does not.*

Using Winamp's Equalizer

When you start Winamp, an equalizer should appear below the main Winamp window (see Figure 9-2). If it doesn't, press ALT-G. You can also click the icon in the upper-left corner of the main window, and then choose Equalizer from the list that appears.

As you can see, the equalizer has ten *bands,* each of which is used to adjust a specific frequency range for the audio you hear.

Click the On button to activate the equalizer (just because it appears doesn't mean it's functioning). Experimentation is the best way to determine which band does what—start a song, raise the volume to a comfortable listening level, and then slide one of the equalizer bands up or down. Some have a barely discernible impact, while others have very pronounced effects.

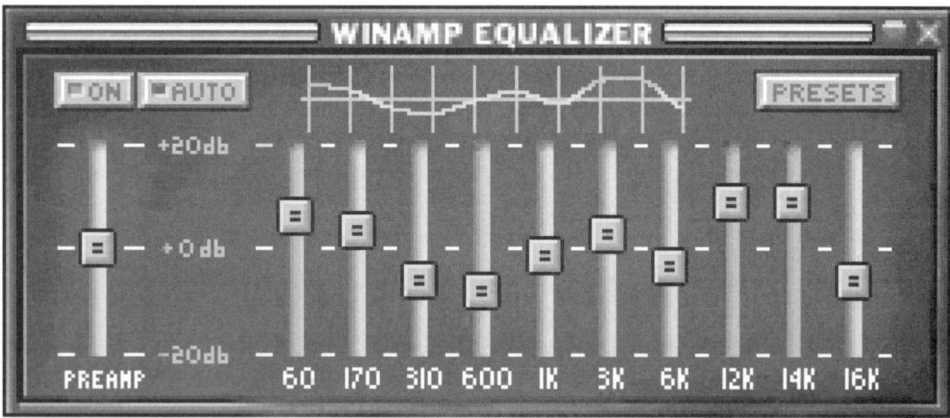

FIGURE 9-2 Winamp's equalizer works just like a traditional stereo equalizer to tweak music frequencies.

You can also load one of Winamp's dozen-plus presets, which automatically place the equalizer bands at settings that are well-suited to specific kinds of music. Here's how:

1. Click the Presets button, then Load, then Preset.
2. In the box that appears, select your desired choice from the list. As you can see, they range from Classical to Techno—something for just about every kind of music.

3. Click the Load button. You'll see the equalizer bands jump to their new settings, and you should hear a change in the song that's playing.
4. If you wish, you can change the Preset settings, and then save your modifications as your own personal preset (just click the Presets button again, followed by Save).

NOTE *It may take a second or two before changes made to equalizer settings are actually reflected in what you're hearing. This is software, not hardware, so there's a bit of processing time involved.*

Using the Windows Media Player Equalizer

To access the equalizer in Windows Media Player, you must first be viewing the Now Playing window. Next, click View | Now Playing Tools | Graphic Equalizer. You'll see the equalizer appear, as shown in Figure 9-3 (taken from Windows Media Player 7—the Windows XP version looks slightly different). Unfortunately, all you see are ten bands—no descriptors of what any of them do. Even the normal descriptors (170, 3K, 16K, etc.) aren't particularly helpful, so our advice is the same regardless: experiment!

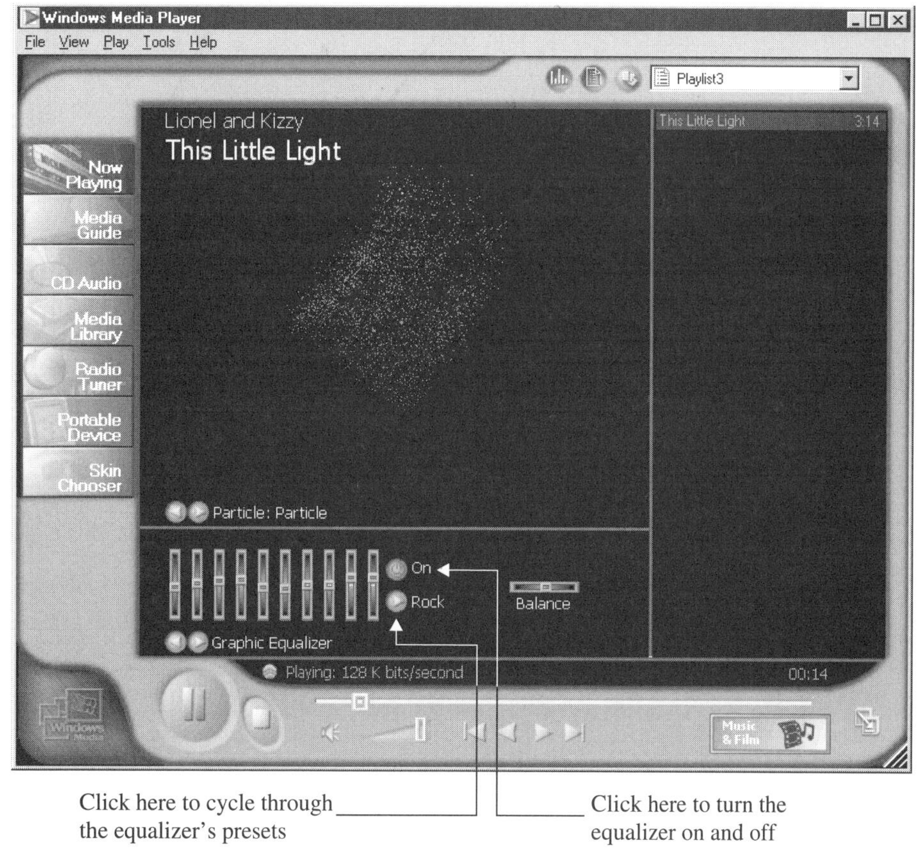

FIGURE 9-3 The equalizer in Windows Media Player isn't labeled well, but at least it's there.

In Windows Media Player 6, the equalizer is pretty well hidden and kind of a pain to work with. We recommend upgrading to a newer version, which you can do at www.windowsmedia.com.

Windows Media Player has eight equalizer *presets* (settings created for particular kinds of music), which you can cycle through by pressing the Presets button (see Figure 9-3). These presets all make very subtle changes to the equalizer—we think most users will prefer creating their own settings. You can do that by using the Custom preset, which will retain your changes even after you exit Windows Media Player. Too bad the software doesn't let you save more than one preset.

NOTE

When you adjust any of the equalizer's ten bands, the preset automatically changes from whatever was selected to Custom.

Choose a Killer Set of Speakers

Rick and Dave disagree wholeheartedly on the subjects of bit rates, sound quality, and the best Star Trek series, but there's one item on which they concur: bundled speakers stink. (And the ones found in notebooks are even worse.)

Many off-the-shelf and mail-order computers come with two- and three-piece speaker systems that just aren't fit for the great tunes you're pumping through them. Sure, a few premium machines come with decent speakers, but by and large, they're low-quality cheapies.

If you spend a lot of time at your PC, it probably makes sense to invest in some really good speakers. Though PC speakers generally aren't designed to rival those

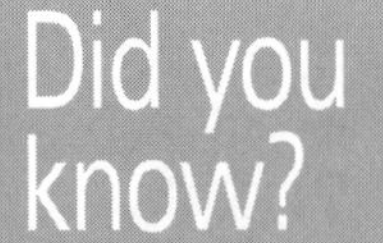

About the Sound Card

As we discussed in Chapter 2, your computer's sound card can be just as important to overall audio quality as the speakers themselves. If you're shopping for a five- or six-piece setup, be sure your sound card has dual speaker jacks. (Many computers have built-in audio subsystems with only one speaker jack, which would mean buying a separate sound card if you want surround-sound speakers.) If you need a new card, we highly recommend the Creative Labs Audigy MP3+, which has a list price of just $99.

found in home theater systems, there are some notable exceptions. Before we catalog them, however, let's look at specific features to watch for when choosing a speaker system.

- **Number of satellites** Any good speaker system is going to be based on a *subwoofer*—a box that sits on the floor and pumps out the bass tones. The *satellites* are the actual speakers. Thus, when we refer to a three-piece system, we mean one subwoofer and two satellites. A five-piece system has one subwoofer and four satellites—two that sit in front of you, two that sit behind (hence the term "surround sound"). A six-piece system adds a center speaker, which is great for live music and DVD movies. We highly recommend a five- or six-piece system because surround sound is leaps and bounds ahead of anything three speakers can accomplish.
- **Size of satellites** So-called flat-panel speakers are increasingly popular these days, not just because they save space on overcrowded desks, but because they look really cool. However, keep in mind that you still get what you pay for. Just because they're thin doesn't mean they sound better than their "fat" counterparts.

- **Location of controls** Believe it or not, some speaker manufacturers put volume, bass, and treble controls on the subwoofer rather than on one of the satellites. Given that the subwoofer usually resides on the floor, tucked well out of arm's reach, this is stupid beyond belief. Make sure the controls are easy to access (some speaker systems have independent control boxes that can be placed on or near your monitor for super-convenient access).

- **Length of cables** Depending on the layout of your room and computer desk, you may want to spread out the positioning of your satellites—especially the rear ones. Thus, make sure the cables are long enough. Consider that they have to travel from the back of your computer to a spot at least a few feet behind you, and that the path probably won't be direct. Plan your setup before making a purchase.
- **Rear-satellite stands** Sometimes the hardest part about working with a surround-sound package is positioning the rear satellites. You don't want them sitting on the floor, and it's rare to have a desk or table that's just where you need it. Fortunately, some five- and six-piece packages come with stands for the rear satellites, so you can easily and effectively position them.
- **Headphone jack** A headphone jack on one of the satellites is a nice touch—it lets you plug in your 'phones without having to reach around the back of your PC to find the jack on your sound card.

So, which speakers are right for you? You have dozens of great packages to choose from, with prices ranging from $60 up to $400. We recommend that you check out some of the reviews at places like Cnet (computers.cnet.com) and ZDNet (www.zdnet.com). In the meantime, here's a look at some of the speakers we like best.

Speakers	Estimated Street Price	Number of Satellites	URL	Ideal For
Altec Lansing AVS500	$60	4	www.alteclansing.com	Bargain shoppers who want a five-piece system
Harman/Kardon SoundSticks	$200	2	www.harman-multimedia.com	Macintosh users who want the coolest-looking speakers on the planet
Klipsch ProMedia 5.1	$400	5	www.klipsch.com	Serious audiophiles who want one of the best computer speaker systems ever created
Logitech SoundMan Xtrusio DSR-100	$150	4	www.logitech.com	Users who want a solid five-piece system at an affordable price
Sonigistix Monsoon MH-505	$179	5	www.sonigistix.com	Users who want a 5.1-channel system that doesn't cost a small fortune

Choose a Killer Set of Headphones

Not everyone in the house/office/building/neighborhood is likely to share your taste in music, so you may have to be mindful of cranking the volume at all hours of the day and night. (Rick, who has a few inconsiderate neighbors, would like to personally remind you that *babies and other people are trying to sleep*!) Fortunately, there's an easy solution: headphones.

There's another scenario that warrants the purchase of some 'phones: replacing the set that came with your portable MP3 player. Just like PCs often come with mediocre speakers, so do players bundle less-than-stellar headphones.

Let's take a look at some of the better offerings for listening in peace:

Headphones	Estimated Street Price	URL	Notes
Grado SR125	$150	www.gradolabs.com	Excellent clarity and fidelity
Koss SportaPro	$30	www.koss.com	A bargain, but beware the short cord
Sennheiser HD 25 SP	$90	www.sennheiser.com	Sealed headphones block out external noise but become uncomfortable after several hours

Headphones That Roam Free

Want to listen in private but not be tethered to your PC? Sounds like you need a set of wireless headphones. Look no further than the UnWired IR1000 (www.laral.com).

Plugging In

As noted in the previous section, a few of the better speaker systems have a headphone jack on one of the satellites, so you can plug right in with a minimum of fuss. What you have to watch for is the type of jack: many premium headphones have 1/4-inch phono plugs, whereas many speakers have the smaller 1/8-inch jacks. (You may encounter the reverse scenario as well.) Radio Shack to the rescue—you can find inexpensive adapters to insure a successful marriage between headphones and jacks.

The infrared base station plugs into your sound card and has a range of 25 feet, so you can roam the room and not have to worry about radio interference. Just one hitch: the headphones have to keep a direct line of sight to the base, so no ducking into another room. The good news is they sell for just $29.99.

Part III

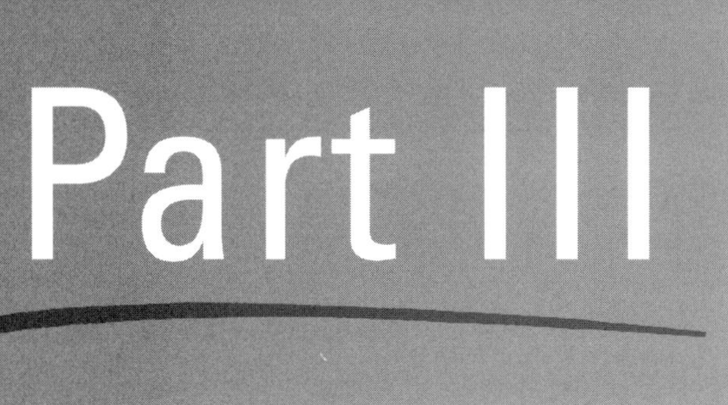

Creating Your Own Music Files

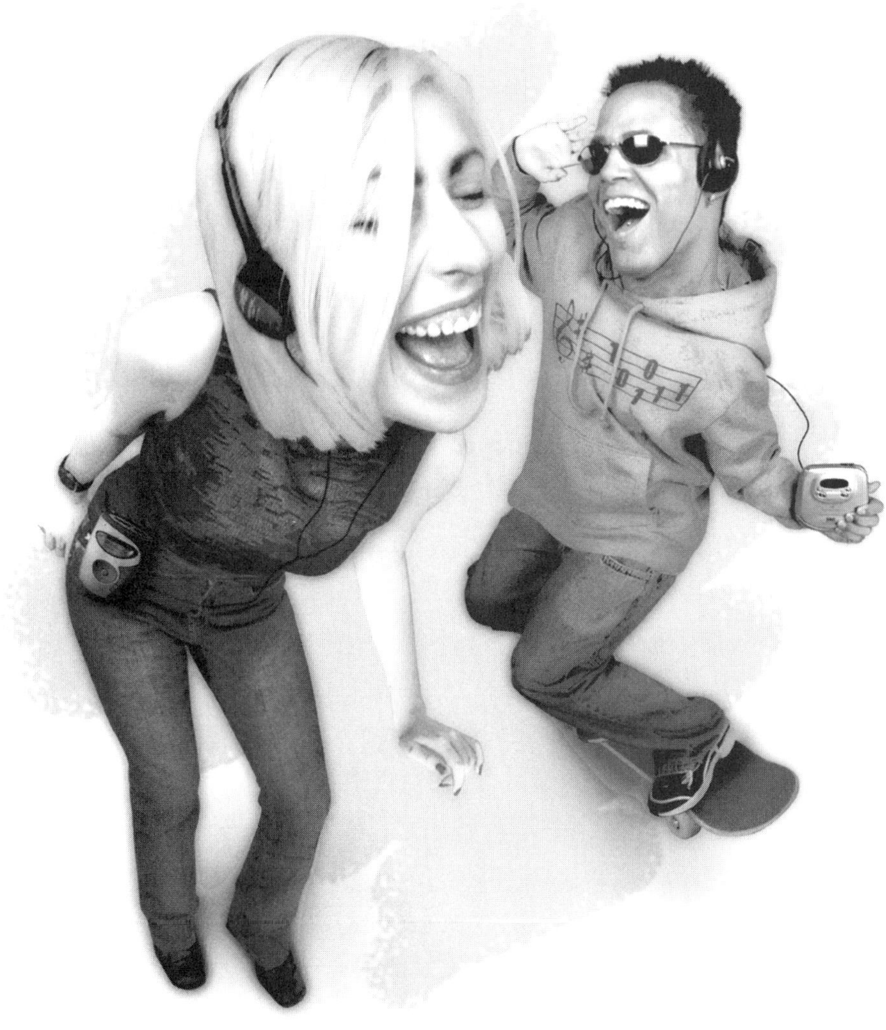

Chapter 10

Ripping Music from a CD

How to...

- Understand how sound propagates in air
- Distinguish between analog and digital audio
- Define the way digital audio is captured and stored
- Measure the quality of digital sound
- Choose between lossy and lossless audio formats
- Select audio capture software
- Rip songs from a CD
- Control the quality of sound files
- Optimize your PC for ripping songs from a CD
- Switch to analog capture if digital isn't working

The term *ripping* confuses people who are new to digital music. It sounds complicated and perhaps even a little violent. In reality, it's a slang term that refers to the process of making a copy of a song, CD, or other musical source—and the technical term is Digital Audio Extraction (DAE). When you rip music, you usually do it digitally, which makes a perfect copy, identical to the original in every way. (This explains why the record companies are a bit nervous.) Sometimes you can't extract the data from a CD digitally, which means your software has to resort to making an analog copy. It's still going to sound very good, and people usually refer to this type of copy as an *analog rip*. Technically, it's not a rip at all because the data isn't being copied bit for bit. See how cranky tech guys can be?

In this chapter, we'll get into the nuts and bolts of copying music. We'll start by discussing the basics of digital music files, move on to preparing your PC for ripping, and finally, actually tear some music off CDs and onto your PC's hard disk. Looking for information on making copies of analog music, like LPs and tapes? Check out Chapter 11 for details on that.

Inside Digital Audio

The best place to start is with a short primer on what sound—and digital audio—is all about. Some of this might remind you of a high school physics class. For others, like Rick, who took classes like hog farming and stenography in high school, this information might be new to you. Either way, we think that it helps to understand what's going on behind the curtain to get the most out of your recording sessions.

Sound Waves 101

No doubt you already know that sound is simply vibration. Something vibrates (like a person's vocal cord, a drum skin, or a guitar string), and that causes the surrounding air to vibrate as well. The air radiates the vibration away from the source of the original sound in ever-expanding waves, and those waves eventually reach your ears.

Of course, the air itself really isn't going anywhere; air molecules get excited from the vibration and jiggle. That "jiggling" transfers the energy of the sound to adjacent air molecules, and so on, until the sound has traveled a great distance. Eventually, those vibrations are received by your ears and interpreted by your brain as sounds.

For our purposes, sound waves have two key characteristics: amplitude and frequency. The *amplitude* of a sound is a way to measure its loudness. In air, loudness is measured in decibels (dB), and it's a unit used to compare the difference in energy level between two sounds. It's logarithmic in nature. For those of you who can't remember Mr. Buchanan's math class, that means higher decibel levels increase exponentially. The threshold of human hearing is 0dB, and every increase of 2dB doubles the actual intensity of the sound.

If a quiet room measures around 40dB, a jet plane measures about 140dB—and that's about ten million times louder.

The other characteristic of sound is *frequency*: a measure of the sound's pitch. Frequency is measured in *hertz,* another term for cycles per second. In fact, the sounds important to people—the ones we can actually hear—are conveniently measured in *kilohertz,* or thousands of cycles per second.

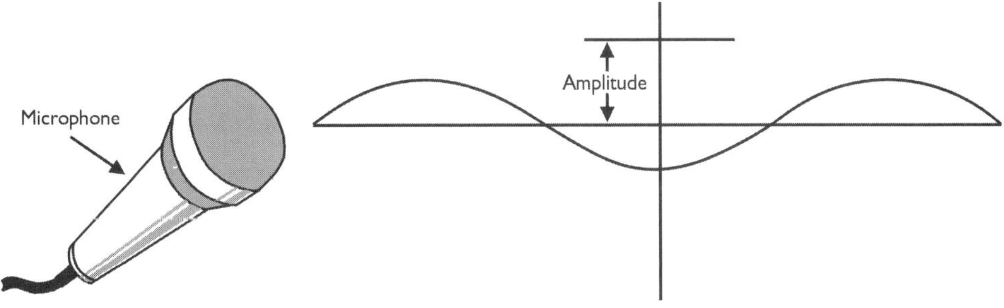

Electric Sound

Now for the clever part. When you record a sound and play it back through an electronic system like a stereo system, sound waves are represented as variations in electric voltage. The process works both ways: When you sing into a microphone, a small transducer converts the vibration of a diaphragm into a voltage that represents the varying sound waves. That current is transferred to the speakers, where a bigger diaphragm vibrates in perfect sync with the voltage, converting the electricity back into sound waves.

Voltage is simply a measure of the electrical "force" in an electric current, and the sound's amplitude is just the voltage. More voltage equals louder sound. The rate at which that amplitude changes forms the sound wave, and hence, the frequency.

Digital Sound

So how does all that get converted to digital music, you ask? Good question. Unlike an analog recording, a digital recording can never be a perfect recreation of the original sound. If that surprises you, consider this: analog recordings continuously vary the voltage to match the original sound wave. A digital recording, by definition, takes regular "samples" of the amplitude at regular time intervals, as you can see in Figure 10-1. The more samples you take, the more accurate the end product will be. Digital audio succeeds because it's possible to take so many samples that the accuracy of the signal is beyond the ability of humans to detect any missing information.

Two factors contribute directly to the quality of any digital sound: the resolution and the sampling rate. Together, these factors allow you to accurately—or inaccurately—reproduce a sound wave digitally. Here's what they are:

Resolution The *resolution* is a measure of the number of values used to represent the amplitude of a wave. Imagine a 1-bit resolution: because a bit has two values (0 and 1), a wave can be either on or off. No matter how loud or soft you played your kazoo, for instance, the sound would vary between maximum and off. The result? It'll sound like syncopated clicking. Obviously, that resolution is poor for any music reproduction. If you used the resolution of CD audio, though, you'd find 16-bit samples—or about 65,000 discrete levels of amplitude in the wave. Figure 10-2 demonstrates what the same sound wave looks like, rendered in two different resolutions.

Sampling rate If the wave is divided longitudinally (so the amplitude is broken into lots of measured values), then it stands to reason that there's another factor to consider: how often you take those measurements. That's the sampling rate. In a nutshell, the *sampling rate* is a measure of how many times each second you take an amplitude reading. The more of those you take, the more accurately you'll be able to depict the waveform. Audio CDs, for instance, use a sampling rate of 44.1 KHz.

The Age-Old Debate: Digital or Analog?

That's the basics of digital audio. As you can see, there's nothing about digital technology that makes it automatically better than analog. Indeed, if your resolution and sampling rate are too low, you can end up with audio that sounds significantly worse than the analog original! That problem actually happens a lot—in fact, sometimes by design. You can try it out for yourself. Record a sample of audio using the Windows Sound Recorder, for instance, at two different qualities, and listen to the difference.

Although the quality of lower samples and resolution suffers, sometimes it's all you need, such as if you're recording phone conversations or AM radio. On the other hand, with enough samples and sufficient resolution, digital becomes the equal of analog.

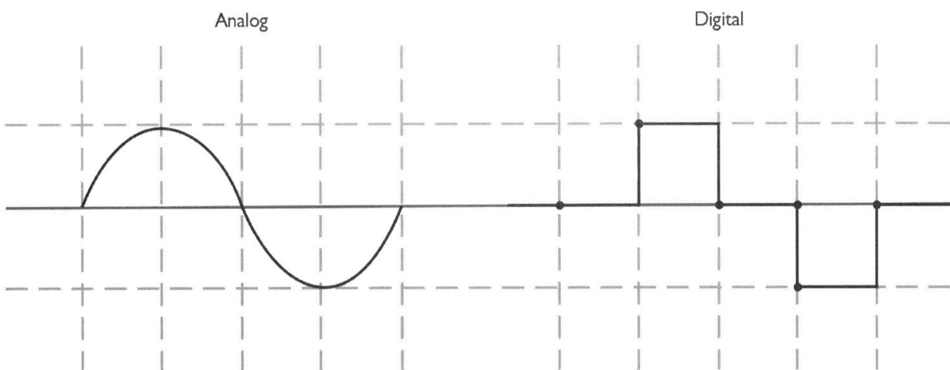

FIGURE 10-1 Garbage in, garbage out: digital audio is only as good as the number and quality of the data samples.

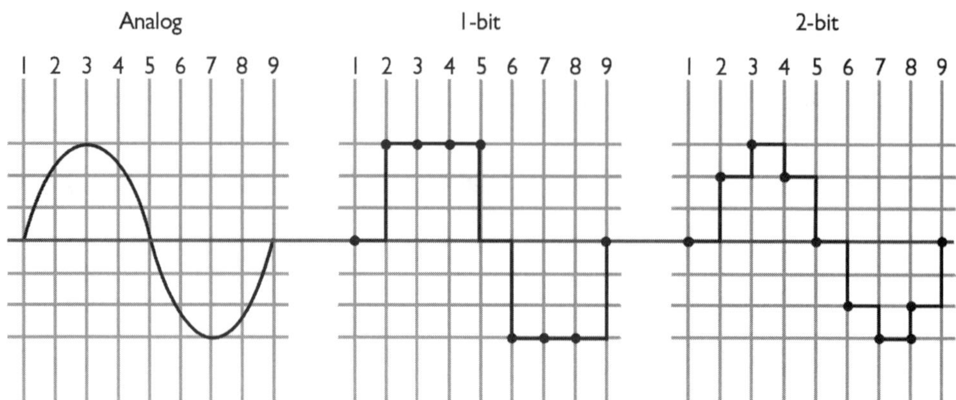

FIGURE 10-2 2-bit audio has four levels of resolution and is more accurate than 1-bit audio.

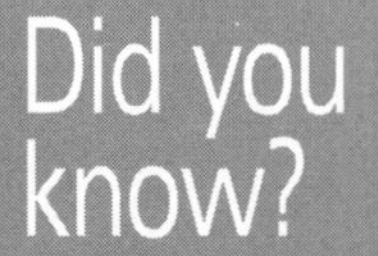

What They Really Mean

What do analog and digital really mean, anyway? As you've already seen, a digital recording isn't, by definition, more accurate or somehow better than its analog equivalent. Here are the dictionary-safe definitions of these two vexing terms:

- **Analog** Data that is represented by continuously variable, measurable, and physical quantities, like voltage or pressure
- **Digital** Data that is represented by discrete integer values

An infinite number of samples and an infinite number of resolution values will generate a perfect reproduction of the original analog source material, but we needn't go that far. Once the sound file's resolution passes a certain threshold, humans can't

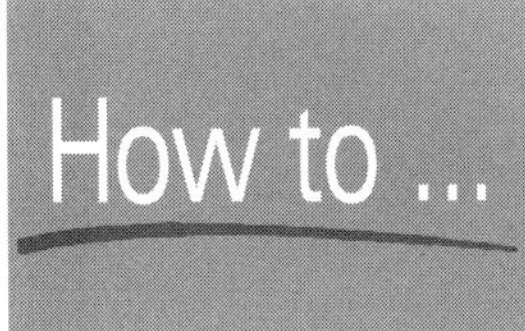

Change Sound Quality

1. Choose File | Properties to open the Properties For Sound dialog box.
2. Click the Convert Now button. You should then see the Sound Selection dialog box.
3. Click the Attributes list box and choose a sampling rate and resolution.

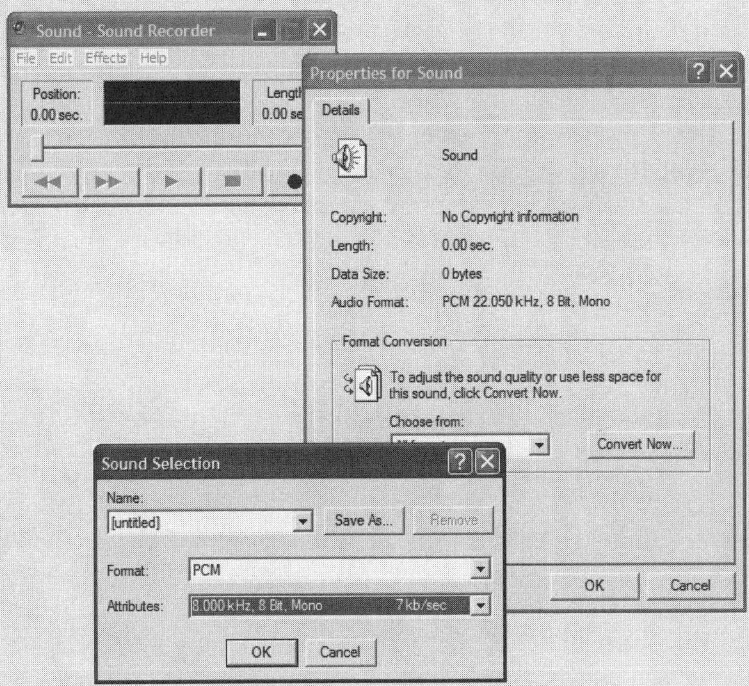

4. Click OK to close the box.

10

perceive any difference between analog and digital. Perhaps a species with better hearing—like the hunter creature in the movie *Predator*—could still tell the difference, but we're making music for us, not them. (*Them,* of course, was a movie about giant ants, and insects don't appear to listen to music at all.) So all you need is some knowledge of human anatomy to determine which resolution will pass muster. Record at that level, and everyone is happy: that's what the recording industry tried to do in the 1970s with CDs.

Many audiophiles think digital audio sounds cold and lacks the "warmth" of analog recordings like LPs. They have a point. It turns out that the audio CD's 16-bit, 44.1 KHz specification was a compromise when it was established in the late 1970s, and if it were redesigned today, it would probably have more resolution and a higher sampling rate. That would almost certainly quell any potential arguments, but for 99 percent of the population, CD audio and the related digital music technologies like MP3 remain more than sufficient for most human ears.

That said, the somewhat fuzzy concept of "warmth" is the only real complaint audiophiles can muster against digital, while digital has some very important advantages over analog. Here are the best aspects of digital:

- **Archive quality** Unlike every form of analog music storage, digital music can last essentially forever. The problem is that LPs and cassettes are *destructive playback media:* every time you listen to one, the act of playing it damages the source material. Played enough times, it'll wear out and not be fun to listen to anymore. Case in point: *Dark Side of the Moon*, by Pink Floyd. That album holds the record for spending the most time on the

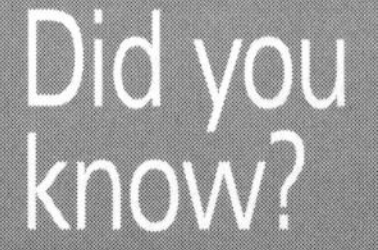

Better than CDs?

Some music companies are actually trying to reinvent the wheel (or, in this case, the CD). Both DVD-Audio (DVD-A) and Super Audio CD (SACD) are emerging technologies that deliver music with more clarity, warmth, and dynamic range, thanks to better resolution and sampling rate. Specifically, these new formats feature 24-bit sampling (instead of 16-bit) and 96 KHz (instead of 44.1 KHz). We doubt many ordinary folks will buy into these new music discs—CDs are just way too popular and do a pretty good job on their own—but it'll be popular with super-fanatical audiophiles who like LPs better than CDs.

Billboard Top 100—about fifteen years, in fact. Its position began to slip only after the rise of CDs. Some industry experts suggest that it sold so well for so long because audiophiles would routinely replace the vinyl regularly when repeated playings made it degrade. When those music lovers switched to CD, further replacements became unnecessary.

NOTE *The actual media, like audio CDs and CD-Rs, have a definite life span. Audio CDs should last for at least 100 years, but some CD-Rs may deteriorate long before that. Inexpensive discs may fail after a decade, whereas most should last for about 50 years or perhaps longer. If you back up or duplicate these discs occasionally, though, the content should be essentially immortal.*

- **Dynamic range** *Dynamic range* is the total range of frequencies that can be stored and reproduced in a given piece of music. Older analog recordings had a fairly limited dynamic range—LPs could reproduce perhaps 80dB and cassettes could muster perhaps 75dB at best. CDs, on the other hand, are engineered with a dynamic range of 96dB. A better dynamic range makes it easier to filter out noise as well, and background noise was always a problem with analog source material. In the world of digital, the signal-to-noise ratio is so high that few people worry about it anymore.
- **Perfect reproduction** Digital sources allow people to make flawless, bit-for-bit perfect copies of music recordings. Of course, this is what worries the music companies and some artists. But the fact remains that this is a big advantage for people who like to make copies of music they actually own.

Digital File Formats

With all that said, there's still another factor to consider: digital music is a generic term that includes a lot of different kinds of file formats. Just like the term *digital picture* could mean TIFF, JPG, BMP, GIF, or any of another dozen computer file formats, digital music could be WAV, WMA, MP3, Liquid Audio, and more. Which do you choose? Well, for a primer on file formats, check back to Chapter 4. What we're going to focus on here is the difference between two important files: WAV and MP3.

Musical Awakenings

Today's question: Which band, album, or event really turned you on to music?

Dave: I'll try to keep this brief, but there's a bit of a story here. I didn't care much about music until I was in my sophomore year of high school. Previous to that, I really didn't listen to any music at all. Not too surprising—all I ever heard was the easy listening instrumentals that came out of Dad's kitchen radio. But in sophomore year, one of my all-time heroes, a teacher by the name of Ray Page, taught a course on music and fine art. No other instructor had such a profound impact on my life: his class introduced me to the likes of Rothko and Pollock and Kandinsky and Mondrian.

As for music, he opened up a world of John Cage and Phillip Glass and Steve Reich. Those styles hit me like the light of a new dawn illuminating a long night. But then he covered the history of rock and played The Beatles' *Abbey Road.* To my growing collection of contemporary classical works like *Einstein on the Beach* and *Music for 18 Musicians,* I added *The Blue Album,* a brilliant compilation of Beatles songs. And that, my friend, was the album that changed everything. The Beatles, it turns out, were a doorway through which I passed into a new plane of musical experience. Oh, but, um, your *Frankie Goes to Hollywood* collection is good, too.

Rick: Wow, man, that is, like, such a totally far-out story. When I hear people talk about music taking them to "a new plane," I just want to lean over and, well, vomit. Music is neither my drug nor my soulmate—it's just a very, very good friend. My tastes have changed and evolved over the years, to the point where I now relish just about every musical style. As much as it pains me to say so, the initial spark came from MTV, which I started watching in the early '80s (before it became the unwatchable garbage heap it is today). Until then, I really wasn't all that interested in music (except for classical, which came from playing classical pieces in the high school band). And as long as I'm confessing, it was Michael Jackson's "Thriller" that really set the ball rolling, musically speaking. [Sound of Dave screaming in agony.] Hey, back then, it was cool to watch his videos and make fun of his clothes—which is exactly what I did.

WAV vs. MP3

If you're a longtime PC user, you've probably already heard of WAV files. Microsoft has long defaulted to the use of WAV files in Windows, but in these MP3-enriched days, the company has established a preference for WMA files instead. Nonetheless, WAV files are still alive and well, and they are important because the format is *lossless.* A lossless file format does not sacrifice any information in the file to compress data or save space. That's not to say that lossless files can't be compressed; they can. But the amount of compression and disk space savings you can get with lossless files is quite small compared to lossy files.

On the other side of the proverbial coin, there's MP3 audio. MP3 is a *lossy* format that is designed to lose information "gracefully" as it is compressed. The compression algorithm strips away information humans can't hear—or can't hear well—to begin with. If you compress an MP3 file very aggressively, though, information important to the music can certainly be lost. The advantage of an MP3 file is that it takes a small fraction of the space required by a WAV file, and it's immediately usable in MP3 players. The downside is that the compression process removes information that is then lost forever.

How big is the file size difference between WAV and MP3 files? This chart can help illustrate:

File Format	File Size for Ten Minutes of Audio
WAV	100MB
128 Kbps MP3	10MB
64 Kbps MP3	5MB

When to Use WAV and MP3

That leads to the question, "When should you choose one format over the other?" This decision is important because we're about to start capturing music from CD (and, in Chapter 11, from analog sources as well), and we need to know which format to select. You can approach the encoding process two ways, as you can see in Figure 10-3 (on page 15). You can convert music from the source to WAV, perform additional steps to the WAV files, and finally, reencode it as MP3. Or you can go directly from the source material to MP3 format. When should you choose the direct route, and when is the more convoluted path appropriate?

In a nutshell, here's all you need to know: in many audio editing programs, MP3 files are not editable, whereas WAV files typically are. Therefore, unless you have audio software that can edit MP3 files, you should capture music in WAV format if you intend to do editing, such as the following:

- Delete dead space at the beginning or end of a track.
- Attach two tracks together to make a single track.
- Clean up songs by adjusting levels or removing noise.
- Fade in and fade out individual songs.

Such edits require a huge amount of hard disk space because WAV files are so large. If you don't plan to make such edits, avoid the intermediate WAV step and encode your music directly to MP3.

Choosing a CD Ripper

You're finally at the point that you can rip music from CDs and store it on your PC in digital format. Which program you use is largely a matter of personal taste, because so many decent ripping programs abound. There are stand-alone rippers and programs that combine ripping, playback, and a variety of other features into a full-service music jukebox.

Here are some of the best stand-alone rippers you can choose from:

Windows	AudioCatalyst (www.xingtech.com)
	AudioGrabber (www.audiograbber.com-us.net)
	Easy CD-DA Extractor (www.poikosoft.com)
Macintosh	MPegger (www.proteron.com)
	SoundJam MP (www.soundjam.com)

Those are all compact, efficient programs that offer a wealth of options for extracting music from CDs and saving the result in either WAV or MP3 format. If you prefer an integrated, all-in-one program though, you probably want to check a jukebox program. That's what we tend to use most often. All the usual suspects—RealJukebox, Windows Media Player, and MusicMatch—are full-featured player/ripper/encoders. For the most part, you can probably be quite happy with any of those programs. If you have a CD-RW drive, it probably came

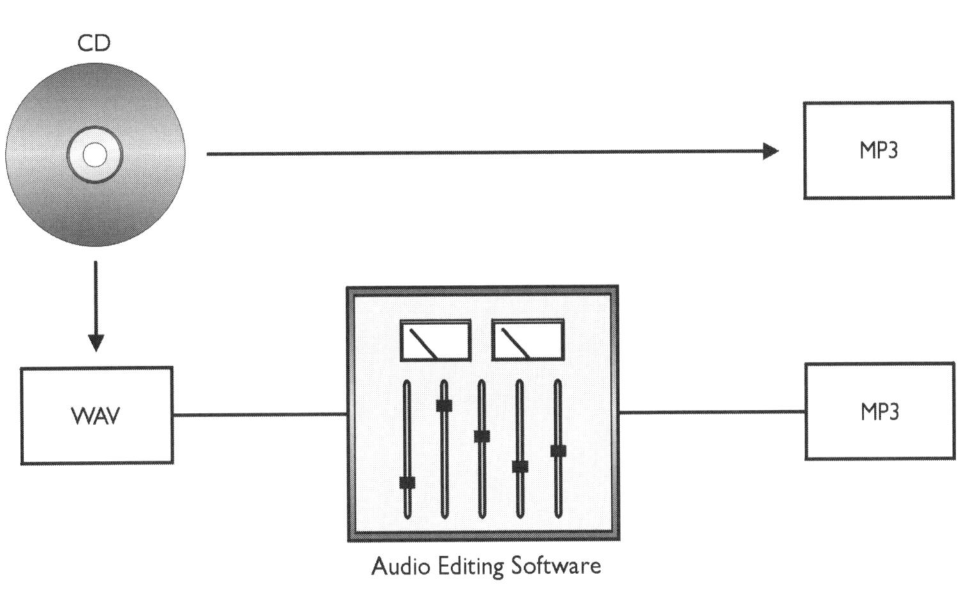

FIGURE 10-3 The two paths to digital audio

with a program like Easy CD Creator. Although it's designed primarily to copy data onto CDs for you, it can also rip music from audio CD. We'll talk about that program in Chapter 12.

TIP *There's an excellent reason to avoid Windows Media Player: it doesn't include MP3 encoding. You can rip music and store it in WMA format, but if you want MP3 capability, that'll cost you some money because it's an upgrade. Other jukebox programs come with MP3 encoding even in the free trial versions.*

Ripping Music

The process of ripping tracks from a CD is pretty straightforward. Here's the rundown.

TIP *See Chapter 13 to learn how to control the filenames and folder structure of ripped and encoded music.*

When you actually rip music from a CD, you might initially be surprised at the speed. Most rippers can read data up to ten times faster than the ordinary playback speed of the song, and some rippers can go much faster—as much as sixteen times, in fact.

The maximum ripping speed is a function of several components, including the maximum speed of the CD-ROM drive, the computer's speed, available memory and hard disk configuration, and the capabilities of the ripping software itself.

NOTE *Keep in mind that the maximum bit rate and even the speed at which you can rip music are limited in the free trial versions of most ripping software. If you download a program like MusicMatch and find that it can't capture the bit rate you need, you can pay the shareware fee and get all of the program's features, including a higher bit rate for the MP3 encoder.*

Using a Jukebox

Ripping music from one of the popular jukebox programs is fast and easy. Before you begin, though, make sure that the encoder is set up the way you like. Specifically, set the file format and sound quality as well as the destination folder for where the music will be stored. By default, any songs you rip will also be automatically added to your music library—that's a convenient feature.

Rip Tracks from a CD

1. Insert a CD in your PC's CD-ROM drive.
2. Start the ripper software.
3. If necessary, specify the file format and bit rate/capture quality that you want to record in.
4. Click the Record button and watch the magic as your computer reads the music from the CD and stores it on your PC in digital form.

Ripping with RealJukebox

In RealJukebox, choose Tools | Preferences to display the Preferences dialog box, and click the Audio Quality tab. You'll see a dialog box like the one in the following illustration, which you can use to specify exactly how the ripped songs will be saved. You need to set these preferences only once, and they will be used for all of your subsequent recordings.

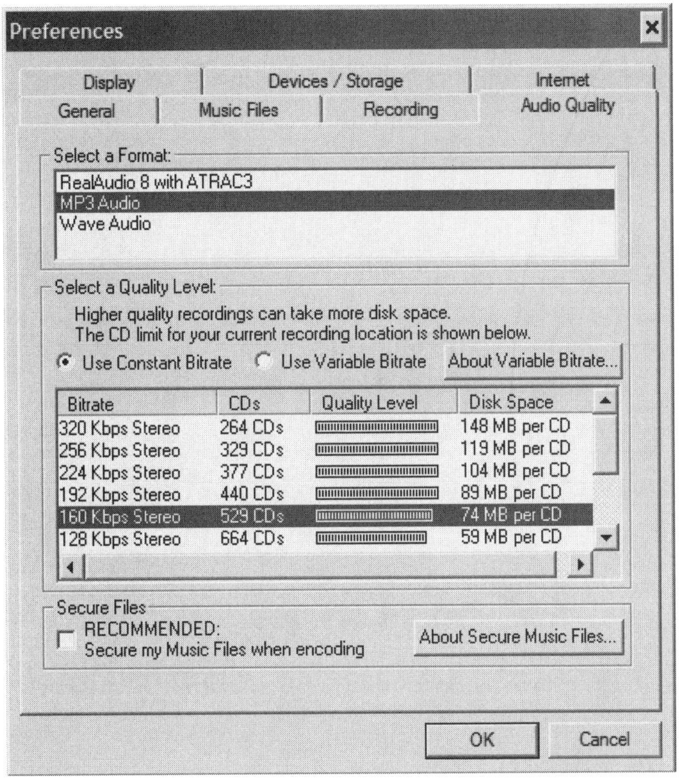

TIP *Some rippers can use variable bit rates. A* variable bit rate *can create smaller, more compact song files because the encoder can vary the bit rate based on the dynamic range of the song; however, some music players can't play tracks recorded with this new capability. As a result, you might want to stick with constant bit rates until you know that all of your hardware and software supports variable bit rates.*

When your preferences are saved, insert an audio CD into your PC and click the red Record button. RealJukebox will automatically rip the songs and store them on your hard disk.

If you don't want to rip all of the songs from a disc, first click the CD button on the toolbar. You should see a list of tracks. Clear any songs you don't want to rip, and then click the red Record button.

Ripping with MusicMatch

If you're using MusicMatch, the procedure is quite similar. To configure your file format and bit rate, choose Options | Settings to display the Settings dialog box, and click the Recorder tab.

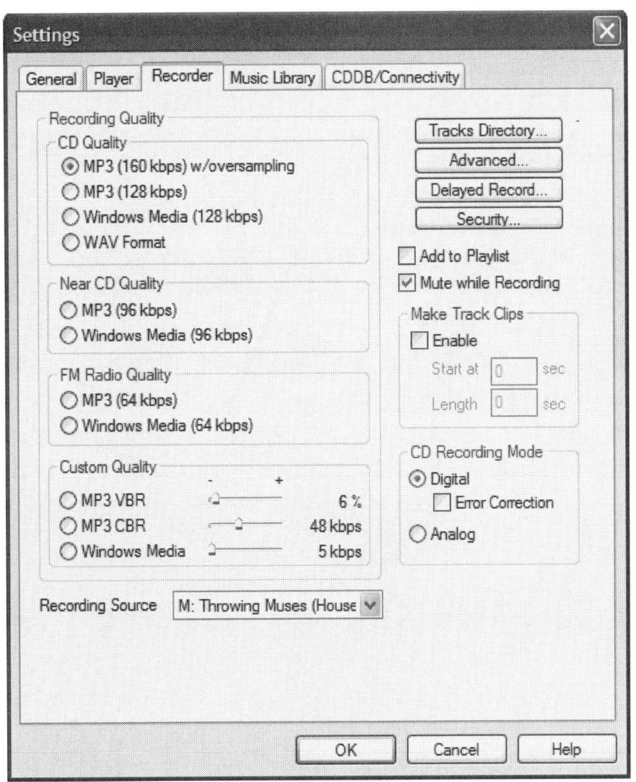

MusicMatch divides the recording quality into a number of areas; CD quality is the top section and includes 160 Kbps, 128 Kbps, and WAV files. If you don't see a bit rate you like, look at the bottom of the dialog box. There's a slider for MP3 VBR (variable bit rate) and MP3 CBR (constant bit rate). Select whichever you prefer and drag the slider to the bit rate you want to use.

Finally, insert the CD and click the central recording button. MusicMatch should open the small Recorder window. Clear any songs you don't want to capture, and click the Record button.

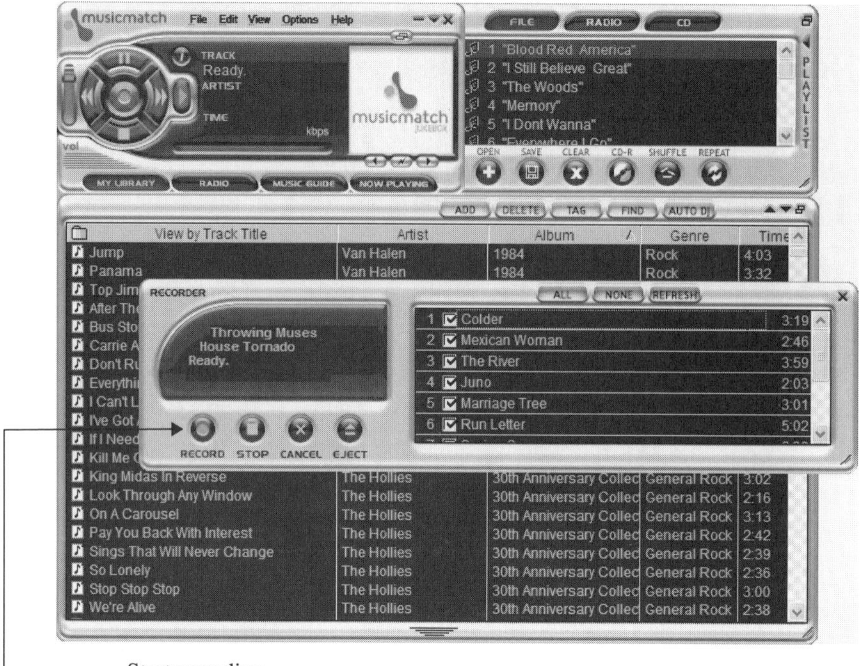

Ripping with Windows Media Player

Unlike the other Jukeboxes, Windows Media Player 8 doesn't support MP3 recording right out of the box. Instead, encoders are treated like little plug-in components in Windows Media Player, and only the WMA file format comes with the basic player. If you want MP3 encoding in this program, you need to upgrade. (For information on how to do that, choose Tools | Options and click the Copy Music tab. Then click the MP3 Information button.) Windows Media Player 7 doesn't have an MP3 encoding option at all.

That said, if you want to create WMA versions of songs, Windows Media Player can do that for you. WMA file compression is similar to MP3, so you don't have to learn anything radically new to do it. To configure the bit rate, choose Tools | Options, and click the Copy Music tab. At the bottom of the dialog box, adjust the slider to reflect the bit rate you want.

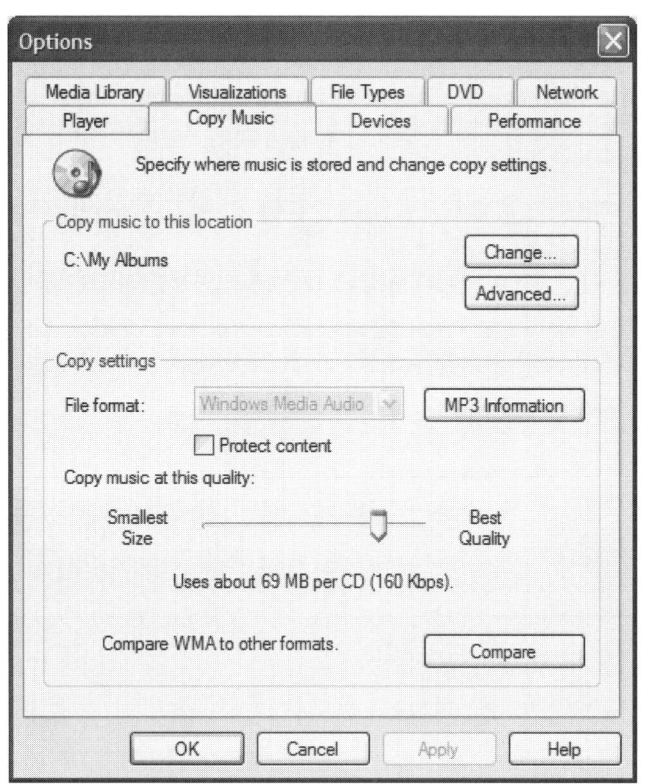

TIP *The WMA file format is a good digital music file system (in fact, the audio quality is sometimes somewhat better than MP3 at the same bit rate), but it's only sporadically supported. Not all software or hardware music players can understand WMA files, so MP3 is a "safer" format to use, at least for now.*

Once your WMA file settings are saved for posterity, you need to record your songs from a CD. Click the Copy From CD button on the toolbar on the left side and clear any songs you don't want to rip. Then click the Copy Music button on the toolbar at the top.

Dealing with Glitches

Of course, ripping audio from CDs is not always a smooth and effortless process. Especially when you first start recording music from CDs, you might run into a few problems. If you have an older CD-ROM drive, it may not be able to keep up with the arduous task of copying data from CDs to your hard disk. Your MP3s might turn out with obvious audio artifacts that clearly don't belong—at any bit rate— or the ripper program might give up in the process of trying to copy songs.

Reinforce Your PC

Especially if your PC is a bit, er, mature, you might have a hard time ripping because of a slow processor, minimal memory, or outdated equipment. Here are some things to check to make the process run more smoothly:

- We recommend having no less than 128MB of RAM in your PC before you start ripping.
- If your hard disk is getting full or is badly fragmented, the computer can have a hard time writing data to the drive while simultaneously trying to read data from the CD-ROM. Run the defrag program on your hard disk at least once a month. To find it, double-click My Computer, then right-click the hard disk and choose Properties. Click the Tools tab of the hard disk's Properties dialog box.

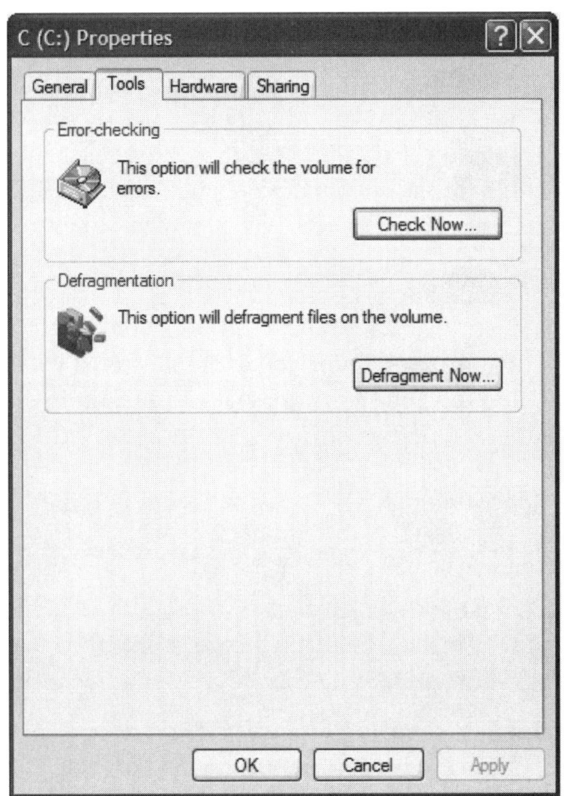

- Your CD-ROM may not be engineered to let rippers read data accurately enough to copy music digitally. But if the CD-ROM drive appears to be at fault, don't give up hope. First, make sure you are running the best and newest drivers for the CD-ROM drive and sound card. Check the manufacturer Web site for updated drivers. If you're up to speed on drivers, you might want to buy a CD-ROM drive or simply upgrade to a new PC.

- Doing too much with your PC can make ripping sessions go awry. Newer gigahertz-speed PCs don't suffer this problem, but older, slower PCs need to do one thing at a time, especially when that one thing is ripping and encoding songs from a CD. Shut down all applications while your ripper is doing its business.

Making Analog Copies

Sometimes, your PC is simply too slow to properly make a good digital copy of a CD. Or, more likely, the source CD is scratched, dirty, or damaged in some way that makes it impossible for the computer to read the data properly for a digital extraction. If you have a CD that you can't copy any way, any how, you need to do an *analog extraction,* also known as an analog rip or an analog copy.

A lot of programs automatically detect when a digital extraction won't work and try to do an analog rip instead. If that's the case, you don't have to do anything —the software will do it for you. But if you aren't having any luck with a regular copy, you might want to force the software to do an analog rip instead. Typically, you can find the analog and digital rip settings in the program's Preferences or Settings dialog box.

You want to avoid making analog copies in favor of digital copies whenever possible, though. Here's why:

- Analog copies take longer. An analog rip takes the complete run time of the song or CD to make the copy, whereas a digital copy can run ten times faster than real time or even better.
- Analog copies aren't true digital copies. They're very high quality, to be sure, but they're not a duplicate of the digital data. It's a slightly higher-tech version of stringing cables around, since the data is converted to an analog signal and then back to digital again. In the process, some background and line noise can be introduced. But on the whole, it's better than not getting the copy at all.

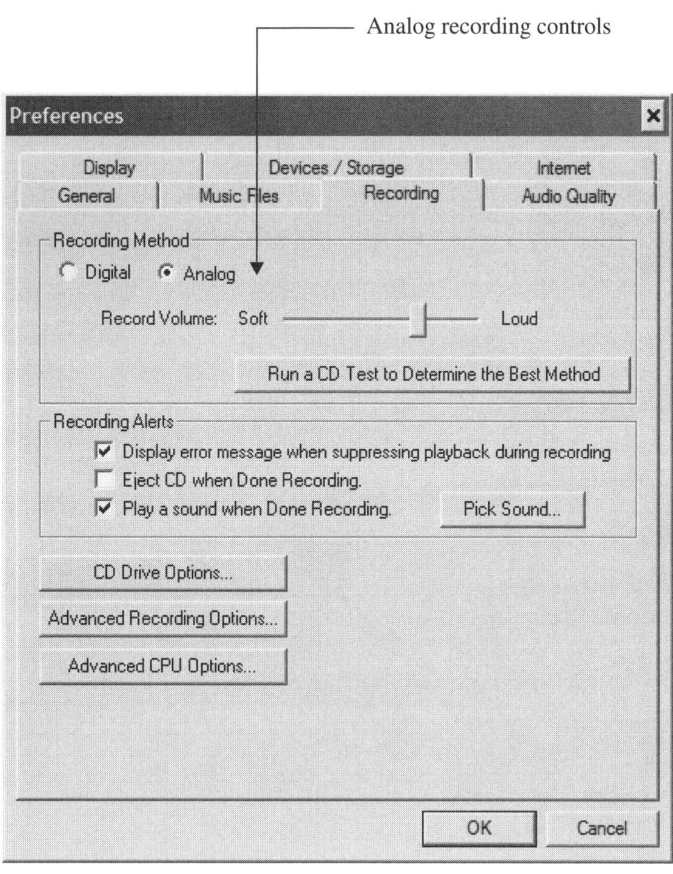
Analog recording controls
Preferences
Display
Devices / Storage
Internet
General
Music Files
Recording
Audio Quality
Recording Method
Digital
Analog
Record Volume:
Soft
Loud
Run a CD Test to Determine the Best Method
Recording Alerts
Display error message when suppressing playback during recording
Eject CD when Done Recording.
Play a sound when Done Recording.
Pick Sound...
CD Drive Options...
Advanced Recording Options...
Advanced CPU Options...
OK
Cancel

Transferring Analog Sources to MP3

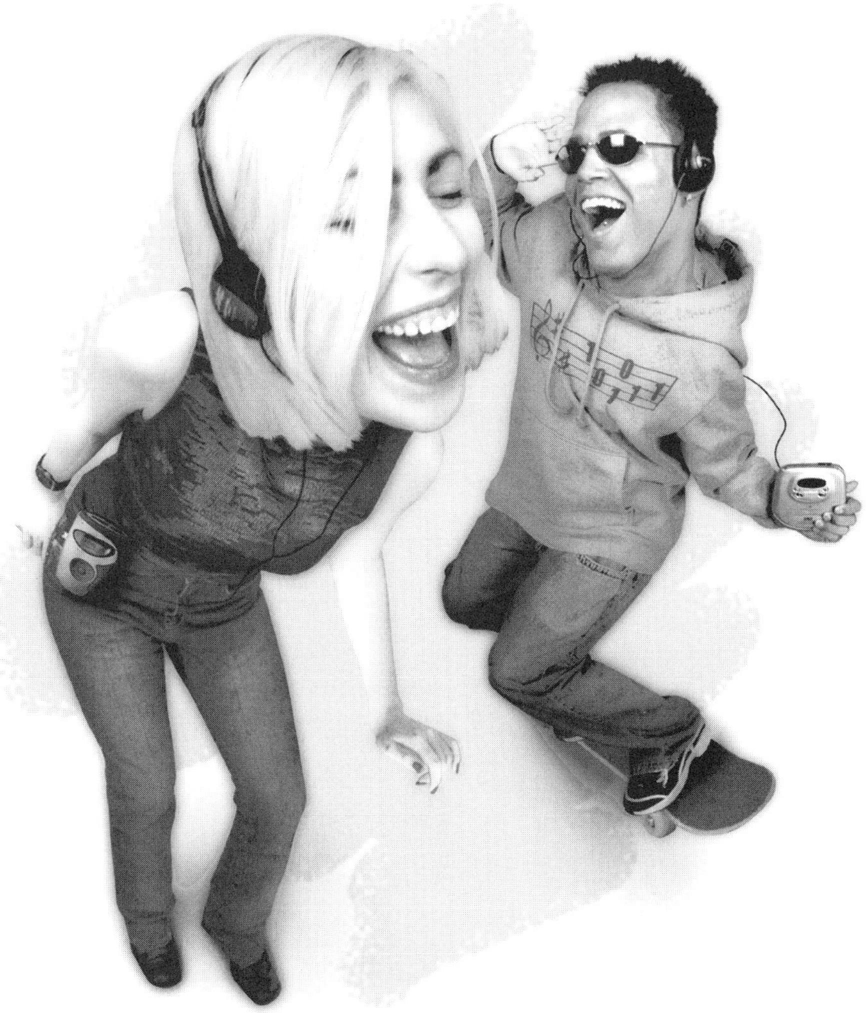

How to...

- Identify audio connections on the PC
- Properly amplify analog source material
- Connect a PC to analog audio gear
- Ensure high-quality signals
- Choose an audio capture program
- Configure Windows to detect your analog audio signal
- Optimally set the audio levels
- Copy analog sound as a WAV or MP3 file
- Batch-convert an LP or cassette's worth of songs
- Capture audio when the source is too far from your PC

As you saw in Chapter 10, making absolutely perfect copies of CDs isn't that hard. Ripping a CD is like making a copy of a computer file; as long as the media on which the file is stored isn't fatally damaged, you can't help but get identical copies every time. Even cloning animals isn't quite that repeatable, regardless of what Darth Vader may have told you when you got that VIP tour of the Imperial cloning vats.

Copying analog sources is something else altogether. The process of making a copy from an analog source, such as LPs and cassettes, is by definition imperfect. You'll get noise, imperfections in the analog media, and the inevitable degradation that occurs just by making a copy. Of course, analog is all we had in the "old days" before digital, and we all seemed to get along just fine. So in this chapter, we'll look at what you need to know to make good-quality recordings of analog material —including live and almost-live audio. You'll also want to read Chapter 12, because that's where you learn how to edit and clean up messy recordings like the ones you'll make here in this chapter.

Making the Connection

While we can talk about the science of analog recording all day long, from a practical standpoint, the real difference between analog and digital recording is the way you hook everything together. But because we're dealing with analog source material, we have lots more options for what to record than just the plain old audio CD. Here are some of the most common kinds of source material you can make recordings from:

- LP (or any kind of vinyl record, for that matter)
- Reel-to-reel
- Cassette tape
- Radio
- Television
- Laser disk
- Minidisk
- PC
- Microphone
- Live events

The list goes on. Heck, you could presumably make digital recordings of 8-track if you were so inclined. But we're pretty sure you won't, for the following excellent reasons:

- The 8-track format is a fairly low-fidelity format. You're better off just buying a CD of that old Sly and the Family Stone tape of yours.
- Those pops when the tape changes tracks are unforgivably loud.
- We're not sure that stereo equipment old enough to support 8-track would have the necessary output jacks.
- When last surveyed, it was found that almost all of the surviving 8-track equipment and tapes were in Rick's basement.

Despite the veritable cornucopia of potential analog sources out there, the way you connect them all to your computer for digital recording is reasonably simple, standardized, and straightforward. Typically, you'll simply connect the audio source, such as a stereo receiver, to your PC's sound card input via an audio output jack.

The process can get somewhat squirrelly if your hardware is a bit nonstandard, but in general, that's pretty much it.

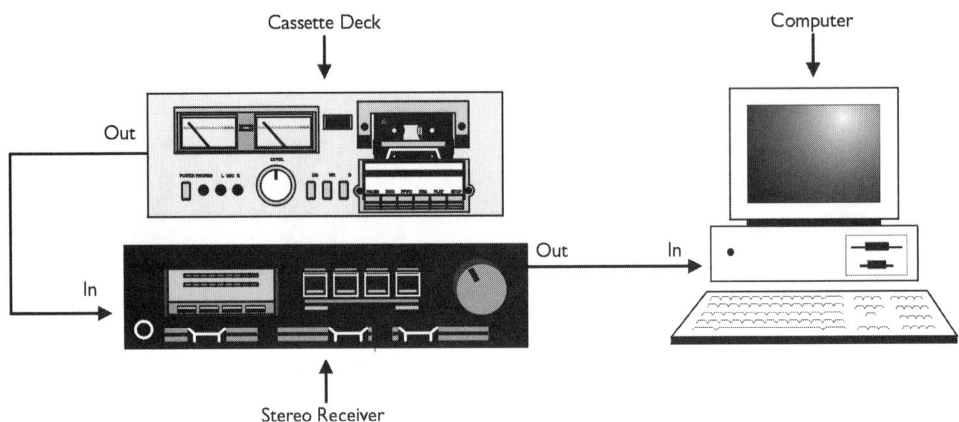

Sound Card Inputs

For us, one of the most frustrating aspects of connecting a PC to an analog sound system is decrypting the sound card. While sound cards vary from manufacturer to manufacturer and even from model to model, one fact is true about all of them: figuring out what each connector does is like making sense of the alien mothership's flight controls before the giant bug monsters discover you've broken out of your cocoon and come to send you back, first to work in the uranium mines, and later, to mate with the Bug Queen.

It helps to use a small flashlight to identify the ports because you'll probably be working in the dark, behind the PC. You might also want to use a small portable vacuum to clean all the dust and cobwebs from the PC's connectors.

The sound card's ports all look alike, and they all have miniscule symbols etched into the backplate in such a way that you can't tell them apart or even figure out which symbol lincs up with which connector. And the whole thing is all the way in back of the PC, in the dark, requiring you to crank your head behind the desk and try to connect stuff with a flashlight in one hand and the cable in your teeth. And the bugs—they're coming... Let's try to make sense of it all.

For starters, depending on which kind of PC you have, your sound system may be on a separate sound card or integrated into the motherboard. An integrated sound system relies on an inexpensive sound chip to provide all the sound management features in your computer, and the inputs are typically located on the back of the case near all of the other connections, like the parallel, serial, USB, and PS/2 ports.

Most computers use a separate sound card, which lies in one of the PC's expansion slots (usually called PCI slots). A separate sound card costs the manufacturer a bit more than integrated sound and takes up an expansion slot that can't be used by something else, but it has the potential to generate much higher-quality audio.

Your sound inputs probably look something like the ones in Figure 11-1, which shows the back of a PC that actually has two sound cards installed. You can see how differently various sound cards are marked. If you're not used to messing around behind the PC, you can find the audio inputs by looking for the 15-pin

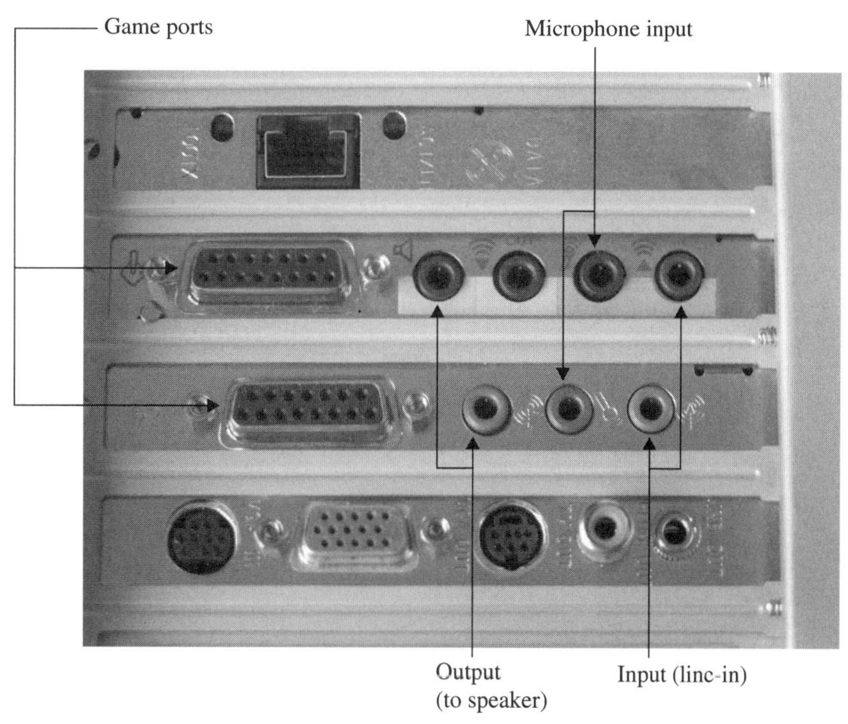

FIGURE 11-1 Typical PC sound card connections

game controller port (which is where you can connect a joystick); if you have a separate sound card, the game controller is almost always on the card, at the end of a row of audio inputs. If you have an integrated sound system, though, the game port may not always be right next to the sound inputs.

Sometimes, you'll run into PCs that have both integrated, on-board audio and an add-in sound card as well. In those cases, the integrated sound is disabled and only the inputs on the sound card are active.

Your PC's sound system should have three important jacks. Some have more. The key connectors are the following:

- **Microphone** This is where you'd plug in a standard, unpowered PC microphone, like the boom mikes that typically come with new PCs.
- **Line-in** This is where you connect line-level components, such as stereo equipment.
- **Output** This is a line-level output most commonly used to send the audio signal to PC speakers. You can also use this connector to send audio to your home stereo or other analog gear, though. Some sound cards have two or more output connectors so you can attach speakers and still have an output available for other purposes.

Analog Source Outputs

At the other end of the equation is your analog source equipment. Typically, this will be some sort of stereo system. To successfully connect the stereo to your PC, you'll need to properly select the right kinds of jacks. Here are the key considerations:

- Preamplify the source material. You can't directly connect a component-level device like a turntable, cassette player, or microphone directly to the PC's sound card. The signal coming from those devices is too low to be properly used by the PC. Instead, connect the component to a stereo receiver or amplifier, and use the output connectors from that device to drive the sound card.
- Use the output connector, not the input connector. Most stereo components have a pair of stereo connectors: one pair for input and another pair for output. Only components capable of both playing and recording have both, though. That means CD players have only output (no input) connectors, but

cassette players have both input and output. You need to be sure you choose the right connectors when you make your connection. A typical amplifier has a matrix of connectors that looks like this:

TIP

Your final recording will be only as good as the source material, but you can cheat a little. If you have access to a graphic equalizer, use it to expand the areas of the audio spectrum that are lacking or deemphasize those that are offensive.

Remember, if you're trying to record audio from an integrated system, the material is already preamplified, and you can go directly from the device to the computer. Here are some examples:

- Recording the audio from a VHS tape when the VCR is built into the television
- Recording a cassette tape that's built into a portable stereo
- Recording an FM broadcast from an AM/FM stereo receiver

But if you're trying to record from a cassette deck that typically attaches to a home stereo, you'll need to put an amp or stereo receiver between the deck and the PC.

If you've dug an old turntable out of the garage to transfer LPs and 45s to MP3 format but have no receiver to make it go, stop by the local Radio Shack. You can get an inexpensive amplifier there that'll do the job.

Cabling It All Together

Great! You've got your analog source and your PC all ready to go. All you need now is a cable to connect them together. Here's the tricky part—your PC's sound inputs are one size and the analog gear is another.

Your PC requires a 1/8-inch stereo miniphone jack. It's a single plug that sends both channels of audio information through the same wire. These jacks are fairly common because they're used not just for computer sound cards, but also to connect headphones to portable music players. Beware, though. Miniphone jacks come in two formats: stereo and mono. You always want to use stereo jacks. Mono jacks are visually different; they have only one insulating band around the metal plug instead of two. You can see them both in the following illustration.

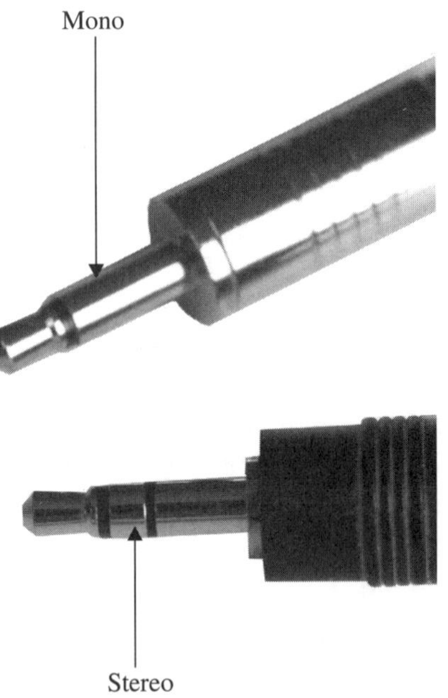

The analog gear uses RCA jacks, which are larger than miniphone jacks and always come in pairs—one each for the left and right channels. They're very standard. All home stereo and home theater systems use RCA jacks to connect various components together. Here's what they look like:

Because the two ends of your setup require different plugs, the standard Y-cable is your best friend. Any electronics, computer, or stereo store can hook you up with a cable like the one in Figure 11-2. It's a Y-cable that features a 1/8-inch stereo miniphone jack at one end and a pair of RCA plugs at the other end.

FIGURE 11-2 The standard RCA-to-miniphone-jack Y-cable allows you to connect your PC to most analog gear.

Cabling Accessories

A few other cable accessories can help you get your gear hooked up as well. Your PC may be quite some distance from your stereo equipment, for instance. If you don't have a single cable that's long enough to reach, you can use several shorter cables, connected by a coupler that's female at both ends. This little gadget, shown in the next illustration, is a real life saver, and it's available from electronics stores like Radio Shack.

Here's another common situation: you may not have enough outputs such that you can dedicate one to your PC for recording. If that's the case, you can "split" a single output so part of the signal goes to your PC and the other part of the signal goes to another component. There are a lot of Y-plugs around in electronics stores. You'll need a pair of them, of course, to reroute both stereo channels. In fact, cables, connectors, and adapters are available at electronics stores like Radio Shack for almost every conceivable wiring quandary. You can convert an RCA jack into a mono or stereo miniphone jack, for instance, or wire a device with a miniphone jack output (like a headphone jack) directly to your PC's sound card with some of these gadgets:

Ensuring a High-Quality Signal

You can use accessories like the coupler we mentioned earlier, but we actually don't recommend it for music. It's fine for spoken word recording, though.

If you plan to make a high-quality recording, you need to keep the analog source material as high quality as possible right up until the moment it gets sucked into the PC. Extremely long wires and gadgets like extenders and Y-plugs degrade the sound slightly, and if you degrade it enough, it'll noticeably affect the final sound.

Indeed, the cabling is an important element in your overall sound. We recommend using quality shielded cables instead of the standard rubber-sheathed stuff you get with most stereo gear. Some audiophiles buy gold-plated plugs. Even though Dave is fanatical about the sound of his audio, he's never really noticed an audible difference with gold plating, however.

If you visit your local stereo equipment store, you'll find shielded cabling from companies like Monster Cable. Figure 11-3 shows the difference between quality audiophile cabling and run-of-the-mill cables.

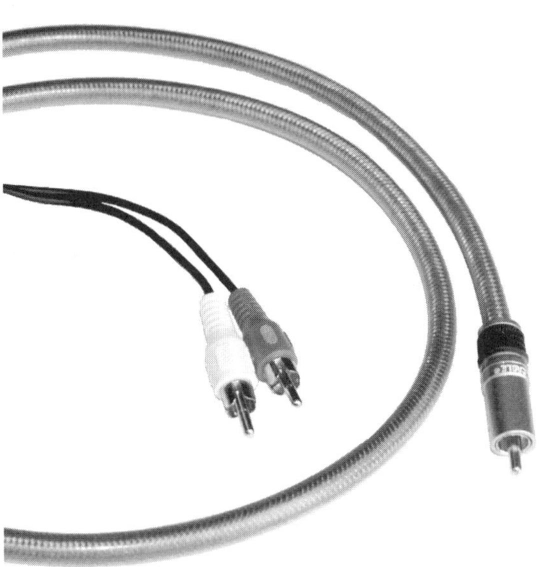

FIGURE 11-3 Dave tends to use Monster Cable for most of his audio projects.

In general, the thicker the cable is, the better it will sound. Thick cable is better able to transfer high-frequency sounds over long distance than thin cable; this is referred to as the cable's *capacitance.* The lower the capacitance (and the thicker the cable), the more full-bodied your sound will be. Thin cables tend to lose the high end of your music. Not surprisingly, quality audiophile cabling covers both bases—capacitance and shielding—for you. While we're making a wish list of cable characteristics, it's worth noting that gold-plated jacks transfer electricity, and hence, your audio, better than ordinary cables, at least in theory. That's another benefit you'll get in higher-quality cables.

For the absolute best sound quality, here are a few other tips you might want to try:

- Keep cables as short as possible. For instance, don't use a 20-foot length of cable if 6 feet will do.
- Keep cables away from each other. If you run cables in parallel, right next to each other, you can generate background noise. Audiophiles try to run cables away from each other at fairly sharp angles when they leave the components and not run them parallel to each other until they're a few feet away from each other. Just don't crimp the cables so much that you actually damage them.
- Don't lay the power cable and signal cables next to each other. This is the same basic premise as the previous tip, only this one is even more important because of how noisy power cords are.

Audio Recording Software

With your analog source securely connected to the PC, now we can take a look at the software you're going to use to make the recording. Unfortunately, all-in-one jukebox recorders like MusicMatch and RealJukebox are designed to capture audio only from digital sources like CD. For analog capture, you'll need one or two new tools.

What about the Windows Sound Recorder, you ask? After all, it's free with Windows. Unfortunately, it records a maximum of 60 seconds, which isn't enough time to capture a complete song.

The Best Music Films

Dave: I just purchased my own DVD of *Almost Famous* since I was getting so tired of renting it over and over. I've seen that movie now about, oh, eight times or so. Part of my infatuation with the movie is that I wish I was Cameron Crowe—but, then again, who doesn't? That notwithstanding, it's also one of the best "music" movies I've ever seen. In fact, I found myself at a party last week shouting, "I am a golden god!" at the top of my lungs after winning a volleyball game. What are your top five music movies? Here are mine:

1. *This Is Spinal Tap*
2. *Almost Famous*
3. *High Fidelity*
4. *The Wall*
5. *A Hard Day's Night*

Rick: Dave always wishes he was someone else: Cameron Crowe, Neo from *The Matrix,* Cap'n Crunch—why can't he just be happy with who he is? Anyway, this promises to be the one list in which we agree on more than one item:

1. *The Commitments*
2. *The Blues Brothers*
3. *Almost Famous*
4. *High Fidelity* (but the book was better)
5. *Singin' in the Rain*

Dave: Brian, our tech editor, points out that we haven't mentioned the granddaddy of all rock movies—*Woodstock*. I'll leave that movie in Brian's capable hands. The only film in all the world more boring than *Woodstock* is the insanely ponderous, 30 minute-long-slow-zoom sequence in Pink Floyd's *Live at Pompeii*. There, I've done it—I've criticized Pink Floyd. I feel so cheap. Excuse me, I need to go take a shower.

A lot of audio recording applications are available, and in general, any application that can save your music as either a WAV or MP3 file will get the job done. We recommend these programs:

- **Sound Forge** This excellent program from Sonic Foundry (www.sonicfoundry.com) has just about every editing and recording feature you could ask for. The downside? It costs about $400. Sound Forge XP is a consumer version of the program with a few less features and a much reduced price tag (about $60).

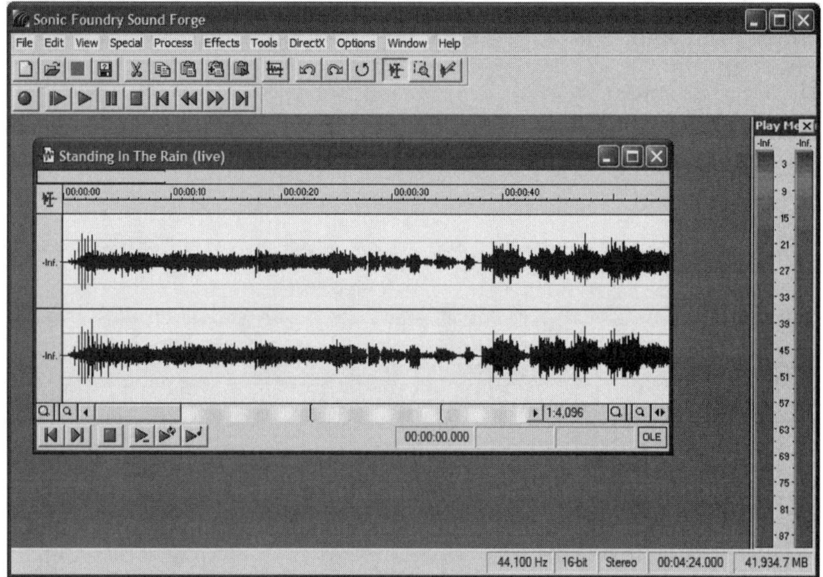

- **Cool Edit 2000** Almost as elaborate as Sound Forge, Dave uses this program regularly when he doesn't need all of the power in Sound Forge. While Sonic Foundry targets Sound Forge at pros, Cool Edit 2000 has all the goods for average consumers who want to tweak their song files as well as up-and-coming musicians who need more power. You can find the program at Syntrillium's Web site (www.syntrillium.com).

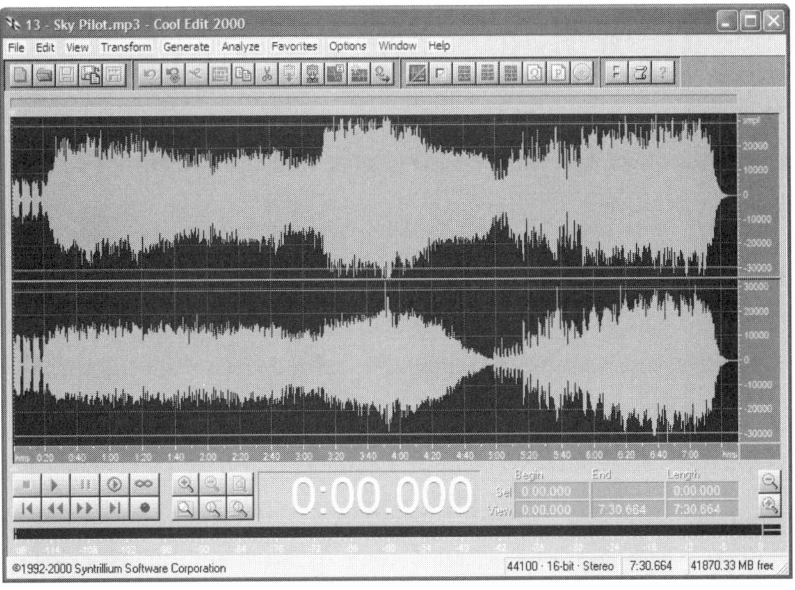

- **Audiotools** If all you're looking for is audio capture without all of the cumbersome editing features in other programs, look into Unrelated Inventions' Audiotools (www.unrelatedinventions.com). This excellent capture program is smart enough to automatically split songs into separate tracks based on sensing the silence between songs. We'll talk about that clever feature again later in "Recording Strategies."

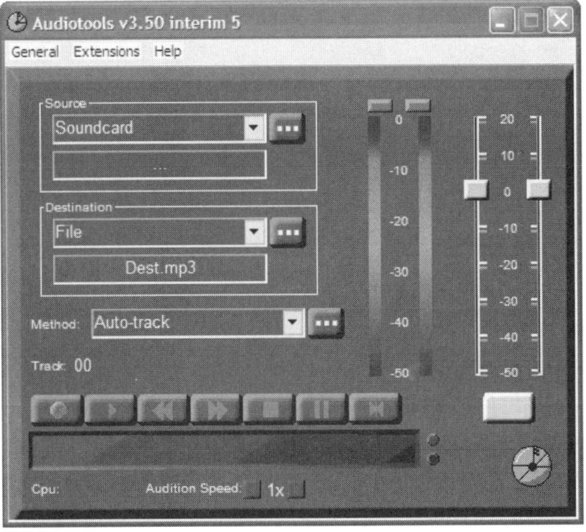

Making the Recording

Let's record some audio. Start the audio capture program that you plan to use and configure all of your cables. Start playing the analog source material. We're not going to record yet—first we need to make sure the PC's sometimes-confusing audio settings are configured properly.

Setting the Recording Device

Your PC might not be configured properly to listen for audio coming into the sound card, especially if it has more than one sound card, sound input device, or microphone attached. Here's a quick test you can do to see:

1. Start the Windows Sound Recorder by selecting Start | Accessories | Entertainment | Sound Recorder.
2. With your analog source playing, click the red Record button on the Sound Recorder. You should see a waveform appear as audio is copied to your hard disk.

If you saw some wave activity, you're fine. Skip to the next section, "Setting Sound Levels." If the recorder sat there mutely, though, with a flat line instead of a wave, you need to do a small bit of surgery. Figure 11-4 shows you what you should be looking for.

FIGURE 11-4 If your sound card is properly configured, you should see the window on the right when you record audio; the one on the left is receiving no signal.

Here's the fix: you need to tell Windows which of your various audio devices is the one it should listen to; it can pay attention to only one at a time. Do this:

1. Select Start | Settings | Control Panel, and then double-click Sounds And Audio Devices in the Control Panel window.
2. Click the Audio tab to display the configuration details for your PC's sound system.
3. Look for the Sound Recording section in the middle of the dialog box. You should see a list box that includes all of the devices currently configured on your PC. They may include sound cards, webcams, microphones, and other audio devices.

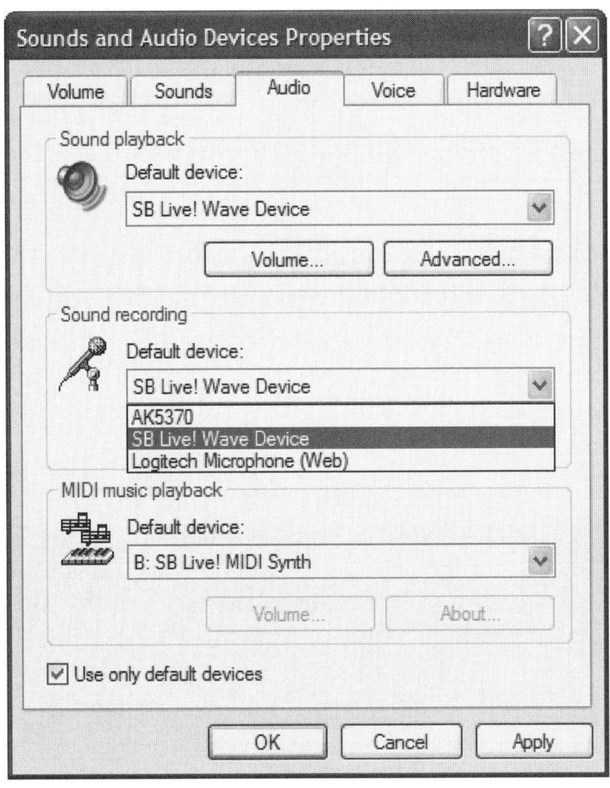

4. From the list, choose the sound card that has the line-in jack to which your analog source is currently attached. It's probably your main sound card, and odds are quite good that it's some variation on a SoundBlaster card.
5. Click OK to close the dialog box.

NOTE *If you have an older card, Windows may ask you to restart the PC.*

If you run the Windows Sound Recorder test again, you should see some waveform activity when you try recording audio. If you don't, it means that you still need to increase the sound level of the sound card's line-in jack. We'll do that next.

Setting Sound Levels

Next, let's optimize the recording level. In a nutshell, you need to set the level high enough so that the signal-to-noise ratio obliterates background noise, but not so high that the level causes clipping and distortion. It's part art, part science, but we'll show you how to do it. First of all, we'll make sure that the line-in jack isn't muted. Then we'll adjust the level to optimize the sound.

1. Select Start | Settings | Control Panel, and then double-click Sounds And Audio Devices in the Control Panel window.
2. Click the Audio tab and then click the Volume button in the Sound Recording section. Be sure to select the Volume button for recording, not playback—they'll give you two different dialog boxes. The Record Control dialog box should open.
3. The Record Control dialog box looks like a mixing board, with sliders for all of the sound card's various inputs. Look for the Line-In column. This controls the volume at which sound from the line-in jack is recorded. If it isn't already selected, click the Select check box at the bottom. Only the selected input will record.

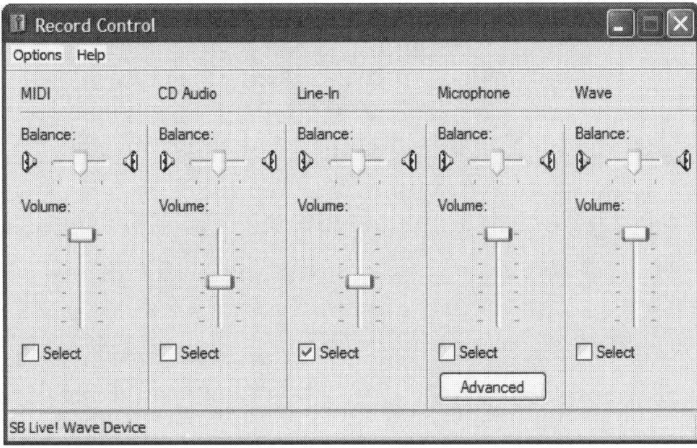

4. Start your audio capture program. The record controller will vary depending upon which program you're using, but it should look more or less like Windows' Record Control dialog box in the sense that it'll let you vary the level at which you're recording the sound.

5. Now it's time to optimize the sound. Arrange the Record Control dialog box on the screen so you can see both it and the record controller in your audio capture program.

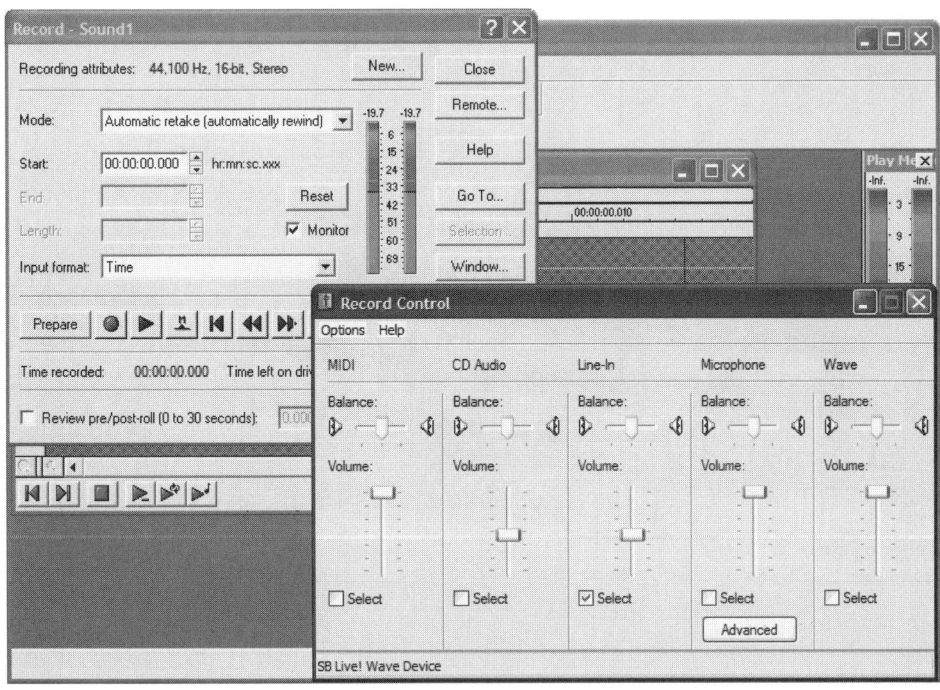

6. The audio level in the audio capture program should fluctuate in response to the sound that's playing on your analog device. Keeping an eye on it, drag the Line-In slider in the Record Control dialog box up or down so it stays consistently high but rarely hits the yellow and never goes into the red. Some audio capture programs will help you by displaying a clipping warning when the sound goes too high. Here's an example of a good audio level on the right and a clipped, distorted signal on the left.

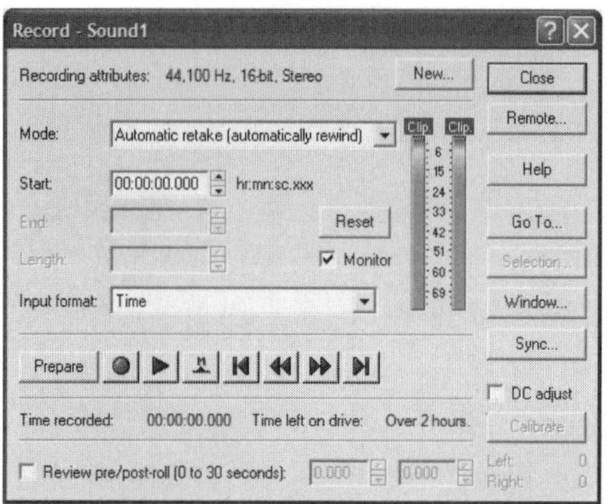

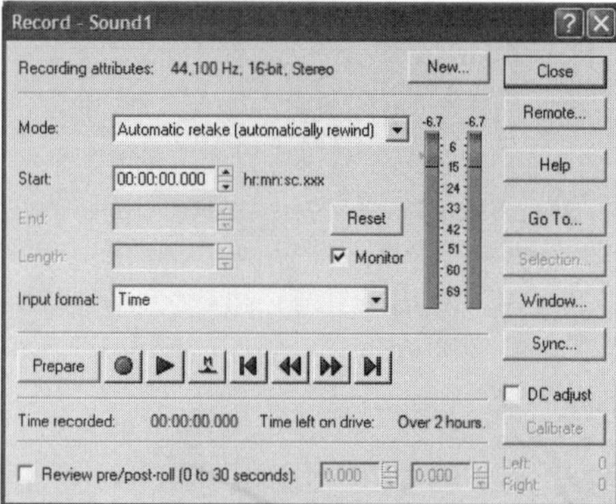

That's pretty much it. When you have optimized the sound, close the Record Control dialog box and you can start recording. There are a few points you might want to remember:

- Listen to an entire song, or sample the loudest, most dynamic parts of the audio you plan to record. That way, you know you've adjusted the level for the worst case, not just the quiet parts.
- Some audio capture programs have their own level controls. If yours does, set the Record Control dialog box for an average position while the level control in the program is also about halfway up. Then fine-tune the level with the programs, which is probably more sensitive.

Recording Audio

Finally! You were beginning to think we'd never get to the good part. This is easy, though. Here's a short checklist:

- Your hard disk should be recently defragmented.
- You should have plenty of hard disk space handy—gigabytes, in fact. While the program captures audio, it'll need enough space to hold uncompressed audio, which adds up to about 10MB per minute. You can do the math, but that means a typical LP will consume about 400–500MB of space.

TIP *You might want to invest in an external hard disk for making audio recordings. You can find some inexpensive yet large hard disks that connect to the PC via USB or FireWire.*

- Make sure that your capture software is ready to go. It should be running, and its record control should be open and ready to start with a single click.
- The analog source should be cued up and as clean as you can make it. If you're recording vinyl, for instance, use a record-cleaning brush to clean the record and make sure the needle doesn't have a collection of dust on it.

Start recording by clicking the appropriate record button on your PC. Then promptly move to the analog gear and start playback. When the recording is done, click the stop button to halt recording and save the audio as either a WAV file or an MP3. Which should you choose? You don't always have a choice. Many audio capture programs save only to formats like WAV, and you'll have to use an encoder to make the transition to MP3 later. But what if you do have a choice? We'll talk about that in the next section, "Recording Strategies."

In the end, you'll have a collection of songs in MP3 format or a collection of WAV tracks. If you have MP3 tracks, you can load them into an MP3 jukebox application and edit the ID3 track information based on the liner notes that accompanied the album.

NOTE *As you might remember from Chapter 6, ID3 tags are automatically part of every MP3 file you create. They store information about the song, like the title, artist, and album name. You can edit the ID3 information so it accurately reflects the music that's playing. ID3 information is visible in most music players on your computer, as well as on many portable music players.*

If, on the other hand, you have a collection of WAV files, you need to convert them to MP3s. After you are finished editing them, you need to use an encoder to convert them all to the more common MP3 format. Any number of programs can encode your WAV files for you. We recommend either AudioCatalyst or MP3 Wave Maker (shown in Figure 11-5, and which you can find at www.mightsoft.com).

Remember that you should configure your encoder to convert your WAV to MP3 at your desired bit rate. If you don't choose a bit rate in the program's preferences, you'll get MP3 songs at the program's default setting, which is probably 128 Kbps.

Recording Strategies

Making digital copies of analog recordings is quite a bit different than ripping CDs. It's more than just the difference between digital and analog technology;

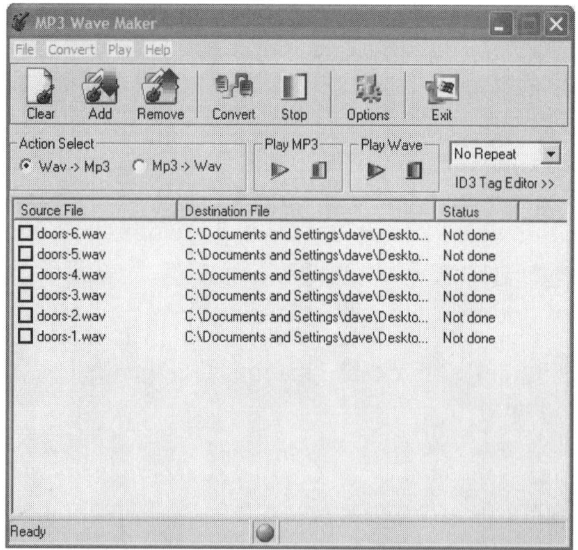

FIGURE 11-5 Good encoders, like MP3 Wave Maker, can batch-process a bunch of WAV files and turn them all into MP3s with a single click of the mouse.

it's also about the fact that there's no CDDB service identifying songs for you, nor is there even an automated process for dividing songs into individual tracks.

CDDB is an online CD database service that's used universally by all the major CD ripping programs. When you rip music from a CD, the program queries CDDB via the Internet and retrieves all sorts of information about the CD, including song titles, artist info, and more. That information is then embedded in the MP3 file in the form of ID3 tags, which then appear on-screen when you play the music. Of course, this whole system doesn't work when you rip music from analog sources, so you need to create the data for the ID3 tags by hand.

Consider this: you copy an LP to WAV format. The result might be that you have a huge 200MB file with five songs in it. What do you do with that? It's not nearly as neat and tidy as ripping songs from CD.

There are two ways to approach the process of copying analog material:

- Make one long recording of an LP side or cassette tape or similar program. The advantage is that it's a fire-and-forget solution. You start recording and have to come back only at the end to stop the recording process. If you choose this approach, you'll need to open the file in an audio editor and cut the file apart into separate songs afterwards.
- Monitor the recording process carefully, stopping recording after each track to save each song in a unique file. The upside here is that you've already created individual song files. But it's also more time-consuming up front, because you need to babysit the copying process.

Either way works, and it's largely a matter of taste. If you choose the first approach, though, you'll typically need to keep the file in WAV format so it can be modified in an audio editing program. Even if you choose the second approach, you may yet need to edit the file, so the WAV format isn't a bad idea all around.

TIP

Dave, who has done a fair bit of this, recommends making a single large file and cutting it up afterwards. He's found that it takes less time to get good-sounding results. You'll end up wanting to trim bits of silence off the ends of songs afterwards anyway, even if you used the second method.

It's worth mentioning that there's another high-tech solution to the babysitting dilemma. Certain programs can automatically sense blank space and save individual tracks as different files. As we mentioned earlier in "Audio Recording Software," we've tried Audiotools, from Unrelated Inventions, and found it works great for just this kind of task. Audiotools can automatically divide an album side or cassette tape into individual tracks for you without your direct input. In the end, all you need to do is rename the files.

Also, remember that there's no way for CDDB to automatically name your songs and add track information. That means you'll need to add those details yourself, manually.

TIP *If you want to record live audio, a number of programs (like Cool Edit and Sound Forge, for instance) let you record a microphone directly from the line-in jack. You can use it to record audio from a laptop in a conference, for example. We also recommend CD-Maker Professional (www.ntcicdmaker.com), because it lets you burn a CD in real time from live incoming audio.*

Do It All with Easy CD Creator

Equipped with Roxio's Easy CD Creator 5 (at www.roxio.com), you can streamline all of your analog recording, processing, and encoding tasks into a single program. The program is very simple to use, and it might be a good alternative to using several different applications to get the job done.

To copy an LP into MP3 format, for instance, follow these steps:

1. Start the SoundStream application and choose Properties from the menu. Click the MP3 tab and choose the MP3 bit rate you want to capture. Click OK to save your changes.

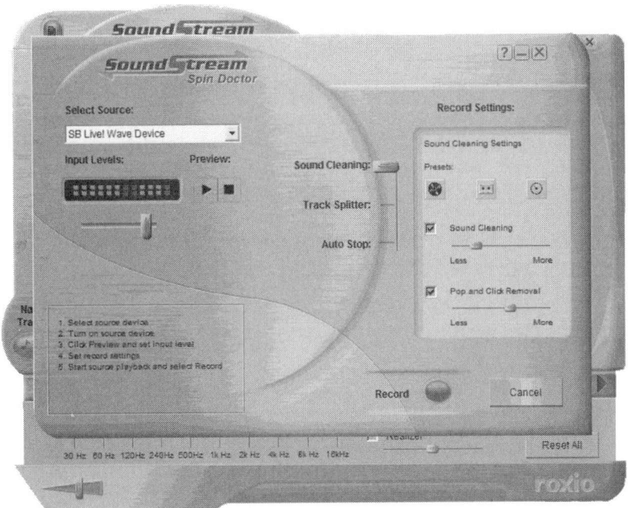

2. Open the options drawer at the bottom of the screen.

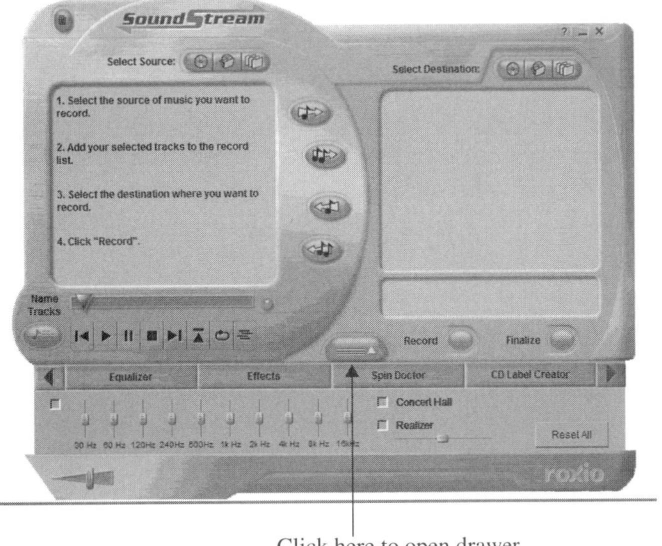

Click here to open drawer

3. Click the Spin Doctor button on the drawer's toolbar. The Spin Doctor screen should appear. Make sure that the correct sound source is selected

and play your analog source. Watching the input level, drag the slider to the left or right to optimize the sound.

4. Now configure the Sound Cleaning, Track Splitter, and Auto Stop settings. Drag the slider to the Sound Cleaning position and choose the preset for LP or cassette.

5. Drag the slider to Track Splitter. You'll probably want to choose the bottom option, Split Whenever Silence Is Detected. With this option selected, the program will create separate MP3 files for each song on the analog source material.

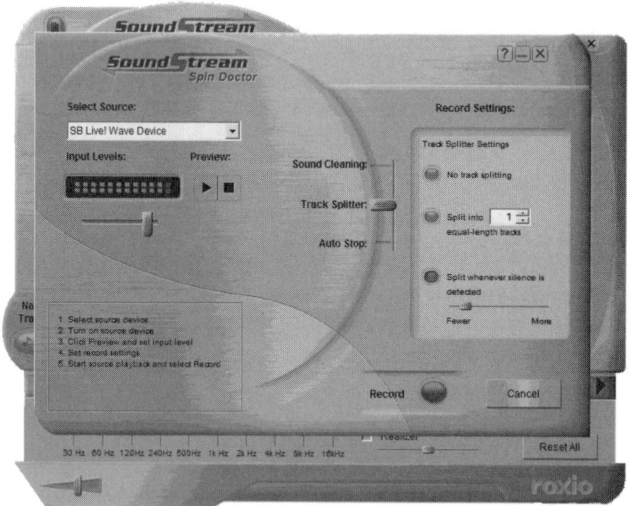

6. Select the Auto Stop position and choose Manual Stop. This option gives you control over when the software stops copying the incoming audio.

7. When you're ready, click the Record button. The Spin Doctor's Record dialog box should appear. Select the location on your hard disk to which you want to save your MP3 tracks by clicking the File button.

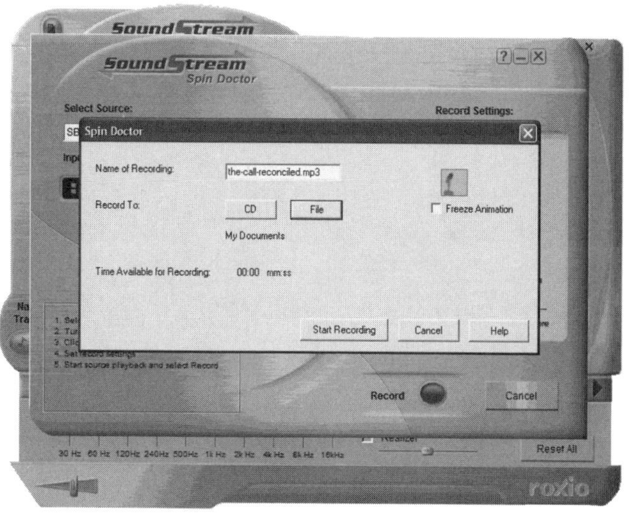

8. Finally, restart the analog source and click the Start Recording button. When the recording is complete, click Stop Recording.

After you stop recording, Spin Doctor will take several minutes to process the sound files. Of course, you'll still need to rename the MP3 files and add the ID3 tag information, because Spin Doctor doesn't know anything about the music you're capturing.

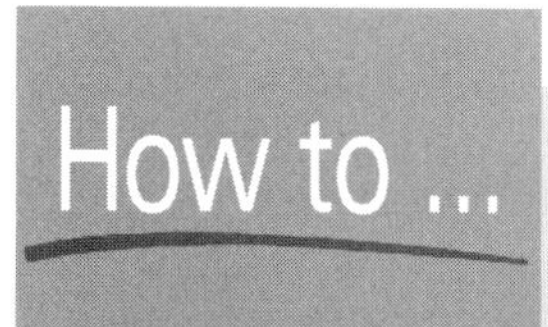

Get Closer to the Source

What if your PC is just too far away from the analog source material to make a reasonable connection? That's when you need to get creative. There are two easy ways to get the job done: borrow a notebook computer or use a portable MP3 player with recording capabilities.

If you choose to use a notebook, make sure it has an audio input jack. Avoid using a microphone input because the voltage level is different, and you'll distort the audio you're trying to record. You also need to install an audio editing program that can capture the music, and the hard disk needs to be ample for the data you're trying to capture. Remember: you should have about

500MB to grab a single LP, and portable PC hard disks are typically somewhat smaller than on the desktop. It can also help if the PC has an Ethernet connection; after you copy an LP, you can bring the notebook into the same room as the PC, transfer the audio quickly via a network connection, then edit, encode, and burn the music on your ordinary desktop computer.

Or there's the possibility of using a portable MP3 player with recording features. Dave loves the Archos Jukebox Recorder, as shown in the following illustration. It's a tiny MP3 player with a 6GB hard disk and inputs for capturing hours of audio directly into MP3 format. Dave has transferred his somewhat sizable LP collection to MP3 in this way. It's easier than hauling a computer into the home theater room. Of course, you still need to manually name the files and enter MP3 ID3 tag data yourself; there's just no getting around that problem.

Chapter 12

Editing, Correcting, and Tweaking Your Audio

How to…

- Ensure a clean, accurate recording before you start copying
- Choose an audio editor
- Cut away unwanted silence at the start of a song
- Add silent leader to the start of your music
- Combine and cut apart songs in an audio editor
- Fade songs in or out
- Clean up noisy tracks
- Optimize the dynamic range of your songs
- Make all of your songs roughly the same volume

If you've tried to make some copies of music based on the advice we've doled out earlier in the book, you may have found that the MP3s, WMAs, or WAV files you end up with are a little too accurate. Often, they include not just the music, but the noise. The hissing, the popping, the rumble—it's all there, especially if you're copying analog source material like LPs and cassette tapes that weren't perfect to begin with.

That's not too surprising. If you're like Dave, you played George Harrison's *All Things Must Pass* and The Cars' debut album to death back in the days of turntables and LPs, and all that resulting damage to the vinyl is faithfully recorded when you make a copy on your PC. In this chapter, we'll talk about how to minimize that unwanted and annoying sound through editing. But we'll also talk about how to make other tweaks and edits to your songs.

Starting Clean

While most of this chapter focuses on how to clean up and repair sound files that have already been ripped and stored on your PC's hard disk, it bears repeating that your finished copy is only as good as the original you started working from. If you find that you have a bad copy on your hard disk, it may be worth your while to rerecord it rather than trying to clean it up digitally. Keep these tips in mind:

- **Start with clean media** Remove dust and grime from vinyl records using a brush or cloth designed for cleaning LPs. You can use diluted rubbing alcohol to work embedded dirt loose from the grooves, but always clean in a circular motion—don't clean across the grooves, or you'll scratch the record. And don't use excessive force when trying to clean the record. Instead, you might want to visit a record store and pick up a cleaning brush designed especially for cleaning LPs. These brushes are great for ensuring that the cleaning agent gets into the grooves.
- **Clean the stylus** In fact, it's not a bad idea to replace the stylus in the turntable, especially if it has been a few years since you last changed it.

TIP *You can look at the needle under a magnifying glass to see if it comes to a sharp, symmetrical point, or if it looks jagged on one side. If it's unsymmetrical or jagged, replace it. A good needle will not do as much damage to the vinyl and will play music more accurately.*

- **If you're recording a cassette, clean the tape heads in the cassette player** You can use a cotton swab to apply a small amount of diluted alcohol, and be sure it's completely dry before use.
- **Use high-quality short cables to connect the analog sound system to the PC** We think it's a really bad idea to use any sort of wireless transmitter to broadcast a signal from the stereo system to the PC; every commercially available wireless system we've tried introduces enough static to make Hendrix roll over in his grave.

Touring an Audio Editor

As we mentioned in Chapter 11, you can rely on a number of audio editors to change your music after it's recorded to the PC's hard disk. You won't find any appropriate software bundled with Windows or the Mac, though. You'll need to use a third-party program. We like both Cool Edit 2000 (www.syntrillium.com) and Sound Forge (www.sonicfoundry.com).

Sound Forge, which is typical of what audio editors look like, is shown in Figure 12-1. An audio file appears in a window; the stereo channels are represented by two waveforms, one for the left channel and the other for the right. The amplitude of the wave—its height—indicates the volume of the sound.

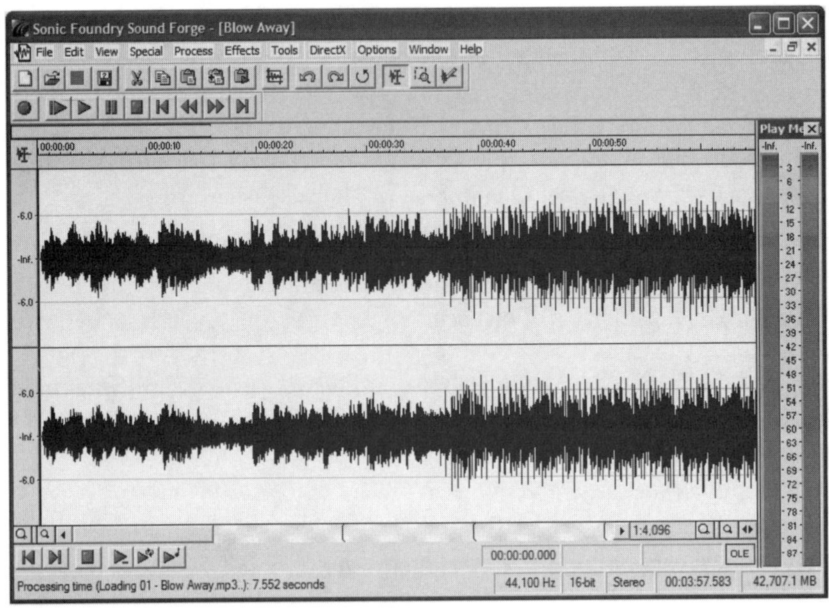

FIGURE 12-1 Sound Forge is an excellent audio editor, but you can use any program with the basic features discussed in this chapter.

Most programs like Sound Forge can be used to capture sound, edit it, and perform a wide variety of effects and transformations via the menu commands. It's fun, for instance, to experiment with features like Reverberation and Chorus, which you can find on Sonic Foundry's Effects menu.

Cutting Up Your Music

The easiest and most common task you'll no doubt need to perform with an audio editing program is simple cut-and-paste jobs. Audio editors let you cut and paste sections of your music files just about as easily as working with text in a word processor. You'll want to use this tool to perform three major tasks:

- **Delete extended silence at the start and end of tracks** This makes songs shorter, and thus, consumes less disk space. Cutting out extended leaders at the start or end can reduce the silence between songs when playing tracks on an MP3 player.

- **Cut an LP side's worth of songs apart into individual tracks** You'll want to do this if you store all of the songs on a cassette or LP in a single file during the recording process to save time.
- **Glue separate tracks together** This can be handy if you have interrelated songs that don't have pauses between them on the original recording. Suppose you ripped the CD version of *The Dark Side of the Moon,* for instance. You might want to make "Brain Damage" and "Eclipse" a single track; otherwise, when you listen to them on your PC or MP3 player, there will be an ugly pause during the transition between the songs, which should really flow seamlessly together.

Deleting Silent Leader

Deleting silence at the start or end of a track is the easiest task you can perform with an audio editor. Load a song into your editor and you'll see something like this:

Use the Zoom tool to magnify the song's waveform so you can see it better. Typically, the Zoom tool looks like a magnifying glass, although some programs also zoom when you roll the scroll bar with your mouse. Zoom in far enough so that the silent region spans the width of the screen, and then click and drag the mouse to select the flat line:

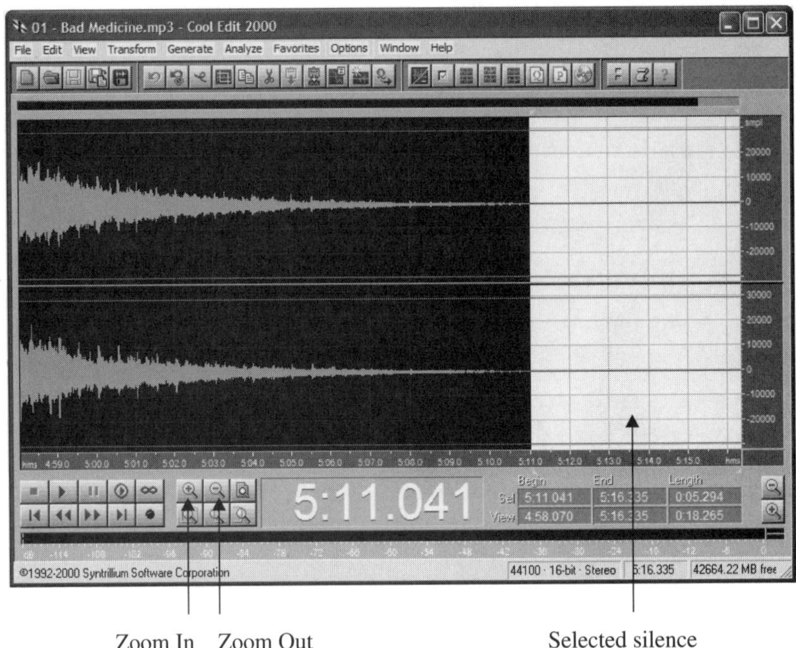

Finally, press the Delete key to cut that selected part out of the track. You can use this same procedure to cut dead space at the end of any track.

If you intend to run a cleanup filter on your music to eliminate noise caused by the LP or cassette, be sure to do it before you trim away all of your silent leader. Many cleanup filters need to use the noise level in the silent part of the track as a baseline to figure out how to clean up the rest of the file.

Inserting Silent Leader

Sometimes you might want to do just the opposite—insert some silent space at the start or end of a track. People tend to want a few seconds of silence between songs, for instance, and you can go too far in cutting out silence.

If you want to stick some dead space at the start of a track, it's usually just a mouse click or two away. In Cool Edit 2000, for instance, load the song you want to change and place the cursor at the very beginning of the track. Select Generate | Silence and choose the appropriate time period. That's it! In Sonic Foundry, place the cursor and choose Process | Insert Silence instead.

TIP

If you record a CD using the Disc-At-Once method (which we explain in Chapter 14), you might need to manually add some silent leader to the start or end of each song.

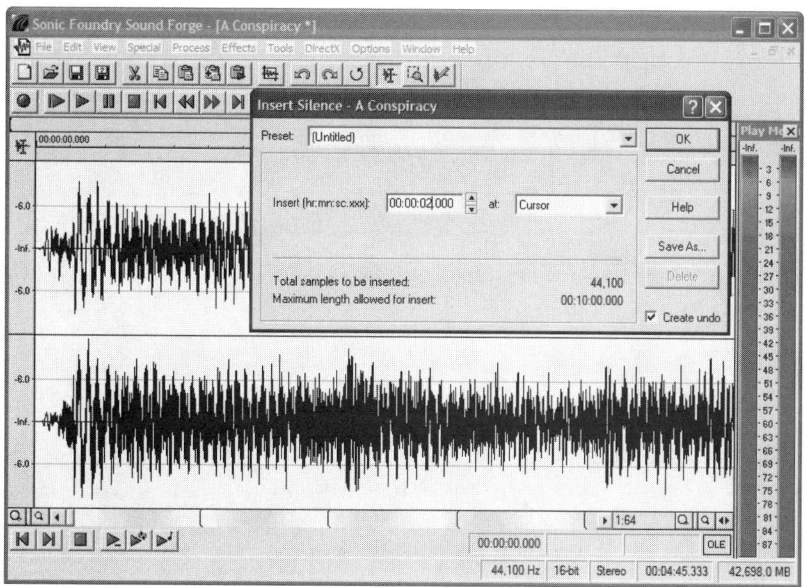

Did you know?

How Much Silence?

People sometimes ask how much silence should be at the start or end of a song. One solution is to simply leave the leader the way it was on the original source material. But if you've created your own song from scratch and converted it to digital format, that's not an option. Typically, the silence between professional tracks varies from .5 to 2 seconds.

Keep in mind that there's a difference between the real leader length and the perceived length of silence that listeners actually hear. The silence often appears to start sooner and last longer because the last fading note of a song is often lost in the background noise of the environment, especially in a noisy car or when the music is playing softly. So don't judge your silent leader by eyeballing the waveform on the computer screen; gauge it with your ears at a volume that represents the way you or others will typically hear it.

Splitting a File into Tracks

If you've captured a half-dozen songs into a single WAV or MP3 file, it's easy to cut them apart now that you've saved them to your PC's hard disk. Open the file in your favorite audio editor and you'll see them separated by little "pinches" of silence, looking something like this:

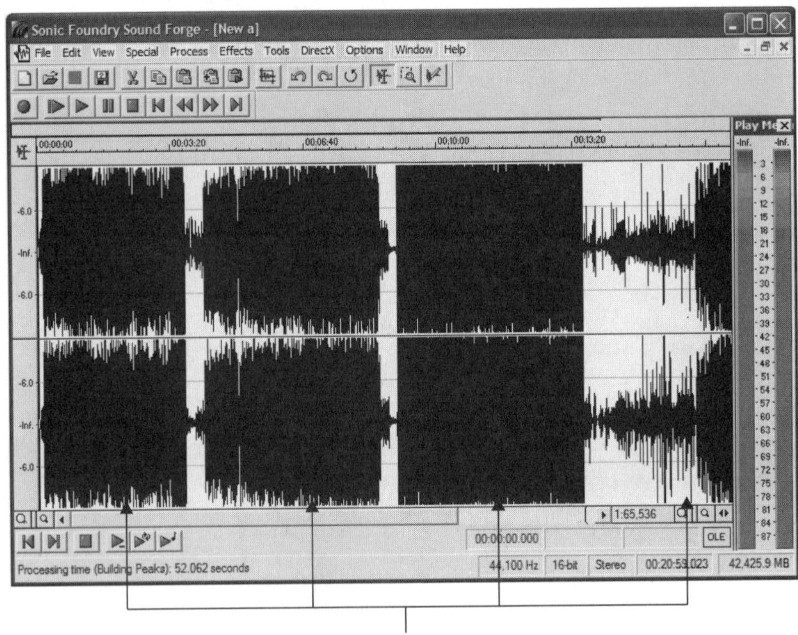

Individual songs

Select a region that goes from the beginning of the first song to the first silence. You don't have to be terribly accurate at this point; indeed, be sloppy and grab too much audio, so you actually select a little of the next song as well.

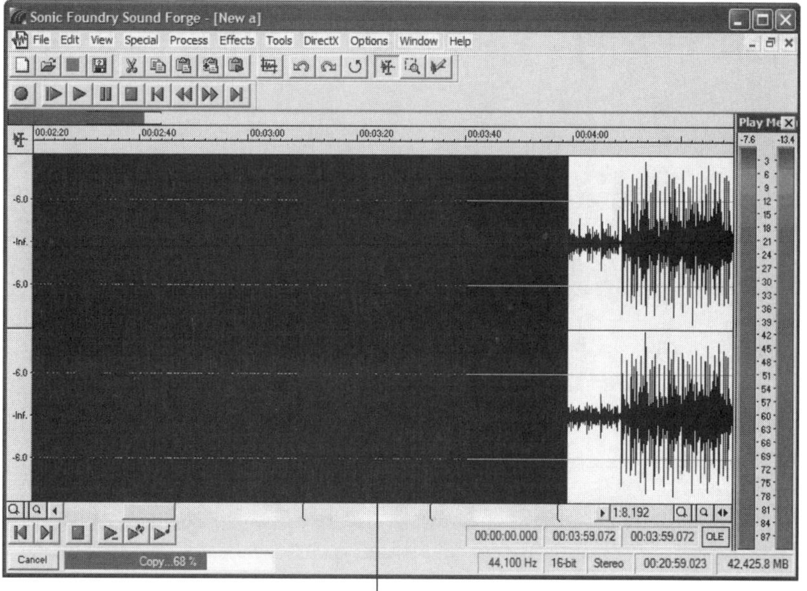

Selected song

Now select Edit | Copy. Don't select Edit | Cut. If you do that, you'll damage parts of the original file that we're not done with yet.

Paste the copied song into a new file. The method for doing this varies from program to program, but it shouldn't be too hard to find. In Sound Forge, it's Edit | Paste Special | Paste To New. In Cool Edit 2000, it's Edit | Paste To New.

Now you've got the first song in its own file, badly edited. Delete unwanted audio and trim the silence to taste. Finally, save the file as an MP3 or WAV file.

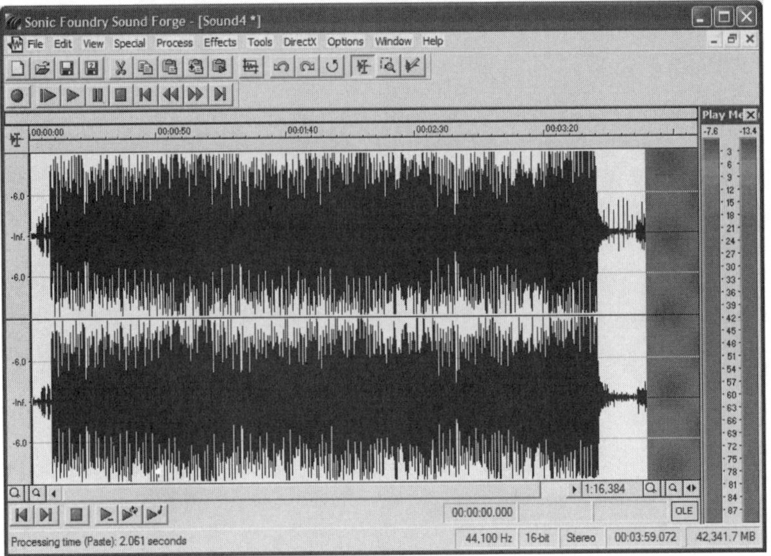

Now it's time to lather, rinse, repeat—you need to copy, paste, and trim each song in the file. When you're done, you don't need the original file anymore. Delete it.

Gluing Tracks Together

So, you've got a bunch of tracks that should transition seamlessly from one to the next, and you cringe every time your MP3 player inserts pauses between them as the next track loads. With an audio editor and a little elbow grease, you can eliminate that problem completely.

Here's all you need to do: open both tracks in your audio editor and select the entire duration of the second track. Select Edit | Copy. Place the cursor at the tail end of the first track and select Edit | Paste. Save the first file—which now contains both songs—and delete the second song from your hard disk.

Selected song

Selected song pasted onto end of previous song

TIP *Some programs display multiple files in one window, while others, like Cool Edit 2000, show only one waveform at a time. If that's the case with your audio editor, you'll need to switch views using the Window menu to work with multiple audio files.*

Fading Your Songs

Sometimes, you might want your song to fade in or fade out instead of starting abruptly—especially if you trim away all of the silent leader at the ends of the track. Fader controls are a common staple in almost every audio editor on the market. In Sound Forge, for instance, you can find the fader by selecting Process | Fade. It's hiding in Cool Edit 2000. Select Transform | Amplify and choose Fade from the presets.

Typically, you have two fading options: you can choose to let the program automatically fade in or out using a linear curve that ramps the volume over a set duration, or you can choose a more sophisticated fade control. In Sound Forge, select Process | Fade | Graphic, and you'll get this dialog box:

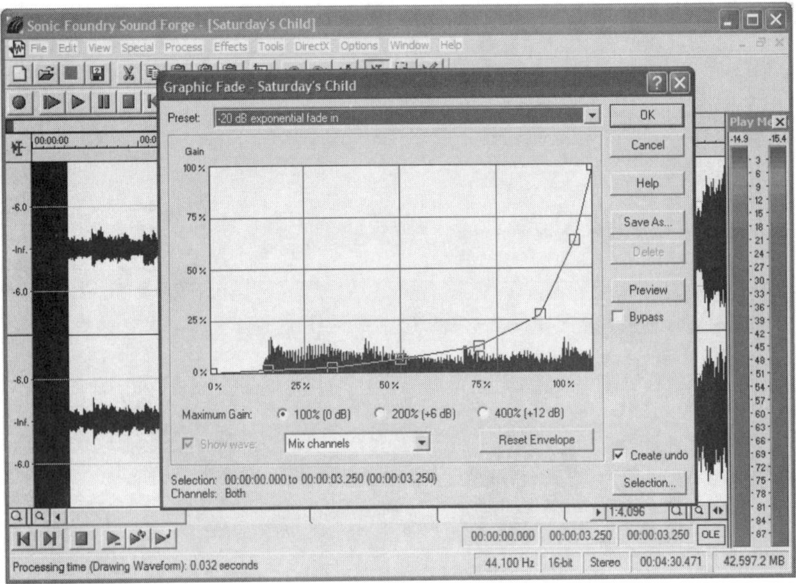

You can drag the curve with the mouse, creating a custom fade curve that acts quickly, slowly, or anything in between.

Taking Jazz Head On

Dave: OK, smart guy. You dis me on a daily basis for not liking jazz. And I'm getting tired of it, so let's duke it out right here, right now. What's so great about this art form? I can say that I once approached jazz with an open mind, but, after taking a survey class that spanned the century-long history of the musical style, I walked away bored out of my skull. Indeed, the only parts of the class I enjoyed were the detours on ragtime and the blues. Every form of jazz, from the pretentious works of Thelonious Monk to the toe-tapping hell-on-earth of big band and swing, is my personal fingernails-on-a-chalkboard. And though you claim that everyone loves jazz, that's clearly not the case. It was considered the work of the devil in the 1920s, and entire generations of people have disliked it. So, either pony up a good argument here, or stop telling me I'm strange for disliking jazz.

Rick: Asking "What's so great about jazz?" is like asking "What's so great about oxygen?" I find it amusing that you profess to liking ragtime and blues, but not big band or swing. They're all in the same family, bub. I think the reason you don't like jazz is that there's no personality—no depressed chain-smoking chicks or controversial bands—associated with it the way there is with rock and roll. And often no lyrics, either. (Apparently, if it's not somber or depressing, it's not for you.) As for "generations of people" who dislike jazz, that is, of course, ridiculous—jazz helped define the '20s and '30s, and kids went ape over it the way they eventually did over rock and roll (which, of course, had its own generations of haters). Asking me to argue why jazz is good is just plain silly. Why don't *you* tell *me* what's so great about Pink Floyd? Blech.

Dave: Ah, I finally understand. As you say, you like jazz because it has no personality. Like Yanni, it's emotionless, personality-free dribble that leaves no marks behind after you've heard it. With that in mind, I can't explain Pink Floyd to you—you'd never understand.

TIP *If you choose the Fade command without selecting a region, most programs will fade the entire song, so it starts at a volume of zero and reaches maximum volume at the very end. You rarely want that. Always remember to select a few seconds of audio at the start of the song before choosing the Fade command.*

Cleaning Up Noisy Audio

When you rip songs from digital sources like CDs, you generally don't have to worry about capturing noise in the ripping process (unless that sound was in the original recording, such as a 60Hz hum in the original recording equipment). But analog captures can include all sorts of glitches, including hiss and crackle sounds from LP recordings, popping sounds from a scratched record, and background rumble from noisy equipment or dirty electrical lines.

A lot of products are available that are designed to clean up your music. In general, your choices are determined largely by which audio editing software you're already using. Here's a brief overview of the most common programs:

- **Audio Cleaning Lab** This stand-alone capture and editing program is an inexpensive alternative to some of the pricier products out there. It does a good job for most folks who don't want to spend a lot of time or money creating a digital music library but need to do a little audio cleanup. (You can find it at www.magix.com.)

- **Sound Forge Noise Reduction plug-in** Probably the most complete sound-filtering system we've seen, this is a DirectX-compatible plug-in for programs like Sound Forge. Several filters are included in the package for cleaning up vinyl, removing hiss, pop, and crackle. There's even a filter that can restore songs that have moderate amounts of clipping caused by recording at too high of a level. Unfortunately, it's the most complicated of the filters, so you'll need to spend some time with the short manual to understand how to get the most out of it. (Check it out at www.sonicfoundry.com.)

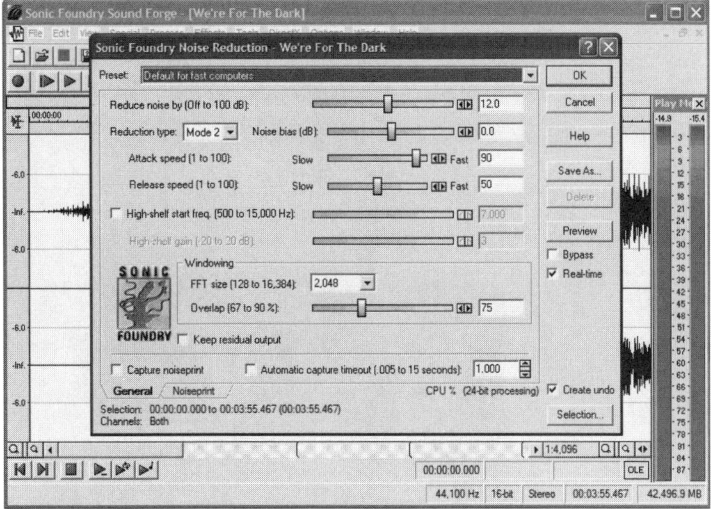

- **Cool Edit Audio Cleanup plug-in** Compatible with Cool Edit 2000, this filter set is—like the plug-in for Sound Forge—very complex. The plug-in takes some practice to use, but it offers a wide array of options for ensuring that you minimize as much noise as possible. (Check it out at www.syntrillium.com.)

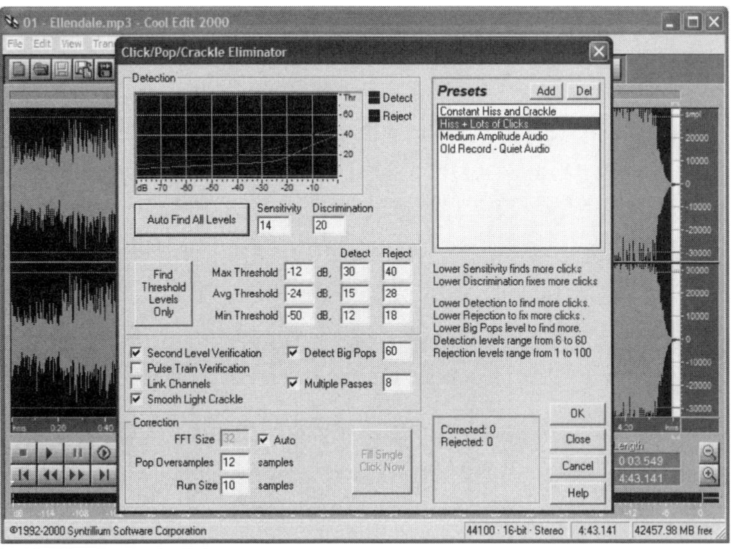

- **Ray Gun** Ray Gun is another inexpensive and fairly simple alternative to more sophisticated tools. It's a DirectX-compatible plug-in, so you can use it with a program like Sound Forge that uses these plug-ins. Ray Gun is also able to run on its own, outside of an audio editing program, though, so you can use it to clean up songs even if you don't own a separate audio editor. As a stand-alone program, however, it imports only WAV files. (You can find it at www.arboretum.com.)

No matter which audio cleanup tool you use, you can take certain steps to get the best results. Be sure to consider these tips:

- Many noise-reduction filters need to sample the silent leader to establish a baseline for how much noise is on the track. If you plan to perform noise reduction, do it before you cut away all of your silent leader.
- If you plan to normalize your audio (see "Optimizing the Dynamic Range" later in this chapter), do that first, before you apply any cleaning tools.
- If you have clipping because the audio was recorded at too high a level, discard the selection and rerecord the audio if possible.
- If you can use several filters to eliminate noise, such as a pop remover, hiss remover, and hum remover, follow any directions the program offers about in which order you should perform the steps. The order can make a difference, because you generally want to enhance a recording before starting to take away portions of it.
- Noise reduction is interactive. You generally have to use your ears to see which settings work best for the music you are cleaning. Listen carefully as

you tweak the settings, because you can easily clean too much and end up damaging the music.

- Compare the cleaned-up song side by side with the original dirty version and make sure you like the result before you overwrite the original or delete it from your hard disk, losing it forever.

Optimizing the Dynamic Range

Or, in English, using *normalization*.

Wait—that's hardly plain English either.

Here's the deal: when you normalize a song, you raise its volume so that it uses the full dynamic range available. This is especially handy for two reasons:

- Some audio you've recorded from digital or analog sources may have been captured at a low level, so the song will be too quiet.
- Different audio tracks, captured at different times with different equipment, or coming from different production standards, will play back at different volumes. Normalizing your music will make sure all of your tracks play at roughly the same relative volume level.

TIP *Normalization is a great tool for fixing songs that were captured at very low audio levels and thus sound far too quiet when you play them.*

Your audio editor may have two or more normalization options. There are two principal ways of optimizing your audio's sound with normalization:

- **Peak level** This setting recalibrates the dynamic range of your song, inflating the levels until the waveform's peaks touch the maximum possible level allowed. This normalization setting is a conservative one to choose; it increases the level of your audio but prevents any possibility of clipping the peaks of your audio.
- **Average RMS** This setting increases the level of the song not by monitoring the peaks, but by monitoring the average loudness of the song. This choice is good when you want to match the apparent loudness of all the songs in your library, but it has a downside. It's possible to clip the peaks of your audio using this setting, so you should be careful and check the waveform for clipping after running the normalization filter.

To normalize your audio file using Cool Edit 2000, select Transform | Amplitude | Normalize. Because Cool Edit supports only peak normalization, you have few options.

Sound Forge has a significantly more advanced normalization tool. You can access it by selecting Special | Normalize.

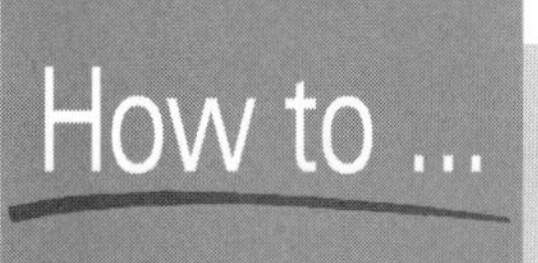

Use Sound Forge

1. Choose Special | Normalize.
2. Choose Average RMS from the top of the Normalize dialog box.
3. Click the Scan Levels button. Sound Forge should scan the song for a few seconds, searching for the loudness levels in the file.
4. Drag the Normalize To slider up or down to set the loudness level. Be sure not to select a level above about –6dB (which corresponds to about 50 percent). Any higher, and you will introduce nasty clipping into your audio file.

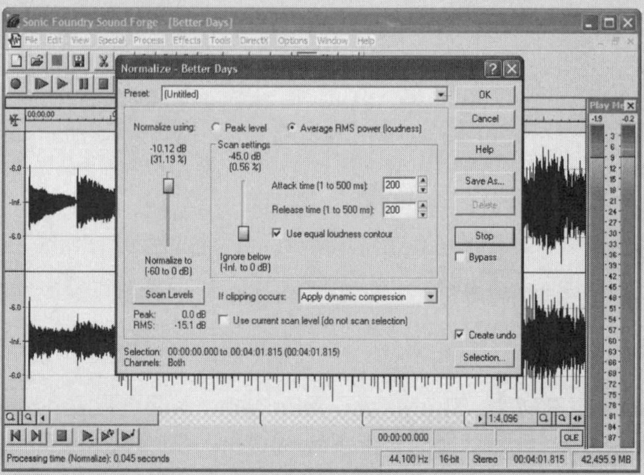

5. Apply the normalization and listen to the song (and look at the waveform). If you don't like the results, you can always undo it and try again.

Chapter 13

Organizing Your Music Files

How to…

- Plan for MP3 storage
- Calculate how much space you need
- Arrange your music into folders
- Select filenames for your songs
- Edit ID3 tag information
- Correct several ID3 tags at once
- Use ID3 tags to play songs in the CD's track order
- Change ID3 tags on the go
- Fix broken file type associations

Digital music is fiendishly addictive. When you start collecting music from the Internet or ripping music from CDs and LPs, you might think that "it's OK, I only need a few songs." As time goes on, though, you'll find yourself moving more and more of your private audio CD collection to the computer, or searching for that old '60s song that's long out of print in record stores, but you're pretty sure Bananarama covered it in the '80s. It becomes an obsession, and your collection will grow like wildfire.

Before you know it, you need to measure your music collection in gigabytes, not megabytes—and that's when having firm control over your songs is important. It's like Rick's paperclip collection. When he only had a few, he could toss 'em all into the same box. Now that he has the third largest collection in Michigan (as certified by the NPCCA—you know, the National Paper Clip Collectors Association), he needs to sort them carefully by size, color, and springiness, lest he never be able to find specific clips again. MP3s are not all that different, and this chapter is designed to keep you on top of your music files.

Planning for MP3 Storage

It's a good thing that digital music didn't come ambling along until the twenty-first century. If it had emerged back in the '80s or even the early '90s, it would never have become popular just because hard disk drives were so small. Around 1990, a 100MB hard disk cost about $400. By 1995, things had certainly improved, but not by leaps and bounds: you could get a 400MB drive for the same price. Today, you can get 100 times that much storage space for a little over $100. That's a good thing, because if you're into digital music, you'll need the space.

As you're already aware, the bit rate that you use to sample your MP3s dramatically affects the total number of songs you can store in a given amount of hard disk space. Higher quality means bigger files, so you need to decide ahead of time what your own personal sweet spot is and collect or rip songs at that bit rate. This is particularly important if you're planning to move the songs to a portable music player with a small hard disk.

TIP

What bit rate do we prefer? Glad you asked. Rick considers 128 Kbps MP3 files to be good enough, and uses that bit rate to maximize his storage capacity. Dave prefers 160 Kbps songs, because they are (to his ear) significantly closer to CD quality—and he has plenty of hard disk space, so it's worth the extra megabytes.

You can use the following chart to help you decide which bit rate to use for your own music collection. But remember: there's no substitute for your own ears. Rip a song with a lot of dynamic range several times, each time with a different bit rate, and compare them with a good speaker system or headphones. Based on that test drive, figure out which bit rate works best for you. Of course, it's important to remember the old adage of garbage in, garbage out. If your source material has pops, scratches, or came from Rick's music library, a higher bit rate won't make the copy sound better, just truer to the original.

Bit Rate	Sound Quality	Average Disk Space for a Dozen Songs (One Album)
64 Kbps	Poor. Somewhere between AM radio and hearing your trained monkey play "Stairway to Heaven" on a kazoo. There are obvious audio artifacts any music lover will run screaming from.	25MB
96 Kbps	Poor. Rick describes it as similar to FM radio, but the old wireless doesn't have the digital whooshing effect you'll hear in the midst of a subtle arpeggio when listening to 96 Kbps MP3s.	40MB
128 Kbps	Average. Near-CD quality, best used in environments when you can't hear the full dynamic range of the audio anyway, like in a car, in an airplane, or when jogging.	50MB
160 Kbps	Excellent. Near-CD quality can fool most people into thinking it's real CD playback.	65MB
192 Kbps	Outstanding. Captures essentially all of the human-perceivable audio information from CD, but the storage cost adds up if you have a lot of songs.	75MB

Organizing Your Songs

When we first started saving MP3 files on our hard disk, we didn't give folder structures or organizational strategies a whole lot of thought. In fact, we essentially dropped all of our songs into one big folder. When we had a dozen tunes, that was OK, but by the time we reached 100 songs, it became a crisis to find specific files and build logical playlists.

We highly recommend dividing your music into folders based on artist and album. Actually, the specific storage scheme you choose is a matter of personal taste, but one thing is for sure: one big folder will eventually become a headache.

Similarly, you might consider a standard file-naming convention. The songs you download from the Internet, for instance, will arrive with whatever hare-brained naming scheme the person who created the file used. Fortunately, you can rename the file yourself. More importantly, songs you rip from your own library can get named properly right from the start.

TIP *It goes without saying that all of your subfolders of music should be centralized in a single folder, such as C:\My Music or C:\My Documents\ My Music. The latter is a handy location if you have an automatic backup program routinely archiving everything in your My Documents folder (and your backup device has the space to accommodate all your music). Keeping it in a single place makes it easy to copy music to portable music players as well.*

Controlling Playback with Filenames

If this all sounds a little, err, retentive, bear with us. A good filing system isn't just for folks who like to keep their pencils sharp and their desks immaculately clean. Instead, the way you store songs on your hard disk influences the order in which they'll actually play back. Or play them back at all. Our tech editor, Brian Nadel, just reminded us of the main character from that great film, *High Fidelity*: always rearranging his music collection. It's a miracle he ever found anything to listen to.

By default, many music players—both on the PC (which we discussed in Chapter 6) and portable music players (discussed back in Chapter 8)—play songs in alphabetical order. We don't know about you, but when we want to listen to Jimi Hendrix's classic *Are You Experienced?,* we don't want the album to kick off with "Are You Experienced?" and wrap up with "Third Stone from the Sun." That just isn't right. We want to hear the album the way Jimi intended it—kicking off with the brilliantly psychedelic riffs of "Purple Haze" and trailing off with the freaky, experimental churning chords of "Are You Experienced?"

Likewise, the way you organize your music into folders is important because it affects the way you play music and build playlists. Portable music players that understand folder structures (not all do) will play all the songs in a single folder, then move on to the next, allowing you to hear *Rubber Soul* followed by *Revolver,* for instance. Sure, you don't have to store your songs in folders to hear them this way, but this strategy makes it a lot easier.

Selecting a Folder Strategy

How should you store your songs? Figure 13-1 shows one of the most common ways of arranging files and folders using Led Zeppelin as an example. Notice that our personal favorite—an Artist folder with Album subfolders—most closely resembles the way you store music in the real world, either by LP, cassette, or CD.

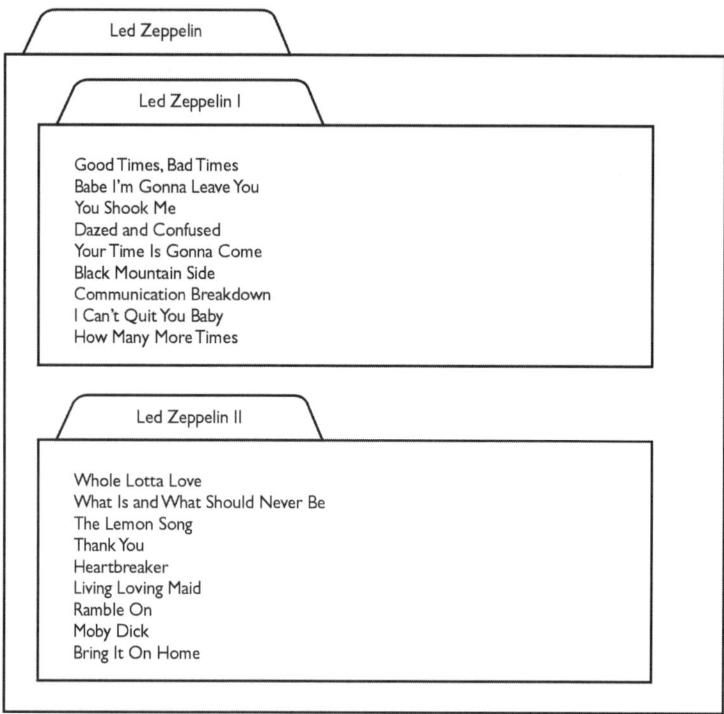

FIGURE 13-1 A consistent folder structure makes it easy to find your music when your collection has grown large.

Fear not: you don't have to manually move files around and rename folders to implement a folder strategy for your music. Most MP3 encoders will do it automatically for you. You just have to tell it what your preference is. Here's how to do it in the most common encoders:

- **MusicMatch Jukebox** Choose Options | Settings and click the Recorder tab. Click the Tracks Directory button and choose to create a sub-path by artist, album, or both.

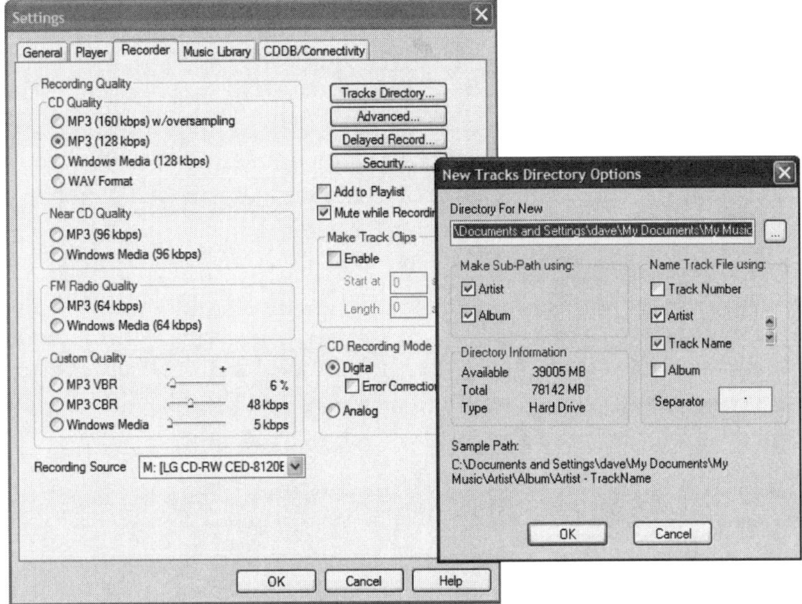

- **RealJukebox** Choose Tools | Preferences, and then click the Music Files tab. Click the Change Sub-Folders button and make a choice from the long scrolling list.

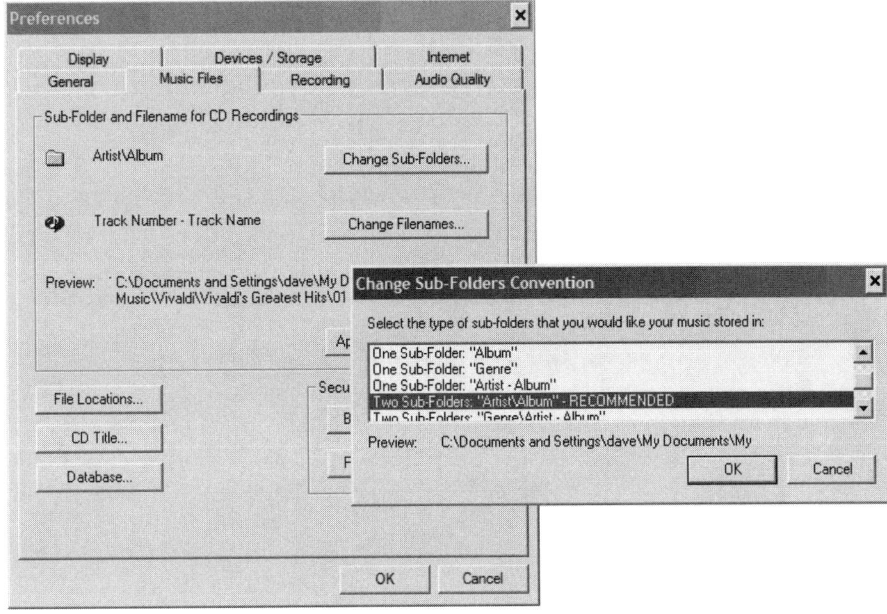

You have no control over the folder structure in Windows Media Player.

Selecting Filenames

Your filename structure is arguably even more important than the way the folders are named. Why? Because, as we mentioned earlier, many players will play tunes in alphabetical order when not told to do otherwise.

If you want to make sure that your tunes play in proper track order by default, use a format that begins with the track number. You can follow that with the track name, album name, artist, or a slew of other details. To keep the titles reasonably short, you might want to go with just the track number and track name, especially if they're already being filed in artist and album subfolders. That's how Dave's music collection is arranged, so a typical folder looks like this:

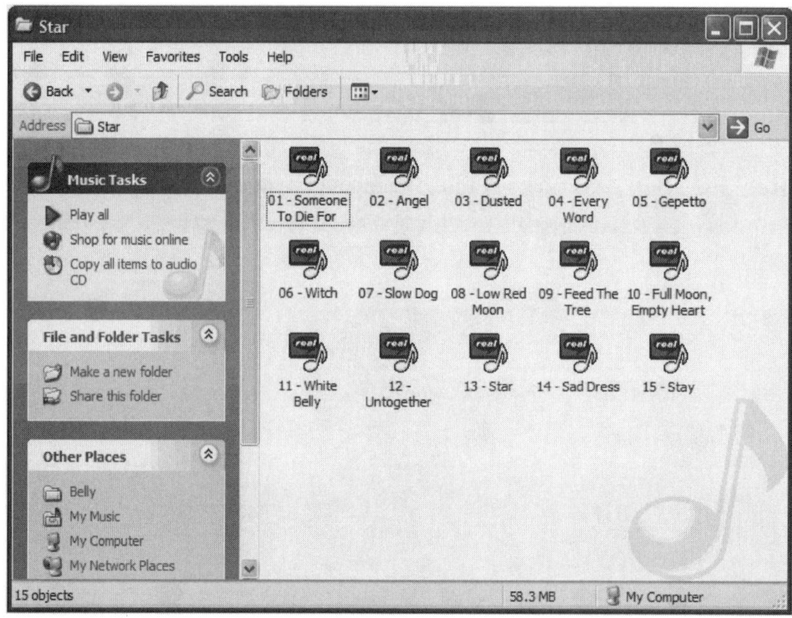

Most encoders give you a fair bit of file-naming flexibility. Here's where you can find file-naming controls in each of the most popular encoders:

- **MusicMatch Jukebox** Choose Options | Settings and click the Recorder tab. Just as if you were setting the folder details, click the Tracks Directory button. You can choose to include details like track number, name, artists, and more. Use the arrows to arrange the order of the elements in the filename and choose the separator to specify what you'd like between each element, such as a dash or a space.

Did you know?

Where Do the Filenames Come From?

When you rip music from CD, most encoder programs access an Internet-based service called CDDB, which stands for CD Database. There, the CD is checked against an exhaustive database to find the artists, album name, song titles, and other details. This information is then used to automatically fill in information about the digital music files you've just created. Some programs won't access CDDB unless you register it, though.

- **RealJukebox** Choose Tools | Preferences, and then click the Music Files tab. Click the Change Filenames button to choose up to four elements to include in the filename.

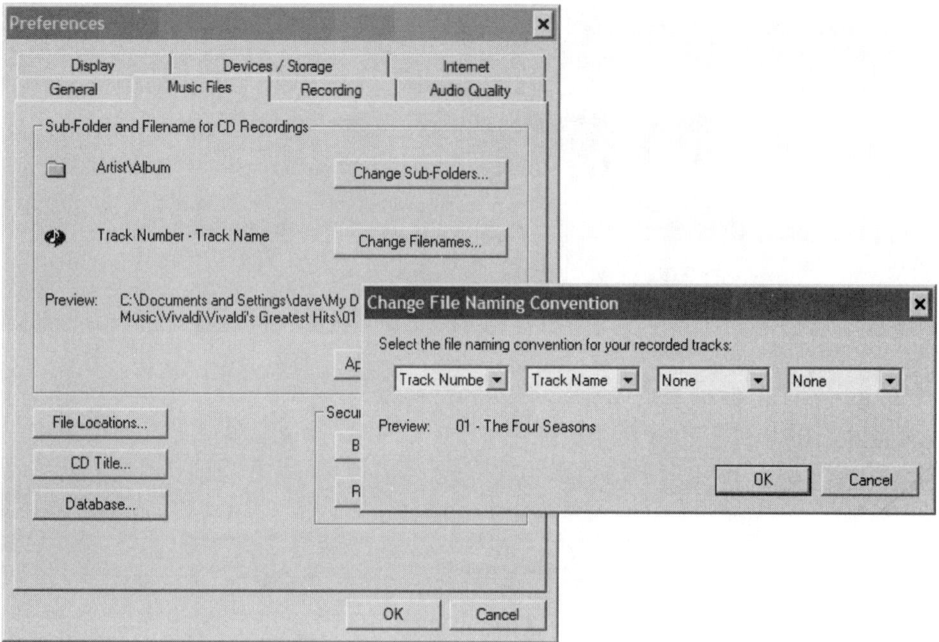

- **Windows Media Player** Choose Tools | Options and click the Copy Music tab. Click the Advanced button to specify which elements to include in the name, as well as the file name order and type of separator.

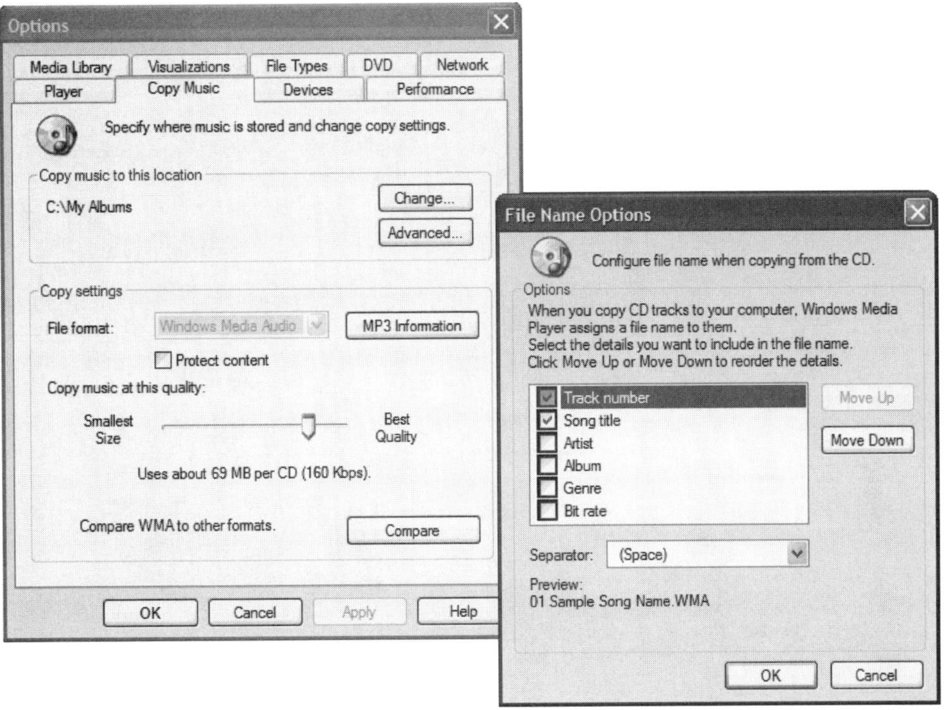

Editing Music File ID Tags

One of the most powerful features in digital music is what's known as the ID3 tag. The *ID3 tag* is a component of the MP3 file that stores information about the song: stuff like artists, album name, genre, lyrics, album art, and a number of other items can be stored here. Unlike audio CDs, that means MP3 tracks have lots of identifying information embedded in them.

When you rip a song from a CD, your encoder should look up all this information from the Internet-based CDDB service and store it in the MP3 file for later use. MP3 players can use the ID3 tag information to display title information in an LCD display. It can be used by karaoke software to display lyrics. It can even be used by music players to show off album art during playback. You can view all the song's ID3 tag information in most music players; here's what it looks like in RealJukebox:

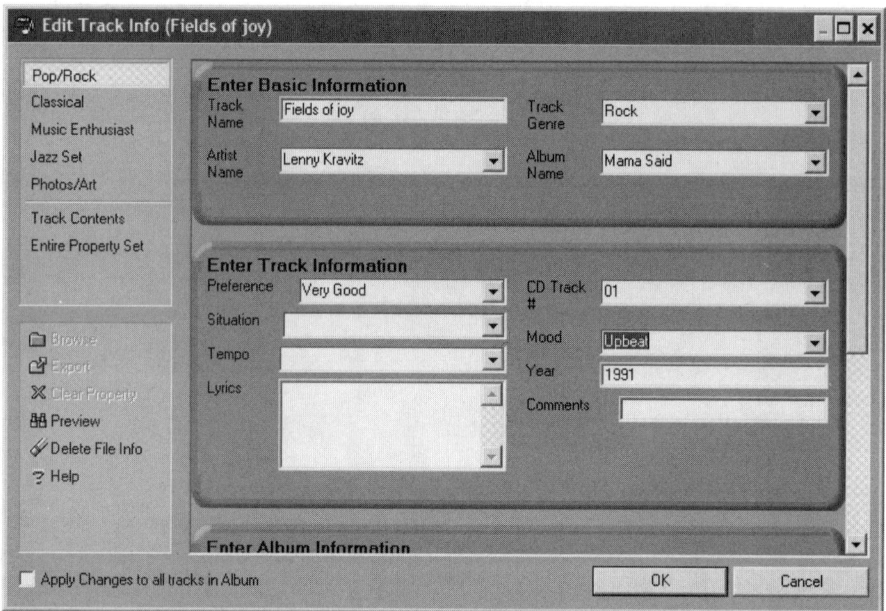

Although your encoder should generate ID3 information for you automatically, sometimes you might want to edit it manually. The CDDB database may have misspelled the artist's name, or perhaps the song titles came through in all capital letters (Dire Straits' *Communique* appears in all caps, for instance, and that kind of thing drives Dave absolutely insane).

The procedure to edit the ID3 info for a song is essentially the same regardless of which program you use: right-click a track in the library and choose the option to edit the track. Here's what you should see in MusicMatch. (You can see RealJukebox in the previous illustration, and Windows Media Player has a much less elaborate mechanism for changing ID3 tag info.)

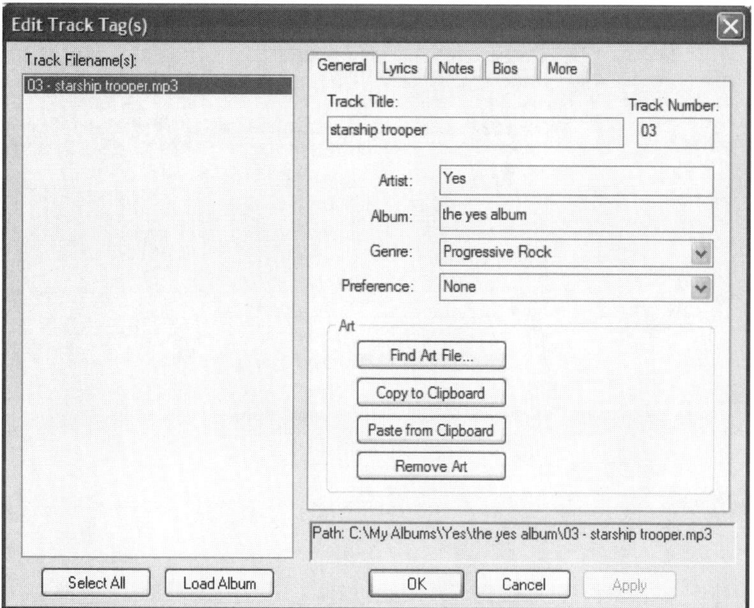

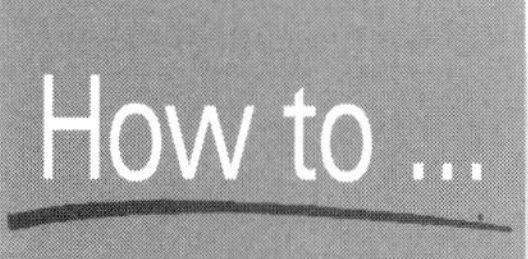

Edit ID3 Tags on Your Handheld PC

Do you have a Palm device, like a Palm V, Handspring Visor, or Sony Clie? If you do, you might like a program called Playster. This little app for any Palm device, which you can find at www.palmgear.com, costs just $10 and is pretty darned cool. Playster searches your hard disk for MP3s and synchronizes the ID3 tags—you know, stuff like the title, artist, genre, year, and other comments—with a database on your Palm. If you download music from the Internet with poorly completed ID3 tag data, you can fill in the blanks at your leisure on your Palm, and the changes get reflected on the PC when you perform an ordinary HotSync. Playster even lets you build and save playlists for your desktop music player software.

When you click OK, the track will be updated with the new information.

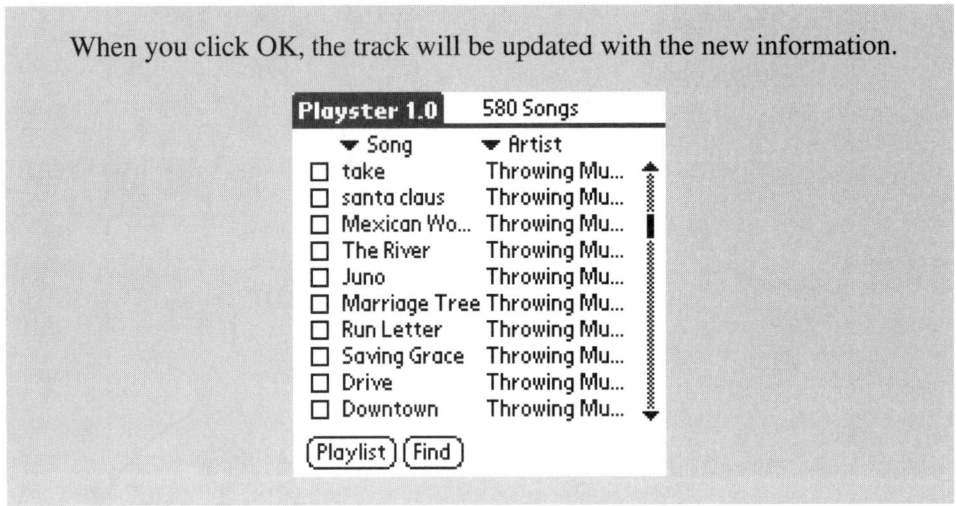

Changing Several Tracks at Once

What if you want to make a global change to a bunch of tracks at once? Take the Dire Straits' *Communique* example we offered earlier. Perhaps you want to select all the tracks on the album and correct the spelling of the album name by typing it only once. Here's what you should do:

- In RealJukebox, select all the tracks you want to edit in the library and right-click. Choose Edit Track Info. You'll see the Edit Track Info dialog box, but some fields (like the track name) are disabled, because you wouldn't want to make that sort of change to a bunch of files at once. Type your change (such as the album name), and click OK. You'll see all the selected tracks in the library updated with this new information.

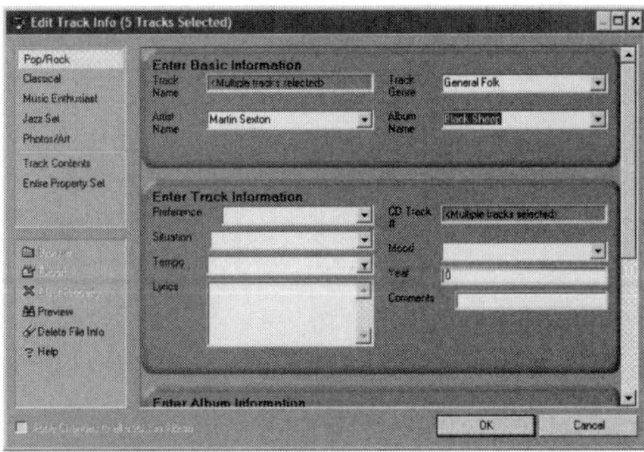

- In MusicMatch, select all the tracks you want to edit in the library and right-click. Choose Edit Track Tag(s). In the Edit Track Tag(s) dialog box, select all of the tracks you want to change by Shift-selecting or Control-selecting them with the mouse. Then find the item in the ID3 tag you want to change (such as the artist, album, genre, or preference), and click the

Brilliant Reasons to Manually Edit Your ID3 Tags

Here are some ways you can use ID3 tags to streamline and organize your MP3 files—and get more enjoyment from your music:

- **Correct errors** CDDB isn't perfect, and you will sometimes run into albums with typos, incorrect capitalization, and other annoying glitches.
- **Turn double albums into single albums** Double albums don't have to be double albums—separated into two separate folders—when they're digital files. Select *The Wall Disc 1* and *The Wall Disc 2*, for instance, and edit the album's ID3 tags so the album title is just *The Wall*. Then change the track numbers on disc 2 so "Hey You" becomes track 14 instead of restarting at track 1, and concludes with "Outside the Wall" as track 26. Finally, use RealJukebox to apply its folder structure rules to your music folder. It'll consolidate the album into a single folder and play each song in sequence, the way Roger Waters would surely have intended if LPs could hold 80 minutes of music.
- **Consolidate onesies** If you download a lot of songs, you may end up with a half-dozen tracks from the same artist, but they're all stored in different folders because each song came from a different album. If you prefer, make your own *Greatest Hits* album—select all the individual tracks and change their album titles to *Greatest Hits*. All the songs will consolidate into a single folder.

Depending on which music player you use, you may need to delete your music library (don't delete the songs off the hard disk, just delete them from the music

check box to select it. Type your change and click OK to save your changes. Remember, if you forget to select the tracks from the list, you'll change only the very first track in the list.

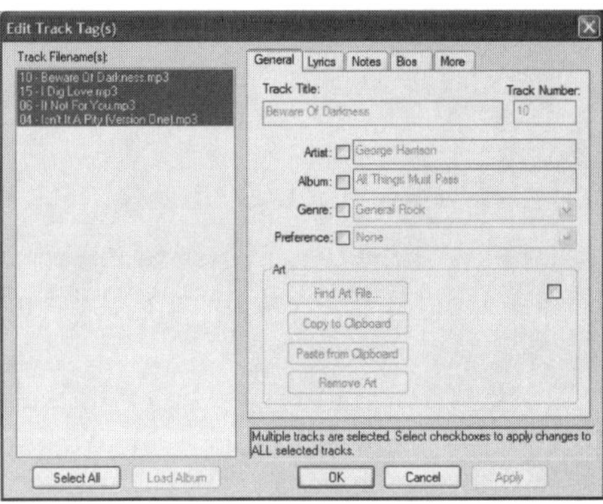

Despite all that effort, albums, if sorted into folders, will still play in alphabetical order. If it's important to you to hear The Cowboy Junkies' The Caution Horses *before* Lay It Down, *you might want to add the year of release before the album title manually, sort of the way your music player automatically adds the track number to the front of the song's filename.*

Fixing the File Type Association

One of the most frustrating aspects of installing and trying various music players in Windows is the fact that many of those programs insist—quite rudely—on taking control of file types like MP3 (which is an MP3 file) and M3U (which is a playlist file). "So what?" you ask. Well, when you double-click a music file, you might want Winamp to open it and start playing. But if you just installed MusicWhiz yesterday and it has taken control of the MP3 file type association, then MusicWhiz will open, not Winamp.

There are two ways to fix this annoying problem:

- Let the program you prefer take back the association. Why do the hard work yourself? Let the program do it. Open the program that you want to own the association and look in its options or preferences. Odds are good that there will be an option for it to reassociate itself with important music-related file types. In RealJukebox, for instance, choose Tools |

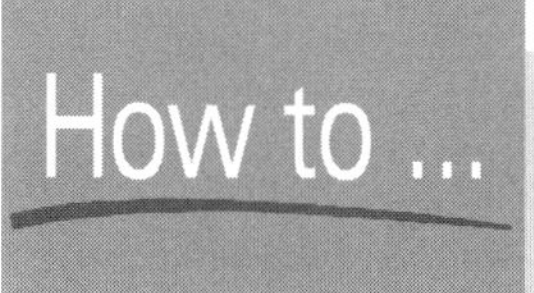

Fix the File Type

1. Open a folder on the Windows desktop. It really doesn't matter what kind of folder you open.
2. Choose View | Folder Options. You should see, not too surprisingly, the Folder Options dialog box.
3. Click the File Types tab. You'll see a long list of file types; these are all the files Windows recognizes.
4. Scroll down until you find the entry for MP3. Unfortunately, it might be called something different, depending on what the last program to associate the file type named it. Look for MP3, MPEG Audio, and similar names. Select it and click the Edit button.
5. In the Actions section, highlight Play and click Edit.
6. Click the Browse button and find your way to the program you want to associate with the MP3 file format. It'll probably be somewhere in the C:\Program Files folder. Make sure you add **%1** to the end. If in doubt, check another file association to make sure you did it right.
7. Click OK to save your changes.

Preferences and click the General tab. You can use the Re-Associate button to "steal back" file associations stolen by other software.

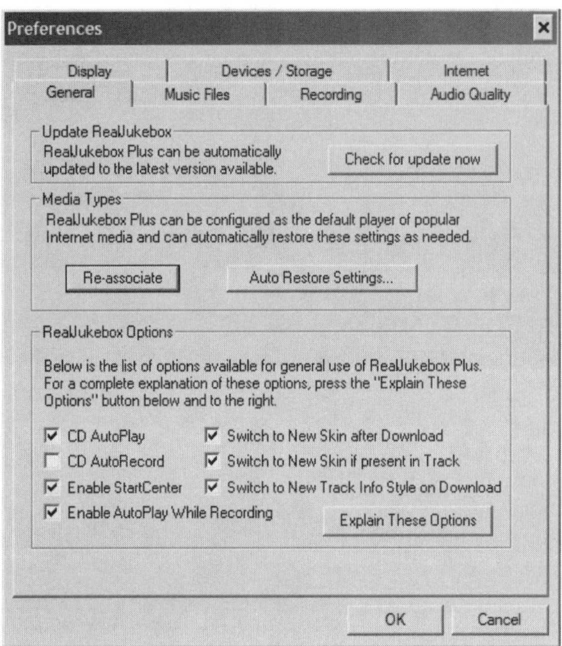

- Use the brute force method. If your music program doesn't have such a feature, or it doesn't seem to work, you can do it yourself. Get out your gardening gloves and sit down in front of your PC, because you're going to have to edit some intimidating-looking configuration boxes. But it's really not that hard.

TIP

If you're using Windows XP, the Folder Options menu item has been moved to the Tools menu. From there, it's actually a bit easier. Click the File Types tab and scroll down to MP3. Then click Change and select the program from the list of suggested options. Click OK and you're done.

The Desert Island Test

Dave: I can't figure out Gilligan's radio. Despite being stranded in the middle of absolutely nowhere, it got crystal-clear broadcasts from Hawaii. And its batteries lasted forever. But assuming we weren't blessed with Gilligan's magic radio, which five absolutely essential albums would we each bring to a desert island? Two ground rules: No double albums allowed, and they have to be artist-released original titles. No greatest hits compilations, Mr. Only-Likes-Top-40. Here are my picks, in no particular order:

1. *Abbey Road* — The Beatles
2. *The Velvet Underground and Nico* — The Velvet Underground
3. *Dire Straits* — Dire Straits
4. *Red Heaven* — The Throwing Muses
5. *The Dark Side of the Moon* — Pink Floyd

Rick: What is truly shocking is that not a single Kristen Hersh album appears on Dave's list, and he worships the very air she circulates through her lungs. (Yes, I know Kristen Hersh is/was the lead singer for Throwing Muses, but that's beside the point.) Here are my picks, also in no particular order:

1. *Dookie* — Green Day
2. *Glass Houses* — Billy Joel
3. *Jagged Little Pill* — Alanis Morissette
4. *Big Bad Voodoo Daddy* — Big Bad Voodoo Daddy
5. *Kamakiriad* — Donald Fagen

Dave: Later in the book, you'll find I came up with five really lame band names. As a preemptive strike to prove I can occasionally come up with a good band name, let me add that Gilligan's Magic Radio is a seriously cool band name.

Part IV

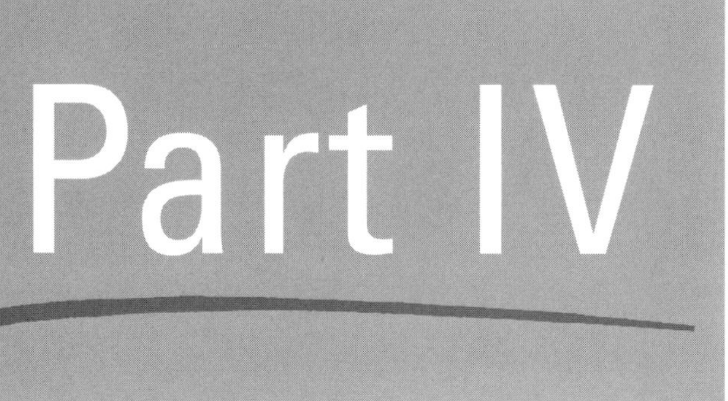

Sharing Your Digital Music

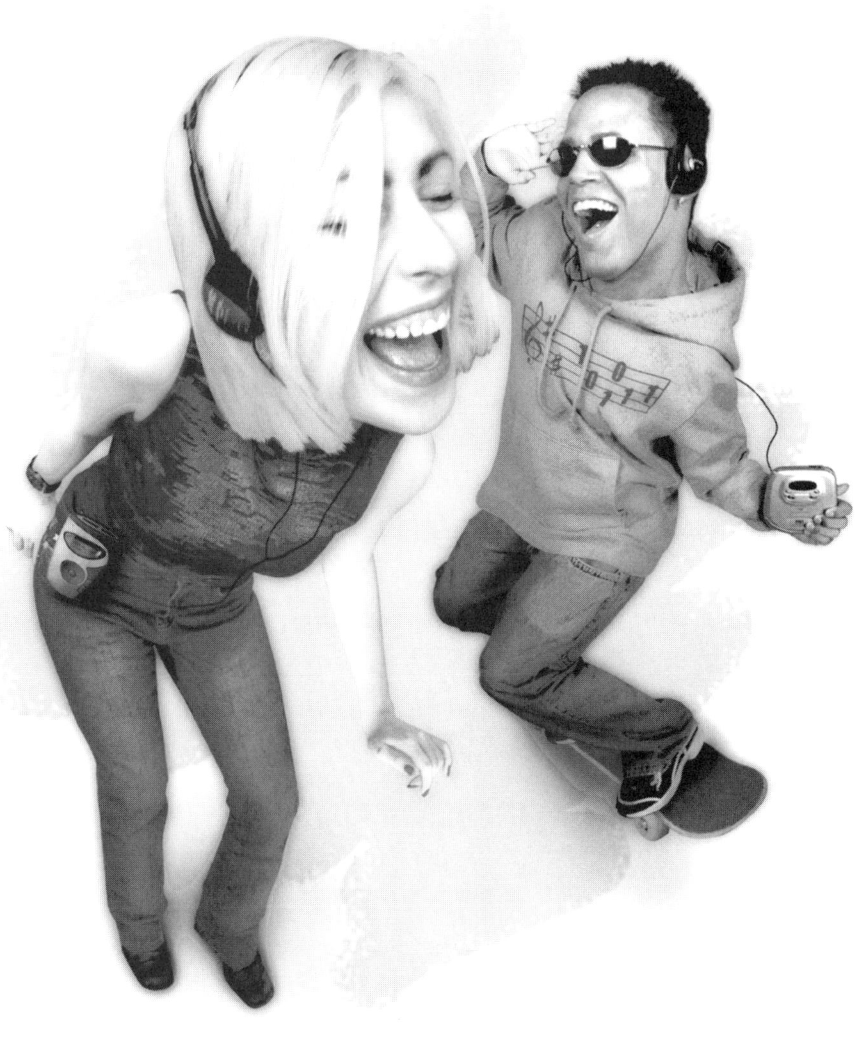

Chapter 14

Converting Music to CD and Streaming Audio

How to...

- Understand the basics of CD burning
- Prepare your computer for CD duplication
- Choose among the many kinds of recordable CDs
- Know which speed to record at
- Choose tracklist and disc-image recording options
- Use sessions when recording CDs
- Burn an Audio CD
- Create an MP3 data CD
- Add streaming audio to your Web site
- Choose the right streaming audio software solution

Until now, this fine book has focused on converting your music to a digital format that you can appreciate on your own PC or on a portable MP3 player. But we haven't talked much about how to convert your music into a format that's useful outside of your basement.

If you're an artist and you want to spread your music around, for instance, you might want to stream your MP3 files from a Web site so future fans can listen to your sound from their own PCs. Or you might just want to convert your MP3 collection into Audio CDs so you can play it in the car or share your own digital mix tapes with friends. In this chapter, we'll take a look at how to turn your digital music into those little silver platters we all call CDs. We'll also take a look at what you need to know to share music through streaming technology.

Getting Started with CD Recording

We tend to think of digital music files like a bucket of snap-together building blocks. You can make them into the combination dinosaur/Toyota 4Runner Morph-o-Block Monster depicted on the box, or you can use the blocks to make all sorts of things the designers never envisioned—speedboats, three-dimensional sculptures of Sandra Bullock, a cityscape of Chicago, or a futuristic moon base.

What are we babbling about? You can use your digital music files to make duplicate copies of Audio CDs. The process of copying data onto a CD is called *burning* a CD, much as ripping is copying data from a CD. By burning your own CDs, you can listen to The Painkillers' *Medicine for the Soul* both at home and in the car, or you can mix and match songs to make your own unique mix-tape discs. If you're a professional musician or you want to become one, you can arrange your tracks and create your own CD masters as well.

As you saw in Chapter 3, we're not breaking the law—personal, noncommercial copies are legal.

Prepping Your Computer

Thankfully, making CDs from digital music files is very simple. Often it's the easiest part of the entire process. The most important element is to be sure your PC is up to the challenge. Like in the ripping and encoding process, you'll need a computer that can handle the workload of transferring data from the computer's hard disk to the CD-RW drive in a steady and uninterrupted fashion. That's an important point: if, for any reason, the computer can't keep up with the rate at which the CD-RW drive needs the data, you get what's known as a *buffer underrun.* The CD you are copying data to is ruined, and you can discard it. It's now a coaster, and not a very good one at that. Glasses tend to get the CD all wet and everything slides around. It's a mess.

Although the majority of CD-RW drives connect to the PC internally using the old reliable IDE connector (the same cable that attaches to hard disks), it's not the only kind of CD-RW drive on the market. Here's a quick overview of the various drive formats you can choose from:

Interface	Typical Write/ Rewrite Speed	Pros and Cons
Parallel port	4X/4X	For older PCs and laptops. It works, but it's very slow. Not recommended.
IDE	16X/10X	Internal devices only. It's easy to install and quite inexpensive. Almost any IDE CD-RW drive will be more than fast enough for your needs.
SCSI	20X/10X	Very fast, but needs a special PC interface card. Worse, it can bc hard to install.

Interface	Typical Write/ Rewrite Speed	Pros and Cons
USB	8X/4X	A reasonable choice if you want an external drive that you can switch among several PCs or attach to a laptop. Easy to install, but sluggish.
FireWire	16X/10X	Among external drives, a FireWire device is quite fast and can be self-powered (so there's no need for an AC adapter), but it needs a PC with FireWire built in or a special FireWire interface card. Sometimes hard to install.

With that in mind, here's a short checklist to get your computer ready to rock:

- **Have enough RAM** In general, we recommend having no less than 128MB of RAM to create CDs. More than that is overkill, because lots of memory benefits users who multitask—and, as you'll see, we don't want you to run multiple programs when you copy.
- **Prepare your hard disk** Remember how we suggested that you defragment your hard disk way back in Chapter 10? The advice still holds. If your PC has to skip around the hard disk to find data when writing to the CD, you can end up with a coaster. Also, make sure that your hard disk has lots of free space—empty the trash and delete large, unneeded files.
- **Check for software updates** It's a good idea to make sure that your PC is using the latest drivers for your CD-RW drive, video controller, and sound system. You might also want to check with the manufacturer's Web site for software updates for your CD software.
- **Minimize running programs** Shut down any applications that you don't have to be running, especially software that can proactively start doing stuff in the middle of the write session. That includes your mail program, antivirus software, and productivity tools like a word processor. Games? Don't even think about it.
- **Don't use the PC** When you start running the CD creation software, back away slowly from the PC. Don't touch the mouse, don't touch the keyboard. Don't run any software. Don't even look at the computer if you can avoid it. The trick is to give your computer some space and let it do its thing without worrying about handling multiple applications.

Choosing Your Discs

If you've ever visited a computer, music, or office supply store, you have no doubt seen that several kinds of discs are available. Specifically, you can choose CD-R or CD-RW discs, and some are clearly marked as audio discs, while others are identified as data discs. How to choose?

CD-R and CD-RW discs are fundamentally different animals. They use different physical mechanisms to record data and have two different applications. The following sections describe the key distinctions between them.

CD-R

CD-R is a common and inexpensive standard for home CD duplication. A CD-R disc can be written once, but read a nearly unlimited number of times. The bottom line is that you cannot erase data from a CD-R and start over; if you no longer need a CD-R or make an error during the copy phase, just throw it away. On the plus side, CD-R discs are very inexpensive; you can get them in bulk for as little as $.50/disc—sometimes even less if you find a deal that includes a rebate. If you buy CDs without the jewel case, you'll save even more money. The jewel case and packaging is virtually the most expensive component.

The physics behind CD-R discs is fairly simple. Blank discs come preconfigured with a microscopically thin layer of photosensitive dye, which is a material that can be burned into little pits when the laser fires. These pits form the zeros, and the unburned regions of dye are the ones in the digital code that is your music. A spiral-shaped track is also engineered into the disc; this track guides the CD-R drive's laser like a toy racecar in a racing track. As the laser follows the track during the burn process, changes in the laser's power create the pits, and when you're done, you have a CD-R that can be read in any ordinary CD player.

CD-RW

Unlike CD-R discs, CD-RWs can be erased and reused just like floppy discs. CD-R discs can't be reused because the burn process destroys the dye, permanently etching pits in the surface. CD-RW discs, on the other hand, use a different kind of material that simply changes state when excited by a laser. The effect is not permanent and can be changed many thousands of times.

The bottom line: the data on a CD-RW is stable until you insert it into the CD-RW drive and intentionally erase or change it. The rewritability comes at a cost, though—each disc sells for several dollars. (Rick claims he's seen them for a buck apiece, but it's important to remember that he lives in a magical place where the normal rules of physics don't always apply. And our tech editor, Brian Nadel, agrees with him. They're both insane, I say!)

Worse, few standard CD players can read a CD-RW disc because they don't reflect the laser light in the player nearly as well as CD-R discs do.

Audio and Data Discs

That said, it should be obvious that you'll want to use CD-R discs most often. You can make CD-RW discs for music that play on your PC, but that's kind of silly: the discs won't work in regular CD players, and the discs are expensive anyway. Stick with CD-Rs. But when you venture into a store, you may find different CD-R packages marked as data discs and as audio discs. What's the difference?

None—except that audio discs are taxed by the Recording Industry Association of America (RIAA) to help compensate copyright holders for lost revenue due to music pirating. In other words, don't buy these discs unless you like making charitable donations to record companies. Data CD-R discs (if they're not explicitly marked as audio discs, assume they're data discs) work just fine.

TIP *Looking for good deals on blank CD-R media? Point your Web browser to PriceGrabber (www.pricegrabber.com), and then drill down into Computers | Accessories | Media Storage. We found a 100-pack selling for just $35, and a 50-pack for just $23.*

CD-R Speed

When it comes to burning discs, faster is better. If it usually takes 20 minutes to create a CD and you can now make the same disc in 5 minutes, you'd take the faster speed, right? Well, four factors contribute to the maximum speed you can burn:

- **Computer performance** If your hard disk, processor, or memory configuration isn't up to snuff, your burn sessions will end in buffer underruns; or it'll default to a slower speed so everything works without a hitch. Make sure your PC is optimized before you start burning.
- **Software limitations** Sometimes the fully registered version of your software will burn faster than the shareware version. It helps to pay for the software you like to get the most out of it.
- **CD-RW drive** For most users, this is the key limitation. CD-RW drives are typically described by a trio of numbers, like this: 12X/10X/32X. The first number refers to the CD-R write speed; the second number is the CD-RW rewrite speed; the third number is the normal CD read speed. You can create discs as fast as your CD-RW drive's performance rating. For more details on CD-RW drives, check out Chapter 2.
- **CD-R disc speed** Discs are manufactured to specific tolerances to perform adequately at certain speeds. A 4X CD-R disc, for instance, should work fine in a 4X drive, and may even work OK at 6X, but ask it to keep up with a drive trying to write at 8X, and you may end up with a coaster. Look up the speed of your CD-RW drive (the first number in the drive's speed stats) and buy discs that are that speed or faster.

Choosing a Data Format

Now that you have your PC configured, a CD-RW drive installed, and a stack of CD-R discs of the proper type and speed handy, it's almost time to record. You have two options available:

14

- **Audio CD** A standard Audio CD—the kind you buy in a music store—is called an Audio CD or, more formally, a Red Book Audio CD. The Red Book specification describes exactly how data is recorded, stored, and read from standard audio discs. Audio CDs can store only about 80 minutes of music because the sound is written in uncompressed WAV files. An Audio CD can be read on virtually any traditional device, though: PCs with CD-ROM drives, CD players, DVD players, car stereos, and more.
- **Data CD** You can also store music on CD-R discs in data form, as if the CD was just a hard disk, floppy, or Zip drive. Instead of Red Book format and uncompressed WAVs, the files are packed in MP3 format. Considering

> CDs can hold 700MB of data, that's about a dozen hours of audio, or a dozen vinyl LPs. Your data CD can be read by your PC's CD-ROM drive, CD-based portable MP3 players, and car stereos with special CD/MP3 playback hardware. But that's it—ordinary car stereos and CD players won't be able to make sense out of the data on these discs.

You can see the difference in the file structure quite readily in Figure 14-1. On the left is what you see when you peer into an Audio CD in Windows. Only a few huge files live in there. An MP3 disc, on the right, can be filled with hundreds of small, compressed MP3 files.

Now that you've decided on a format, let's start burning.

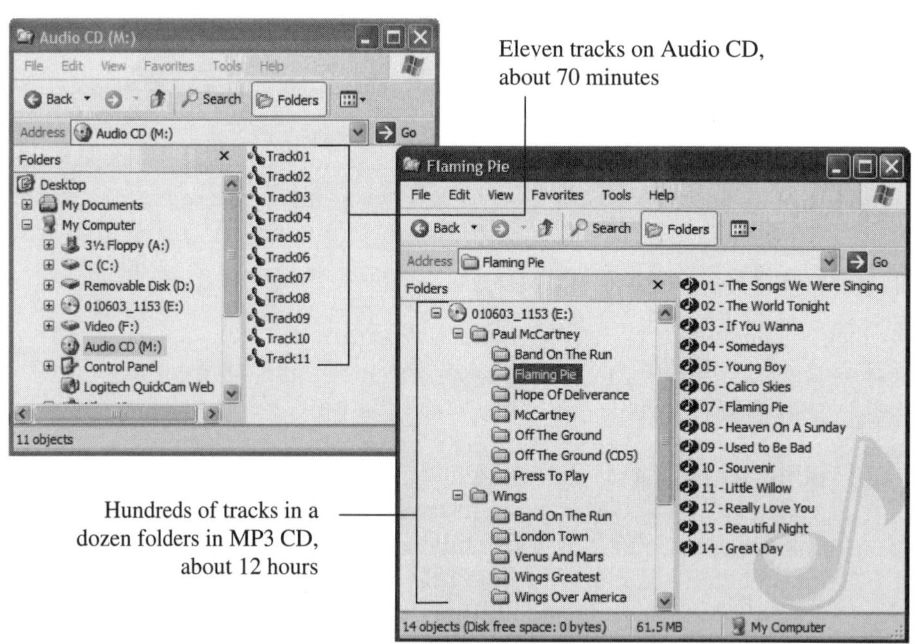

FIGURE 14-1 MP3 CDs hold a lot more music, but they are playable only in a limited number of devices.

Recording with Easy CD Creator

One of the most popular tools for making recordings on CD is a program called Easy CD Creator, from Roxio. It's bundled with the majority of CR-RW drives and is also available on its own in computer stores and via the Internet (www.roxio.com). Truth be told, we don't think there's a good reason to mess with anything else; Easy CD Creator is simply an excellent program.

Prior to version 5.0, Easy CD Creator was sold by Adaptec.

Choosing Recording Options

Whether you use Easy CD Creator or another program, though, you need to select a number of key recording options before you go too far, so let's look at the major decisions you need to make.

Record from Image or Playlist

This decision is fundamentally important. Most of the time, you'll just record a CD from a playlist (or tracklist) of song files on your hard disk. The computer will have to feed data to the CD-RW drive, switching from one track to the next in a continuous stream of data to keep the CD-RW drive happy. Most PCs can handle this without a glitch, but some slower PCs can burn coasters in this way, especially if the CD-RW drive is trying to copy data very fast—like 10X or 12X.

Your alternative is to avoid writing directly from the individual tracks to the CD. Instead, you can create a CD disc image file first. In Easy CD Creator, you arrange the songs you want to record (more on that later) and then select File | Create CD Hard Drive Image. The software will create a "virtual" CD on your PC's hard disk. Later, select File | Record CD From CD Image to burn that single, finished, large file to your CD-R disc.

The advantage of the image method is that it's almost foolproof, even in situations where your PC chokes trying to make CDs the normal way with a very fast CD-RW drive. The downside is that CD images are huge; they're the same size as the finished CD, which is 650MB. You'll need to have a lot of free hard disk space for this strategy to work.

NOTE

Because an image takes up a lot of disk space and is used only once, using this technique can often fragment a hard disk very quickly and require more maintenance.

Track- or Disc-At-Once

You can burn the CD using either of two recording methods, Track-At-Once or Disc-At-Once. In general, you'll probably want to use the Track-At-Once method unless you are duplicating the disc and the production facility specifically requests a Disc-At-Once master. Here's the difference between these methods:

- **Track-At-Once** recording is less demanding on your PC because it allows the CD-RW drive to turn off the laser and "breathe" between tracks. This method automatically inserts a two-second pause between songs.
- **Disc-At-Once** recording leaves the laser on and records the entire disc in a single pass, meaning there's more required of the PC and the CD-RW drive. Older PCs may burn coasters using this method. Disc-At-Once also avoids the two-second pause between tracks, so if you want a silent leader between tracks, you'll need to add it manually to the individual music files using audio editing software (as discussed in Chapter 12).

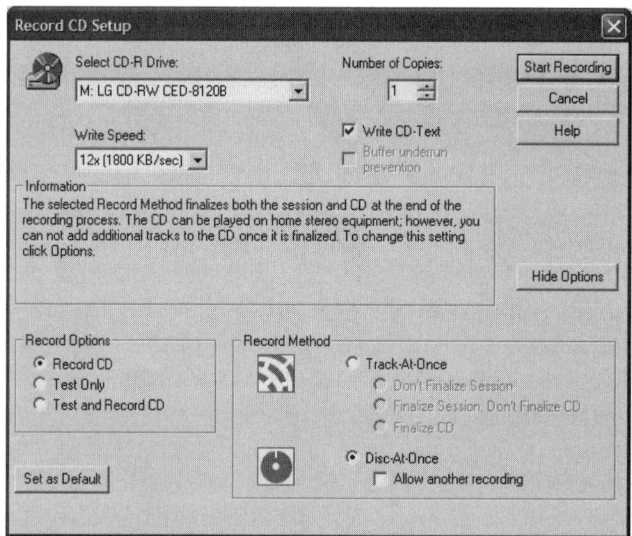

Understanding Sessions

The last major option you need to consider is disc sessions. *Sessions* are exactly what they sound like: you can record some data to CD in one session and return later to add more data to a different session.

Unfortunately, it's slightly more complicated than that. First of all, CD players recognize only the first session on a disc. So if you want to mix Audio CD and MP3 on the same disc, you can do that, but all the Audio CD files need to go into the first session.

After closing the session and creating a new session, you can put anything—MP3s, Word files, ham sandwiches, whatever—into another session and the CD player won't know or care. But any Audio CD tracks that end up in later sessions will likewise be invisible to the player.

That's why programs like Easy CD Creator give you some options. You can typically perform any of these actions when burning the CD:

- **Don't finalize the current session** That's right, you can leave the current session open. If you later add more tracks to the CD, they'll go in the same session and be visible to the CD player.
- **Finalize the session but don't finalize the CD** This closes the current session after writing tracks to the CD, so you can return later and put other stuff in a new session that's invisible to traditional CD players. If the CD is still "open," you can't play it in a CD player, but a PC will be able to read all the data just fine.
- **Finalize the CD** This closes the current session and finalizes the CD at the same time, making it readable in a CD player.

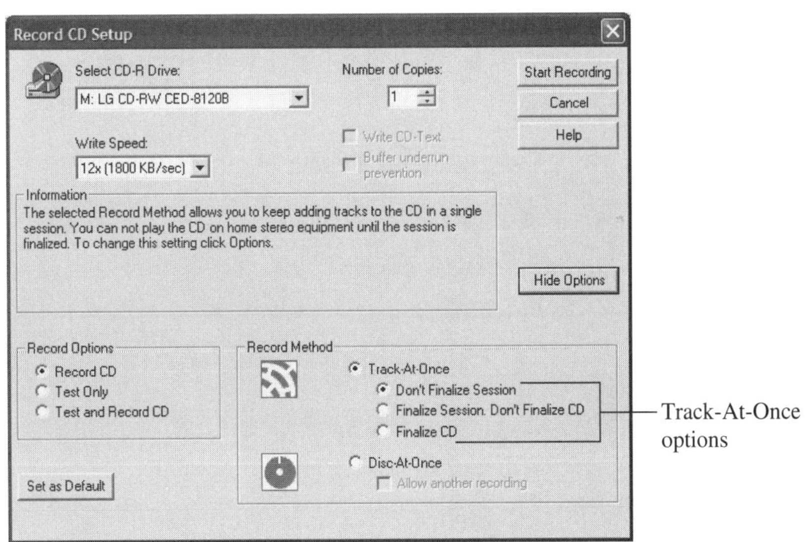

14

A CD player can read only the stuff stored in the disc's first session, but a PC can access the whole hamhock (to coin a new phrase). And while a PC can read data on an open CD just fine, you'll need to finalize the CD for it to be readable in a CD player.

Burning a CD

After all that, the actual mechanics of creating a music CD are pretty simple. Let's use Easy CD Creator 5 to walk through the process:

1. With Easy CD Creator already running, choose File | New CD Project | Music CD from the menu. You'll see your hard disk folders up top and a blank tracklist below.

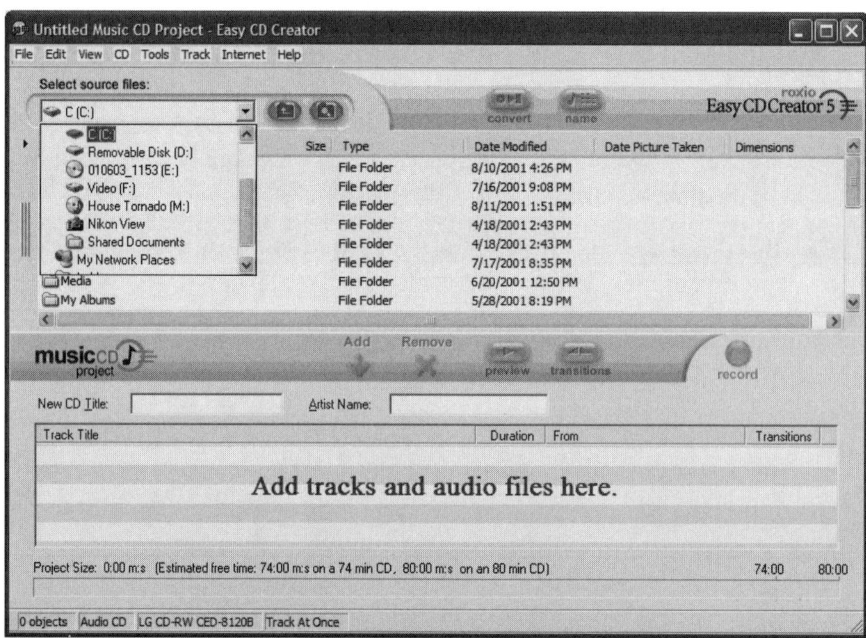

2. Locate songs on your hard disk and drag them to the track pane in the lower part of the window. Drag-and-drop each song that you want to include on the CD.

TIP *If you want to add every song in a particular folder to the CD, you can just drag-and-drop the folder instead.*

3. Arrange your songs by moving them with the mouse. You can arrange them in any order you like.
4. If you want to delete a song from the tracklist, simply select it with the mouse and press the Delete key. It won't delete the song from your hard disk, just from the future CD's playlist.
5. Keep an eye on the project size at the bottom of the screen. Don't exceed the maximum time allowed for the CD.

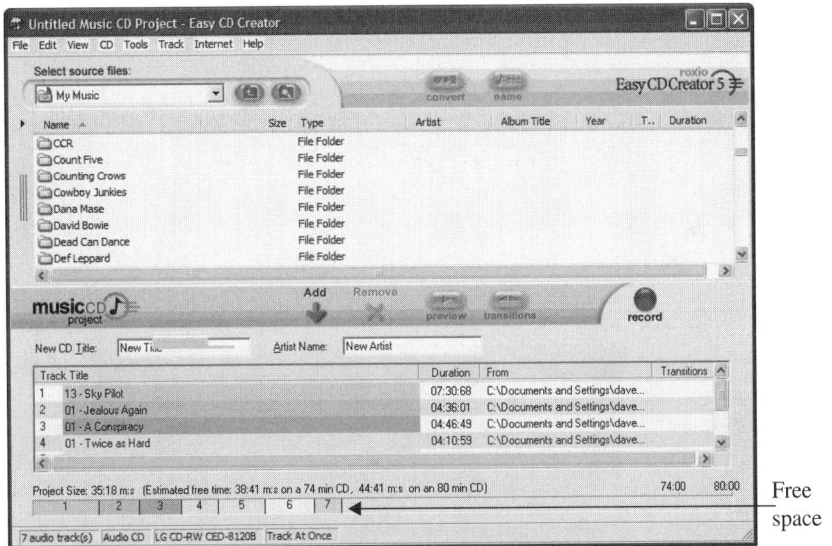

6. Some CD burners have transition effects. In Easy CD Creator 5, for instance, you can click the Transition button to make songs fade in and out.

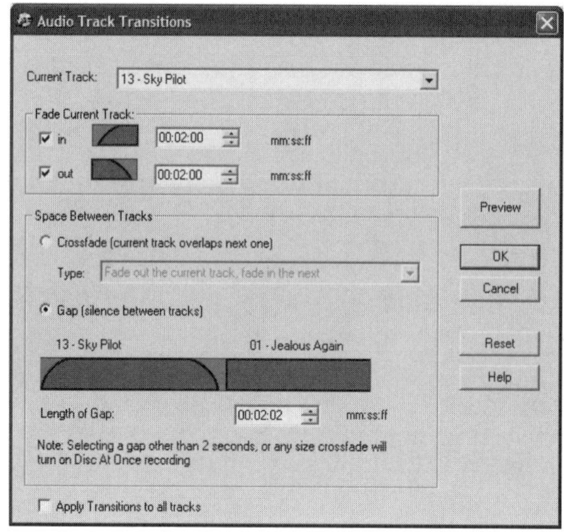

7. When all of your songs are arranged properly, it's time to record. Make sure there's a fresh, blank CD-R disk in the CD-RW drive and click the Record button.

If you want to record a CD image on your hard disk, don't click record—choose the appropriate option from the File menu.

8. In the Record CD Setup dialog box, make sure the CD-RW drive is selected and the write speed is no greater than the speed of the CD-R disc in the drive. Click the Options button.

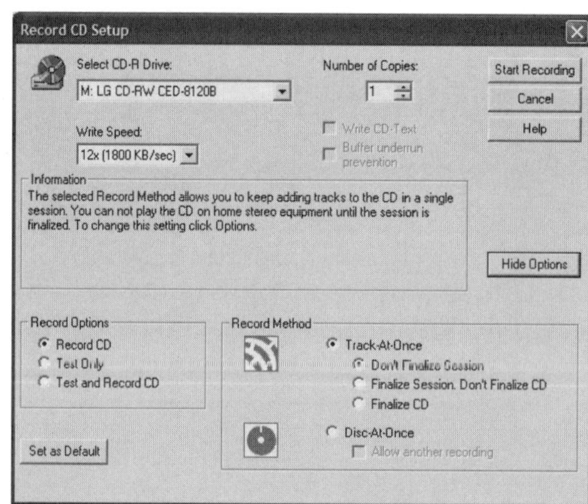

9. If you've never recorded before, you might want to run a performance test first. If you don't mind wasting a CD-R (they're cheap, after all), just go ahead and choose to record the CD. Also, select the Track-At-Once and session preference or choose Disc-At-Once.
10. Click Start Recording and leave your PC alone until it's done.

Making a Disc Image

As we mentioned before, you might want to make a disc image of the CD instead of writing the data to CD one track at a time. This strategy can help if you have a sluggish computer or a pokey hard disk. To do that, follow the directions for burning a CD until step 6, but don't click the Record button. Instead, do this:

1. Choose File | Create CD Hard Disk Image.

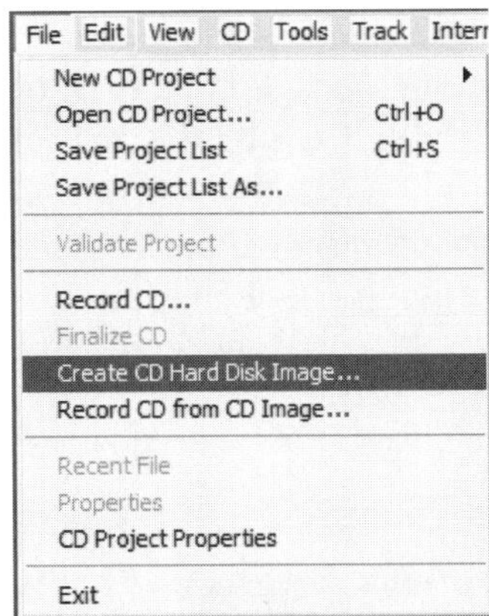

2. Select the location on your hard disk to save the image.

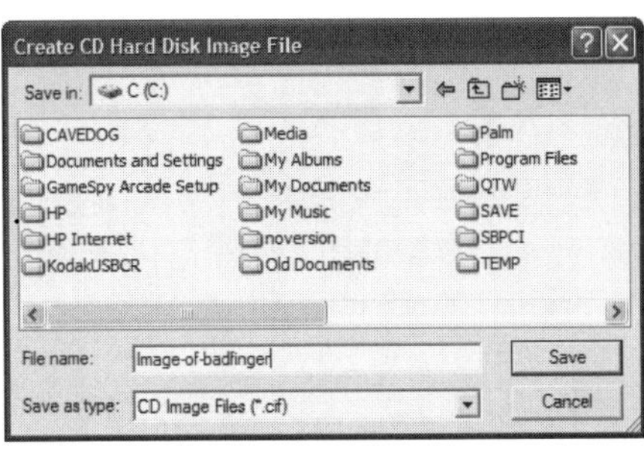

3. When the program is done writing the file, choose File | Record CD From CD Image.
4. Select the file you created in step 2.
5. Configure the Record CD Setup and click the Start Recording button.

Making an MP3 CD

The advantage of Audio CDs is that they'll play in any CD or DVD player—but because the data is stored in an uncompressed format, you get only about an hour's worth of music. If you have a player that can read data CDs loaded with MP3s, you might want to use that format instead. A typical CD-R filled with MP3s can play for about 11 or 12 hours. That can change your whole approach to music storage.

Filing-System Issues

Nothing is ever as simple as it should be, of course. In this case, you have to choose from two different filing systems. By default, most CD burners make CDs in a format known as *Joliet.* But it won't always do the trick for you. Here's the scoop:

- Joliet-formatted CDs support long filenames (like "02-My Baby Is Sweeter" for instance, from the inimitable John Mayall collection). Joliet-formatted CDs work in Windows PCs and most portable MP3 players we tried, but they don't work in Mac systems. If you want the disc to work across all platforms, try the next choice.
- ISO-9660 CDs work pretty much everywhere. The downside is that they don't support long filenames. Instead, they use the old 8+3 DOS convention. John Mayall's classic "My Baby Is Sweeter" becomes, in ISO-9660, "MYBABY~1.MP3." If you use a numbering system at the start of the filename, it gets worse: "02-MYB~1.MP3." So, if you have to rely on the ISO-9660 format, be careful to rename your files to be as understandable as possible.

Another important issue is that regardless of which format you use, most players will attempt to play music from the MP3 CD in alphabetical order. As a result, you might want to use filename and folder-name conventions with numbers at the beginning so they're ordered for playback the way you want. Even if you use the strategies discussed in Chapter 13 to number individual tracks, you might want to manually preface album names by year of release. Otherwise, Collective

Soul's *Blender* will play before *Dosage,* but anyone can tell you that they should be the other way around.

Making the MP3 CD

Creating a CD with MP3s is easy. Instead of using a program like Easy CD Creator in Music CD mode, you can simply create your CD in Data CD mode. Or, if your CD burner software has it, you can choose MP3 CD mode; either way, you're simply treating the CD like a floppy disk and copying data files.

Using Easy CD Creator, the process is similar to—but easier than—creating a music CD. Select File | New CD Project | Data CD and drag song files to the lower pane. When you're ready to burn the disc, click the Record button and configure the record options. Click Start Recording.

The Monkees Weren't so Bad

Dave: You may be surprised to hear me say this, but The Monkees are a closet favorite of mine. Sure, everyone knows they were a product of anonymous corporate greed: four actors thrown together for a show designed, in a fit of Hollywood high-concept design, to be a weekly TV version of the three-minute "Money Can't Buy Me Love" scene in the classic film *A Hard Day's Night,* designed expressly for 13-year-old girls. But The Monkees were so much more than that. They were all accomplished musicians: they indeed could (and sometimes did) play their own instruments. They created some of the tastiest pop songs of the decade (I still love "Sweet Young Thing" and "She," for instance). But they also made some totally overlooked music that pushed the cultural envelope. "Mommy and Daddy" is still worth a listen, even today. Too bad the band's heyday was already over by the time it was released. Heck, we all know that Mike Nesmith invented the music video, and for that, I can even forgive Davy's regrettable appearance on *The Brady Bunch.*

Rick: You realize this destroys every argument you've ever made about music. The Monkees were a manufactured band long before the Backstreet Boys you so despise. "She" wasn't even written by The Monkees (few of their popular songs were). And I can't believe you'd defend a band that so flagrantly ripped off your precious Beatles. Your crazy flip-flopping has forced me to go on the offensive, Monkee-wise, which is unfortunate, because I quite like The Monkees. Saw them live during their '80s comeback tour, in fact. Would you please go back to your predictable pop-bashing and let those of us who like pop get on with our lives?

Unlike in the Music CD mode, dragging a folder full of music to the CD will copy the folder and its contents, not just the contents. This allows you to organize the music on the CD into folders by artists, album, genre, or any other system you want to use.

Streaming Your Music from the Web

No doubt you know about streaming audio. By *streaming,* we mean that the music plays as it is downloaded to your computer—you needn't wait for the entire 3MB or 5MB file to arrive. In this way, it's like listening to the radio using the Internet, and we discussed this from a listener perspective back in Chapter 6.

You may not realize that it's a pretty simple task to create your own streaming music. Here are a few reasons why you might want to stream music from a Web site:

- It's easy. We'll show you how you can create an audio stream in less than 10 minutes.
- You get instant gratification. If you're an artist who's trying to make music available to fans via your Web site, streaming your tunes allows people to be listening within seconds of clicking a link instead of waiting for an entire song to download.
- You can protect your song. Streaming technology keeps end users from saving a copy of the song on their hard disks. While it's possible, with enough effort, to steal the song, it keeps basically honest folk from uploading your music to Napster-like music-sharing services.

Stream Without Extra Software

Lots of programs are available that let you package ordinary MP3 files into streaming audio, but you can do it without spending a penny or downloading anything. All you need is a Web design program, a way to upload files to the Web (such as with a file transfer protocol (FTP) program), and the Notepad program that comes with Windows. Here's what you need to do:

1. Upload the song that you want to stream to your Web site. We recommend putting it in a special folder, but you can put it anywhere. Using Dave's Web site as an example, you could put your song called Reservoir.mp3 in a folder called Music, as in http://www.bydavejohnson.com/music/reservoir.mp3.

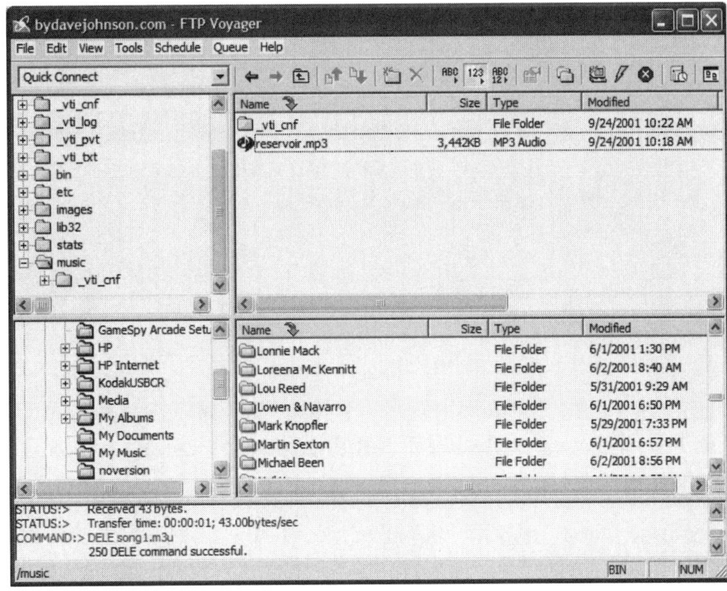

2. Now you need to create a file that tells Web browsers to stream the audio file instead of simply playing it. Open a plain, ordinary text editor like Notepad and create a line that details the exact file path to the MP3 file you just uploaded. Following the example we started with, all you should see in Notepad is this: http://www.bydavejohnson.com/music/reservoir.mp3.

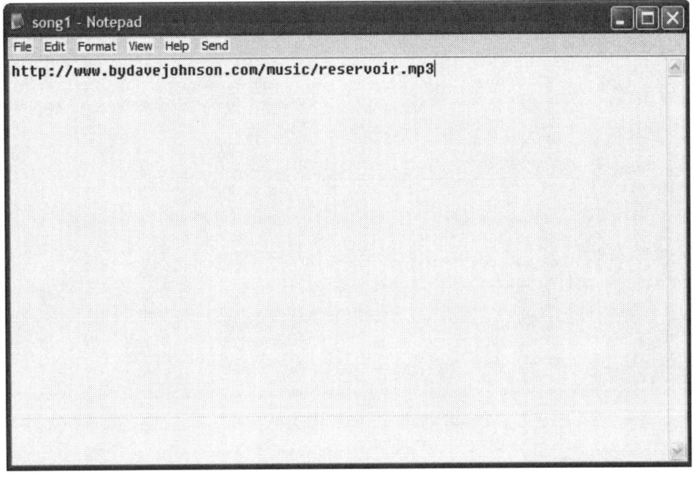

3. Save the file. Name it anything you like, but it needs to have an .m3u file extension. By default, Notepad will give the file a .txt file extension, so you have two choices: track the file down after you save it and change its extension in DOS (that's the hard way), or use quotes around the filename when you save it in Notepad to begin with (the easy way). Type something like this, **song1.m3u**, and click Save.

The name of the MP3 file doesn't have to appear in the M3U filename, although you might want to include it so various streaming files are easier to keep track of later.

4. Upload the M3U file to your Web site. You might want to put it in the same folder as the MP3 file itself, but that's not essential.
5. Create the Web page. Make it as simple or elaborate as you like, but the key ingredient is a link to the song in question. Create a link that says something like this: Listen To Reservoir. Link the word "Reservoir" to the M3U file.

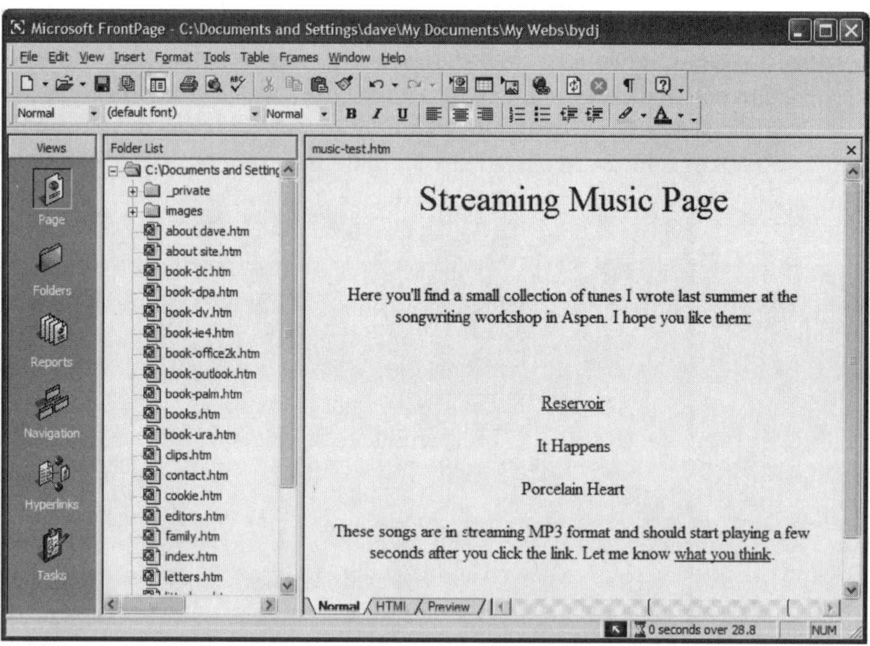

6. Save your Web page and upload it to your Web server.

That's it. Now go ahead and test it. Open a Web browser, surf to the page you just created, and click the link. The song should start playing.

There are a few disadvantages to creating streaming audio this way. For starters, it's all very manual. You have to create the M3U file, build the links, and so on. You might not be interested in that kind of interaction with a Web site.

In addition, you need to encode your MP3 song for whatever bit rate you want to stream the song at. This is important. If you stream a 128 Kbps MP3 file, it'll consume a lot of bandwidth and work well only on computers that have fast broadband Internet connections; slow modem users will just hear lots of annoying stuttering. As a result, you need to encode your streaming audio at a lower bit rate, like 64 Kbps or even slower. It can be a pain to maintain several copies of the same song to accommodate slower Web users.

Finally, M3U streaming isn't extremely efficient, and if too many people try to listen to the song simultaneously, your Web server won't be able to keep up. That's why there are some commercial alternatives to building your own M3U files.

Using Streaming Production Software

A variety of programs are available that help you encode digital audio (and video, for that matter) into a streaming format for the Web. If the M3U approach we just talked about isn't up your alley, try one of these programs:

RealProducer

This excellent program lets you encode digital music and video files into the fairly ubiquitous RealPlayer format. The program also includes a Web page builder that can create and publish a Web page with all the hard work of integrating the streaming audio already done for you.

RealProducer is particularly appealing because in addition to a commercial version (RealProducer Plus, for $199), there's a somewhat more limited, free version as well, called RealProducer Basic. If you want to try your hand at streaming audio from a Web site, definitely give RealProducer Basic a shot. You can download it at www.realnetworks.com.

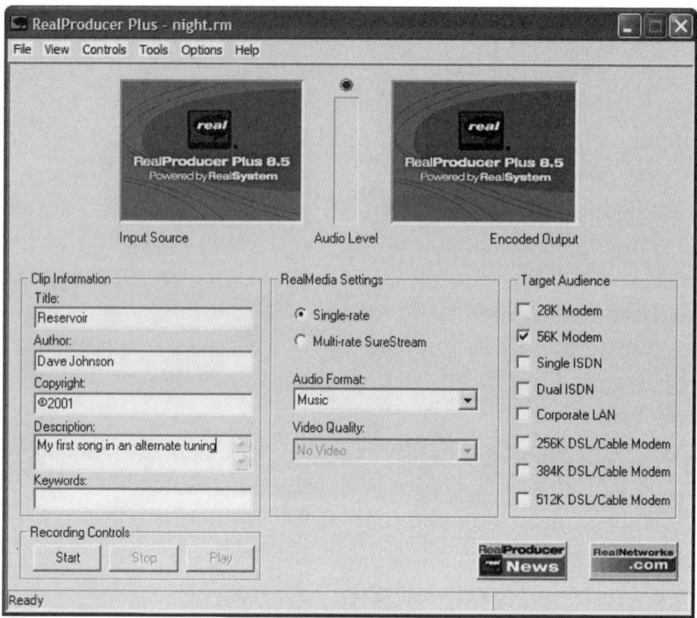

Stream Anywhere

Although there's no free version of Sonic Foundry's Stream Anywhere like there is of RealProducer, this program has other advantages. We especially like the fact that Stream Anywhere includes audio editing tools. You can load an audio file into Stream Anywhere and cut away parts at the beginning or the end, as well as establish a fade-in and fade-out. You can normalize the audio and even adjust equalization levels.

When you're ready to burn your audio into the final streaming format, Stream Anywhere also has more options that RealProducer. You can create ASF streaming files (which work with Windows Media Player) or more traditional RealPlayer files. Stream Anywhere is available for $149 from www.sonicfoundry.com.

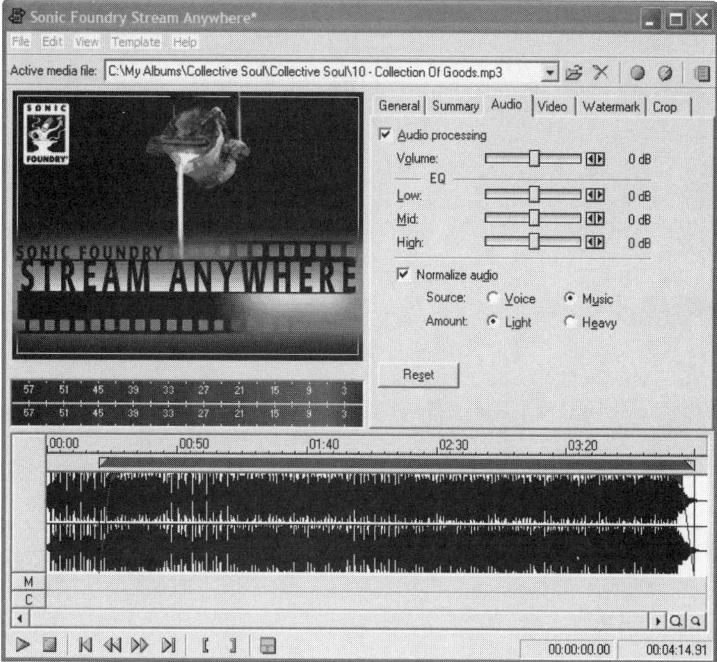

Chapter 15

Sharing Your Music Online

How to...

- Find an audience for your music on MP3.com
- Copyright your music on MP3.com
- Make money from your music on MP3.com
- Promote your music on MP3.com
- Get your songs played on Internet radio stations
- Broadcast your music worldwide using SHOUTcast

So you've just blown your savings to put your musical stylings on a CD, and now you need a big record company to come along with lots of money and a ticket to stardom. Sorry to break this to you, but fame and fortune aren't going to come knocking on your door. You need to get out there and share your sound with the world. Then you can make the big bucks, attract the attention of major record labels, land a huge contract, and wind up in the third row with your fingers crossed at next year's Grammy awards.

MP3.com (www.mp3.com) hasn't produced any success stories quite like that, but it has helped plenty of virtual unknowns sell their albums, attract a worldwide audience, and even land contracts with major labels. If you're hoping to make it as a musician, MP3.com should be one of your first stops.

As discussed at length in Chapter 4, MP3.com is a music portal that gives users access to over a million songs and provides a wealth of digital-music services. For the artist, however, MP3.com is also an unparalleled resource for promotion, sales, licensing, and even copyright protection. In this chapter, we introduce you to these and other Artist services. We also tell you more about SHOUTcast (first discussed in Chapter 6), a free service that enables you to create an Internet radio station where you can broadcast your music to the world.

What MP3.com Can Do for You

At the risk of sounding like PR weasels, we think MP3.com is the single best Internet resource for the budding band or musician. Whether you're a gal with a guitar or the trumpet player in a six-piece jazz ensemble, you'll find a wealth of invaluable resources at this site. Let's take a look at some of the highlights.

The Premium Artist Service

While many of MP3.com's Artist offerings are free, there are benefits to enrolling in the company's $19.99-per-month Premium Artist Service (PAS). For instance, all uploaded songs must be approved for content, and PAS membership moves them to a priority queue for faster processing. Similarly, your songs are reviewed first for inclusion in special MP3.com promotions (CDs, radio shows, newsletters, and the like) that can lead to greater exposure. PAS also enables you to participate in the Payback for Playback program, which lets you earn money each time an MP3.com visitor plays one of your songs.

Payback for Playback

As you learned in Chapter 4, you can listen to streaming songs while perusing MP3.com. If you're enrolled in the Payback for Playback program (which requires a PAS membership), you earn half a cent every time a listener plays one of your songs. Half a cent may not sound like much—and it isn't—but consider that MP3.com receives nearly three million page views per week. According to the company, one artist earned $37,000 in the program. That's not bad for doing absolutely nothing.

The Copyright Wizard

It's your music. You wrote it, you performed it, you own the rights to it. But unless you're also a lawyer, you probably have no idea how to go about copyrighting it. MP3.com's Copyright Wizard is designed to take the hassle (and high cost) out of the process by walking you through the necessary steps. You don't have to fiddle with paper forms, and the whole procedure takes only about 10 minutes. You can receive up to $150,000 in statutory damages if there's an infringement on your copyright. MP3.com charges $69.95 for the registration of a CD or collection of songs, and that includes the manufacturing of a CD copy of your work, an audit of your online registration forms, and more.

The Music Licensing Program

Just imagine hearing your song the next time you see a commercial for Diet Coke. MP3.com's Music Licensing Program makes your music available to producers, directors, ad agencies, and other folks in the movie, TV, and commercial businesses. Cash, connections, and exposure are among the possibilities, and you have total control over whether you accept or reject offers. Annual membership in the program costs $25.

The CD Program

This is one of MP3.com's core programs, and the one that's most likely to put money in your pocket. Put simply, you upload your songs to MP3.com, and the company turns them into a CD (one that contains both CD audio and MP3 files) that can be purchased directly from your Artist page. The CD will include a jewel case, a four-color insert booklet you can create yourself, and multimedia features for PC users. Buyers can also opt to purchase a netCD, which deposits your songs into their MP3.com library. (This costs buyers less because there's no CD to manufacture, and enables them to listen immediately because there's no CD to be delivered.) You earn a full 50 percent of each CD and netCD sold. MP3.com handles all the production, processing, shipping, and so forth. Better still, it costs nothing to participate in this program, and you can yank your CD if you sign a big record deal. MP3.com even provides you with reports so you can track your sales.

Promo Auctions

With over 150,000 artists vying for attention on MP3.com, how can you put your name in front of more listeners? One way is with Promo Auctions, which let you bid to win placement on high-profile areas of the site. At press time, MP3.com offered eight separate auctions, meaning you have the option of marketing yourself in whatever way you think is best. For instance, you can try to win a spot on the MP3.com home page, which could give you exposure to up to three million visitors. And then there's the Payola Auction, in which you vie for one of ten weekly spots on your song's top-genre page.

Promoting Your Music on Ampcast.com

If MP3.com is the Hollywood of online music, Ampcast.com (www.ampcast.com) is the Telluride Film Festival. It's a small, respectable, independent site that allows music fans to hear and download songs from a growing community of artists. For the artist, it offers a royalty program that's potentially much more lucrative than MP3.com's, plus a comprehensive CD program.

Becoming a registered artist on Ampcast.com costs $25 annually. That entitles you to the following.

Royalties

Ampcast.com pays you six cents every time a listener downloads one of your songs. It's not a fortune, but it beats the half cent you get from MP3.com (though, admittedly, MP3.com draws quite a bit more traffic).

The CD Program

Ampcast.com manufactures shrink-wrapped CDs on demand, meaning you don't pay anything up front. There are too many details to cover here, but there are

Five Best Band Names We Just Made Up

Rick: One of Dave's favorite hobbies is making up band names. Yes, he does need to get out more. But in the spirit of indulgence, I hereby serve up my own list of band names that don't exist (as far as I know) but should:

- The Balled-Up Socks
- That's Good Squishy
- The Manic-Depressive Girl Band with Lead Singer Who Will Soon Leave to Produce Even More Manic-Depressive Solo Records
- There Is No Spoon
- The Groundskeeper Willies

Dave: I'm touched that Rick would think to include this topic in the book, but I point out that he has, once again, ripped off one of my ideas and called it his own. "There Is No Spoon"? Come on!!! That's mine! Anyway, here goes:

- Spock's Brain
- Psychedelic Depression
- Worms!
- Hillary's Butler
- The Jazz Stoppers

numerous production options and prices available—and it ultimately falls to you to set the sale price of your CD. Ampcast.com sells the CDs directly through your page on the site.

Ad-Free Pages

No distracting banner ads appear on your personal Ampcast.com page. That helps present a more professional look to visitors to your page.

Ratings and Sales Data

Ampcast.com provides charts based on listeners' ratings, not the number of "listens" or downloads. Ostensibly, that gives you better feedback about your music than MP3.com's system, which does focus on the number of listens or downloads. Additionally, Ampcast.com charts the activity of your music and provides sales tracking and reporting.

Fast Song Approval

The service promises approval of your uploads "within minutes." MP3.com doesn't specify how long it takes to get approval, but receives "several thousand" songs per day. You do the math.

Concert and Event Calendars

Your fans need to know where and when to find you. Here's a simple and effective way to add a calendar to your Artist page.

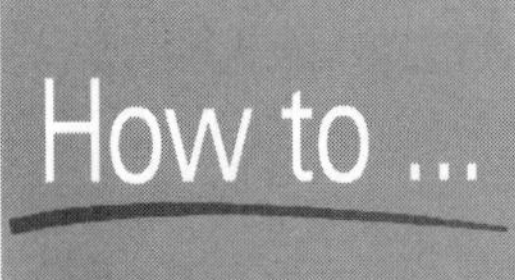

Convert Your CD into MP3 Files

Although we addressed this in Chapter 11, it bears repeating here. If you've decided to sell your music online via a service like MP3.com or Ampcast.com, the single most important step is turning your songs into MP3 files (so you have something to sell). Assuming you already have a CD, it's a pretty simple matter—just grab a utility like CDex (available from www.download.com). In one fell swoop, it rips songs from CDs and converts them to MP3 files ready for uploading. And it's a freebie!

Getting Your Songs on Internet Radio

Before the days of MTV, a band or artist was most likely to be "discovered" on the radio. That happens to a lesser extent these days, but it still happens. Problem is, you can't just send your CD to the local station and expect it to get played. (You might have some luck with college stations, assuming your music qualifies as alternative.) Thank goodness for the Internet, the great equalizer. As discussed in Chapter 6, Internet radio stations are plentiful and varied—and if you play your cards right, they could help you hit the big time (or at least a bigger small time).

If you need proof that Internet radio can lead to sales, consider something that happened to Rick while researching this book. While listening to a big band station, he heard a song by female jazz vocalist Lavay Smith, instantly fell in love with her sound, located her Web site, and ordered one of her CDs on the spot.

So, how do you get your songs played on the major Internet radio stations? Unfortunately, because many stations have playlists that come directly from major music labels and/or distributors, sometimes the only way onto the list is to be an artist signed with one of those labels. We can't tell you how to accomplish that (that's what your agent is for), but we can tell you how to get your songs played on the Internet—by broadcasting them yourself.

Create Your Own Internet Radio Station on SHOUTcast

Any good self-promoting Web site for a band or artist should include some music samples that listeners can easily access. Making a few songs available for download is one obvious option—but if you'd rather sell the cow than give the milk away for free (OK, so we butchered the metaphor—we haven't had our coffee yet), consider creating your own Internet radio station.

This process is relatively easy thanks to SHOUTcast, a Winamp offshoot (see Chapter 6) that enables you to broadcast streaming MP3 files—effectively creating a custom Internet radio station. The tools you need to accomplish this are free—the only costs are a bit of time and study. Oh, you also need a computer—preferably a spare one that's not being used for anything else—and a broadband Internet connection.

Installing the SHOUTcast Plug-In for Winamp

The first step in creating your SHOUTcast station is downloading and installing a small plug-in file for Winamp. Here's how:

1. Visit the SHOUTcast Web site (www.shoutcast.com).

2. Click the Download SHOUTcast link, and then find and download the SHOUTcast Source for Winamp DSP plug-in—a small file that acts as a bridge between the Winamp software and your SHOUTcast server (that is, your PC).
3. Verify that Winamp is not running, and then double-click the downloaded file to install it. Follow the instructions presented.
4. Start Winamp, press CTRL-P to open the Preferences window, and then click the DSP/Effect item under Plug-Ins. You should see SHOUTcast Source For Winamp in the right pane.

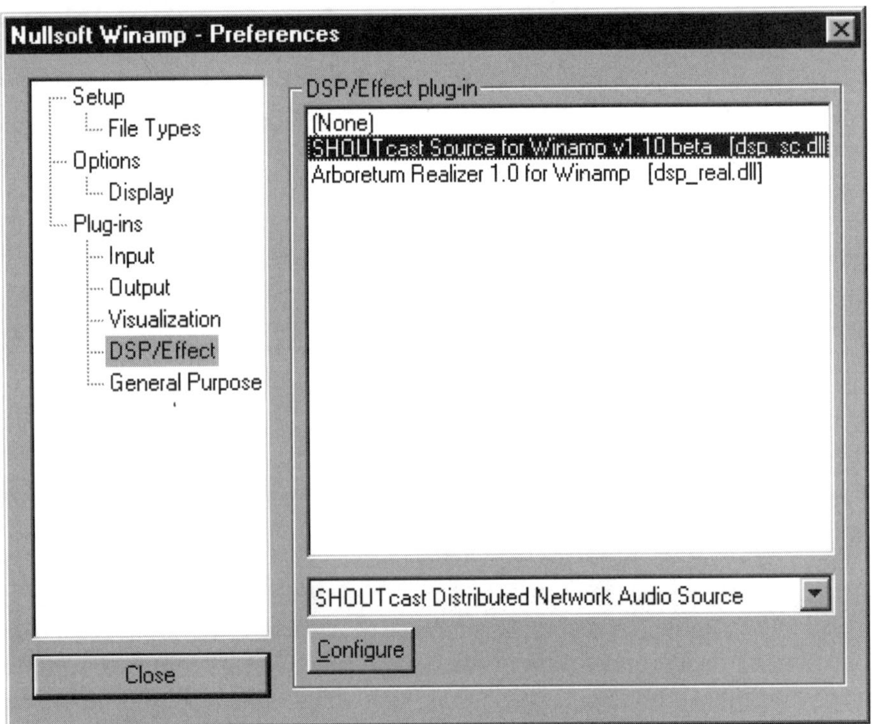

Installing the SHOUTcast Server Software

The second software element is SHOUTcast Server, which is available for a variety of platforms (including Windows 9x/NT/2000, FreeBSD, Linux, and Solaris—sorry, Mac users). You can download it from the SHOUTcast Web site. Follow the installation instructions presented there.

As you'll find amidst those instructions, configuring your SHOUTcast server can be a bit complicated. Unless you're a card-carrying IT guru, you may need to enlist the help of a friend or contractor who specializes in this sort of thing. Anyone worth their salt should be able to get your server up and running—and provide you with the link that will ultimately end up on your Web site—within two hours.

When that step is complete, you'll be able to select the MP3 files you want to be a part of your station—and even broadcast live events.

Promoting Your Sound

How to...

- Get your CD into stores
- Get a UPC code for your CD
- Accept payment for your music
- Select a duplication service for your CD
- Make your Web site distinctive
- Promote yourself with press releases
- Contact your fans via e-mail
- Make the most of advice from independent artists

Now what? You're a musician. Maybe you have your sights set on *Star Search.* (Is that show still on the air? We really have no idea...) Or maybe you just like creating tunes in your basement and want some friends to hear them. Whatever the case, being able to create your own CD full of original music and actually promoting yourself are two very different tasks. And artists, by their very nature, often are the worst at self-promotion.

This last chapter of the book takes a look at some of the "Now what?" issues that might help you build awareness of your art. To write this chapter, we did all the normal research, but Dave also chatted with a half dozen of the most exciting independent artists around today: people who not only have a great sound, but who know how to use technology to their best advantage. Hopefully, there's something in this chapter to help you on your road to musical success.

Selling Your CD

Recording a CD—even in a basement studio—can be only half the battle. Unless you want to simply hang it on the wall and admire its circularness, you may want to duplicate the discs and sell them. It's not hard to put your music up for sale, but it entails a little extra work after the music is mixed and laid down onto the CD.

Online Stores That'll Sell Your CD

Online music and media stores are a good place to establish sales, because you don't have to deal with the traditional distribution and sales channels of "brick and mortar" stores. Many online stores will stock your CD. The following sections describe a few of the most common.

Amazon.com

Amazon works with lots of independent publishers and artists through the Advantage program. Products sold through the Amazon Advantage program are bought and advertised exactly the same way as mainstream products like Harry Potter books and Nirvana albums, but Amazon deals directly with you to get shipments of CDs. The Advantage program is free to enter, and you get a percentage of all sales. For information, visit www.amazon.com/advantage.

MP3.com

While MP3.com has had its share of legal worries over the last few years, it remains one of the top locations for MP3 listeners, with about 10 million visitors per month. The site is a massive library of independent artists arranged by music genres (see Figure 16-1). You can add your band to the site for free. Each artist site lets visitors listen to your music online in streaming format as well as purchase your CDs. In fact, MP3.com even has the ability to duplicate and sell discs for you (see Chapter 15).

FIGURE 16-1 You can make your own home on MP3.com so new fans can find you.

Your Own Site

You have a Web site, right? You can sell your CDs from your own online home, although you'll need to take care of some of the gory business details that the big guys would otherwise do for you. Most importantly, you need to come up with a payment system.

Essential Resources for Musicians

We asked The Painkillers' Cherish Alexander for a list of the top seven (why seven? Don't bother us with trivialities) online resources that she'd recommend for budding musicians trying to make it in the music business. Here's what she gave us:

1. The Velvet Rope (www.velvetrope.com)
2. Mi2n (www.mi2n.com)
3. Band Radio (bandradio.com)
4. Artist Direct/Ultimate Band List (ubl.artistdirect.com)
5. Andrew's Entertainment Industry Contacts (www.geocities.com/SunsetStrip/Club/1484/menu.htm)
6. Internet Music Resource Guide (www.specialweb.com/music)
7. Music Business Solutions (www.mbsolutions.com)

Accepting Payment

If you choose to sell your music through your own site, you'll need to work out some way to accept payment from customers. Depending on how much money you care to invest, how much hassle you want to put your customers through, and the overall sales volume you expect, you have three options: you can choose just one or implement all three.

Personal Check

A lot of artists' Web sites accept personal checks. This is the easiest solution from your point of view, but it has some disadvantages:

- **Check writing is a hassle** When you buy something on the Web, you typically want to click a few times and be done. A check must be mailed, though, which means the transaction can't be completed on the Web site. That can cost you sales—some folks will just give up rather than write a check and pop it in the mail.
- **Delayed gratification** Not only does a check take a few days to travel through the mail, but you might want to let it clear before mailing off your CD, and that can add up to a few weeks to complete the transaction.
- **You're liable** If you don't wait for the check to clear, it can be hard to recover the money for a bounced check if you mail off your CD and later find you got stiffed.

Credit Card Processing

Online credit card processing has gotten a lot easier in the last few years, and most local banks as well as a lot of online services can help you set up a merchant account. The downside is that merchant accounts cost money, and low CD sales may not really make up for the recurring costs of having the account to begin with. If you're still interested, check out charge.com or your local bank for details on creating a credit card merchant account. If you don't sell many discs, you might be better off letting MP3.com sell your music for you.

PayPal

Billed as "the way to send and receive money online," PayPal is the closest thing on the Internet to electronic money. PayPal is a sort of online bank that allows people to e-mail cash back and forth, and PayPal takes care of the details of transferring funds in and out of real bank accounts. You can use your Web site to accept PayPal payments. Many online users already know about and use PayPal (it's popular on eBay, for instance) and will happily send you PayPal funds, which you can withdraw easily to convert into real money.

Finishing Touches for Your CD

Just because you've recorded about 70 minutes of music doesn't mean the disc is done. You still need to worry about mastering and duplication, artwork, and legal/technical details to get it into a store. Consider some of these tips.

Mastering and Duplicating Discs

While you don't have to deliver a CD-R version of your audio CD in finished form to a duplicating service, that's increasingly common. If you prefer, though, many duplicators accept music in a variety of formats, including DAT and analog tape. If you choose to master your own disc, though, you should check with the duplicator to make sure you're sending a disc in the form they need. Some duplicators require Disc-At-Once instead of Track-At-Once format, for instance; see Chapter 14 for details on the difference between the two.

More CD duplication services are out there than you can shake a really big stick at. Be sure you do some comparison shopping and know exactly what you're buying. Here are some of the options CD duplicators can offer you:

- **Plain CDs** By omitting the jewel case, you can cut costs, but you'll have little in the way of packaging.

- **Silkscreened CDs** CDs with 1-, 2-, or 3-color silkscreen artwork finish provide nice packaging. You can finish the CD with a silkscreen logo or graphic, although this can add significantly to the price. Check out examples of silkscreened CDs in Figure 16-2.
- **Packaging** If you can deliver the appropriate artwork to the duplicator, you can have 1- to 4-color sleeves, inserts, lyric sheets, and shrinkwrap.

Typical CD pricing should look like this. If the quotes you get for a duplication are dramatically different, you might want to ask some questions.

CD Quantity	CD Costs (Includes Silkscreen Artwork)	Packaging Costs (Jewel Case and 2-Color Art)
1000	.65 each	.24 each
5000	.55 each	.24 each
10,000	.50 each	.20 each

FIGURE 16-2 Artwork doesn't have to be elaborate to make a real impact.

It's a good idea to order a preproduction demo of your pressing and try it out on a few different CD players to make sure it checks out OK. Also, make sure the company will replace defective discs. Some duplicating companies have questionable quality control.

Getting a Universal Product Code (UPC) Number

If you've never created a CD before, you'll need to learn how to get a UPC number (like the one in the following illustration) to put on your disc; without it, you can't sell it in an online (or offline) store.

The *UPC* is the 12-digit code that appears on the back of all music jewel cases. The Uniform Code Council (UCC) assigns UPC numbers; to get your own UPC number, you need to join the UCC and apply. For more information about UPC codes and to join the UCC, visit www.uc-council.org.

Once you have been assigned a UPC number, you need to integrate it into your jewel case design. Many graphic design companies can create a UPC label for you. Unlike the UPC itself, it costs only a few dollars to get a UPC file made. For a good list of companies that do this work, visit www.isbn.org/standards/home/isbn/us/barcode.html.

Promoting Yourself

There's no such thing as too much promotion. You might feel like a heel when you set up a stack of CDs at a show or send out an e-mail advertising a gig, but trust us—your fans appreciate the effort.

Write a Press Release

The world may be going digital, electronic, and virtual, but the good old press release will never die. At least, we hope not. Press releases constitute the majority

Cool Things to Do with Your Site

There's little doubt that you should have a Web site. But once you pay $35 to register a domain name, what do you actually do with it? Here are some elements you might consider implementing on your site:

- A newsgroup-like forum for fans to chat not just with you, but with each other.
- A signup feature so people can add themselves to your fan mailing list.
- A store where fans can buy your CD and other merchandise.
- Streaming audio and video. If you have radio interviews, music videos, or a single, be sure to make it all accessible on the Web site.
- Tour information. When are you playing? Where? Your Web site should always have the newest and most accurate information about live shows. You can even link to a tour search engine like Pollstar.com.
- A download center where fans can find images, video clips, and music samples.
- Press releases and news clips. If magazines and newspapers print good stories about you, display it proudly on your site.
- Press contacts. People like us need to interview people like you. It's the great circle of life—you record a CD, we interview you, music lovers read the review, and then they buy the CD, thus becoming fans. But none of that happens unless you post, at a bare minimum, your e-mail address —or even better, a phone number. But we understand that without a professional publicist on your payroll, it may be difficult to put a phone number on a Web site for all the world to see.

of our heating material in winter. When your band plays a new venue, releases a single, wraps a CD, revamps the Web site, wins a battle of the bands, sneezes, or does anything else even vaguely newsworthy, write a press release. You can post it on your Web site, mail it to any friendly members of the media you know, hit local radio stations, music Web sites, fanzines, and even music stores. Be sure to make the press release look professional and include detailed contact information. Books are available written expressly to teach novices how to draft killer press releases. Invest in one.

Write to Your Fans

Some artists are reluctant to e-mail their fans, but think about it—that's why they gave you their e-mail address to begin with. Don't saturate their inbox daily with news and ramblings, of course, but be sure to keep your fans up-to-date on tour dates, the status of your latest CD, and just the occasional personal update (like the e-mails from Diana Darby and The Painkillers that follow). Once again, trust us: fans like hearing from their favorite bands, especially if it looks personal and genuine.

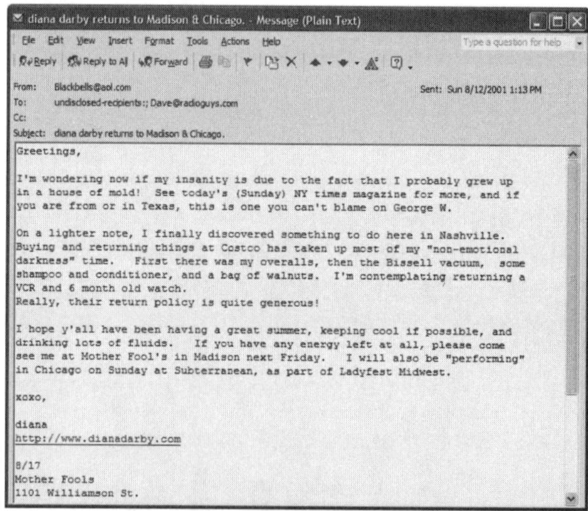

diana darby returns to Madison & Chicago. - Message (Plain Text)

From: Blackbells@aol.com Sent: Sun 8/12/2001 1:13 PM
To: undisclosed-recipients:; Dave@radioguys.com
Cc:
Subject: diana darby returns to Madison & Chicago.

Greetings,

I'm wondering now if my insanity is due to the fact that I probably grew up in a house of mold! See today's (Sunday) NY times magazine for more, and if you are from or in Texas, this is one you can't blame on George W.

On a lighter note, I finally discovered something to do here in Nashville. Buying and returning things at Costco has taken up most of my "non-emotional darkness" time. First there was my overalls, then the Bissell vacuum, some shampoo and conditioner, and a bag of walnuts. I'm contemplating returning a VCR and 6 month old watch.
Really, their return policy is quite generous!

I hope y'all have been having a great summer, keeping cool if possible, and drinking lots of fluids. If you have any energy left at all, please come see me at Mother Fool's in Madison next Friday. I will also be "performing" in Chicago on Sunday at Subterranean, as part of Ladyfest Midwest.

xoxo,

diana
http://www.dianadarby.com

8/17
Mother Fools
1101 Williamson St.

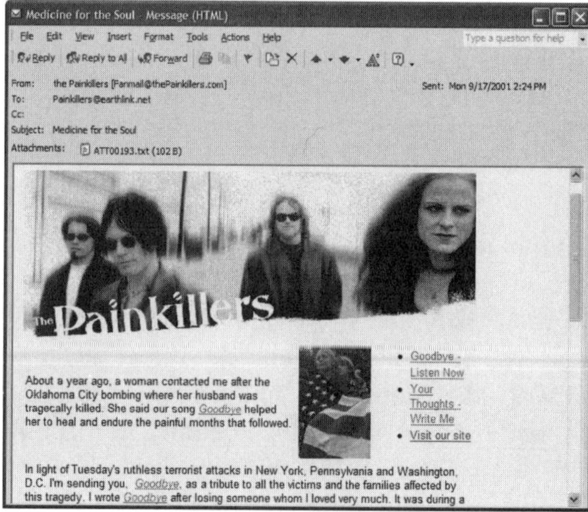

Medicine for the Soul - Message (HTML)

From: the Painkillers [Fanmail@thePainkillers.com] Sent: Mon 9/17/2001 2:24 PM
To: Painkillers@earthlink.net
Cc:
Subject: Medicine for the Soul
Attachments: ATT00193.txt (102 B)

The Painkillers

About a year ago, a woman contacted me after the Oklahoma City bombing where her husband was tragecally killed. She said our song Goodbye helped her to heal and endure the painful months that followed.

- Goodbye - Listen Now
- Your Thoughts - Write Me
- Visit our site

In light of Tuesday's ruthless terrorist attacks in New York, Pennsylvania and Washington, D.C. I'm sending you, Goodbye, as a tribute to all the victims and the families affected by this tragedy. I wrote Goodbye after losing someone whom I loved very much. It was during a

Music That Burns Your Fingers

Dave: Back in Chapter 9, Rick was looking for music to unwind. He asked me about my favorite tunes to mellow out after having a tough day at the office. I don't like to mellow out. I want music that grabs me by the shirt, lifts me up in the air, and demands that I pay attention. So, Rick, what five songs wrinkle your shirt? Here are five of the best that spring to my mind:

- "Pearl" — The Throwing Muses (I'd like to remark that this could well be the best rock-and-roll song ever.)
- "Psychotic Reaction" — The Count Five
- "The End" — The Beatles
- "Murder" — David Gilmour
- "Tremble" — The Call

Rick: Hey, look at that! I've actually heard of one of your choices! But who are these "Beatles" you keep referring to? Anyway, I've already listed the songs that I find energizing. (Although I called them "funky," which obviously ruffled your feathers. Is that the same thing as "wrinkling your shirt"?) Therefore, I have nothing to contribute to this list except my endless wonderment that you like such a diverse array of music—but not jazz.

From the Experts

Rarely in the course of writing a book do unrelated national or world events seep into the narrative of a chapter. For one thing, it disturbs the flow of the prose. For another, it "dates" the book, and that's something most authors don't want to do. Nonetheless, we feel the need to explain the circumstances of this last chapter.

First of all, no one understands the reality of surviving in the music world better than the artists themselves. As a result, when mapping out this book, we had planned to chat with a few independent artists who thrive despite the lack of major label support. With that in mind, Dave compiled a list of artists to include in the book.

Unfortunately, the timing of this book was such that we talked with each of these musicians in the very week following the World Trade Center and Pentagon bombings in September 2001. It was a difficult time to talk about something like music; at such a time, writing about music can feel trivial. Actually, writing about anything can feel trivial. Not surprisingly, each and every artist we spoke to was on the same emotional roller coaster ride. In addition to talking about the great human loss to this planet, though, we managed to find out how these outstanding, world-class artists capitalize on technology to help them succeed in a world where marketing dollars and corporate image are often more important that the music itself.

Kristin Hersh

Counting backwards I count you in
I don't remember him I don't remember

In time I rope you in again
I try and turn you back through him
I built a tower in my bones
I spill the mortar through my home

Don't let your heartbeat keep you safe
No telling what keeps me awake
One hundred fingerprints I hear
A hundred linger in my ear

Measure fortune killing time
"Counting Backwards" — *The Real Ramona*

As the driving force behind the college radio favorite The Throwing Muses, Kristin Hersh knows what it's like to be a rock star. But in recent years, her more personal and (if it's possible) even more eclectic brand of semiacoustic music as a solo artist has led her to nurture her fan base without the support of a major label.

Kristin, assisted by her husband/manager Billy O'Connell, has perhaps the most aggressive and innovative Internet presence we've ever seen.

As part of the Throwing Music Web site, Kristin delivers all the ordinary stuff, like news and tour dates. But her message board is an example of just how thoroughly artists can embrace fans, offering them an open forum for talking about anything: the artist, music, and life in general. The Throwing Music board is a largely unmoderated place for people to chat about anything. Fans do indeed come to the site to chat about all sorts of topics, and with rare exception, everyone gets along and has a good time. That's because, as BillyO says, "When you meet someone that's a Throwing Muses fan, you're probably going to have other things in common." Kristin isn't a frequent visitor to the message board—her duties as a mom and a musician keep her quite busy—but she takes the time to visit on occasion. Her assessment of the board: "It's like having a room in the back of the house I never knew I had, and a bunch of people are in there throwing a party."

Kristin has been on the cutting edge of technology with a number of clever innovations. Finishing up a second year, the Works In Progress (WIP) program has been a resounding success. Works In Progress is a subscription MP3 program: for $15/year, subscribers get access to a new song each month. Some songs are new, as in the flurry of demos she released that would eventually find their way onto new studio albums like *Sky Motel* and *Sunny Border Blue.* Other songs were alternate versions or demos of older Throwing Muses tunes.

Is a WIP-like program worthwhile for you? Here's what BillyO had to say about it: "It paid for itself in the very first month. The cost is so low that if we ever decided not to continue doing it, saying it was too expensive would be a lousy excuse. There were a few early costs, like taking credit cards, but these days, you could actually do it all with PayPal. The recording costs are already paid, so it's like bootlegging our own material."

Some programs didn't work out quite as planned. Last year, Kristin introduced the idea of a Strange Angels program to the fans that frequent her Web site. Strange Angels were intended to be grassroots promoters who could help Kristin with advertising for shows and albums locally throughout the country. But BillyO says, "I backed away from the idea. I don't like the idea of creating a hierarchy of fans. That's not what the site is about." Instead, they've implemented an alternative that you can probably try yourself quite easily. Kristin and BillyO have, in a sense, made everyone a "strange angel"—fans can download tour posters and other material from the Web site and post them locally. It's an inexpensive way to vastly increase the promotional potential of the band while also letting fans participate in the process: a win/win situation all around.

Kristin is at www.throwingmusic.com.

Peter Himmelman

You don't dance with your broken bones
You don't sing when you're alone
You don't fly when the air's so thin and all this weight is closing in
Hey this is the taste of freedom yeah this is how it feels
When fate picks you to get
Crushed beneath the wheels

All the things that you've learned this far
Could not have prepared you for where you are
So take your compass and face the east
To the ruins of the temple and the wrath of the beast
Hey I said the evening is falling like a hundred tons of steel
Now and then we get
Crushed beneath the wheels

If I could do it I would gladly bear your pain
But I know anything I do would be in vain
You must believe me when I say this all will pass
But for the moment your poor heart must feel like glass and I say
Hey this is the taste of freedom yeah this is how it feels
When fate picks you to get
Crushed beneath the wheels

"Crushed" — *From Strength to Strength*

"I'm not the flavor of the week," says Peter Himmelman, "and I may never be." That doesn't keep this dynamic artist—who started as the front man for punk act Sussman Lawrence and later came into his own as a sort of spiritual rock-and-roll troubadour—from being the most talented musician that mainstream America has never heard of.

Peter's Web site is a work in progress, and he is using a group of Web designers to realize his vision of how he'd like to interact with his fans. "I like communicating with people, but I don't really like to travel," he says. "I see the Web site as a starting place to give me the ability to sort of be in many more places at once. I always saw myself as being very good on TV, for example, interacting with a lot of people at once." In particular, Peter thinks that an effective Web site for artists is one that breaks the rules and becomes very personal. "It's the cold impersonal hand of technology yielding to personal choice in a paradoxical way."

How does Peter blend the cold and the personal? By offering commissioned songwriting. "It's an offshoot of a business I had when I was about 18 years old called Time Capsules. It was like a commissioned portrait. I would write a song based on people's input. It wasn't necessarily a funny song, though some were, but maybe a beautiful ballad, for example. Maybe about a wedding or an anniversary. It will be part of the Web site. People can commission me to write a song for them. If you're aware of my shows, you know I'm somewhat uniquely qualified to do something like this.

"We'll come up with a completely finished master-quality CD, even with artwork. I keep thinking of artists like Rembrandt, for example. I keep wrestling with the problem that people who don't know my work might think it's some sort of novelty act or cheap thing, but it's something all artists have done; lots of great art has been commissioned. I taught a song school for a few years, for example. I stress that for a song, a work of art to manifest itself, you need to have a specific reason for it to exist, and though it sounds sort of cold, one of the biggest motivators is time or money. It's easier to come up with something. Now that I'm not on a record deal, for example, no one is insisting for me to come up with a record every year, so I don't. The specificity of the need manifests the work much more quickly."

Time is a major obstacle for Peter as he tries to grow his Web site. As the man behind all of the music on the television show *Judging Amy,* Peter has to balance his solo career—and its promotion through the Internet—with a demanding production schedule. He tries to answer all of the e-mail people send him via the site, for instance, but that can be difficult considering his schedule. He also says that he has a goal to set up a camera in his studio and deliver Webcasts to fans. "People would write in and I might make up a song live on the spot for someone in Alaska, maybe. You can be in people's homes and touch them without leaving the studio. I just have to make some time."

Peter highlights the importance of understanding how to capitalize on a fan base, wherever it might be. "The *Judging Amy* Web site gets about 40,000 hits a day. I need to get a link to my site to help fans interested enough in the show to maybe discover a new world through my site."

Finally, Peter cautions that interacting with fans through the Net is fundamentally different than playing live—and that can lead to uncomfortable situations, as in the case of online stalkers. "There are a few people that seem to have extra time on their hands and want me to contribute something to their lives that's not realistic. I don't share personal stuff with people, except in my songs, which are very intimate. But that's very protected. I play somewhere for an hour-and-a-half and share, and then I'm gone. It's protected. You can leave, go on to the next town, you're totally in control."

Peter is at www.peterhimmelman.com.

Diana Darby

Well you dream that you are riding
On a horse made out of glass
And it shatters underneath you
And you can't find your way back
And you'd like to be a dancer
And your breasts are double D
And you smile
At all your teachers
'Cause you want so bad to please
Oh, Amelia

Well you walk into the window
And you feel the other side
And the voice
That guides your conscience
Is a psychopathic liar
And your friends are baking cookies
And your mother's at the pool
And your father's taking valium
And you hate your rich high school
Oh, Amelia

Well the watchman
Sleeps beside you and you can't stay in your skin
And you burn your feet
With matches
Till the memory comes again
And you hear the doorknob
Turning
And you'd like to drive a car
But you can't get past September
And you don't know who you are
"Amelia" — *naked time*

Psychedelia isn't dead. But under the command of Diana Darby, it is less about expanding your consciousness and more about confronting those jagged things deep inside us. Her light, wispy voice is a ruse, because the pain she sings about is as haunting as her guitar licks.

Diana's debut album was released in 2000, and her Web site is a bit different than many. It is a glimpse at Diana the person, but, like her music, it's through a glass, darkly. "I thought it was important to show other sides of myself," she says. That means you'll find some unusual pages on this site, such as a lengthy tour journal, which Diana writes on her own. "I thought it would be fun to let people see what it's like to be on the road." And since Diana is first and foremost a poet, you can find examples of her poetry there as well. The effect is very powerful. While some artist sites end up looking like little more than single-product record stores, Diana's site seems to invite fans to get to know the woman behind the guitar. Sure, you can buy *naked time* at the site, but the main focus seems to be on meeting the artist. Diana's site takes both the artist and the fan seriously.

Although she has a sizable database of fans, Diana acknowledges that she needs to be better about using it. Her infrequent personal notes to fans keep people informed about her travels and studio details, but not often enough to be of a lot of value. Indeed, she says it's a good lesson for how artists should think about themselves in relation to their fans. "I need to be better about sending e-mail out more often. I guess I'm shy. The whole concept of keeping in contact with my fans is not something I'm used to. I'm used to being a writer and living in my own internal world. I've never been a marketer, it's not who I am. But as an artist, you need to look at it as just talking to people who want to hear from you."

There's no doubt that technology has leveled the playing field for independent artists. Mark Linn, Diana's producer, says that getting a credit card processing account was an important accomplishment for him with Diana's site. "Before that, if someone wanted a record, they had to send a check. This has made things much easier, and people are much more likely to buy when they visit the site."

Mark also says the Web site can be an important tool for helping one-time promotional events be available to visitors well past their ordinary lifetime. "Diana did an interview on NPR, and we put it up on the site so it didn't just die. The show can live on and people can continue to hear it." Indeed, the site lets visitors listen to streaming audio from shows and interviews—and that can make all the difference for an artist who gets short bursts in the national spotlight and needs to have the most leverage from those appearances as possible.

Diana is at www.dianadarby.com.

Cherish Alexander, The Painkillers

Now that you're here, in your disguise
Feeding the cancer of my intellect
Holding the knife to the ulcer in my stomach

Now that you're gone, I'll be alright
Now we are distanced by the open sea
Bluer than I may ever appear to be

My choice to survive let it be tonight
All the stars in the sky in between the dark and light
and the night coming down can we stay where we're found
Everyone's falling down can we stay in our ground
Where we are found

So mean what you say, say what you mean
Maybe it will help on your recovery
of all that you find there of all your mysteries

These treasures you find, hold them real tight
Planting a seed into it let it grow
Cause I never stay there in the comfort of all the pain

"In Between" — *Medicine for the Soul*

They're loud and they're in your face. But the L.A.-based Painkillers also have soul, thanks to the brutally honest and introspective songwriting from lead singer Cherish Alexander.

The band started slow with establishing an Internet presence, but they did it early—over four years ago. Their first stab at a Web site was through a friend, but at every point along the way, the band—and Cherish, in particular—has been very closely connected to the process. "It's hard not to become actively involved in the Internet," she says.

Indeed, Cherish takes a surprisingly hands-on approach to promotion. "I set goals for myself. Today, maybe, I'll get my pictures and music posted on ten Web sites. There's tons of webzines and fanzines out there. Another day, I'll get a list of those and send off a CD to ten of them." Indeed, it sometimes seems like she goes above and beyond the call of duty. She explained to me how she'll visit Yahoo.com and look up bands who are similar to The Painkillers. From there, she can figure out where those bands are linked and then try to get her own band linked to those sites as well. Her advice? "Set goals for yourself, and do a little something every day."

The Painkillers have a national following, thanks, in part, to being featured on the soundtrack for the television series *The Crow*. But while many bands don't seem to know exactly how to use their mailing list, Cherish does. She aggressively stays in touch with her fans through e-mail. When The Painkillers were competing for the Tonos.com Rock Songwriting Challenge at the start of 2001, they actively e-mailed fans to visit the site and vote on several occasions. The result? The band won, resulting in even more exposure. Says Cherish, "You can send out 100 e-mails and only reach three people, but if you do reach three people, that's better than nothing."

Cherish makes the time to answer all of her fan mail personally, something that's time-consuming but essential to her philosophy of touching people's lives. Like Peter Himmelman, though, she notes that on rare occasion, she encounters people on the Internet who can be problematic. "Recently, I sent an e-mail to our fans with my song 'Goodbye' after the World Trade Center tragedy. It's a song I wrote about something that happened to me, when I lost my boyfriend a few years ago." Indeed, the song is a moving farewell to someone who has passed away, and the difficulty of letting go and moving on with one's own life. Says Cherish, "I got e-mail from a few people who just said we were taking advantage of the tragedy."

Cherish is at www.thepainkillers.com.

Dana Mase

Rain comes down through the trees
Crimson-colored memories
Something like the autumn leaves of time.
Raindrops falling from the sky
Raindrops falling from my eyes
Memories are like the ageless oaks.
Every time I think of you , the Autumn seems to know

I watch the leaves as they fall down
Trace their paths onto the ground
Somewhere in the end they find their peace.
Somewhere deep inside my mind
I trace a dusty path through time
Wonder if you've found your sweet release.
Every time I think of you, the Autumn seems to know.

You left me one autumn afternoon
I watched that day turn to years.
Now every time the Autumn seems to call me
It's you I hear,
It's you I hear.
"The Autumn Seems to Know" — *Sitting with an Angel*

Who is Dana Mase? Her four albums paint a picture of a contemplative woman who, unlike most of us, is extremely comfortable with her spirituality. That permeates her music: without sounding like she's singing from the synagogue, she sings about life, her faith, and her irrepressible sense of optimism. She does it all with a musical sensibility that could only come from growing up with both Joni Mitchell and the Beatles.

What makes Dana unique, though, is how cleverly she embraced the Internet at a time when most people were still trying to figure out what a modem was. Her Web site was, no doubt, one of the very first erected by an independent artist. Dana is convinced that technology has allowed her to flourish without major label support: "The site is a great way to promote my music to the whole world. Otherwise, fans wouldn't have access to my music. The Internet gives me a lot of control. It lets me be independent."

One example of this independence from a major label manifested itself in the wake of the terrorist attacks. "After this horrible thing that has happened, I wrote an inspirational song. I got together with the musicians and everything was totally free. The musicians, the studio, the artwork, it's all free. We'll sell it through the Web site and every cent of the profit will be donated. I can do that because I don't have a guy over me telling me I have to give him 50 percent. And it's all because of the Internet."

Barry Mase, Dana's manager, was there at the beginning of Dana's recording career in 1994, helping make sense out of the brand new Web. "As independents, we were just trying to find our way. I had, at the time, stumbled onto newsgroups. And I always knew if we could get music in front of the people, it would do well."

So Barry and Dana tried a risky but clever promotion. After finding newsgroups dedicated to similar artists, they posted messages offering free copies of Dana's second album, *Sitting with an Angel.* The hook: pay if you like the album; otherwise, simply throw it away. Says Dana, "I have faith in human nature. People will do the right thing." Indeed, it was a highly successful promotion and introduced Dana to thousands of new fans.

When Dana offered her "shareware" CDs in 1995, the Internet was new to many people and spam wasn't yet a serious issue. Today, an artist hoping to try a similar giveaway would need to be very careful, or people could react negatively to such offers. In fact, Dana has moved to a new style of Internet promotion: her own affiliate program. Web sites that link to danamase.com can reap a bounty for every CD sale Dana makes.

Dana keeps breaking the rules because, she says, there are no rules to break. "The music biz isn't like being a lawyer, where you go to college, then you get a degree and go practice law. In music, you have to be driven and creative. If you're not driven, forget it. And don't forget—when one door shuts, another door always opens."

Dana is at www.danamase.com.

Appendix A Internet Radio Stations

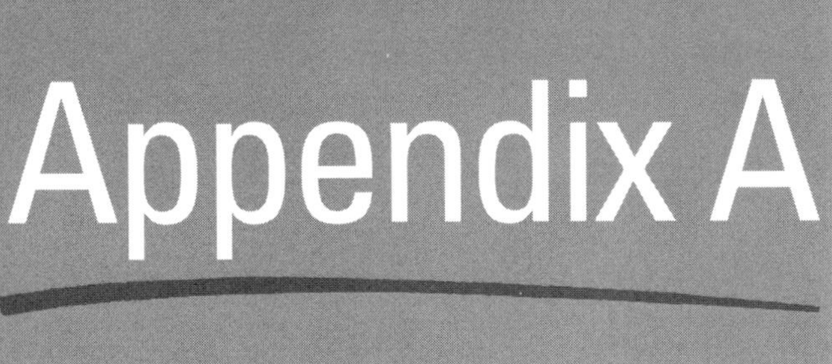

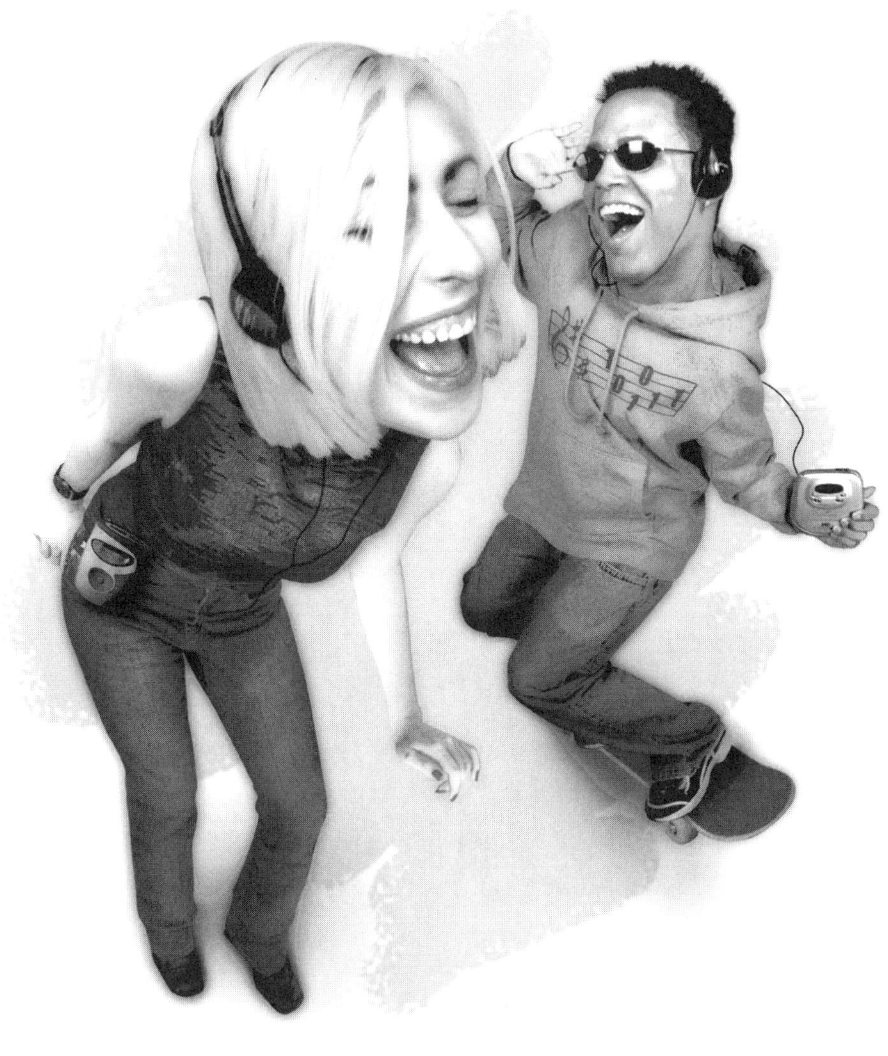

General/Networks

Excite radio

http://music.excite.com/

This subsection of Excite.com lets you tune in various Internet stations.

SonicNet.com

www.sonicnet.com

SonicNet, part of the MTVi Group, can connect you with specialty radio stations playing everything from Blues and Folk to Classical and World/International.

WindowsMedia.com

www.windowsmedia.com

The Web-based version of the hundreds of stations featured in Windows Media Player.

Yahoo!Radio

Radio.yahoo.com

This subsection of Yahoo! steers you to a wide variety of stations, all of them categorized in the familiar Yahoo! style.

News/Sports/Talk

ABC News

www.abcradio.com/radio/newsradio/index.shtml

The Internet news branch of the ABC/Disney Go Network.

Ananova

www.ananova.com

An all-purpose news site, featuring late-breaking news, weather, entertainment, and sports, featuring the now-famous virtual newscaster.

Australian Broadcasting Corporation

www.abc.net.au/newsradio

The news from Down Under.

BBC World News

www.bbc.co.uk/worldservice/audio

Internet radio news from the British Broadcasting Corporation.

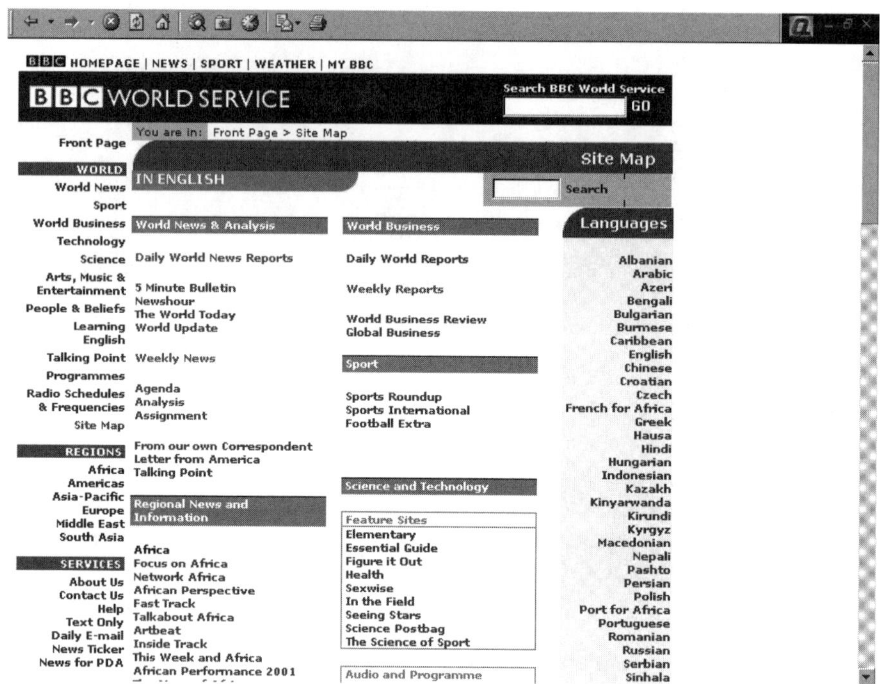

Bloomberg.com

www.bloomberg.com

Excellent business news coverage.

C-SPAN: Watch And Listen Now

www.c-span.org/watch

Hear live news coverage from C-SPAN.

CBC Newsworld

www.cbc.ca/news/live

News from the Canadian Broadcasting Corporation, featuring text, audio, and video.

Christian Science Monitor Audio Briefs

www.csmonitor.com/audio/audio.html

Internet radio news and commentary from *The Christian Science Monitor*.

CNN

www.cnn.com/audioselect
www.cnn.com/videoselect

CNN's site offers live streaming audio and video news coverage.

The Economist/E-Vision

www.economist.tv

Global views and opinions from *The Economist*.

FOX News Video

www.foxnews.com/video

Streaming video from the FOX News network.

KCRW.org

www.kcrw.org

Los Angeles public radio station featuring an eclectic schedule of news, locally and nationally produced music, public affairs, political analysis, and cultural programs.

ListenToTheNews.com

http://listentothenews.com

Streaming audio news and information from around the globe.

Major League Baseball

www.mlb.com

For $9.95 a year, you can listen to all the Major League Baseball you want!

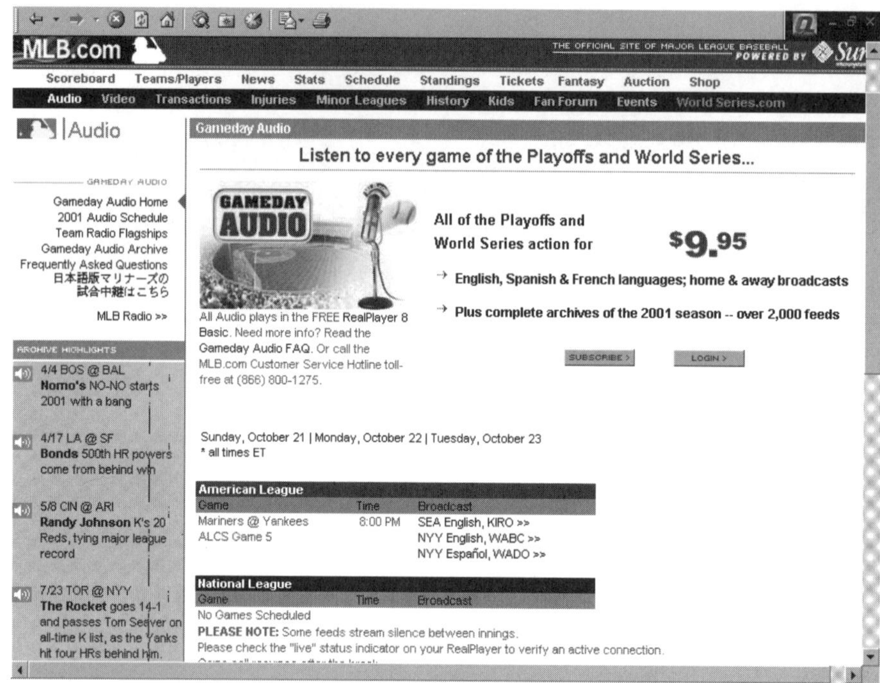

MicroRadio.Net

www.microradio.net

Streaming updates from various sources with a focus on international events and independent journalism.

MSNBC

www.msnbc.com

Another great site for business news.

MSN Chat Radio

http://chat.msn.com/default.msnw

Chat with others in the Microsoft community.

Naked News

www.nakednews.com

Yes, this is the site you've heard about. News read by male and female anchors who actually strip during the broadcast.

National Public Radio News

www.npr.org/news

News and programming from NPR, the network of 600+ public radio stations across the U.S.

Radio Deutsche Velle

www.dwelle.de/english/Welcome.html

This German site has a great English-language news service.

ReporterTV.com

www.reporterTV.com

News on the entertainment industry.

United Nations Radio

www.un.org/av/radio

The UN's site features daily news in English, French, and Spanish.

The World

www.theworld.org

This site, based on the popular show from Public Radio International, features live news coverage.

WorldNewsTV.com

www.foreigntv.com/worldnews

Daily video updates from across the world.

Classical

Beethoven.com

www.beethoven.com

This Internet radio station and streaming audio content provider aims to be "the best place on the Internet for lovers of classical music to listen, read, learn, play and interact with each other."

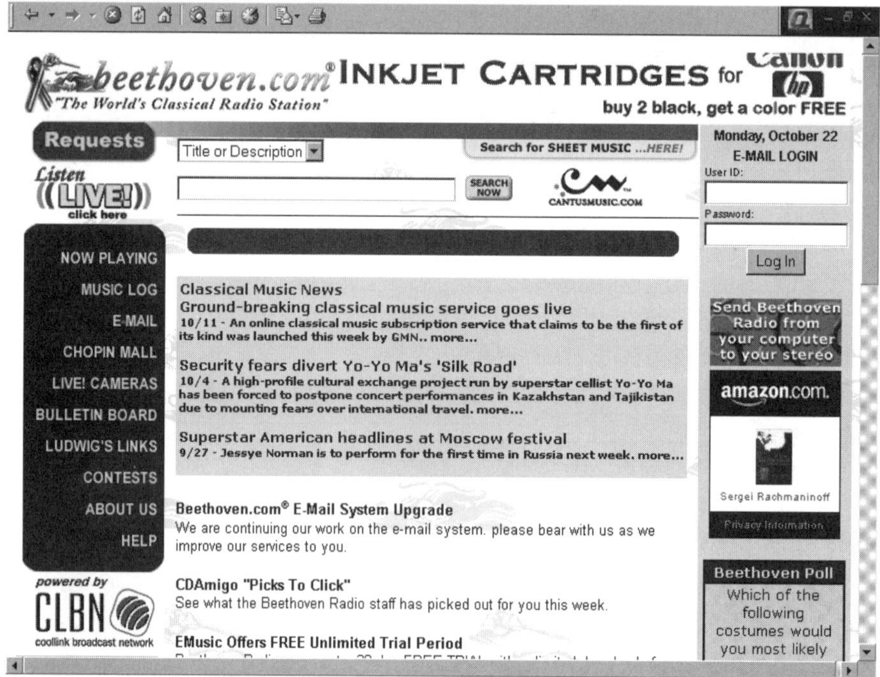

Broadcast.com: KLASI

www.broadcast.com/radio/continuous_classical/KLASI

Classical music 24 hours a day, with no commercial interruptions.

ClassicalRecordings.net

www.classicalrecordings.net

Provides audio broadcasts, music reviews, and profiles of the noteworthy conductors and classical artists.

From the Top

www.fromthetop.org

This public radio series, which aims to encourage and celebrate the development of youth through music, features teenage classical musicians from across the United States.

Online Classics

www.onlineclassics.net

This London-based station offers recorded and live concerts, ballet, opera, and musicals.

OperadiO

www.operadio.com

Another U.K. site devoted to classical music, OperadiO focuses on opera, chamber, and other types of classical music.

Rudas Superstar Theater

www.superstartheater.com

An online showcase for new and emerging opera and classical artists from around the world.

Web Concert Hall

www.webconcerthall.com

Venue for new performers to make their work known and appreciated. In addition to classical broadcasts, this station also features news, reviews, and music history.

XLNC1

www.xlnc1.org

This site celebrates the memory of Alejandro Diaz-Guerra, a Mexican broadcasting professional who started 15 radio stations in Mexico before he died in 1969. Features continuous classical music broadcasting.

Country

Dedicated Country

www.dedicatedcountry.com

This station offers a real-time request line.

NetRadio Country

http://www.netradio.com/country/

Comprehensive site featuring broadcasts of contemporary country artists.

Sugar in the Gourd

www.sugarinthegourd.com

Continuous broadcasting of country artists, including Appalachian, String Band, and Balladry.

TwangCast

www.twangcast.com

Provides online country music. An Austin, Texas–based site dedicated to the world of Americana Music, alternative country, bluegrass, and classic country from indie artists.

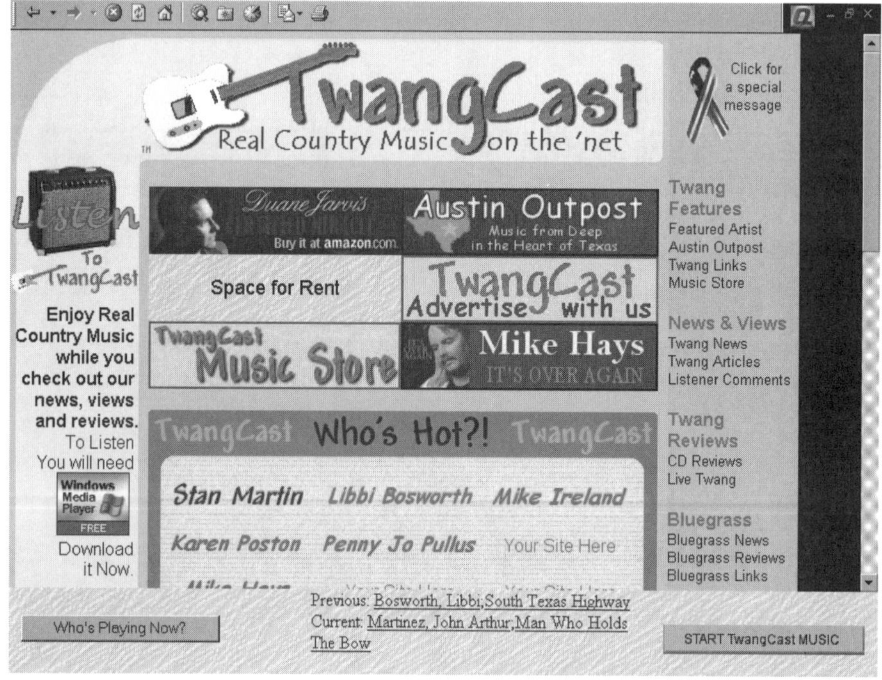

Hip-Hop/Electronic/Dance

aminoRadio

www.aminoradio.com

Free-form and live electronica.

Bassment Online Radio

www.thebassment.com

Drum'n'bass, hip-hop, music reviews, and more.

Beta Lounge

www.betalounge.com

Audio and video webcasts of dance music.

BoomBox.net

www.boombox.net

Streaming media featuring hip-hop and drum'n'bass.

CN Soho Live

www.cnsoholive.co.uk

Dance music of all sorts.

Dance Radio

www.dance-radio.net

This site broadcasts the latest dance music.

Danceportal.co.uk

www.danceportal.co.uk

Weekly live webcasts from underground UK nightclubs.

Deeprhythms.com

www.deeprhythms.com

Deep house mixes, updated weekly.

DezMix Muzik

www.dezmix.com

New York City–style underground house music mixes.

Digitalnoise.com

www.digitalnoise.com

New York–based station playing drum'n'bass, ambient, experimental, hip-hop, and more.

downtempo.org

www.downtempo.org

Slow-motion music including downtempo, ambient, and trip-hop.

Dublab

www.dublab.com

Funk, hip-hop, electronic, and experimental.

Eternal Trance

www.eternaltrance.tempo.fm

House, trance, club, and dance music.

Factory 188

www.factory188.com

Shoutcast and RealAudio feeds of downtempo, trip-hop, and drum'n'bass.

FlareSound

www.flaresound.com

Downtempo, house, breakbeats, and acid jazz.

Freaknet2000

www.freaknet2000.com/mixes

Techno, hip-hop, and house music mixes.

Gaia Live

www.gaialive.co.uk

A British site featuring weekly shows, reviews, and downloads.

Global Sound Kitchen

www.globalsoundkitchen.com

Music from the UK underground club scene. Garage, ambient, drum'n'bass, and hip-hop.

Groovetech

www.groovetech.com

Radio and club broadcasts of hip-hop and trip-hop music.

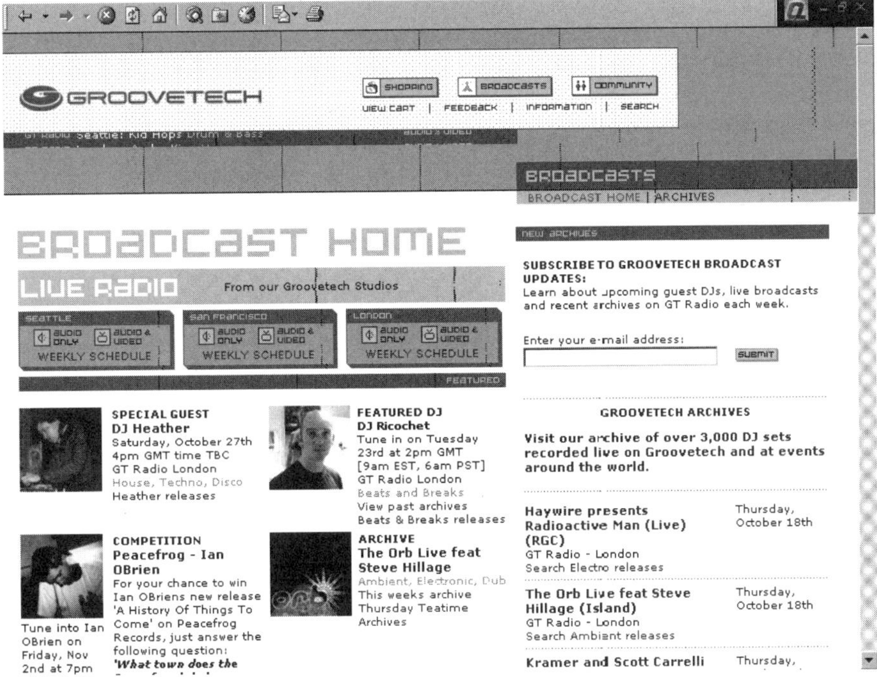

Houzepage

www.houzepage.com

Local rave DJs playing house, trip-hop, and techno.

LiveDJs.com

www.livedjs.com

San Francisco electronic music DJs. Includes chat room, message board, schedule, and archives.

Labyrinth

www.labyrinthdetroit.com

Gothic, industrial, retro, techno, house, and drum'n'bass nights. Site features live webcasts.

Mix of the Week

www.mixoftheweek.com

Hip-hop, trip-hop, house, funk, and soul.

Monkey Radio

www.monkeyradio.net

Continuous broadcast of dance, techno, and trip-hop music.

Netmix.com

www.netmix.com

Hip-hop and techno DJs, reviews, and interviews with artists.

Omega Dance Radio

www.omegadanceradio.com

Live broadcasts of dance music.

Pulse Internet Radio

www.pulseradio.net

Live broadcasts and DJ mixes.

Radio Free Underground

www.stitch.com

Live broadcasting of techno, gothic, industrial, and ambient music.

Radio Technologix

www.technologix.org

Toronto-based station featuring live broadcasts, DJ mixes, and local dance club information.

Radiokook

www.radiokook.com

Features music from Club Electronica Organica.

RadioValve

www.radiovalve.com

Continuous broadcasting of DJ mixes, interviews, and reviews.

ReMixRadio

www.remixradio.com

Streaming media playback from independent techno artists and DJs.

SafeHouse Live

www.safehouselive.com

An online rave with dance and hip-hop music.

SomaFM

www.somafm.com

Ambient, downtempo, and lounge music.

Soundselective

www.soundselective.com

This station focuses on independent imports.

Studio FM

www.studiofm.cjb.net

Dutch site playing dance music from Belgium and the Netherlands.

UK Rumble

www.ukrumble.com

Twenty-four-hour live dance music, webcam, interactive chatroom, and more.

The Womb

www.thewomb.com

This site is "dedicated to the progression of electronic music and digital culture."

JAZZ

All That Jazz Radio

www.jazz-radio.fm

Streaming interviews, music, and more with host Brian Parker.

Blue Note Radio

www.bluenote.com

Blue Note Radio is a showcase for Blue Note Records, the iconic jazz record label founded in 1939.

ejazz.fm

www.ejazz.fmsite.html

Offers 20 audio channels, jazz chat, downloads, and more.

Jazz From Lincoln Center

www.jazzradio.org

Jazz concerts from New York City's renowned music halls.

JazzManMusic.com

www.jazzmanmusic.com

Smooth jazz.

PuroJazz

www.purojazz.com

The site is in Spanish. Mainstream jazz, featuring tributes to John Coltrane, Miles Davis, Dexter Gordon, and other good stuff. Live and webcast.

Radio Free New Orleans

www.neworleansonline.comneworleansmusicrfno.html

Traditional jazz, cajun music, and more.

Radio There

www.there1.com

Jazz and blues, focusing on new releases.

RadioNation

www.rnation.com

Mostly R&B, some hip-hop jazz programming.

SkyJazz

www.skyjazz.com

Jazz programming, news, and more.

R&B/Soul

Key 56 Radio

www.key56internetradio.com

LiquidSoulRadio.com

www.liquidsoulradio.com

Neo-soul, R&B, jazz, and hip-hop.

HotMixx

http://www.hotmixx.com/

Hip-hop, R&B, and soft jazz.

Rnaton

www.rnation.com

R&B, with some hip-hop and jazz programming.

Royal Groove

www.royalgroove.com

Soul, funk, and jazz. Includes record reviews and archives of past shows.

Solar Radio

www.solarradio.com

Funk, soul, and some jazz programming.

Soul 24-7

www.soul24-7.com

Just as the name promises, this station broadcasts soul and R&B music around the clock.

UrbanHitzRadio.com

www.urbanhitzradio.com

Rock/Pop

3WK Underground Radio

http://www.3wk.com

Explores music as art.

Alligator

www.alligatorrecords.com

Features contemporary blues and roots rock musicians.

The ARTISTdirect Network

www.artistdirect.com

ARTISTdirect aims to facilitate interaction between fans and their favorite artists.

Billboard Radio

www.billboardradio.com

Weekly top 100 show.

BryceRadio.com

www.bryceradio.com

Features top 40 news, shows, and multimedia.

Capitol Broadcasts

www.capitolbroadcasts.com

Features new music and videos from Capitol Records.

DiscJockey.com

www.discjockcy.com

Music from the '40s through today. Listeners request and dedicate their favorite songs.

Digital Club Network

www.dcn.com

Provides fans of both established and new alternative rock artists with live performances 24 hours a day, 7 days a week.

DJ Mix

www.djmix.com

This site boasts the world's leading DJs and promises to be "your one stop source for all info related to dj culture and the electronic music lifestyle."

Energy 94

www.energy94.com

Dance music station.

F.A.K.E. Radio

www.fakeradio.com

An eclectic mix of music and talk. International DJs play everything from hip-hop to bebop.

Frenzy Radio

www.frenzyradio.com

Features underground hardcore, metal, and deathcore.

GoGaGa

www.gogaga.com

Free-form eclectic music and entertainment.

HardRadio

www.hardradio.com

Commercial-free hard rock radio.

Health and Happiness Show

http://whichthat.tripod.com/hnhshow.htm

Rock, hip-hop, jazz, noise, and more.

Hijackradio.com

www.hijackradio.com

Streaming and customizable live-feed formats including alternative, rap, latin, R&B, and country.

House of Blues

www.hob.com

Concert venue serving up an assorted combination of "international pleasant cuisine" and music.

IndiePopRadio.com

www.indiepopradio.com

Indie pop and rock, reviews, interviews, and much more.

IndieRadio.org

www.indieradio.org/

Indie music including experimental, power pop, dream pop, emo, and electronic pop.

InfoWeb Radio

www.infoweb.net/radio/

Free-form space, classic rock, fusion, jazz, and other musical styles. Also features comedy and talk radio.

K-Metal Radio

www.k-metal.com

Heavy metal radio.

KEEE Radio

www.keee.com

Radio broadcast accepting song requests from listeners.

KIIS-FM

www.kiisfmi.com

Streaming music, music videos, and movie trailers.

KNAC

www.knac.com

Hard rock.

Late Bar Radio

www.latebarradio.com

All Duran Duran, all the time.

LosDudes

www.losdudes.com

Live rock and roll broadcast playing listeners' song requests.

Luxuria Music

www.luxuriamusic.com

Downloads and soundtracks for lounge music, spaghetti westerns, and surf music.

M97FM

www.m97fmjakarta.com

Classic rock.

Machine(x)Soul

www.machineandsoul.com

Synthpop, electro, and darkwave radio show webcast. Features interviews, artist biographies, and musical event listings.

NetRadio.com

www.netradio.net/channels/newwave

New Wave channel.

New Wave Netcast

www.freshproducemusic.com/1980/NewWave.html

All '80s, all the time.

OldiesCentral.com

www.oldiescentral.com

Top 40 music from the '50s through the '80s.

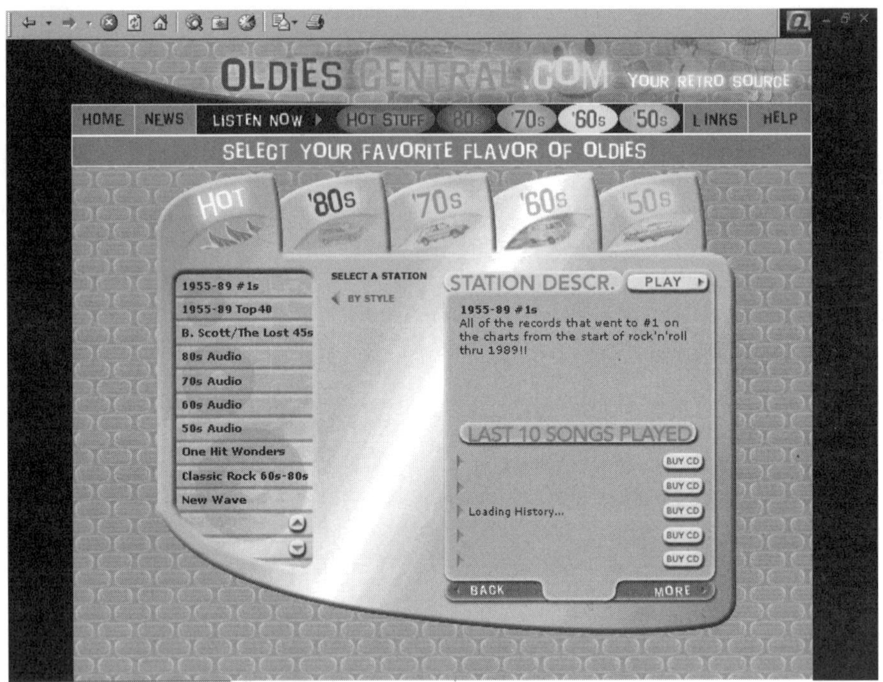

ON-AIR Music Channels

www.on-air.com

Concert webcasts, streaming media, and more.

Power FM

www.powerfm.com

Dance and pop music.

Progradio.com

www.progradio.com

Progressive music from international artists.

Radio Free Music Archive

http://radiofreemusic.coolsite.com

Self-produced music. Listeners can submit their CDs for one month's free posting.

Radio Free Radio

www.radioFREEradio.com

Commercial and independent music.

Radio Good

www.radiogood.com

Alternative rock, independent label bands.

Radioactiva

www.radioactiva.com

A Spanish site featuring pop music.

RadioAlbany.com

www.radioalbany.com

Top 40 tunes.

Raw Energy Radio

www.rawenergy.com

Punk rock.

The Retro Cocktail Hour

http://kanu.ukans.edu/retro.html

Lounge music, cocktail jazz, or in their words, "the likable, eager-to-please instrumental pop of the 1950s and '60s."

RockTime Radio

www.broadcast.com/radio/continuous_rock/RockTime

Rock from the '70s, '80s, and '90s.

Rolling Stone Radio

www.rollingstone.com

The classic rock music magazine's site features 12 different music channels.

RTN Radio

www.rtnradio.com

Classic rock from the '70s and '80s.

SonicNet FlashRadio

www.flashradio.com

Part of the MTVi Group, this site features several channels spanning many genres: Alternative, DJ, Electronic, Guitar Rock, Hip Hop, Pop, and Remix.

Stardog Radio

www.stardogradio.com

Alternative rock music.

Summer of Love

www2.orangesunshine.com/orangesunshine/

Psychedelic music from the '60s.

SwankRadio

www.swankradio.com

Cocktail, bachelor pad, space age, and lounge music.

Swanktown

www.swanktown.com

Big band, swing, and lounge artists.

Treasure Island

www.treasureislandoldies.com

Oldies—tune in for latest scheduled show times.

Virgin Radio

www.virginradio.co.uk/

Classic tracks.

We Kick The Underground

www.wktu.com

Not to be confused with the popular New York City station WKTU (103.5 FM), this site aims "to spread the dance music vibe on a global scale."

Appendix B Top Web Sites for MP3 Dowloads

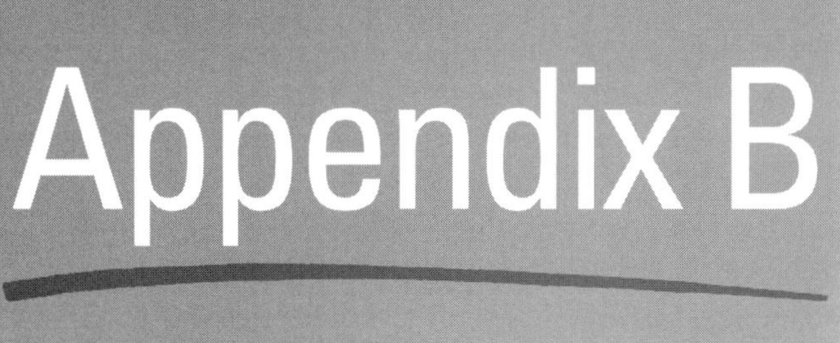

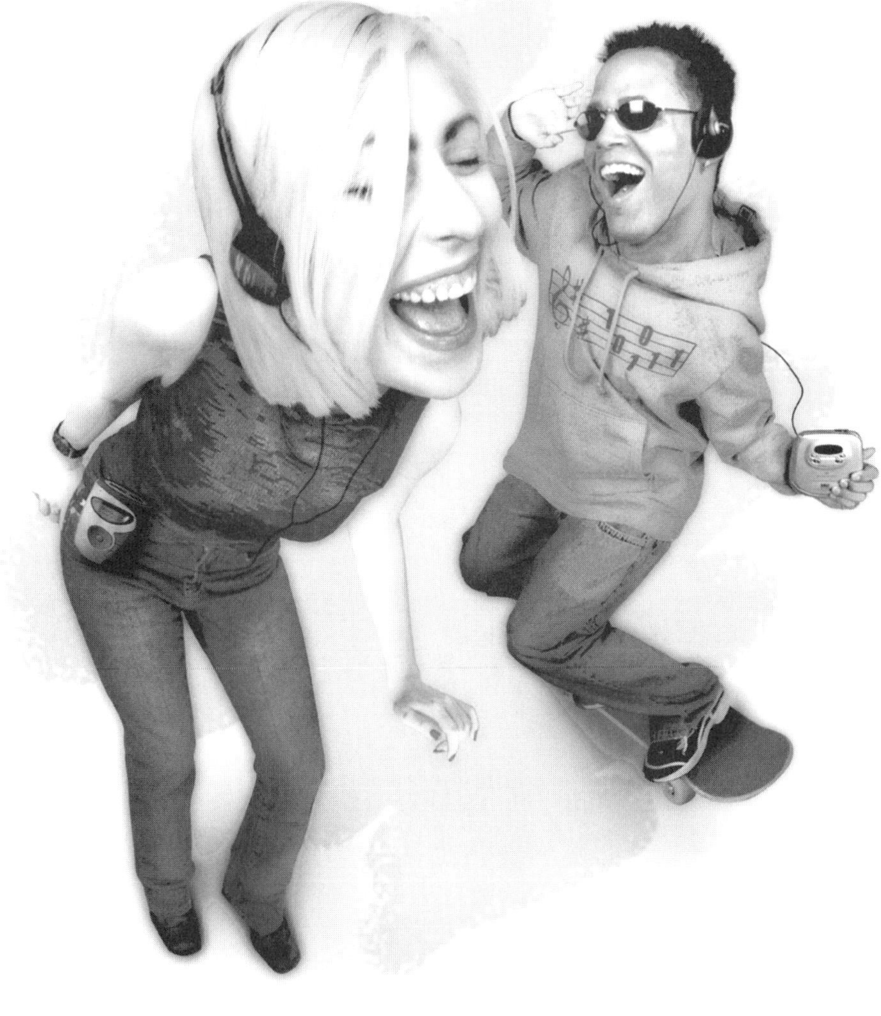

There's no experience in the entire world quite like discovering new music. Sure, your CD collection is fine, but meeting and falling in love with a new song is a magical experience. Rick routinely runs out of music stores shouting "New music! New music!" when a new Christina Aguilera album comes out. Dave often daydreams about what it would be like to have been an adult in 1967, able to hear *Sgt. Pepper's Lonely Hearts Club Band* when it played on the radio for the very first time. (For the record, he was three years old at the time.)

NOTE *Downloading copyrighted music without permission from the song's owner can be illegal. Check out Chapter 3 if you have any doubts about the legality of using these sites. And please read the artist interviews in Chapter 16—they are the people you're affecting right in the wallet if you do choose to download unauthorized music.*

Internet sites that let you download music make it easier than ever to get music with that new car smell. Here's what we recommend for your surfing and downloading pleasure.

Napster

www.napster.com

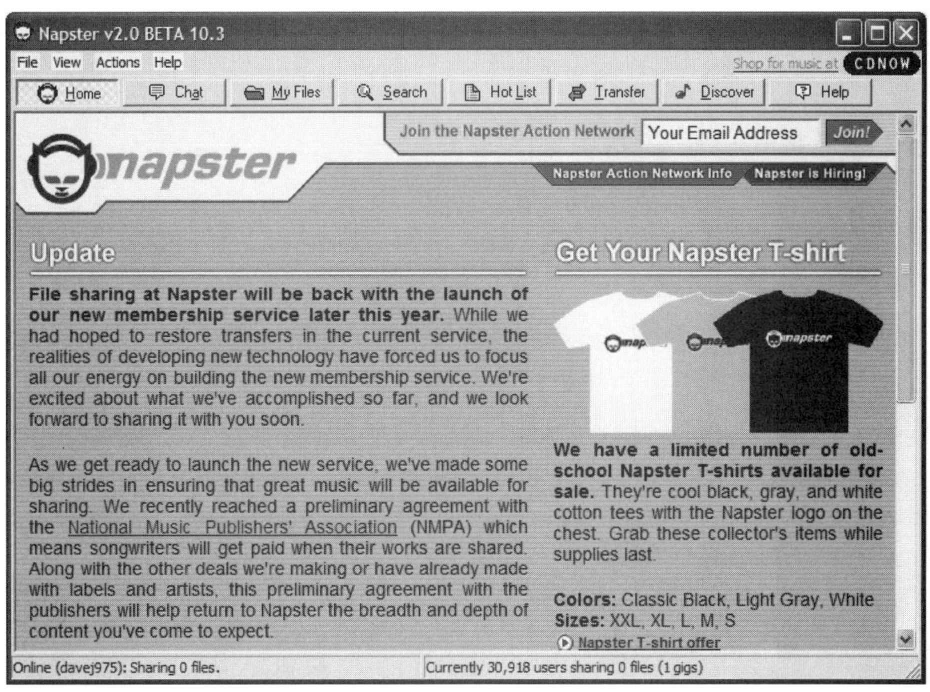

FIGURE B-1 Napster

Once the undisputed ruler of online file sharing, Napster is considered by many to be the ultimate expression of evil because it allowed ordinary folks to download songs for free, circumventing copyright and royalty payments. But many people—including some musicians, to be perfectly honest—applauded the way Napster eroded the draconian control of the record labels. Alas, that's all gone now. As we write this, Napster is retooling itself as a subscription membership service that lets you download music for a cost. Once, Napster had the best interface on the planet for finding and downloading music. Only time will tell if it's still worth visiting.

Morpheus

www.musiccity.com

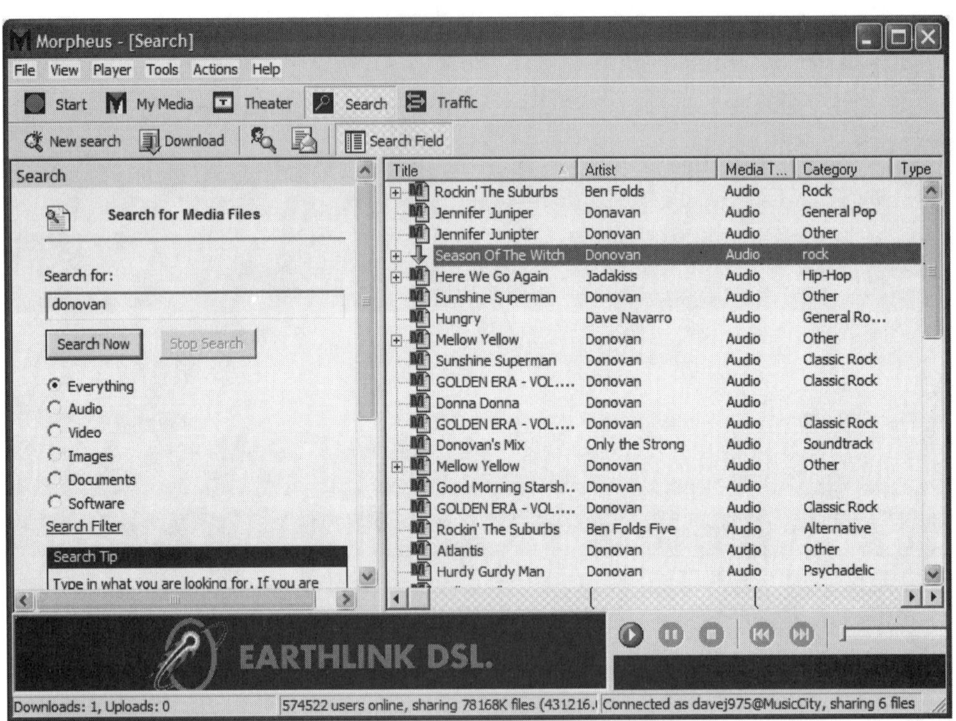

FIGURE B-2 Morpheus

One of the most popular file-sharing successors to Napster, Morpheus makes it easy to find and download music via the Internet. It's still free, and it's likely to survive a legal assault better than Napster because there's no central server coordinating file transfers—it's all done PC-to-PC. To use Morpheus, you need to download and install a program that serves as a download and file management tool. It's available for download at the Web site.

Aimster

www.aimster.com

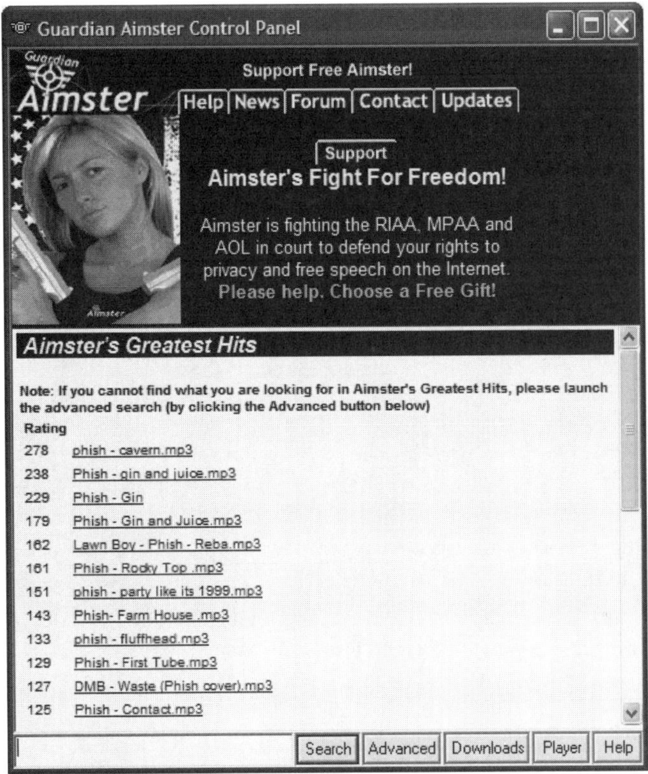

FIGURE B-3 Aimster

Aimster takes a personal approach to file sharing—it allows you to establish buddies and share music with them. Buddies can be people you already know and invite to the service, or they can be new buddies you meet on Aimster. Aimster makes it easy to search for potential buddies with common interests. But if, like Rick, you're antisocial and don't like talking to other people, Aimster might not be for you. Aimster requires you to chat with potential buddies before you can start downloading their out-of-print copy of *Autumn Leaves* by the now-defunct band Tonto's Expanding Headband.

iMesh

www.imesh.com

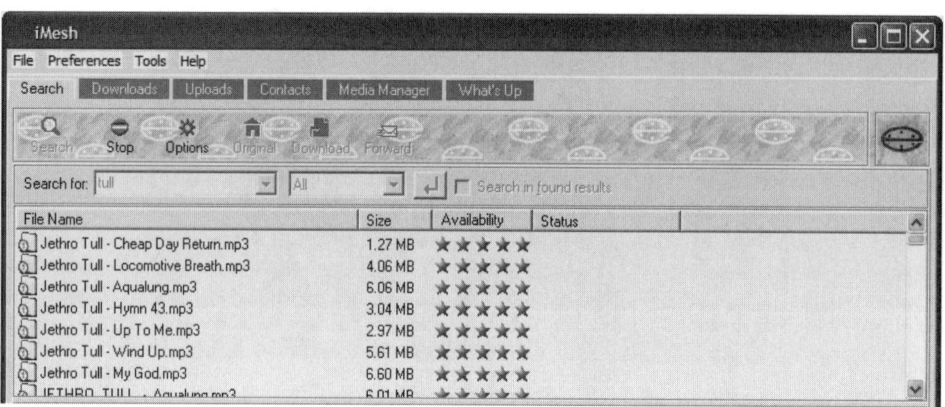

FIGURE B-4 iMesh

Like Napster, this service opens up your desktop archives so you can freely exchange files with other users. But while Napster handles only music files, iMesh lets you transfer audio, video, and image files. Another cool feature: when you disconnect from the Internet or close iMesh, all your partially downloaded files are saved, to be resumed from the exact place they stopped the next time you connect.

KaZaA

www.kazaa.com

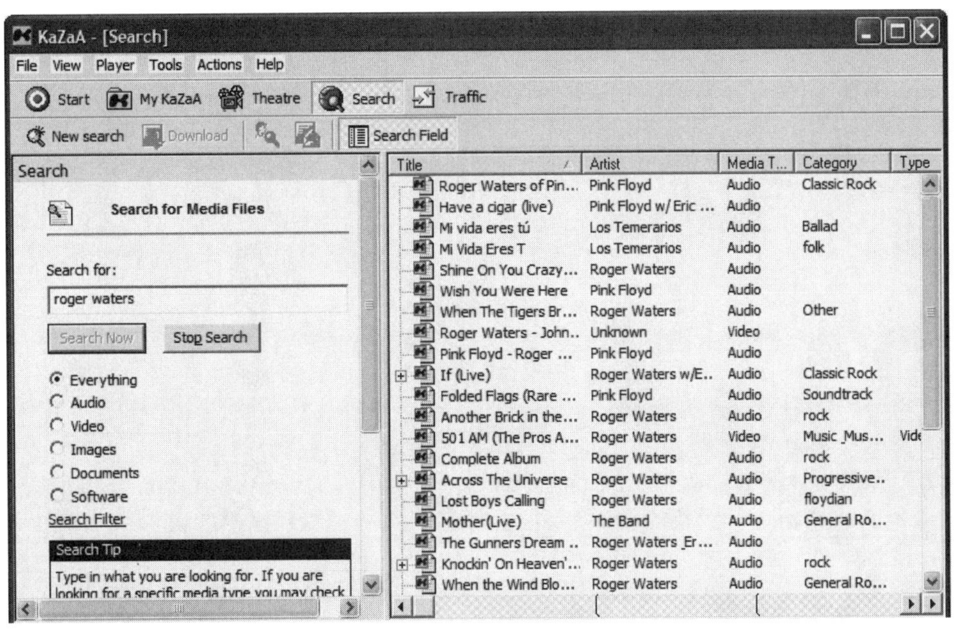

FIGURE B-5 KaZaA

KaZaA Media Desktop allows users to search, download, and play all sorts of media files, including audio, video, and images. The KaZaA Media Desktop is a full-featured peer-to-peer file-sharing application, like a next-generation version of Napster. You can search, download, organize, and play media files (including audio, video, images, and documents). KaZaA has a powerful search engine where you can search by a number of criteria including categories, artists, and titles. Search results are grouped together, so the same file will be displayed only once. KaZaA downloads from several sources simultaneously, thus speeding up the download, and downloads can be resumed if your connection to the Internet is broken in the midst of the download.

Audiogalaxy

www.audiogalaxy.com

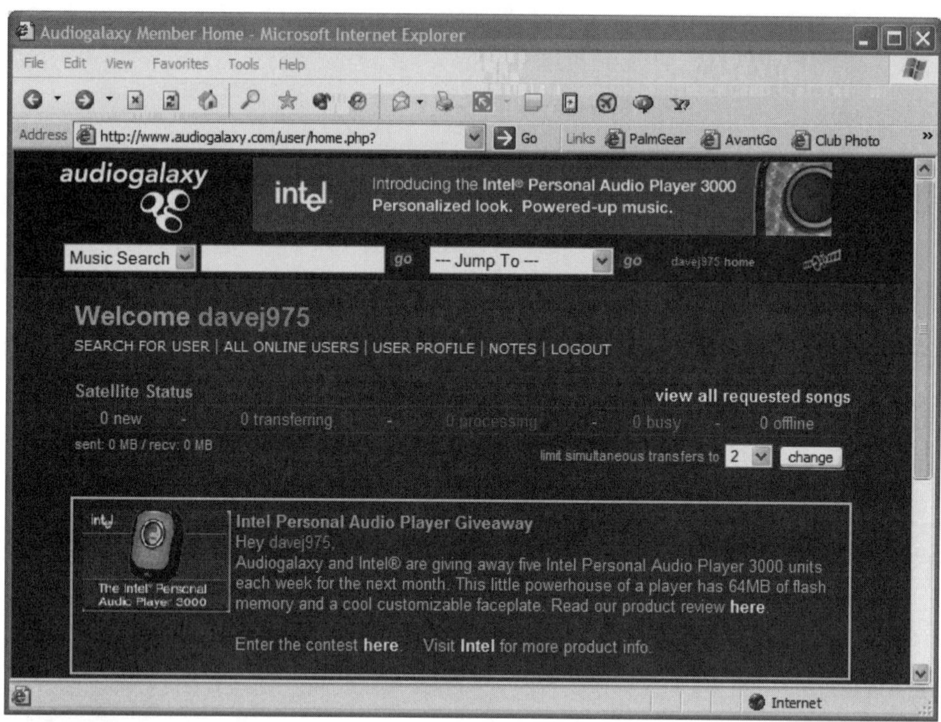

FIGURE B-6 Audiogalaxy

Audiogalaxy is a full-featured music Web site that includes news, artist profiles, music downloads, and community features like discussion boards. Audiogalaxy Satellite is a small program that allows you to share your music with friends and other users on Audiogalaxy. Audiogalaxy Satellite has a few very cool features: It supports autoresume, which picks up a download that was interrupted due to a loss of Internet connectivity. Even better, you can request offline files. If nobody is currently sharing the file you want, you can select it anyway; once someone comes online with that file, you will automatically start receiving it from them.

BearShare

www.bearshare.com

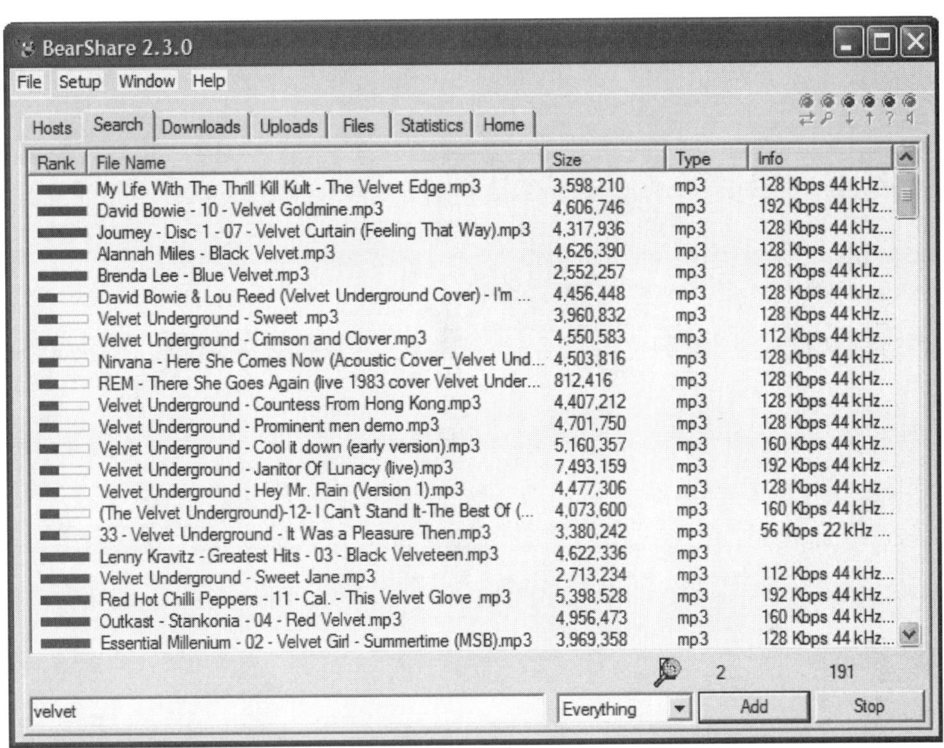

FIGURE B-7 BearShare

Remember Gnutella? It was one of the early competitors to Napster. And while many people used it, it never had the appeal of Napster. Now BearShare, which sounds all warm and fuzzy, is a file-sharing program built on Gnutella technology. That means that BearShare can act like a client to give you access to the Gnutella network of files. Several Gnutella clients are out there—like LimeWire, Newtella, and ToadNode—but we think BearShare is probably the best of the bunch. BearShare lets you share all kinds of files, not just music, and it lets you autoresume interrupted downloads. The program can also be set to automatically seek out (or avoid) users with very fast or slow modems.

WinMX

www.winmx.com

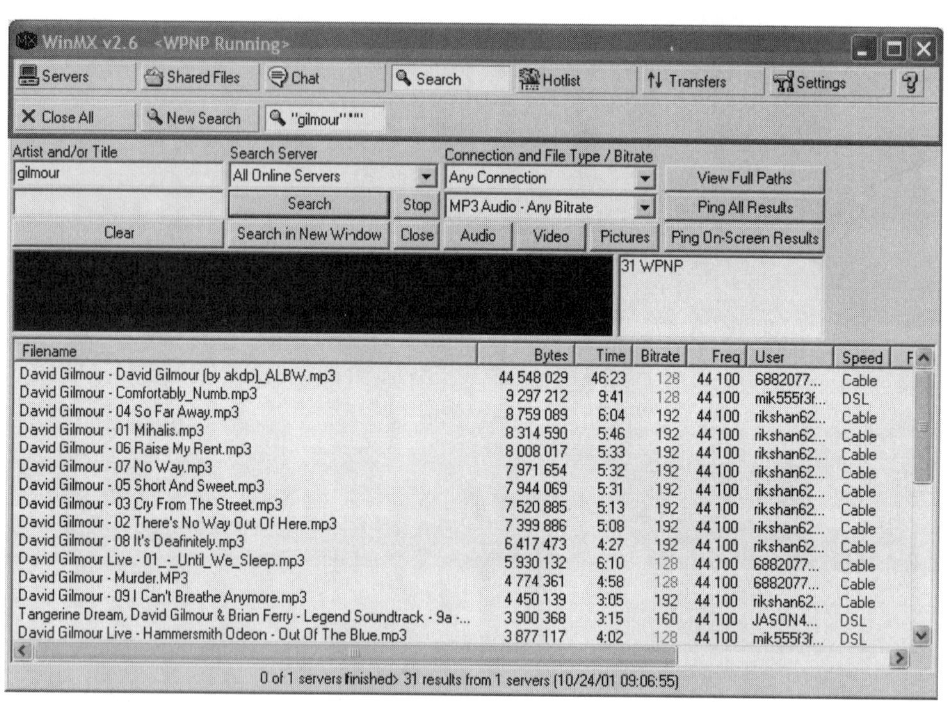

FIGURE B-8 WinMX

WinMX isn't a household name, but it offers you access to a vast, decentralized network of music, video, and other files. It allows you to simultaneously connect through the decentralized WinMX Peer Networking Protocol (which lets you ping other users' computers directly, without going through a central server) and to many networks based on OpenNap and Napster protocols. This means you can search the files of more users than with most other file-sharing programs and, consequently, get better results.

Appendix C

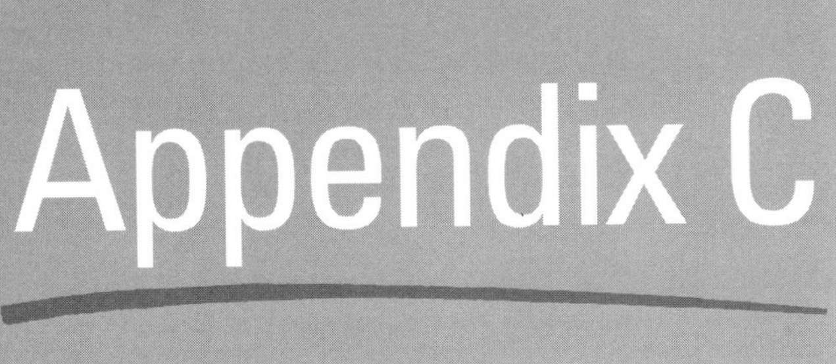

In Search of Storage Space

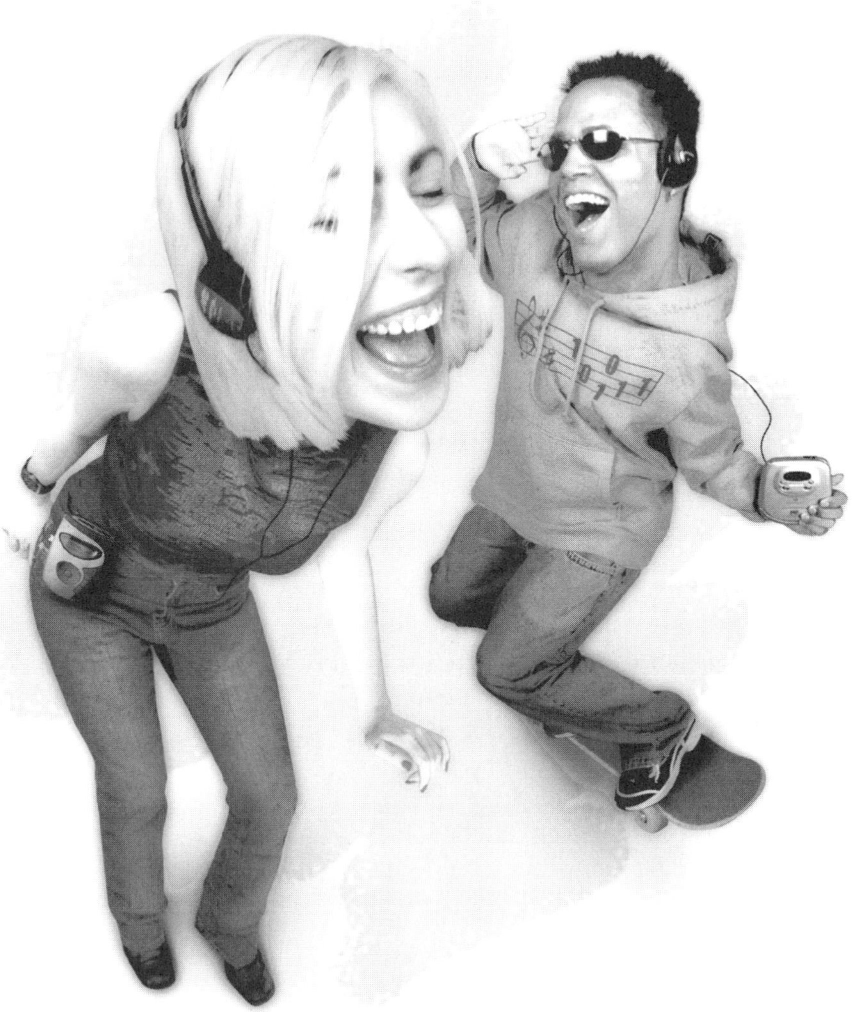

There's a saying where Dave comes from (which is Jersey City, in case you were wondering) that goes something like this: "Your boom box can never be too loud, and your computer can never have too much free disk space." We're not really sure about the first part of that old saying, but there's a lot of truth in the second part. PCs that are even only a few years old will no doubt run out of disk space all the time, especially if you start collecting a lot of music on your PC.

Think of this storage malady as the computer equivalent of bookshelves sagging under the weight of accumulated records or CDs. With high-quality digital music taking up about a megabyte a minute, a 10GB hard disk fills up faster than you can say "Rick, never e-mail me anything from Big Bad Voodoo Daddy ever again." Thankfully, you can increase a computer's capacity in a number of ways to make it ready for the digital music age. Along the way, you can make your PC the equivalent of an unlimited digital jukebox.

Unfortunately, external and removable storage devices come and go faster than members of Menudo. After all, who can remember SyQuest cartridges and IBM's 2.8MB floppy disk? The key is to pick the one that suits your needs, budget, and music storage habits. At 1.4MB, the floppy disk can hold about 90 seconds of music, but there are higher-capacity variants, the most popular of which is Iomega's Zip disk. This megafloppy can hold up to 250MB, although most Zip drives can read only the older 100MB disks. If cost is your greatest concern, the drives are dirt cheap, although the disks are quite expensive per megabyte, compared to the competitors.

In the next few pages, we'll talk about several kinds of storage systems: optical storage systems like recordable CD and recordable DVD, hard drives like Zip, Jaz, and Peerless, plus "virtual" drives you use via the Internet.

Optical Storage

For most, the fastest, easiest, and cheapest way to break through the hard-disk barrier is to keep music on recordable CDs. Most new computers come with a CD-RW drive, and you can pick one up for an older PC for as little as $100 in a computer store. CD-R discs (which cost less than $1 apiece) have a capacity of 700MB, which is good for about a dozen hours. That's a hard price/performance ratio to beat.

Is there a downside? There sure is. If you have lots of music on many different CD-Rs, you'll have no shortage of discs to manage. For instance, Brian Nadel, this book's technical editor, has six CDs that contain Grateful Dead bootleg shows, and he never knows what's on each until he puts the disc in his computer. Dave has copied many of his 400 CDs to MP3 format and then to CD-R, and while his entire Beatles collection fits on one CD, that still means he has over two dozen

CDs to keep track of. Plus, the lifetime of recordable CDs varies, so it's not the "till the end of time" archive that you may think it is.

Rewritable DVDs, which are just making their way into desktop PCs, are a good next step. These discs hold a little less than 5GB and, like CD-RW media, can be rewritten many times. The downside is that although recordable CDs can be played on any but the oldest computers, at the moment, only three DVD standards exist, none of which are fully compatible with each other. Worse, DVD discs can't be played in cars, portable music players, or 90 percent of the other places you'd routinely like to listen to music. This leads to the unenviable situation of recording music on one drive that cannot be listened to on another. However, its capacity is impressive, although the media is still quite expensive: as we write this, a single DVD-R costs about $12.

External Hard Disks

Don't neglect to consider the wide variety of external hard disks you can choose from, as well. These drives are similar to the drive that came inside your computer. Because of its easy setup and installation, one of our favorites is Pockey (www.pockeydrives.com). It's a complete hard disk—much like what you'd find inside a notebook computer—but connects to a PC or Mac via a USB plug. The capacity is currently limited to 20GB, but expect that to rise over time; its cost is $250. Plug in the drive to a computer, and a new drive letter appears on the computer's screen, ready to be filled with Bob Mould, Dead Can Dance, or The Call. Store 'N Sync on the drive at your own risk. Downside? The Pockey runs a little slower than the computer's native drive.

A similar solution is the BUSLink hard disk (www.buslink.com). BUSLink disks come in much larger capacities—as high as 60GB—and are available in both USB and FireWire varieties. FireWire is very fast but costs a little more; USB has the advantage of being relatively inexpensive.

If even that isn't enough, consider a removable hard disk. Here, the only constraint is the number of drive cartridges you have. You can choose from two major devices, both from Iomega (www.iomega.com). The venerable Jaz drive can hold 1GB or 2GB per cartridge, and the drive can connect via a USB, SCSI, PC card, or FireWire interface. The downside is cost. While the drive itself costs $350, the 2GB cartridges sell for $125 each. Ouch. That gets expensive very quickly.

Iomega's latest drive is called Peerless, a name that is only slight hyperbole. The idea behind Peerless is that you buy a base station for each interface you want to use; they are available for USB and FireWire at the moment, but if it catches on, expect to see a lot of other kinds of devices down the road. You can plug 10GB or

20GB cartridges into the base station. With a 20GB cartridge, the USB-based Peerless sells for $350, and the cartridges cost $200 or $160 depending on whether you want the 10GB or the 20GB variety.

Online Storage

Reluctant to install hardware on your computer? USB and FireWire gadgets are pretty painless, but we don't blame you if you'd rather avoid connections, drivers, and expansion ports altogether.

If that sounds like you, consider online storage. Here's the basic idea: you send your music (and any other data you want to store, for that matter) over a high-speed Internet connection to a secure storage site where your data hangs out and generally waits patiently until you want to listen to it. While this storage scheme is essentially limitless, most of the companies that offer this service limit you to around a gigabyte of storage space. The good news is that with the right plan, you can share your music with others; the bad news is that while startup costs are low, using online storage is a subscription plan that you pay for monthly.

The largest online storage firm is Xdrive (www.xdrive.com), and it offers a number of different plans, some of which integrate quite nicely with Windows XP. Regardless of which method you choose to stash your digital tunes, make sure you have an organization scheme because all bytes look alike.

Storage Schemes at a Glance

Type	Capacity	Price	Pros/Cons
Recordable CD	700MB	$.25 per disc	So cheap, it's almost free. Because CD-R discs play in almost every kind of entertainment and computer gadget ever made, it's also virtually universal.
Recordable DVD	4.8GB	$25 per disc	The next step after CDs, this high-capacity media holds a lot of data, but it's expensive and far from universally compatible.
External hard disk	20GB–60GB	$250–$600	Inexpensive and simple to install, an external hard disk can add a fixed capacity quickly and easily.
Iomega Zip drive	250MB	Drive: $100 Disc: $5	A virtual standard for removable storage, the Zip drive is sluggish and expensive for storing music. Most drives can work only with the older 100MB cartridges.
Iomega Jaz drive	2GB	Drive: $350 Cartridge: $125	Jaz's 2GB capacity limit seems a little antiquated these days.
Iomega Peerless drive	10GB or 20GB	Drive and 20GB cartridge: $350 10GB cartridge: $160	The latest in removable storage, Peerless combines high capacity with a reasonable price tag. Even so, it gets expensive to collect lots of cartridges.
Virtual online storage	Unlimited	1GB: $50 per month	Forget about external drives and cartridges; store your data on the Internet. It's very convenient but extremely expensive, and it requires a high-speed Web connection to be effective.

Appendix D

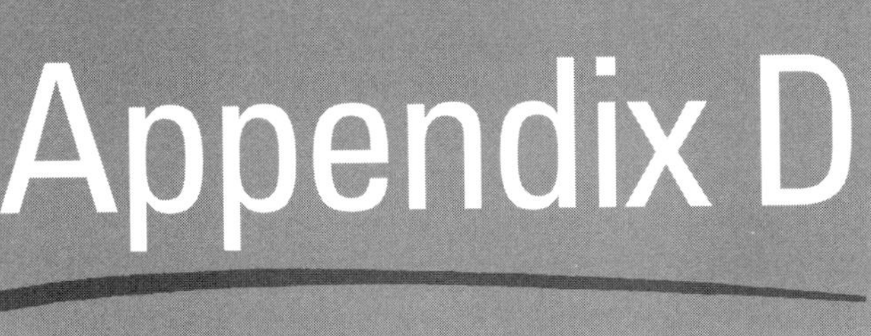

Portable Player Memory Cards

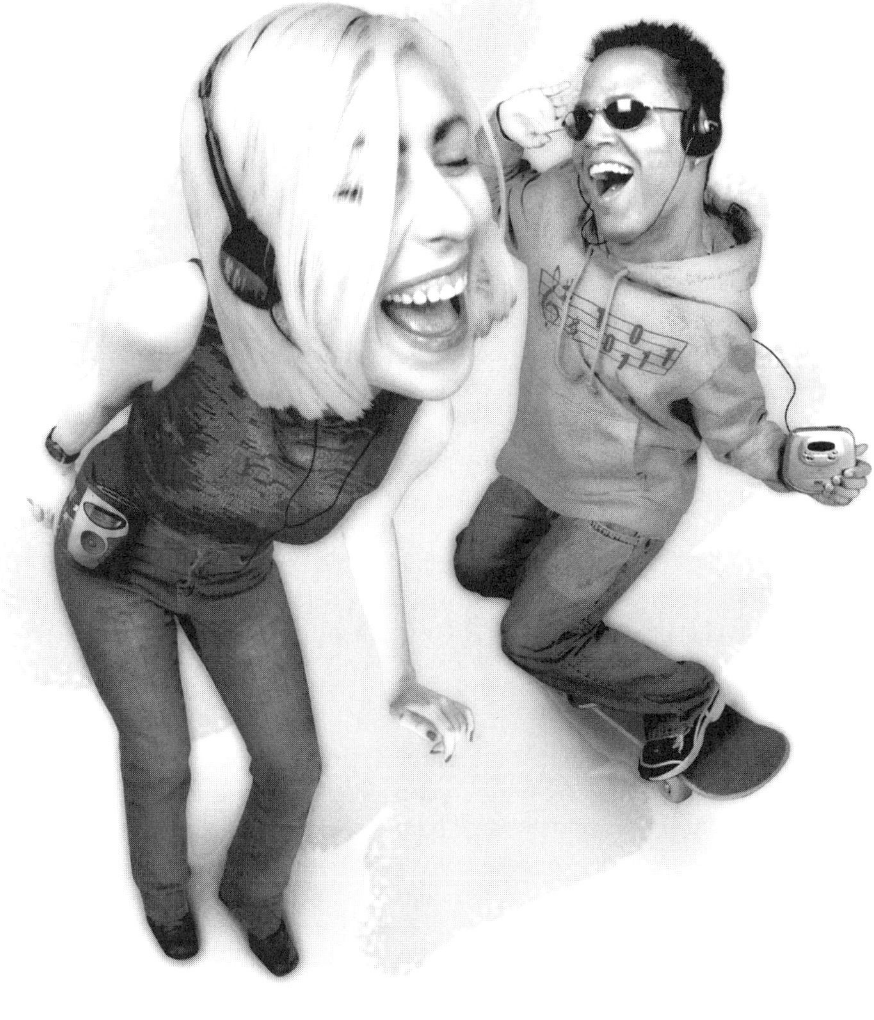

While the music world has pretty much standardized on MP3 as the digital format of choice, those that make and sell portable players have not reached the same level of agreement when it comes to the modules that store the music. Early players didn't have to worry about memory-card standardization because they shipped with a small, fixed amount of memory (typically a meager 32MB), and that was pretty much that. More recent players include a slot that lets you insert removable modules that can store as much as a gigabyte of music, making them portable jukeboxes. And everyone, it seems, uses a different kind of memory card.

To the uninitiated, it might seem as if there is a different kind of card format for every player on the market, although there are really only five major formats that grace MP3 players: CompactFlash (CF), SmartMedia (SM), Memory Stick, Secure Digital (SD) cards, and MultiMedia cards (MMCs). They differ in terms of capacity, price, and how easy it will be to get them to talk to a computer. Here's a rundown of what you should know about these cards.

Memory Cards 101

While they all seem to appear totally different, memory cards are similar in two regards: they are all fairly small, and under the surface, they all use something called *flash memory*. Why flash? Flash memory is a slightly more expensive version of the RAM that stores data in your computer, but it has an important difference: it doesn't lose the data it holds when the power is turned off. This allows the cards to be written to when connected to a computer and then hold the data until you're ready to listen to it. In fact, these modules are nearly indestructible and are not bothered by weather, loud noise, moisture, or barking dogs.

There are two types of flash memory: NOR and NAND. Quite thankfully, it doesn't really matter what the acronyms stand for. You might want to know, though, that NAND flash is much quicker for writing new data to a card, and consequently, it's the most popular type of chip used in these memory modules.

CompactFlash

Created primarily for digital cameras, the largest of the five cards is CompactFlash, which is actually related to those big PC cards (also known as PCMCIA cards) used in notebook PCs. The modules are about the size of a matchbox, yet can hold up to 512MB (about eight-and-a-half hours of MP3 music) of flash memory on a single card. It may be the largest card around, but it can hold only four times the amount of music that most of the other cards can, and it's only large in comparison to the others. It's actually pretty small. It's the biggest kid on the block, though, because CompactFlash cards can use up to eight separate memory chips. The other guys typically use just one chip for all memory storage. For that reason alone, it will lead in terms of capacity and price for the near future.

CompactFlash has another advantage: speed. Although it won't help during playback, a fast chip can make the transfer to the card go faster. The latest advance in CompactFlash is called Ultra, which can be written at up to 2.8 Mbps—about four times that of other memory cards. Unfortunately, Ultra cards are quite a bit more expensive, although you can expect prices to come down as the format catches on.

SmartMedia

About the same time that CompactFlash made its debut in the heady days of the mid-1990s, another format arrived as well: SmartMedia. SmartMedia was found almost exclusively in digital cameras until MP3 players came along. These cards are paper thin, eerily flexible, and have a series of gold contacts at the bottom. They use a single memory chip and also require some extra electronics on the reading and writing end to move the data, which makes the card reader more expensive and bulky compared to CompactFlash cards. On the downside, the largest capacity is limited to 128MB, or about two hours of music. It is also much more fragile; we have heard from several folks who have lost data to damaged SmartMedia cards.

Memory Stick

The chewing gum size of the Memory Stick standard is an industrial designer's dream come true. Rather than building the player around a wide and thick memory card, the Memory Stick card lets designers go thin, leading to players like the Sony Network Walkman, which is the size of a magic marker. This rigid purple card can be had in sizes up to 128MB, but these cards are half again as expensive as CompactFlash modules.

Secure Digital/MultiMediaCards

In contrast, MultiMedia and Secure Digital cards are similar in appearance and generally interchangeable, but not 100 percent compatible with each other. The less-expensive MMC format will not work in an SD device or card reader, although SD cards will work with most MMC equipment. The SD format is built around a postage stamp–sized module that holds a single memory chip and is currently limited to 128MB of storage space. It's the darling of handheld computer makers (like Compaq and Palm) as well as the latest MP3 players from Japan, because the cards are small, light, and the king of power conservation.

Security and Memory Cards

For piracy-crazed music makers, the newest designs have built-in protection. Memory Stick devices, for instance, have an encryption mechanism called Magic Gate that can protect copyrighted music, and SD cards have built-in cryptographic security. The problem is that there is no single standard yet, so we're just going to have to wait for the music industry to decide which standard they will embrace.

Memory Cards at a Glance

Type	Max Capacity	Price Per Megabyte (Approximate)	Our Prognosis
CompactFlash (CF)	512MB	$.88	This memory card offers the largest capacity and the best price point of all the formats. It'll probably stay that way for some time to come, but CompactFlash will eventually be displaced by newer, cooler formats like SD. The IBM Microdrive hard disk delivers a huge capacity in the larger Type II–style CompactFlash card.
SmartMedia (SM)	128MB	$1.35	One of the oldest and lamest formats, SM cards will soon be outmoded due to cost and capacity limitations.
Memory Stick	128MB	$1.32	Sony's proprietary format is slowly branching out with new card makers. Unfortunately, only Sony makes the goods, and Memory Stick has little that's uniquely better than other formats like CF or SD. Use it if you have Sony gear; otherwise, there's no particular reason to like (or dislike) it.
MultiMedia Card (MMC)	64MB	$1.10	While it's essentially the same as SD, the MultiMediaCard won't last much longer due to industry politics.
Secure Digital (SD)	128MB	$1.80	Ultimately, SD cards will probably be the overall winner due to tiny size and built-in encryption. The maximum capacity of SD will be limited for the next few years, and the cards will also be somewhat expensive—but eventually, SD will be cheap, spacious, and plentiful.

Index

A

Acer iRhythm, 106
Adaptec Easy CD Creator 4, 25
Aimster Web site, 347
Alexander, Cherish, 312–314
Altec Lansing AVS500 speakers, 21
Amazon.com
    downloading music from, 47, 49, 63–64
    finding music on, 64
    selling your CD through, 297
Ampcast.com, 288–290
    CD program, 289–290
    general features, 290
    royalties, 289
Amplitude, 171
Analog audio, 194–220
    cables used for, 200–204
    checklist for recording, 212–213
    clean media tips for, 222–223
    connecting to, 194–196
    definition of, 174
    digital audio vs., 173–177
    Easy CD Creator for recording, 216–219
    getting close to source of, 219–220
    output connectors for, 198–199
    recording process for, 208–220
    saving recorded files from, 213–214
    setting the recording device for, 208–210
    software for recording, 204, 206–207
    sound card inputs for, 196–198
    sources of, 195
    strategies for recording, 214–216
    volume settings for, 210–212
Analog rip, 170, 190–191
Apple iTunes player, 9
Archive quality media, 176–177
Archos Jukebox player/recorder, 124, 220
ASF streaming files, 283
Audible Advisor, 137
Audigy MP3+ sound card, 19–20, 162
Audio
    analog, 194–220
    digital, 14, 170–180
    editing, 222–238
    quality issues, 154–166
    streaming, 66, 96–97, 278–283
Audio cable, 26
Audio CDs
    burning, 272–276
    creating with MP3 files, 276–277
    data CDs vs., 266, 267–268
    disc types and, 265–266
    getting a UPC number for, 302
    making a disc image, 275–276
    mastering and duplicating, 300–302
    preparing to record, 262–267
    promoting, 302–304
    recording options for, 269–271

ripping music from, 181–191, 290
selling your own, 296–300
sessions on, 270–272
software for creating, 25
Audio Cleaning Lab, 234
Audio discs, 266
Audio editors, 223–224
cleaning up noise with, 233–237
deleting silent leaders with, 225–226
fading music in and out with, 231–232
inserting silent leaders with, 226–227
normalizing audio files with, 237–238
pasting tracks together with, 230–231
splitting files into tracks with, 228–230
Audio files
converting, 154–156
digital formats for, 177, 179–180
normalizing, 156–158
Audio Home Recording Act (AHRA), 33, 34, 35
Audio tracks
pasting together, 230–231
splitting files into, 228–230
AudioCatalyst, 214
Audiogalaxy Web site, 350
AudioStocker plug-in, 157
Audiotools program, 207, 216
AudioTron, 145–146
Average RMS setting, 237

B

Band names, 289
Beam-it feature (MP3.com), 54–55
BearShare Web site, 351
Belkin 4-Port USB Hub, 21
Bit rates
file storage and, 241–242
getting information on, 63
Internet radio, 99
sound quality and, 158, 241
variable, 183
Blue Note Radio, 105
Bonzaroo.com, 101
Bootleg recordings, 36
Broadband Internet connection, 29
Internet radio and, 99
Broadcasting, online, 97
Buffer underrun, 25, 263
Burning CDs, 262–278
data format for, 267–268
discs for, 265–266
making a disc image for, 275–276
MP3 CDs, 276–277
options for, 269–271
preparing your computer for, 263–264
speed considerations, 266–267
steps in process of, 272–276
BUSLink hard disk, 355

C

Cables (audio)
accessories, 202
analog source to PC, 200–204
inside PCs, 26
MP3 player to stereo, 149
PC to stereo, 140–142
quality of, 203–204
Cache, 25
Capacitance, 204
Car MP3 players, 11–12, 124–129, 131
hard disk players, 126–127
in-dash receivers, 125–126
portable player adaptability, 122–123, 127, 129
wireless transmitter for, 129
See also Portable MP3 players
Cassette tapes. *See* Analog audio

CD burners, 22, 269–278
    See also Easy CD Creator
CD players, playing MP3s on, 115, 123
CD Programs
    Ampcast.com, 289–290
    MP3.com, 288
CDDB (CD Database) service, 247, 249, 253
CDex utility, 290
CD-R discs, 265
    audio vs. data, 266, 267–268
    burning speed of, 266–267
    storing music on, 354–355, 357
CD-ROM drives, 189–190
CD-RW discs, 266
CD-RW drives, 22–26
    choosing, 23–25
    formats of, 263–264
    installing, 25–26
    legality of, 38
    speed of, 267
CDs
    data vs. audio, 266, 267–268
    types of, 265–266
    See also Audio CDs
Children's music, 55
Clarke, Graham, 55
Classical music radio stations (Internet), 324–325
Cleaning up noise, 233–237
    programs and plug-ins for, 234–236
    tips and guidelines for, 236–237
CompactFlash (CF) cards, 130, 360–361, 362
Compaq iPAQ, 135
Compression, 6
Computers
    determining memory on, 17
    listening to MP3s on, 9, 10
    music player software for, 70–93
    portable MP3 player connections to, 116–117
    preparing to burn CDs, 263–264
    ripping music from CDs on, 188–190
Concert and event calendars (Ampcast.com), 290
Converting audio files, 154–156
Cool Edit 2000 program, 206–207, 223
    Audio Cleanup plug-in, 235
    editing audio files, 226, 229, 231
    normalizing audio files, 238
Copy-protection technology, 39–40
Copyright issues
    copy protection and, 39–40
    legal controversy surrounding, 32–37
    See also Legal issues
Copyright Wizard (MP3.com), 287
Costs
    of memory cards, 133
    of MP3 players, 72
Country music radio stations (Internet), 326
Credit card processing, 299

D

Dance music radio stations (Internet), 327–331
Darby, Diana, 310–312
Data CDs, 266, 267–268
Decibels (dB), 171
Decompression songs, 157
Defragmenting hard disks, 189, 264
Deleting silent leaders, 225–226
Destructive playback media, 176–177
Dial-up Internet connection, 29, 30
Diamond Multimedia Systems, 33, 34, 120
Digisette Duo-64 MP3 player, 122–123
Digital audio, 14, 170–180
    advantages of, 176–177
    analog audio vs., 173–177

definition of, 174
explained, 170–173
file formats for, 177, 179–180, 181
resolution of, 172
ripping music from CDs, 180–191
sampling rate of, 172–173
Digital Audio Extraction (DAE), 142, 170
Digital music sites, 47–58
Amazon.com, 47, 49, 63–64
downloading music from, 63–64
finding music on, 51–52, 53, 64
list of sites, 58
MP3.com, 50–57
See also File-sharing services
Digital Signal Processing (DSP), 122
Disc sessions, 270–272
Disc-At-Once recording, 227, 270
Download.com, 71
Download managers, 30
Downloading music
choosing version to download, 64–65
file-sharing services for, 58–67
finding songs, 51–52
legality of, 38
music sites for, 47–58
playing downloaded songs, 50
process of, 63–64
top Web sites for, 344–352
Duplicating CDs, 300–302
DVD-Audio (DVD-A), 176
DVD players, playing CDs with MP3s on, 150–151
DVD-R discs, 355, 357
Dynamic range, 177
optimizing, 237–238

E

Easy CD Creator, 25
burning CDs with, 272–276
choosing recording options in, 269–271
creating MP3 CDs with, 277
making a disc image with, 275–276
recording analog audio with, 216–219
Edison, Thomas, 4
Editing audio, 222–238
audio editors for, 223–224
cleaning up noise, 233–237
cutting up music, 224–225
deleting silent leaders, 225–226
fading music in and out, 231–232
inserting silent leaders, 226–227
normalizing audio files, 237–238
pasting tracks together, 230–231
splitting a file into tracks, 228–230
Electronic music radio stations (Internet), 327–331
Electronic sound, 172
E-mail, sending music links via, 57
Emerson, Ralph Waldo, 4
Encoders, 214, 244, 246
Equalizers, 74, 158–162
Winamp, 159–160
Windows Media Player, 161–162
Ethernet, stereo/computer link via, 146, 148
Ethical issues, 36, 37
Evolution NeckPhone, 115
External hard drives, 19, 355–356, 357

F

Fading options, 231–232
Fast song approval service (Ampcast.com), 290
Fictional band names, 289
File formats
digital audio, 177, 179–180
See also specific file formats
File type associations, 254–256

Filenames
  controlling playback with, 243
  options for selecting, 246–249
  origin of information on, 247
File-sharing services, 58–67
  file sizes on, 65
  fundamentals of using, 59
  Gnutella Network, 60
  grouping songs on, 66
  hackers and, 60
  how to choose, 66
  LimeWire program, 60–66
  list of sites, 67
  quality ratings on, 65
  top Web sites, 344–352
  See also Sharing your music
Films, music, 205
Finding
  digital music, 51–52, 53, 64
  Internet radio stations, 100–101, 104
  shared music files, 62
Firewalls, 60
Flash memory, 360
Folders, organizing MP3 files in, 243–245
Freeware, 71
Frequency, 171
Funky songs, 27
FusionOne Web service, 57

G

Gigabyte (GB), 18
Global Positioning System (GPS), 136
Gnutella Network, 60
Graphic equalizers. *See* Equalizers
Grouped option, LimeWire, 66

H

Hackers, and file-sharing software, 60
Handspring Visor, 136
Hard disk MP3 players, 126–127
Hard drives, 18–19
  defragmenting, 189, 264
  external, 19
  recommended for MP3s, 18
  recording analog audio to, 213
  storing MP3 files on, 241–242, 355–356, 357
  used for ripping music, 189
Hardware issues, 16–26
  CD-RW drive, 22–26
  hard drive, 18–19
  processor, 17
  RAM, 17–18
  sound card, 19–20
  speakers, 20, 21
  USB ports, 20–22
Headphones, 165–166
Hertz (Hz), 171
Hewlett-Packard Jornada, 135
Hi Fi Play option (MP3.com), 57
High-capacity MP3 players, 115
Himmelman, Peter, 308–310
Hip-hop radio stations (Internet), 327–331
History
  of MP3 controversy, 32–37
  of recorded music, 4–5
Home Phoneline Networking Alliance (HPNA), 146, 148
Home stereo systems, 12–13, 140–151
  AudioTron link to, 145–146
  cable link to, 140–142
  DVD players in, 150–151
  Internet radio played on, 147–148
  list of MP3 items for, 151
  plugging portable MP3 players into, 149–150
  Rio Receiver link to, 148–149
  wireless link to, 142–144

I

ID3 tags, 249–254
  editing, 250–254

explained, 249–250
globally changing, 252–254
manually changing, 253
Palm devices and, 251
viewing, 250
Illegal activities, 38–39
Image method, 269, 275–276
iMesh Web site, 348
In-dash receivers with MP3, 125–126
InnoGear MiniJam MP3 player module, 136–137
Installing
CD-RW drives, 25–26
LimeWire program, 61
Instant Listening option (MP3.com), 55–56
Intel Pocket Concert player, 115
Internet
broadband connection to, 29
CDDB service on, 247, 249
modem connection to, 29, 30
radio stations on, 318–342
See also World Wide Web
Internet radio, 96–111
creating your own station, 291–293
custom radio shows, 105–108
explained, 96–97
finding stations on, 100–101, 104
general guidelines for, 111
getting your songs on, 291–293
high-speed access to, 99
home stereo systems and, 106, 147–148
legality of, 38
listening to, 97–99
MusicMatch Radio MX, 109–110
portable appliance for, 147–148
Preset list, 103–104
RealJukebox and, 108–109
SHOUTcast service, 110–111, 291–293
sound quality of, 99
sources of, 97
stations on, 318–342
Webcasting via, 111
Windows Media Player and, 100, 101, 102–104
See also Radio stations
Iomega Jaz drive, 355, 357
Iomega Peerless drive, 355–356, 357
iRhythm appliance, 106, 147–148
iTunes music player, 85–86

J

Jaz drive, 355, 357
Jazz music, 105, 232–233
Internet radio stations, 332–333
Joliet format, 276
Jukeboxes, 71

K

KaZaA Media Desktop, 349
Kima Wireless Systems, 129, 143–144
Kristin Hersh, 306–308

L

Leaders
deleting, 225–226
determining length of, 227
inserting, 226–227
Legal issues, 8–9, 32–41
copy protection and, 39–40
ethical issues and, 36, 37
history of MP3 lawsuits, 32–37
illegal activities, 38–39
legal activities, 38
MP3.com litigation, 34–35
Napster litigation, 35–37
Rio MP3 player controversy, 33, 34
LimeWire program, 60–66
downloading, 60
Grouped option, 66

installing, 61
launching, 62
limitations, 63
Quality ratings, 65
tips on using, 64–66
Link-It wireless transmitter, 129
Linn, Mark, 312
Liquid Audio format, 48
Listening to MP3 files
on car players, 11–12
on computers, 9, 10
on home stereos, 12–13
on portable MP3 players, 9, 10
See also Playing downloaded music
Lo Fi Play option (MP3.com), 56
Lossless files, 179
Lossy files, 179
LPs. *See* Analog audio

M

M3U files, 280–281
Macintosh platform
music players for, 85–90
operating system issues, 26–28
Web site on MP3 for, 17
Macrovision, 39
Magic Gate encryption, 362
Mase, Barry, 315–316
Mase, Dana, 314–316
Mastering CDs, 300–302
Meaningful songs, 128–129
Memory
flash, 360
getting information about, 17
portable MP3 player, 115–116, 130–133, 360–362
recommended for playing MP3s, 17–18
required for burning CDs, 264
used for ripping music, 189
Memory cards, 130–133, 360–362
CompactFlash, 130, 360–361
comparison of, 133, 362
Memory Stick, 132–133, 361
MultiMediaCard, 131–132, 361
Secure Digital, 131–132, 361
security and, 362
SmartMedia, 130, 361
Memory Stick, 132–133, 361, 362
Microdrives, 130
Miniphone jacks, 200
Modem Internet connection, 29, 30
Monkees (group), 277
Monster Cable, 203
Morpheus Web site, 346
MP3.com, 50–57, 286–288
Beam-it feature, 54–55
CD Program, 288
children's music section, 55
Copyright Wizard, 287
downloading music from, 50–57
finding music on, 51–52, 53
Instant Listening option, 55–56
lawsuit against, 34–35
Music Licensing Program, 287–288
My.MP3 service, 52
Payback for Playback program, 287
Premium Artist Service, 287
Promo Auctions, 288
selling your CD through, 297
song options on, 56–57
MP3 files, 5
benefits of, 8
converting WAV files to, 214
copy protection for, 39–40
creating audio CDs with, 276–277
downloading, 46–67, 344–352
editing ID3 tags, 249–254
hardware issues, 16–26
Internet connection issues, 29–30
legal issues, 8–9, 32–41
listening to, 9–14
operating system issues, 26–28

saving analog recordings as, 213–214
sound quality issues, 154–166
sources of, 7–8
splitting into tracks, 228–230
storing, 241–242, 354–357
streaming, 278–283
top Web sites for, 344–352
WAV files compared to, 179–180, 181

MP3 players. *See* Music players; Portable MP3 players
MP3 Wave Maker, 214
MPEG (Moving Picture Experts Group), 5
MPLAY music player, 87–88
MultiMediaCard (MMC), 131–132, 361, 362
Music films, 205
Music Licensing Program (MP3.com), 287–288
Music players, 70–93
considerations for choosing, 70–72
equalizers for, 74, 158–162
features common to, 73–74
finding on the Web, 71
iTunes, 85–86
Macintosh-based, 85–90
MPLAY, 87–88
MusicMatch Jukebox, 82–85, 88–90
playlists for, 73, 77, 78–79, 84–85, 89–90
RealJukebox, 80–82
skins for, 73, 89, 90–92
viewing ID3 tag information in, 250
visualizations for, 74, 92–93
volume controls for, 90
Winamp, 75–76
Windows Media Player, 76–80
Windows-based, 72–85

Music sites, 47–67
digital music sites, 47–58
file-sharing services, 58–67
independent musician sites, 305–316
lists of, 58, 67
top download sites, 344–352

Musicians
essential resources for, 298
examples of independent artists, 305–316
finishing touches for CDs by, 300–302
methods of sharing your music, 286–293
promotional tips for, 302–304
selling your CD, 296–300

MusicMatch Jukebox
creating playlists in, 84–85, 89–90
editing ID3 tags in, 251, 253–254
file-naming options, 247
interface, 83, 88
Macintosh version, 88–90
organizing folders in, 244–245
playing music with, 84, 89–90
Radio MX features, 109–110
ripping music from CDs with, 184–186
Windows version, 82–85

My.MP3 service, 52, 55, 57

N

Napster, 345
lawsuit against, 35–37
"legal" alternatives to, 39

Neo Jukebox MP3 player, 115, 124
Network radio stations (Internet), 318–319
News radio stations (Internet), 319–323
Noise cleanup, 233–237
programs and plug-ins for, 234–236
tips and guidelines for, 236–237

Normalizing audio files, 156–158, 237–238

O

O'Connell, Billy, 307
One-Click Audio Converter, 155–156
Online broadcasting, 97
Online storage, 356, 357
Online stores, 296–298
Operating system issues, 26–28
Optical storage, 354–355
Optimizing dynamic range, 237–238
Organizing music files, 240–257
- controlling playback, 243
- editing ID3 tags, 249–254
- file-naming options, 246–249
- fixing file type associations, 254–256
- folder strategy, 243–245
- planning for MP3 storage, 241–242

P

Packaging CDs, 301
Painkillers (group), 312–314
Palm OS devices
- editing ID3 tags on, 251
- options for choosing, 136, 137
- playing MP3s on, 23, 133–134, 136–137

Pasting audio tracks together, 230–231
Payback for Playback program (MP3.com), 287
Payments, accepting from customers, 298–300
PayPal, 299–300
PCI slots, 197
PDAs. *See* Personal Digital Assistants
Peak level setting, 237
Peerless drive, 355–356, 357
Peer-to-peer file sharing, 39
Perfect reproduction, 177
Personal computers. *See* Computers
Personal Digital Assistants (PDAs)
- editing ID3 tags on, 251
- options for choosing, 135, 136, 137
- playing MP3s on, 23, 133–137

PhatNoise Car Audio System, 12, 127
Playing downloaded music, 50
- choosing music player software, 70–72
- Macintosh-based music players, 85–90
- Windows-based music players, 72–85
- *See also* Music players; Portable MP3 players

Playlists, 73, 77
- MusicMatch Jukebox, 84–85, 89–90
- recording CDs from, 269
- Windows Media Player, 78–79

Playster program, 251
Plug-ins
- for cleaning up audio, 234–236
- for Internet radio, 99, 291–292
- for normalizing audio files, 156–158

Pocket PCs
- options for choosing, 135
- playing MP3s on, 23, 133–135

Pockey hard disk, 355
Pop music radio stations (Internet), 335–342
Pornography, 59
Portable MP3 players, 9, 10, 114–124
- batteries for, 117–118
- budget-minded, 120–121
- car stereo adaptability, 122–123, 127, 129
- CD players combined with, 123
- comparison of features, 120
- connecting to PCs, 116–117
- flying with, 127
- legal issues related to, 33, 34, 38
- long-playing, 122, 124
- memory in, 115–116, 130–133, 360–362
- PDAs used as, 23, 133–137

plugging into home stereos, 149–150
preparing for travel, 119
special features of, 118–119
turning PDAs into, 23
types of, 114–115
voice recorder in, 121
Web resources on, 120
wireless transmitter for, 129
See also Car MP3 players

Premium Artist Service (MP3.com), 287
Preproduction demo, 302
Presets
equalizer, 160, 162
Internet radio, 103–104
Press releases, 302–304
Processor requirements, 17
Promo Auctions (MP3.com), 288
Promoting your music, 302–304
examples of, 305–316
press releases for, 302–304
writing to your fans, 304
See also Selling your CD; Sharing your music
Properties for Sound dialog box, 175

Q

Quality issues. *See* Sound quality
Quality ratings, LimeWire, 65

R

R&B radio stations (Internet), 334–335
Radio stations (Internet), 318–342
classical music, 324–325
country music, 326
creating your own station, 291–293
general/networks, 318–319
hip-hop/electronic/dance music, 327–331
jazz music, 332–333
news/sports/talk, 319–323
R&B/soul music, 334–335
rock/pop music, 335–342
See also Internet radio
Radio Tuner feature (Windows Media Player), 100, 101, 102–104
RadioMOI.com, 105–108
features, 106–107
problems with, 108
RAM. *See* Memory
Ratings service (Ampcast.com), 290
Ray Gun plug-in, 236
RCA Lyra RD2211 MP3 player, 122
Real audio format, 66
RealJukebox, 66, 80–82
controls for, 80
editing ID3 tags in, 250, 252
file-naming options, 248
fixing file type associations in, 255–256
organizing folders in, 245
playing music with, 82
ripping music from CDs with, 183–184
tuning into Internet radio with, 100, 108–109
RealPlayer files, 283
RealProducer program, 281–282
Rechargeable batteries, 117–118
Record Control dialog box, 210–212
Recording analog audio, 194–220
cables used for, 200–204
checklist for, 212–213
clean media tips for, 222–223
Easy CD Creator used for, 216–219
getting close to audio source for, 219–220
making connections for, 194–196
output connectors for, 198–199
process of, 208–220
saving recorded files, 213–214
setting the recording device for, 208–210

software for, 204, 206–207
sound card inputs for, 196–198
strategies for, 214–216
volume settings for, 210–212
Recording CDs. *See* Burning CDs
Recording Industry Association of America (RIAA), 33, 266
Red Book Audio CD, 267
Resolution, 172
Rio 800 MP3 player, 121–122
Rio Car MP3 player, 126
Rio One MP3 player, 120–121
Rio PMP300 MP3 player, 33, 34
Rio Receiver, 12, 13, 106, 148–149
Rio Volt CD/MP3 player, 115, 123
Ripping music from CDs, 170, 181–191
CDDB service and, 247, 249
choosing a ripper program, 180–181
dealing with glitches, 188–190
making analog copies, 190–191
MusicMatch used for, 184–186
RealJukebox used for, 183–184
steps in process of, 182
variable bit rates and, 183
Windows Media Player used for, 186–188
Rock music radio stations (Internet), 335–342
Rock Songwriting Challenge, 314
RockSteady plug-in, 156–157
Roxio Easy CD Creator. *See* Easy CD Creator
Royalties (Ampcast.com), 289

S

Sales data (Ampcast.com), 290
Sampling rate, 172–173
Satellite speakers, 163, 164
Searching. *See* Finding
Secure Digital (SD) cards, 131–132, 361, 362
Security
file-sharing software, 60
memory card, 362
Selling your CD, 296–304
accepting payment, 298–300
examples of, 305–316
getting a UPC number, 302
information resources for, 298
mastering and duplicating discs, 300–302
online stores for, 296–298
promoting yourself, 302–304
See also Sharing your music
Sessions, 270–272
Shareware, 71
Sharing your music, 286–293
on Ampcast.com, 288–290
on Internet radio, 291–293
on MP3.com, 286–288
See also File-sharing services; Promoting your music
SHOUTcast service, 110–111, 291–293
installing the SHOUTcast plug-in for Winamp, 291–292
installing the SHOUTcast Server software, 292–293
Silence
deleting silent leaders, 225–226
determining length of, 227
inserting silent leaders, 226–227
Silkscreened CDs, 301
SIMM doubler, 18
Skins, 73, 89
changing, 90–92
explained, 91
SmartMedia cards, 130, 361, 362
Smith, Lavay, 100
Software
audio recording, 204, 206–207
CD-creation, 25
CD-ripper, 180–181
checking for updates of, 264

Sonicnet.com, 101
Sony Clie N760C, 136
Sony VAIO Music Clip MC-P10, 115
Soul music radio stations (Internet), 334–335
Sound App MP3 player, 156
Sound Blaster Audigy MP3+ sound card, 19–20, 162
Sound cards, 19–20
 connecting analog sources to, 196–198
 speaker jacks for, 162
Sound editors. *See* Audio editors
Sound Forge program, 206, 223–224
 editing audio files, 226, 229, 231
 Noise Reduction plug-in, 234–235
 normalizing audio files, 238
Sound quality, 154–166
 bit rates and, 158
 converting audio files, 154–156
 digital vs. analog, 173–177
 equalizers and, 158–162
 headphones and, 165–166
 normalizing audio files, 156–158
 PC functions for changing, 175
 sound cards and, 162
 speakers and, 162–164
Sound Selection dialog box, 175
Sound waves, 171–173
SoundsGood MP3 player module, 136, 137
SoundStream application, 216–219
Speakers
 headphone jacks on, 164, 165
 recommendations for, 20, 21, 164
 sound quality and, 162–164
Speed
 of burning CDs, 266–267
 of CD-RW drives, 24, 267
 of Internet connections, 29–30, 99
Splitting files into tracks, 228–230
Sports radio stations (Internet), 319–323
Stereo systems. *See* Home stereo systems
Stereo-link device, 140–142
Storage space, 354–357
 external hard disks, 355–356
 online storage, 356
 optical storage, 354–355
 planning for MP3 files, 241–242
 summary chart, 357
Strange Angels program, 307
Stream Anywhere program, 282–283
Streaming audio, 66, 278–283
 Internet radio and, 96–97
 production software for, 281–283
 reasons for using, 278
 steps for creating, 278–280
 testing, 281
Subwoofer, 163
Super Audio CD (SACD), 176

T

Talk radio stations (Internet), 319–323
Throwing Music Web site, 307–308
Track-At-Once recording, 270
Tracks. *See* Audio tracks
Transfer2Device option (MP3.com), 57
Transition effects, 273–274
Tucows.com, 71
TV show theme songs, 13–14

U

Ultraportable MP3 players, 114–115
Universal Product Code (UPC) number, 302
UnWired IR1000 headphones, 165–166
USB ports, 20–22, 140
Uzelac, Tomislav, 5

V

Variable bit rates, 183
Visualizations, 74, 92–93

Voice recorders, 121
Volume controls
 for analog recording, 210–212
 for music players, 90

W

WAV files, 6
 converting to MP3 files, 214
 MP3 files compared to, 179
 saving analog recordings as, 213
 splitting into tracks, 228–230
 when to use, 179–180, 181
Web sites. *See* World Wide Web
Webcasting, 111
Winamp, 75–76
 equalizer, 159–160
 main controls, 75
 playing music with, 76
 SHOUTcast plug-in for, 291–292
 window shade mode, 76
Windows Media Audio (WMA) format, 7, 154, 186–187
Windows Media Player, 9, 76–80
 controls for, 79
 creating playlists in, 78–79
 equalizer, 161–162
 file-naming options, 248–249
 folder structure in, 246
 playing music with, 78–79
 Radio Tuner option, 100, 101, 102–104
 ripping music from CDs with, 186–188
Windows platform
 music players for, 72–85
 operating system issues, 26–28
Windows Sound Recorder, 204, 208
Winmodem, 30
WinMX Peer Networking Protocol, 352
WinRip Enhanced Download option (MP3.com), 57
Wireless headphones, 165–166
Wireless systems
 for car stereos, 129
 for home stereos, 142–144
Works in Progress (WIP) program, 307
World Wide Web
 broadband connection to, 29
 CDDB service, 247, 249
 developing your own Web site, 303
 digital music sites on, 47–58
 examples of independent artists on, 305–316
 file-sharing services on, 58–67
 finding MP3 software on, 71
 Internet radio stations on, 318–342
 modem connection to, 29, 30
 promoting your music on, 296–316
 selling your CD on, 296–298
 sharing your music on, 286–293
 streaming music from, 278–283
 top MP3 download sites on, 344–352
Writing to your fans, 304

X

X10 MP3 Anywhere 2000, 145
Xdrive online storage, 356
XM Radio, 100

Y

Y-cable, 201

Z

Zappa, Frank, 4
ZoneAlarm utility, 60

INTERNATIONAL CONTACT INFORMATION

AUSTRALIA
McGraw-Hill Book Company Australia Pty. Ltd.
TEL +61-2-9417-9899
FAX +61-2-9417-5687
http://www.mcgraw-hill.com.au
books-it_sydney@mcgraw-hill.com

CANADA
McGraw-Hill Ryerson Ltd.
TEL +905-430-5000
FAX +905-430-5020
http://www.mcgrawhill.ca

GREECE, MIDDLE EAST, NORTHERN AFRICA
McGraw-Hill Hellas
TEL +30-1-656-0990-3-4
FAX +30-1-654-5525

MEXICO (Also serving Latin America)
McGraw-Hill Interamericana Editores S.A. de C.V.
TEL +525-117-1583
FAX +525-117-1589
http://www.mcgraw-hill.com.mx
fernando_castellanos@mcgraw-hill.com

SINGAPORE (Serving Asia)
McGraw-Hill Book Company
TEL +65-863-1580
FAX +65-862-3354
http://www.mcgraw-hill.com.sg
mghasia@mcgraw-hill.com

SOUTH AFRICA
McGraw-Hill South Africa
TEL +27-11-622-7512
FAX +27-11-622-9045
robyn_swanepoel@mcgraw-hill.com

UNITED KINGDOM & EUROPE (Excluding Southern Europe)
McGraw-Hill Education Europe
TEL +44-1-628-502500
FAX +44-1-628-770224
http://www.mcgraw-hill.co.uk
computing_neurope@mcgraw-hill.com

ALL OTHER INQUIRIES Contact:
Osborne/McGraw-Hill
TEL +1-510-549-6600
FAX +1-510-883-7600
http://www.osborne.com
omg_international@mcgraw-hill.com